VERGIL

Aeneid Book 7

The Focus Vergil Aeneid Commentaries

For intermediate students
Aeneid 1 • Randall Ganiban, editor: Available now
Aeneid 2 • Randall Ganiban, editor: Available now
Aeneid 3 • Christine Perkell, editor: Available now
Aeneid 4 • James O'Hara, editor: Available now
Aeneid 5 • Joseph Farrell, editor: Available now
Aeneid 6 • Patricia A. Johnston, editor: Available now
Aeneid 7 • Randall Ganiban, editor: Available now
Aeneid 8 • James O'Hara, editor: Available now
Aeneid 9 • Joseph Farrell, editor: In preparation
Aeneid 10 • Andreola Rossi, editor: In preparation
Aeneid 11 • Charles McNelis, editor: In preparation
Aeneid 12 • Christine Perkell, editor: In preparation

For advanced students
Aeneid 1-6 • Ganiban, general editor; Perkell, O'Hara, Farrell, Johnston, editors: Available now
Aeneid 7-12 • Ganiban and O'Hara, co-general editors; Farrell, Rossi, McNelis, Perkell, editors: In preparation

VERGIL

Aeneid Book 7

Adapted from the
Commentary of T. E. Page

Randall T. Ganiban

focus an imprint of
Hackett Publishing Company, Inc.
Indianapolis/Cambridge

A Focus book

Focus an imprint of
Hackett Publishing Company

Copyright © 2021 by Hackett Publishing Company, Inc.

All rights reserved
Printed in the United States of America

24 23 22 21   1 2 3 4 5 6 7

For further information, please address
    Hackett Publishing Company, Inc.
    P.O. Box 44937
    Indianapolis, Indiana 46244-0937

    www.hackettpublishing.com

Library of Congress Control Number: 2021934960

ISBN-13: 978-1-58510-994-4 (pbk.)
ISBN-13: 978-1-58510-997-5 (PDF ebook)

The paper used in this publication meets the minimum requirements of American National Standard for Information Sciences—Permanence of Paper for Printed Library Materials, ANSI Z39.48–1984.

Table of Contents

Preface	vii
General Introduction to Vergil's *Aeneid*	1
Introduction to *Aeneid* 7	12
Latin Text and Commentary	17
Appendix 1: Vergil's Meter	134
Appendix 2: Stylistic Terms	141
Bibliography	157
Vocabulary	173
Index	214

List of Maps

Map 1: The Wanderings of Aeneas	15
Map 2: The Catalogue of Italian Troops (*Aeneid* 7.641-817): Leaders and Locations	106

Preface

This volume is an introductory commentary on *Aeneid* 7 for use at the intermediate level or higher. It provides a generous amount of basic information about grammar and syntax so that students of varying experience will have what they need to translate the Latin. At the same time, it addresses issues of interpretation and style so that readers at all levels will have a richer experience of the poem. Finally, it includes extensive bibliographic notes to help them pursue areas of special interest. I hope that this combination of information will offer a useful alternative to other student editions (often targeting the secondary school level) and will be particularly useful to intermediate Latin students at today's colleges and universities.

This commentary takes as its starting point the valuable school edition of *Aeneid* 7 by T. E. Page in *The Aeneid of Virgil: Books VII-XII* (1900). Page's notes have been pared down, revised, updated, or omitted, while new notes and introductory material have been added throughout. I have also consulted a wide range of editions of Book 7; those by Conington, Fordyce, Williams, and Horsfall have been particularly helpful. As with other volumes in our series, the introduction, bibliography, appendices on meter and stylistic terms, and general index are new. The vocabulary was generated by and adapted from the Bridge (https://bridge.haverford.edu) with the generous permission of Professor Bret Mulligan of Haverford College. The Latin text used is that of F. A. Hirtzel (Oxford, 1900) with the following differences in readings: 307 *Lapithas...Calydona merentem* for *Lapithis...Calydone merente*, 543 *conversa per auras* for †*convexa per auras*†, 586 *pelago rupes* for *pelagi rupes*, 684 *pascis* for *pascit*, 695 *Aequosque* for *aequosque*, 737 *premebat* for *tenebat*, 773 *poenigenam* for *Phoebigenam*.

It is with pleasure that I offer thanks to a number of people who have read various portions of this edition and have given helpful advice: my colleagues in the Classics Department at Middlebury College (Jane Chaplin, Pavlos Sfyroeras, Chris Star, and Marc Witkin); Carrie Bryant, who was a research assistant at an early stage of this project and whose work was generously funded by Middlebury College; my Latin students at Middlebury who tested portions of the commentary at various stages and gave me invaluable feedback; my collaborators on the larger *Aeneid* 7-12 commentary project (Joe Farrell, Charlie McNelis, Jim O'Hara, Christine Perkell, and Andreola Rossi), with whom I have been very privileged to work; Andreola Rossi, who offered excellent suggestions on the commentary as it was being completed; Jim O'Hara, who has graciously read multiple versions of this commentary; Claire Ennen Ganiban, who helped with formatting the vocabulary; and Elizabeth Ennen, who has provided timely advice and support. Whatever flaws or errors remain are mine alone.

I would like to give special mention to Jim O'Hara. His generosity, wise counsel, and expertise have been boundless. I have benefited tremendously from working with him and am fortunate that he is the coeditor of these *Aeneid* 7-12 volumes. I am also grateful to Ron Pullins, founder of Focus Publishing, who came up with the idea to create this new *Aeneid* commentary series and was kind enough to give me the opportunity to help in its development; and to Brian Rak of Hackett Publishing, who has overseen the second half of this project with patience, encouragement, and judiciousness.

Randall T. Ganiban
Middlebury College

optimis fratribus sororibusque

General Introduction to Vergil's *Aeneid*

Vergil's lifetime and poetry

Publius Vergilius Maro (i.e., Vergil)[1] was born on October 15, 70 BCE, near the town of Mantua (modern Mantova) in what was then still Cisalpine Gaul.[2] Little else about his life can be stated with certainty, because our main source, the ancient biography by the grammarian Donatus (fourth century CE),[3] is of questionable value.[4] The historical and political background to Vergil's life (by contrast) is amply documented and provides a useful framework for understanding his career. Indeed, his poetic development displays an increasing engagement with the politics of contemporary Rome, an engagement that culminates in the *Aeneid*.

Vergil lived and wrote in a time of political strife and uncertainty. In his early twenties the Roman Republic was torn apart by the civil wars of 49-45 BCE, when Julius Caesar fought and defeated Pompey and his supporters.[5] Caesar was declared *dictator perpetuo* ("Dictator for Life") early in 44 BCE but was assassinated on the Ides of March by a group of senators led

---

[1] The spelling "Virgil" (Virgilius) is also used by convention. It developed early and has been explained by its similarity to two words: *virgo* ("maiden") and *virga* ("wand"). For discussion of the origins and potential meanings of these connections, see Jackson Knight (1944) 36-7 and Putnam (1993) 127-8 with notes.

[2] Cisalpine Gaul, the northern part of what we now think of as Italy, was incorporated into Roman Italy in 42 BCE. Mantua is located ca. 520 kilometers north of Rome.

[3] This biography drew heavily from the *De poetis* of Suetonius (born ca. 70 CE).

[4] Horsfall (1995: 1-25; 2006: xxii-xxiv) argues that nearly every detail is unreliable.

[5] The Social (or Marsic) War of 91-88 BC, which took place two decades before Vergil's birth, also looms large in the second half of the *Aeneid*. See 641-817 n.

by Brutus[6] and Cassius. They sought to restore the Republic which, they believed, was being destroyed by Caesar's domination and intimations of kingship.[7]

The assassination initiated a new round of turmoil that profoundly shaped the course of Roman history. In his will, Caesar adopted and named as his primary heir his great-nephew Octavian (63 BCE-14 CE), the man who would later be called "Augustus."[8] Though only eighteen years old, Octavian boldly accepted and used this inheritance. Through a combination of shrewd calculation and luck, he managed to attain the consulship in 43 BCE, though he was merely nineteen years of age.[9] He then joined forces with two of Caesar's lieutenants, Marc Antony (initially Octavian's rival) and Lepidus. Together they demanded recognition as a Board of Three (*triumviri* or "triumvirs") to reconstitute the state as they saw fit, and were granted extraordinary powers to do so by the Roman senate and people. In 42 BCE they avenged Caesar's murder by defeating his assassins commanded by Brutus and Cassius at the battle of Philippi in Macedonia, but their alliance gradually began to deteriorate as a result of further civil strife and interpersonal rivalries.

Vergil composed the *Eclogues*, his first major work, during this tumultuous period.[10] Published ca. 39 BCE,[11] the *Eclogues* comprise a sophisticated

---

6 Kingship was hateful to the Romans ever since Brutus' own ancestor, Lucius Junius Brutus, led the expulsion of Rome's last king, Tarquin the Proud, in ca. 509 BCE, an act that ended the regal period of Rome and initiated the Republic (cf. *Aeneid* 6.817-18, 8.646-48). In killing Caesar, Brutus claimed that he was following the example of his great ancestor—an important concept for the Romans.

7 For the reasons behind Caesar's assassination and the fall of the Republic, see the brief accounts in Scullard (1982) 126-53 and Shotter (2005) 4-19.

8 See below.

9 By the *Lex Villia annalis* of 180 BCE, a consul had to be at least forty-two years of age.

10 Other works have been attributed to Vergil: *Aetna, Catalepton, Ciris, Copa, Culex, Dirae, Elegiae in Maecenatem, Moretum,* and *Priapea*. They are collected in what is called the *Appendix Vergiliana* and are generally believed not to have been written by Vergil.

11 This traditional dating, however, has been called into question by some through reevaluation of *Eclogue* 8, which may very well refer to events in 35 BCE. See Clausen (1994) 23-27.

collection of ten pastoral poems that treat the experiences of shepherds.[12] The poems were modeled on the *Idylls* of Theocritus, a Hellenistic Greek poet of the third century BCE (see below). But whereas Theocritus' poetry created a world that was largely timeless, Vergil sets his pastoral world against the backdrop of contemporary Rome and the disruption caused by the civil wars. *Eclogues* 1 and 9, for example, deal with the differing fortunes of shepherds during a time of land confiscations that resonate with historical events in 41-40 BCE.[13] *Eclogue* 4 describes the birth of a child during the consulship of Asinius Pollio (40 BCE) who will bring a new golden age to Rome.[14] By interjecting the Roman world into his poetic landscape,[15] Vergil allows readers to sense how political developments both threaten and give promise to the very possibility of pastoral existence.

The *Eclogues* established Vergil as a new and important poetic voice, and led him to the cultural circle of the great literary patron Maecenas, an influential supporter and confidant of Octavian. Their association grew throughout the 30s.[16] The political situation, however, remained precarious. Lepidus was ousted from the triumvirate in 36 BCE because of his treacherous behavior. Tensions between Octavian and Antony that were simmering over Antony's collaboration and affair with the Egyptian queen

---

12 Coleman (1977) and Clausen (1994) are excellent commentaries on the *Eclogues*. For a discussion of the pastoral genre at Rome, see Heyworth (2005). For general interpretation of the *Eclogues*, see Hardie (1998) 5-27 with extensive bibliography in the notes, Volk (2008a), and Smith (2011).

13 Octavian rewarded veterans with land that was already occupied.

14 This is sometimes called the "Messianic Eclogue" because later ages read it as foreseeing the birth of Christ, which occurred nearly four decades later. The identity of the child is debated, but the poem may celebrate the marriage between Marc Antony and Octavian's sister Octavia that resulted from the treaty of Brundisium in 40 BCE; this union helped stave off the immediate outbreak of war between the two triumvirs. For more on this poem, see Van Sickle (1992) and Petrini (1997) 111-21, as well as the commentaries by Coleman (1977) and Clausen (1994).

15 In addition to the contemporary themes that Vergil treats, he also mentions or dedicates individual poems to a number of his contemporaries, including Asinius Pollio, Alfenus Varus, Cornelius Gallus, and probably Octavian, who is likely the *iuvenis* ("young man") mentioned at 1.42 and perhaps also the patron addressed at 8.6-13.

16 For the relationship between Augustus and the poets, see White (2005). White (1993) is a book-length study of this topic. For an overview of literature of the Augustan period from 40 BCE14 CE, see Farrell (2005).

Cleopatra eventually exploded.¹⁷ In 32 BCE, Octavian had Antony's powers revoked, and war was declared against Cleopatra (and thus in effect against Antony as well). During a naval confrontation off Actium on the coast of western Greece in September of 31 BCE, Octavian's fleet decisively routed the forces of Marc Antony and Cleopatra, who both fled to Egypt and committed suicide in the following year to avoid capture.¹⁸ This momentous victory solidified Octavian's claim of being the protector of traditional Roman values against the detrimental influence of Antony, Cleopatra, and the East.¹⁹

Vergil began his next work, the *Georgics*, sometime in the 30s, completed it ca. 29 BCE in the aftermath of Actium, and dedicated it to Maecenas. Like the *Eclogues*, the *Georgics* was heavily influenced by Greek models—particularly the work of Hesiod (eighth century BCE) and of Hellenistic poets such as Callimachus, Aratus, and Nicander (third-second centuries BCE). On the surface, it purports to be a poetic farming guide.²⁰ Each of its four books examines a different aspect or sphere of agricultural life: crops and weather signs (Book 1), trees and vines (Book 2), livestock (Book 3), and bees (Book 4). Its actual scope, however, is much more ambitious. The poem explores the nature of humankind's struggle with the beauty and difficulties of the agricultural world, but it does so within the context of contemporary war-torn Italy. It bears witness to the strife following Caesar's assassination, and sets the chaos and disorder inherent in nature against the upheaval caused by civil war (1.461-514). Moreover,

---

17 In addition to the political conflicts, there were also familial tensions: Antony conducted a decade-long affair with Cleopatra, even though he had married Octavia, Octavian's (Augustus') sister, as a result of the treaty of Brundisium in 40 BCE (see n. 14 above). Antony divorced Octavia in 32 BCE.

18 For the history of the triumviral period, see the brief accounts in Scullard (1982) 154-71 and Shotter (2005) 20-27; for more detailed treatments, see Syme (1939) 187-312, Pelling (1996) and Osgood (2006). For discussion of the contemporary artistic representations of Actium, see Gurval (1995).

19 This ideological interpretation is suggested in Vergil's depiction of the battle on Aeneas' shield (8.671-713).

20 Recent commentaries on the *Georgics* include Thomas (1988) and Mynors (1990). For interpretation, see the introduction to the *Georgics* in Hardie (1998) 28-52 with extensive bibliography in the notes, and Volk (2008b). Individual studies include Wilkinson (1969), Putnam (1979), Johnston (1980), Ross (1987), Perkell (1989), Nappa (2005), and Thibodeau (2011). For allusion in the *Georgics*, see Thomas (1986), Farrell (1991), and Gale (2000).

Octavian's success and victories are commemorated both in the introduction (1.24-42) and conclusion (4.559-62) of the poem, as well as in the beginning of the third book (31-39). Thus once again, the political world is juxtaposed against Vergil's poetic landscape, but the relationship between the two is not fully addressed.[21]

Octavian's victory represented a turning point for Rome's development. Over the next decade, he centralized political and military control in his hands. He claimed to have returned the state (*res publica*) to the senate and Roman people in 27 BCE.[22] His powers were redefined, and he was granted the name "Augustus" ("Revered One") by the senate. It is true that he maintained many traditional Republican institutions, but in reality he was transforming the state into a monarchy. So effective was his stabilization and control of Rome after decades of civil war that he reigned as *Princeps* ("First Citizen") from 27 BCE to 14 CE, creating a political framework (the Principate) that served the Roman state for centuries.[23]

Vergil wrote his final poem, the *Aeneid*, largely in the 20s, during the first years of Augustus' reign, when the Roman people presumably hoped that the civil wars were behind them but feared that the Augustan peace would not last. The *Aeneid* tells the story of the Trojan hero Aeneas. He fought the Greeks at Troy and saw his city destroyed, but with the guidance of the gods and fate he led his surviving people across the Mediterranean to a new homeland in Italy.[24] As in the *Eclogues* and *Georgics*, Vergil interjects

---

21 The overall meaning of the *Georgics* is contested. Interpretation of the *Georgics*, like that of the *Aeneid* (see below), has optimistic and pessimistic poles. Otis (1964) is an example of the former; Ross (1987) the latter. Other scholars, such as Perkell (1989), fall in between by discerning inherent ambivalence. For discussion of these interpretive trends, see Hardie (1998) 50-52.

22 Augustus, *Res Gestae* 34.

23 For general political and historical narratives of Augustus' reign, see the relatively brief account in Shotter (2005); longer, more detailed treatments can be found in A. H. M. Jones (1970), Crook (1996), and Southern (1998). A classic and influential book by Syme (1939) paints Augustus in extremely dark colors. For broader considerations of the Augustan age, see the short but interesting volume by Wallace-Hadrill (1993) and the more comprehensive treatments by Galinsky (1996, 2005) and Wallace-Hadrill (2008). For the interaction of art and ideology in the Augustan Age, see Zanker (1988).

24 For general interpretation of the *Aeneid*, see the recent overviews provided by Hardie (1998) 53-101, Perkell (1999), Anderson (2005), Johnson (2005), Fratantuono (2007), and Ross (2007). For the literary and cultural

his contemporary world into his poetic world. In the *Aeneid*, however, the thematic connections between these two realms are developed still more explicitly, with Aeneas' actions shown to be necessary for and to lead ultimately to the reign of Augustus.

Vergil was still finishing the *Aeneid* when he was stricken by a fatal illness in 19 BCE. The ancient biographical tradition claims that he traveled to Greece, intending to spend three years editing his epic there and in Asia, but that early on he encountered Augustus, who was returning to Rome from the East, and decided to accompany him. Vergil, however, fell ill during the journey and died in Brundisium (in southern Italy) in September of 19 BCE. The *Aeneid* was largely complete but had not yet received its final revision. We are told that Vergil asked that it be burned, but that Augustus ultimately had it published. While such details regarding Vergil's death are doubted, the poem clearly needed final editing.[25] However, its present shape, including its sudden ending, is generally accepted to be as Vergil had planned.

Vergil and his predecessors

By writing an epic about the Trojan War, Vergil was rivaling Homer, the greatest of all the Greek poets. The *Aeneid* was therefore a bold undertaking, but its success makes it arguably the quintessential Roman work because it accomplishes what Latin poetry had always striven to do: to appropriate the Greek tradition and transform it into something that was both equally impressive and distinctly "Roman."

Homer's *Iliad* tells the story of the Trojan War by focusing on Achilles' strife with the Greek leader Agamemnon and consequent rage in the tenth and final year of the conflict, while the *Odyssey* treats the war's aftermath by relating Odysseus' struggle to return home. These were the earliest and most revered works of Greek literature, and they exerted a defining influence on both the overall framework of the *Aeneid* and the close details of its poetry. In general terms, *Aeneid* 1-6, like the *Odyssey*, describes a hero's return (to a new) home after the Trojan War, while *Aeneid* 7-12, like the *Iliad*, tells the

---

backgrounds, see Martindale (1997), Farrell (2005), Galinsky (2005), and Lowrie (2010).

25 We can be sure that the poem had not received its final revision for a number of reasons, including the presence of roughly fifty-eight incomplete or "half" lines. See commentary note on 7.129.

story of a war. But throughout the *Aeneid*, Vergil reworks ideas, language, characters, and scenes from both poems. Some ancient critics faulted Vergil for his use of Homer, calling his appropriations "thefts." Vergil, however, is said to have responded that it is "easier to steal his club from Hercules than a line from Homer."[26] Indeed, Vergil does much more than simply quote material from Homer. His creative use and transformation of Homeric language and theme are central not only to his artistry but also to the meaning of the *Aeneid*.

Though Homer is the primary model, Vergil was also influenced significantly by the Hellenistic Greek tradition of poetry that originated in Alexandria, Egypt, in the third century BCE. There scholar-poets such as Apollonius, Callimachus, and Theocritus reacted against the earlier literary tradition (particularly epic which by their time had become largely derivative). They developed a poetic aesthetic that valued small-scale poems, esoteric subjects, and highly polished style. Hellenistic poetry was introduced into the mainstream of Latin poetry a generation before Vergil by the so-called "neoterics" or "new poets," of whom Catullus (ca. 84-ca. 54 BCE) was the most influential for Vergil and for the later literary tradition.[27]

Vergil's earlier works, the *Eclogues* and *Georgics*, had been modeled to a significant extent on Hellenistic poems,[28] so it was perhaps a surprise that Vergil would then have turned to a large-scale epic concerning the Trojan War.[29] However, one of his great feats was the incorporation of the Hellenistic and neoteric sensibilities into the *Aeneid*. Two models were particularly important in this regard: the *Argonautica* by Apollonius of Rhodes, an epic

---

26 *facilius esse Herculi clavam quam Homeri versum subripere* (Donatus/ Suetonius, *Life of Vergil* 46).

27 Clausen (1987, 2002), George (1974), Briggs (1981), Thomas (1988, 1999), and Hunter (2006) display these influences, while O'Hara (1996, expanded reprint 2017) provides a thorough examination of wordplay (important to the Alexandrian poets) in Vergil.

28 The *Eclogues* were modeled on Theocritus' *Idylls*; the *Georgics* had numerous models, though the Hellenistic poets Callimachus, Nicander, and Aratus were particularly important influences.

29 For example, at *Eclogue* 6.3-5, Vergil explains in highly programmatic language his decision to compose poetry in the refined Callimachean or Hellenistic manner rather than traditional epic. See Clausen (1994) 174-5.

retelling of the hero Jason's quest for the Golden Fleece,[30] and Catullus 64, a poem on the wedding of Peleus and Thetis. Both works brought the great and elevated heroes of the past down to the human level, thereby offering new insights into their strengths, passions, and flaws, and both greatly influenced Vergil's presentation of Aeneas

Of Vergil's other predecessors in Latin literature, the most important was Ennius (239-169 BCE), often called the father of Roman poetry.[31] His *Annales*, which survives only in fragments, was a historical epic about Rome that traced the city's origins back to Aeneas and Troy. It remained the most influential Latin poem until the *Aeneid* was composed, and provided a model not only for Vergil's poetic language and themes but also for his integration of Homer and Roman history. In addition, the *De Rerum Natura* of Lucretius (ca. 94-55/51 BCE), a hexameter poem on Epicurean philosophy, profoundly influenced Vergil with its forceful language and philosophical ideas.[32]

Finally, Vergil drew much from Greek and Roman[33] tragedy. Many episodes in the *Aeneid* share tragedy's well-known dramatic patterns (such as reversal of fortune), and explore the suffering that befalls mortals often as

---

[30] On the influence of Apollonius on Vergil, see the important book by Nelis (2001).

[31] Ennius introduced the dactylic hexameter as the meter of Latin epic. Two earlier epic writers were Livius Andronicus who composed a translation of Homer's *Odyssey* into Latin, and Naevius who composed the *Bellum Punicum*, an epic on the First Punic War. Both Naevius and Livius wrote their epics in a meter called Saturnian that is not fully understood. For the influence of the early Latin poets on the *Aeneid*, see Wigodsky (1972), and on Ennius, Goldschmidt (2013).

[32] See Hardie (1986) 157-240 and Adler (2003). The influence of the Epicurean Philodemus on Vergil (and the Augustans more generally) is explored in the collection edited by Armstrong, Fish, Johnston, and Skinner (2004). For Lucretius' influence on Vergil's *Georgics*, see especially Farrell (1991) and Gale (2000).

[33] The earliest epic writers (Livius, Naevius, and Ennius; see above) also wrote tragedy, and so it is not surprising that epic and tragedy would influence one another. Latin tragic writing continued into the first century through the work of, e.g., Pacuvius (220-ca. 130 BCE) and Accius (170-ca. 86 BCE). Their tragedies, which included Homeric and Trojan War themes, were important for Vergil. However, since only meager fragments of them have survived, their precise influence is difficult to gauge.

a result of the immense and incomprehensible power of the gods and fate.³⁴ As a recent critic has written, "The influence of tragedy on the *Aeneid* is pervasive, and arguably the single most important factor in Virgil's successful revitalization of the genre of epic."³⁵

The *Aeneid* is thus indebted to these and many other sources, the study of which can enrich our appreciation of Vergil's artistry and our interpretation of his epic.³⁶ However, no source study can fully account for the creative, aesthetic, and moral achievement of the *Aeneid*, which is a work unto itself.

The *Aeneid*, Rome, and Augustus

While Aeneas' story takes place in the distant, mythological past of the Trojan War era, it had a special relevance for Vergil's contemporaries. Not only did the Romans draw their descent from the Trojans, but the emperor Augustus believed that Aeneas was his own ancestor.³⁷ Vergil

---

34 Cf., e.g., Heinze (1915, trans. 1993: 251-8). Wlosok (1999) offers a reading of the Dido episode as tragedy, and Pavlock (1985) examines Euripidean influence in the Nisus and Euryalus episode. Hardie (1991, 1997), Panoussi (2002, 2009), and Galinsky (2003) examine the influence of tragedy, particularly in light of French theories of Greek tragedy (e.g., Vernant and Vidal-Naquet 1988), and draw important parallels between the political and cultural milieus of fifthcentury Athens and Augustan Rome. On tragedy and conflicting viewpoints, see Conte (1999), revised now in Conte (2007), and Galinsky (2003).

35 Hardie (1998) 62. See also Hardie (1997).

36 See Farrell (1997) for a full and insightful introduction to the interpretive possibilities that the study of intertextuality in Vergil can offer readers. For a general introduction to intertextuality, see Allen (2000). For the study of intertextuality in Latin literature, see Conte (1986), Farrell (1991) 1-25, Hardie (1993), D. Fowler (1997), Hinds (1998), and Edmunds (2001). For Vergil's use of Homer, see Knauer (1964b), Barchiesi (1984, in Italian), Gransden (1984), Cairns (1989) 177-248, and Dekel (2012). Knauer (1964a), written in German, is a standard work on this topic; those without German can still benefit from its detailed citations and lists of parallels. For Vergil's use of Homer and Apollonius, see Nelis (2001).

37 Augustus' clan, the Julian gens, claimed its descent from Iulus (another name for Aeneas' son Ascanius) and thus also from Aeneas and Venus. Julius Caesar in particular emphasized this ancestry; Augustus made these connections central to his political self-presentation as well. See, e.g., Zanker (1988) 193-210 and Galinsky (1996) 141-224.

makes these national and familial connections major thematic concerns of his epic.

As a result, the *Aeneid* is about more than the Trojan War and its aftermath. It is also about the foundation of Rome and its flourishing under Augustus. To incorporate these themes into his epic, Vergil connects mythological and historical time by associating three leaders and city foundations: the founding of Lavinium by Aeneas, the actual founding of Rome by Romulus, and the "refounding" of Rome by Augustus. These events are prominent in the most important prophecies of the epic: Jupiter's speech to Venus (1.257-96), Anchises' revelation to his son Aeneas (6.756-853), and the scenes on the shield Vulcan makes for Aeneas, discussed in the commentary on Book 8 (8.626-728). Together these passages provide what may be called an Augustan reading of Roman history, one that is shaped by the deeds of these three men and that views Augustus as the culmination of the processes of fate and history.[38]

This is not to say that the associations among Aeneas, Romulus, and Augustus are always positive or unproblematic, particularly given the ways that Aeneas is portrayed and can be interpreted.[39] To some, Vergil's Aeneas represents an idealized Roman hero, who thus reflects positively on Augustus by association.[40] In general this type of reading sees a positive imperial ideology in the epic and is referred to as "optimistic" or "Augustan." Others are more troubled by Vergil's Aeneas, and advocate interpretations that challenge the moral and spiritual value of his actions, as well as of the role of the gods and fate. Such readings perceive a much darker poetic world[41] and have

---

38 See O'Hara (1990), however, for the deceptiveness of prophecies in the *Aeneid*, as well as the notes in his commentary on Book 8 to *Aen*. 8.40-1, 341, 533, 626-728, 629, 652, 720-8.
39 For general interpretation of the *Aeneid*, see n. 24 (above).
40 This type of reading is represented especially by Heinze (1915, trans. 1993), Pöschl (1950, trans. 1962), and Otis (1964). More recent and complex Augustan interpretations can be found in Hardie (1986) and Cairns (1989).
41 See, e.g., Putnam (1965), Johnson (1976), Lyne (1987), and Thomas (2001). Putnam's reading of the *Aeneid* has been particularly influential. Of the ending of the poem he writes: "By giving himself over with such suddenness to the private wrath which the sight of the belt of Pallas arouses, Aeneas becomes himself *impius Furor*, as rage wins the day over moderation, disintegration defeats order, and the achievements of history through heroism fall victim to the human frailty of one man" (1965: 193-4). For a different understanding of

been called "pessimistic" or "ambivalent."[42] Vergil's portrayal of Aeneas is thus a major element in debates over the epic's meaning.[43]

Randall Ganiban, Series Coeditor

Aeneas' wrath, see Galinsky (1988). For *furor* and violence in Book 7, see commentary notes on lines 312, 386, 607, 609, and passim.

42 For a general treatment of the optimism/pessimism debate, see Kennedy (1992). For a critique of the "pessimistic" view, see Martindale (1993a); for critique of the "optimistic" stance and its rejection of "pessimism," see Thomas (2001), and for brief historical perspective on both sides, see Schmidt (2001). For the continuing debate over the politics of the *Aeneid* and over the Augustan age more generally, see the collections of Powell (1992) and Stahl (1998).

43 Indeed some readers also question whether it is even possible to resolve this interpretive debate because of Vergil's inherent ambiguity. See Johnson (1976), Perkell (1994), O'Hara (2007) 77-103, and Conte (2007). Martindale (1993a) offers a critique of ambiguous readings.

Introduction to *Aeneid* 7

At the beginning of Book 7, Aeneas finally reaches Latium on the western coast of Italy, where he is fated to found a city and ultimately become the ancestor of the Romans. His world, however, is quickly engulfed by violent fury, when the goddess Juno incites a war that will dominate the remainder of the poem. Book 7 thus initiates the so-called "Iliadic" half of the epic, Aeneas' war in Italy (see "Vergil and his predecessors" in the General Introduction), and, despite the greater attention given by modern readers to the powerful events of the first half of the epic, Vergil introduces Books 7-12 as his more weighty undertaking: *maior rerum mihi nascitur ordo, | maius opus moveo* (44-5). Within these books Aeneas' character, the nature of his fate, the quality of his leadership, and the meaning of his *pietas* will be put to the test in new and consequential ways.

Book 7 can be divided into three sections. In 1-285 Aeneas arrives in Latium with the hope that his travails might finally be coming to an end: a possible alliance with King Latinus and potential marriage to the princess Lavinia both point in this direction. Such hope, however, is soon shattered in 286-640, when Juno bristles at and retaliates against Aeneas' incipient success. She calls the Fury Allecto up from the underworld to incite violence that will overtake Italy. After describing the war's outbreak, Vergil concludes in 641-817 with a catalogue of the Italian leaders, troops, and cities that will battle the Trojans.

Homeric epic continues as the dominant model, though Vergil's intertextuality is complex as always. Vergil's Juno and Allecto in Book 7 are illustrative examples. When Juno sees that Aeneas has arrived in Latium, she is so enraged that she calls up the Fury Allecto from the underworld to start a war against him. The scene is modeled on *Odyssey* 5, where Poseidon spies Odysseus sailing on a raft toward Ithaca and sends a storm that shipwrecks him among the Phaeacians. But much more is involved. Vergil's Allecto, for example, may have intertextual connections to Homer; however, she has greater roots in Greek tragedy (see 286-640 n.). In addition, Juno now has important *intra*textual models (i.e., models from earlier in the *Aeneid*), since her actions in Book 7 look back to Book 1, but with an important difference: whereas her fury there had been embodied in the storm that shipwrecked Aeneas at the epic's opening, now in Book 7 she resorts to an actual Fury to create a storm of war. Vergil's Juno in Book 7 thus surpasses the violence of her actions in Book 1—as well as of her model Poseidon from the *Odyssey*. In the process, we are presented with a struggle over the meaning of Aeneas' actions in Italy: Is he a second Paris, stealing another man's woman (i.e., taking Lavinia from Turnus) and thus motivating a second "Trojan War"? Is he a pious hero following through with the commands of fate? Or is he something else?

What Aeneas represents will be contested by characters throughout Books 7-12, but the issues involved also reflect debates earlier in the epic, especially in Book 4. For example, just as Vergil does not definitively state whether or not Aeneas and Dido were married, so Book 7 creates ambiguity as to whether Turnus and Lavinia have, in some sense, been engaged. And just as Dido (though not Aeneas) had been forced by Cupid and Venus to fall in love in Book 1, so Turnus is infuriated by Allecto to fight Aeneas (cf. 286-640 n.), while Aeneas fights because of his commitment to fate. Might Turnus, like Dido, be viewed as a tragic figure, one who suffers, at least in part, because of the gods, fate, and Aeneas' understanding of them? Our interpretation of Turnus' predicament will surely be influenced by our interpretation of Dido's.

Juno's actions are also implicated in the epic's larger treatment of gender and use of tragic intertexts. Juno (throughout the epic) and Allecto (in Book 7) pose the greatest threats to the fulfillment of fate and to Jupiter's control of the cosmos. Indeed, women in Book 7, even if they are not explicitly allied with Juno, generally represent some kind of challenge—emotional, political, military—to Aeneas. Book 7 opens with the loss and burial of Aeneas' dear nurse Caieta and closes with Camilla, the impressive Volscian warrior and Trojan opponent. Lavinia lies at the heart of the Italian war because of her relationship to Turnus, whom Lavinia's mother, Amata, supports with startling fierceness. And of course the central portion of the book is dominated by Juno and the Fury Allecto. The oppositions between male and female, Olympian and Infernal realms, order and disorder are strongly influenced by the treatment of gender with respect to divine rule and cosmic order in Greek tragedy, particularly Aeschylus' *Oresteia*.

Finally, Book 7 is centrally concerned with presenting ancient Italy—its many regions, peoples, and customs (as seen especially in the Catalogue of Turnus' allies, 641-817 n.). But the land of Italy plays a special role in the story not simply because this is where Aeneas must fight, but also because Italy will ultimately be subsumed by Rome. Thus continual references to the geography and customs of Italy always remind us that the people who are bitter enemies of Aeneas will ultimately be reconciled to Rome's power, as Vergil makes clear in his question to Jupiter at 12.503-4: *tanton placuit concurrere motu, | Iuppiter, aeterna gentis in pace futuras?* ("Was it your will, Jupiter, that nations later to exist in eternal peace should clash in such great upheaval?") On the one hand, then, we see that religious and political traditions such as the gates of Janus (607 n.) and the *curia* of the Latins (173-5 n.) draw patriotic connections between Rome and its ancient Italian past. On the other hand, the reader cannot ignore Rome's bitter historical wars in Italy throughout the Republic, particularly the horrific Social War of 91-88 BCE and the civil wars of the first century BCE (cf. 641-817 n., and "Vergil's lifetime and poetry" in the General Introduction). Vergil's Italian war might thus be viewed as a proto-civil war.

In short, Book 7 both continues earlier themes and identifies those that will dominate Books 7-12. Aeneas will be put to the test. Each reader has to decide whether or not Aeneas is ultimately able to resist the destabilizing fury of Juno and the violence of war, and to embody those ideals that would make him a *Roman*—and not Homeric—hero.

For general interpretation, see Heinze (1915: 171-92 = 1993: 142-55), Fraenkel (1945 = 1990), Otis (1964), Anderson (1969, 2005), Gransden (1984), Fredericksmeyer (1985), Mack (1999), Fratantuono (2007), Ross (2007), Fletcher (2014) 217-32, Stahl (2016) 347-430. For intertextuality, see Knauer (1964b) and Nelis (2001). For the gods, see Feeney (1991) 162-80 and Hershkowitz (1998) 95-105. For the importance of Italy, see McKay (1970), Jenkyns (1998) 463-514, and Fantham (2009). For the Italian war as a proto-civil war, see Pogorzelski (2009) and Marincola (2010).

Randall Ganiban, *Series Coeditor*

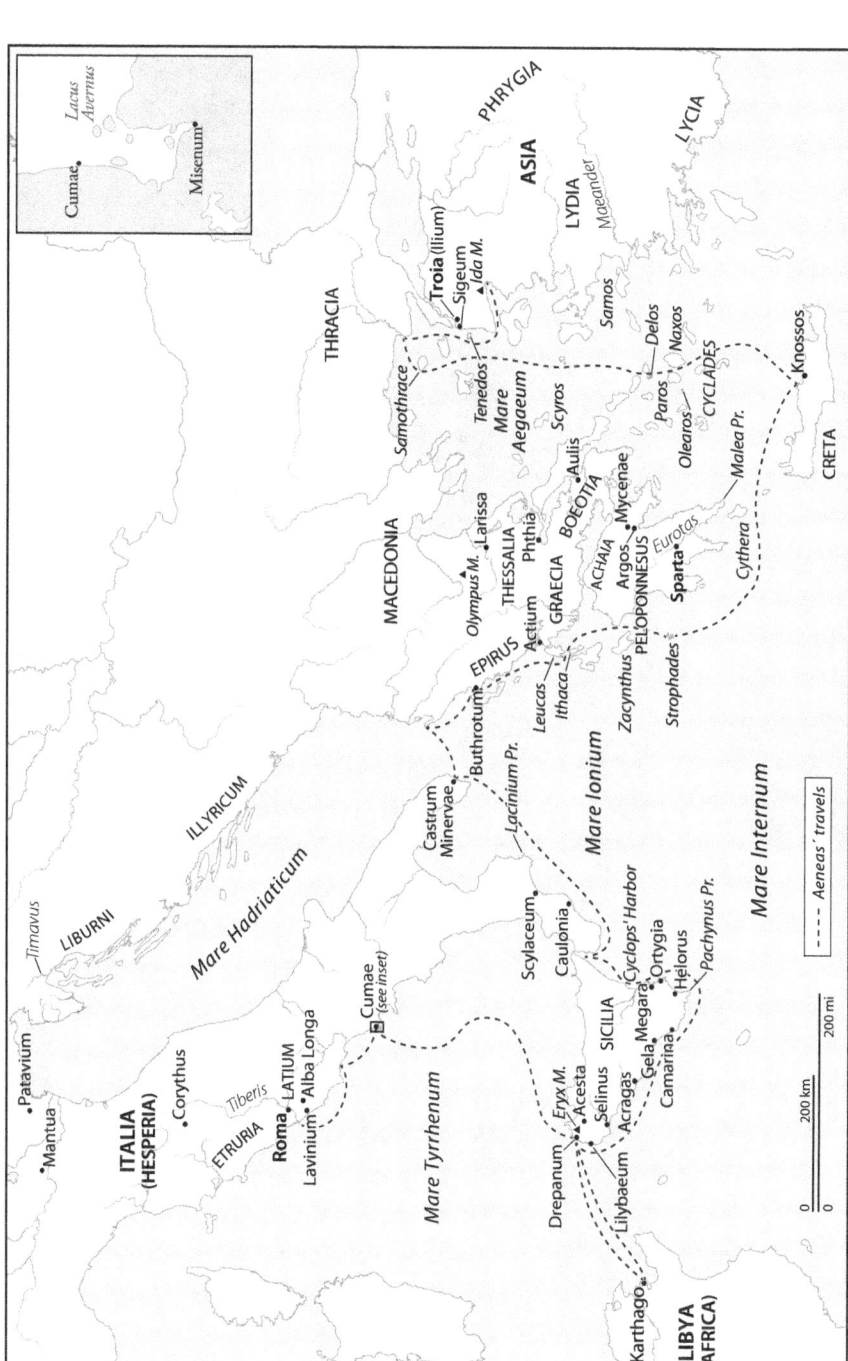

Map 1: The Wanderings of Aeneas

LIBER SEPTIMUS[1]

1-285: Aeneas' arrival in Latium and alliance with Latinus

Vergil describes Aeneas' arrival in Latium, the situation there, and the prospective alliance between King Latinus and Aeneas. The book opens on a calm note, with the Trojans sailing to Latium, but even so the landscape contains latent threats: Aeneas skirts but does not land in the realm of the sorceress/goddess Circe, and thus avoids the fate suffered by Odysseus and his crew in Odyssey 10 (see 10-24 n.). The potential danger in Italy, however, will be realized soon thereafter, when Juno enters the scene (see 286-640 n.).

With the reference to the Circe episode, Vergil extends Aeneas' "Odyssey" from the end of the first half of the epic into the second, thereby blurring the firm distinction we might have expected between the so-called Odyssean and Iliadic halves of the *Aeneid*. The poet complicates matters further by deferring his proem to the second half of the epic until lines 37-45 (see n.), in which he announces his new and "more weighty" martial theme.

As the new half of the epic begins, we learn of the political situation in Latium under King Latinus. His reign is described as one of peace, though that characterization is perhaps thrown into question by intimations of regional strife (cf. 45-6 n.). His role in the Aeneas story was traditional, but the details varied, as

---

[1] *Please note:* When reference is made to a passage from *Aeneid* 7, the line number alone is given, without the book number (e.g., "cf. 110"), along with reference to the note on that passage, if relevant (e.g., "cf. 110 n."). When reference is made to another book of the *Aeneid*, the number of that book is given as well (e.g., "cf. 6.203"). Reference to notes in other commentaries is made by using the last name of the commentator (details of the editions cited can be found in the bibliography). References to *Allen and Greenough's New Latin Grammar* (see Mahoney (2001) in the bibliography) are provided by abbreviation and section number (e.g., AG §471c). *FRH* refers to *The Fragments of the Roman Historians* (Cornell (2014)), *FRL* to *Fragmentary Republican Latin* (Goldberg and Manuwald (2018)), *OLD* to the *Oxford Latin Dictionary* (2nd ed. 2012) with s.v. (*sub verbo*) indicating the dictionary headword, and *VE* to *The Virgil Encyclopedia* (Thomas and Ziolkowski (2014)), an invaluable resource. Terms marked with an asterisk (e.g., chiasmus*) are defined in Appendix 2 on stylistic terms; for metrical features, see Appendix 1 on meter.

can be seen from the three most important extant historiographical sources. In the *Origines* of Cato (second century BCE, only fragments survive; see *FRH* 3.65-6), the Trojans arrive in Latium and are granted land by Latinus, who also gives his daughter Lavinia in marriage to Aeneas; in response, Turnus wages a war against Aeneas in which Latinus is killed in the first battle (the side taken by Latinus, however, is unclear). Vergil's contemporary Dionysius of Halicarnassus (*Antiquitates Romanae* 1.57-60) records a peaceful reception of Aeneas: though Latinus almost attacks the Trojans upon their arrival, he is dissuaded from doing so both by the sight of their army and by a divinely sent dream; instead, he grants the Trojans land and alliance, and together they successfully attack the Rutulians, with whom Latinus is in the midst of a war. Latinus then gives his daughter Lavinia to Aeneas in marriage. Livy (1.1-2), another contemporary of Vergil, offers two different accounts of what happens after the Trojans arrive in Latium, plunder the area, and take land: in one, Latinus attacks the Trojans, loses, and forges peace and a marriage alliance with Aeneas; in the other, Latinus forges a treaty without fighting first, and gives Lavinia in marriage to Aeneas—in response, Turnus, who had been engaged to Lavinia, wages war against the Trojans and Latins and is defeated, though Latinus dies in battle.

Vergil was thus faced with a varied tradition, one that allowed him to mold the stories of Latinus, Aeneas, Turnus, and Lavinia to his own needs. In lines 1-285, Vergil creates a Latinus whose reign is seemingly peaceful, and who becomes an important Italian voice proclaiming the fated nature of Aeneas' presence in Italy. And while it is never explicitly stated that Lavinia and Turnus have been engaged, Vergil incorporates conflicting viewpoints that create ambiguity, thereby complicating our understanding of the competing claims of both the Trojans and (especially) the Latins/Rutulians, who at times view Aeneas as trying to steal someone else's bride—and thus as another Paris, who had made off with Menelaus' wife Helen. The Trojans have finally reached the land in Latium prophesied to them; however, they will quickly realize that their troubles are not over but in a sense just beginning. For 1-285 in general, see Boas (1938), Reckford (1961), Nelis (2001) 267-87, and Fletcher (2014) 217-32. For historiographical sources, see especially Casali (2010) 46-50 and Stahl (2016) 354, 359-71.

1-4. Aeneas performs funerary rites for Caieta, his nurse, thus providing an aetiology for the name of the place where she was buried.

At the end of Book 6, Aeneas exited the underworld at Cumae and traveled to the port of Caieta (*ad Caietae...portum* 6.900, the penultimate line of Book 6). Vergil begins Book 7 with an aetiology* (an explanation of the origin or cause of a name, custom, etc.) retroactively revealing that Caieta (modern Gaeta) was named after Aeneas' nurse, who died while the Trojans were there. Lines 1-4 are written in the form of a funeral epitaph and serve as a symbolic turning point in the narrative: as the Trojans are about to reach their fated land in Latium, they

TV quoque litoribus nostris, Aeneïa nutrix,
aeternam moriens famam, Caieta, dedisti;
et nunc servat honos sedem tuus, ossaque nomen
Hesperia in magna, si qua est ea gloria, signat.
  At pius exsequiis Aeneas rite solutis, 5

leave their Trojan past behind. For Caieta, see Putnam (1970), Mack (1999) 135, Thomas (2004) 140-1, Dinter (2005), Skempis (2010), Seider (2012) 241-7, Fletcher (2014) 218-21.

1-2. **TV:** Vergil begins by addressing Aeneas' deceased nurse *Caieta* (1-4 n.). No other book of the epic opens with an apostrophe*, which here adds emotional power to the start of the epic's second half. Interestingly, despite the prominence given her in these lines, Caieta does not actually appear as a character anywhere in the *Aeneid*. **quoque:** "also"; that is, Caieta is like Misenus and Palinurus, also minor figures who died earlier during the voyage from Troy to Latium, and whose names, as we learned in Book 6, were given to places associated with their deaths—Cape Misenum (6.234-5) and Cape Palinurus (6.381). With *quoque*, Vergil explicitly connects Books 6 and 7—and thus the two halves of the epic. **litoribus nostris:** dative, indirect object after *dedisti*. Notice how *nostris* connects Aeneas' time to Vergil's own; such connections are characteristic of aetiological* poetry (Horsfall). **Aeneïa nutrix...Caieta:** *Aeneïa* (four syllables) is a grand adjectival form, perhaps coined by Vergil, and modifies *nutrix*, "Aeneas' nurse." The name Caieta is seemingly derived from the Greek verb *kaiein* ("burn"), an etymology* perhaps referring to the burning of her pyre (as seemingly suggested in Ovid, *Metamorphoses* 14.443-4). **aeternam moriens famam:** note the oxymoron* involved in the juxtaposition of *aeternam* and *moriens* (modifying *tu/Caieta*); the connection between *fama* and death is explored further in line 4, where Vergil seemingly questions the value of fame.

3. **nunc:** like *nostris* in line 1 (see 1-2 n.), *nunc* emphatically connects Vergil's own day to the Trojan past. **servat:** "guards"; cf. 6.507 *nomen et arma locum servant*, describing the burial place of the Trojan Deïphobus, whose disfigured shade meets Aeneas in the underworld. **honos...tuus:** the older and original nominative form of *honor* elevates the poetic tone. **sedem:** *sedes, -is,* f. in general means "seat" but here (Caieta's) "grave," "burial place" (*OLD* s.v. *sedes* 6a).

4. **Hesperia:** from Gr. "Western land" used, from the Greek perspective, to describe Italy. It therefore had an elevated tone in Latin, was used by Roman poets as early as Ennius in the second century BCE (see "Vergil and his predecessors" in the General Introduction) to indicate Italy (cf. *Annales* fragment 20 in Skutsch and in *FRL* 1), and had been mentioned as the ultimate goal of Aeneas' wanderings at 1.530, 2.781, 3.163, and 4.355. **si qua est ea gloria:** "if this is any glory (to you, Caieta)"; *qua* ("any"), indefinite adjective following *si* and modifying *gloria*. Vergil raises the question of whether such glory means anything to the dead (see, e.g., G. W. Williams (1983) 209).

5-24. Aeneas sails at night and avoids the potential dangers of Circe.

5. **At:** "But," refocusing the poet's perspective back on Aeneas, and thus implying the unusual nature of the preceding four-line apostrophe* to Caieta that initiated Book 7 (see 1-4 n.). The phrase *At pius Aeneas* recurs at several other important junctures in the narrative (cf. 1.305, 4.393; 6.9, 232; 12.311). **pius exsequiis Aeneas...solutis:** note the interlocking word order* involved in these two adjective + noun phrases. Aeneas is immediately described with his

aggere composito tumuli, postquam alta quierunt
aequora, tendit iter velis portumque relinquit.
aspirant aurae in noctem nec candida cursus
luna negat, splendet tremulo sub lumine pontus.
proxima Circaeae raduntur litora terrae,   10

---

essential epithet *pius* (used of him twenty times in the epic), as he performs "with proper religious observances" (*rite*, adverb) Caieta's burial rites (expressed in two ablative absolutes, *exsequiiis...solutis, aggere composito*); *exsequiae* (*-arum*, f. pl.) are "funeral rites."

Throughout the epic, Vergil defines Aeneas by his *pietas*, though this virtue is never fully explained. It involves duty to and affection for one's family, country, and gods. It is a defining component of moral leadership, just action, and heroism. In Books 7-12, the competing conceptions and demands of *pietas* come into conflict at several important moments, such as Aeneas' slayings of Lausus (10.783-832) and of Turnus (12.919-53).

6. **aggere composito**: ablative absolute, "with the mound (of the grave, *tumuli*) constructed." **quierunt**: a syncopated* (or contracted) form of *quie(ve)runt* (from *quiescere*, "be quiet").

7. **aequora**: *aequor* is literally a "level surface" but is often used to mean "sea," as here (cf. also 27-8 n.). **tendit iter**: *tendere* can mean not only "stretch" but also "direct" or "aim" (e.g., a weapon, glance, or, as here, a "journey," *iter, itineris*, n.). Note the chiastic* structure of *tendit iter* and *portumque relinquit*, two phrases that express a similar idea and thus might be considered a *dicolon abundans** (also called theme and variation*).

8-9. **aspirant aurae…**: note the assonance*, alliteration* and consonance* in these lines, as well as the effective juxtaposition of *noctem…candida*. Vergil creates a beautiful backdrop as the Trojans approach the realm of the goddess-sorceress Circe. **in noctem**: "(blow on, *aspirant*) into the night." **nec candida… | luna negat, splendet…**: note the litotes* (the description of something by negating its opposite, i.e., *nec…negat*) and the asyndeton*, which further heightens the interplay between light and darkness. **cursus**: accusative plural. **tremulo**: "quivering," capturing the effect of moonlight reflected on the sea.

10-24. Circe's realm. Aeneas reaches the land of the goddess Circe (sorceress and daughter of the Sun, *Solis filia* 11), as the Trojan seer Helenus had prophesied at 3.386. Circe lives on a promontory on the coast of Latium (10; cf. *Circaeum…iugum* 799), usually associated with Mount Circeo, though Helenus had called it an "island" (*insula*) at 3.386 (as it was in Homer, who, however, placed it in the east). The passage looks back to *Odyssey* 10, where half of Odysseus' men are turned into pigs by the goddess, until he, with Hermes' aid, forces her to return the men to their human form. Aeneas, by contrast, avoids such suffering, though he seems to do so unwittingly: at 21-4 Neptune simply guides the Trojans safely past Circe's island (see 23 n.). Vergil thus implies the differing challenges and natures of the two heroes, Aeneas and Odysseus. For more on Circe in Book 7, see notes on 189-91, 282; Putnam (1970 = 1995b), Mack (1999) 136-8, Nelis (2001) 262-5, Thomas (2004) 141-6.

10-14. Circe is described with an elaborate amount of artful hyperbaton* (any distortion of normal word order): e.g., noun-adjective patterns that are interlocking and enclosing as well as two golden lines* (10 and 14). The passage that follows (15-20), describing the men she transformed into animals, lacks such stylized word patterns and thus provides both a syntactic

dives inaccessos ubi Solis filia lucos
adsiduo resonat cantu, tectisque superbis
urit odoratam nocturna in lumina cedrum
arguto tenuis percurrens pectine telas.

---

and a stylistic contrast between the descriptions of the sorceress-goddess and of her victims (see 15-18 n. for other contrasting features).

10. **proxima...raduntur litora:** *rado* (3) means "scrape" or "graze" (here perhaps "skirt," Goold), and the adjective *proxima* ("nearest," "next") might be construed adverbially ("next"), i.e., "Next, the shores of Circe's land are skirted." **Circaeae:** adjectival form of *Circe* (cf. 10-24 n.). Note that this is a highly stylized golden line* (an artful arrangement of two interlocking adjective + noun phrases with a verb in the middle).

11. **dives:** nominative singular adjective, "rich," modifying *filia*. **inaccessos:** "inaccessible." This word is attested for the first time here (also in 8.195, of Cacus' lair). **Solis filia:** "daughter of the Sun," i.e., Circe, cf. 10-24 n. Note the interlocking* adjective + noun phrases (*dives...filia* and *inaccessos...lucos*).

12. **adsiduo...cantu:** "continual song," ablative of means; singing is a traditional component in descriptions of women at work, one that here helps mask the danger that the sorceress Circe poses. (Note that at *Odyssey* 10.220-3 Circe is also singing and weaving, cf. 10-24 n.) **resonat:** "makes resound," a rare transitive usage, taking *inaccessos...lucos* (11) as object. **tectis... superbis:** ablative of place without preposition; *tectis* here with the sense of "palace" (see 59 n.). Though *superbus* often has a negative connotation ("haughty," "arrogant"; cf. *debellare superbos* 6.853, Anchises' advice to Aeneas in the underworld), it can also be used positively, as it is seemingly here ("magnificent") and at 8.721 (of Augustus' Palatine Temple of Apollo, which is depicted on Aeneas' shield).

13. **odoratam...cedrum:** *cedrum* is feminine (*cedrus, -i,* f.); note the hyperbaton*, whereby this adjective-noun phrase encloses another phrase (*nocturna in lumina*). The pleasing smell of burning cedar (also in *Odyssey* 10.59-60; see notes on 10-24, 12, and 15-18) is another detail that contrasts with the actual danger Circe poses. **nocturna in lumina:** *in* with accusative here indicates purpose, "for night-time light," i.e., to provide light at night. For the juxtaposition of darkness and light, see 8-9 n.

14. **arguto...pectine:** ablative of means; *pecten (-inis,* m.) must here mean "shuttle," not the more usual "comb," while *arguto* ("rustling") describes the noise made by the shuttle as Circe moves it through the *tenuis telas*, as she weaves. **tenuis...telas:** accusative plural after *percurrens*, modifying Circe (*filia Solis* 11); *telas* here means the "warp," i.e., the threads running lengthwise in a weaving loom. Thomas (1985) suggests that *tenuis* ("thin," "fine") might convey the well-established metaphor* for the fineness and artistry of Hellenistic poetry (see "Vergil and his predecessors" in the General Introduction). **percurrens:** here "passing through." For more on weaving details, see Fordyce ad loc. This is another golden line* (10 n.), one that Vergil adapts from his earlier poem, *Georgics* 1.294 *arguto coniunx percurrit pectine telas* (of a farmer's wife weaving at night). (See Thomas (1985) and Henkel (2011) on the complex intertextuality involved.)

hinc exaudiri gemitus iraeque leonum 15
vincla recusantum et sera sub nocte rudentum,
saetigerique sues atque in praesepibus ursi
saevire ac formae magnorum ululare luporum,
quos hominum ex facie dea saeva potentibus herbis
induerat Circe in vultus ac terga ferarum. 20

15-18. These lines differ in style from 10-14 (see n.). They are structured by an elaborate tricolon* built on three historical infinitives (*exaudiri, saevire,* and *ululare*); such infinitives usually have an imperfect tense meaning, take nominative subjects (AG §463), and here add vividness to the decription of the humans whom Circe has transformed into animals. After the beauty and controlled calm of the description of Circe's home and weaving in 10-14, we get the horror of the magically transformed beasts. Vergil has reversed the order from that in the corresponding Homeric scene, where we first are told of the animals (which are tame) and then see Circe singing at her loom (*Od.* 10.210-23; see 10-24 n.).

15. **hinc exaudiri gemitus iraeque:** *exaudiri* is a historical infinitive (see 15-18 n.); *gemitus iraeque* are nominative subjects of *exaudiri* and can together be construed as an instance of hendiadys* (the expression of one idea through two terms joined by a conjunction), thus "angry roars" (of lions). The succession of long syllables at the start of this line perhaps emphasizes the transition to and introduction of the animals/transformed men. For the phrasing, cf. 6.557-8 *hinc exaudiri gemitus et saeva sonare | verbera* (of the sounds emanating in the underworld from Tartarus, which is overseen by the Fury Tisiphone). The echo may thus suggest the potential danger of Circe.

16. **vincla:** = *vincula,* "fetters"; accusative object of *recusantum.* **recusantum...rudentum:** genitive participles modifying *leonum* (15). *Recusantum* is from *recuso* (1), "refuse," "protest"; *rudentum* is from *rudo* (3), "roar," which is used literally of animals, though metaphorically of humans as well—here both usages are present, since Vergil describes men transformed into animals.

17-18. **saetigeri:** "bristle-bearing" (from *saeta* "bristle" and *gero* "bear"), an epic compound modifying *sues* (*sus, suis,* m./f., "pig"). **praesepibus:** "pens" or "cages" (*praesepe, -is,* n.). **saevire...ululare:** historical infinitives (cf. 15 n.) with nominative subjects *sues* and *ursi* in 17 and *formae* in 18; note the onomatopoeia* inherent in *ululare* ("howl"), particularly resonant here, since these humans in their animal form cannot speak. Note also the effective assonance* of the line (e.g., *magnorum...luporum*) which perhaps further underscores the howling. **formae magnorum luporum:** the use of *formae* ("forms," "shapes") in this phrase—instead of simply *magni lupi*—may look forward to the revelation in 19-20 that the animals are actually men whom Circe has transformed into their current animal forms.

19-20. **quos...induerat Circe in vultus...:** the relative pronoun *quos* refers back to the animals/former men just described, "whom Circe had clothed (*induerat*) in the 'faces' or 'features' (*in vultus*)." **dea saeva:** the goddess' fierce nature is made explicit; for *saeva,* see 511-12 n. (Odysseus calls her "dread goddess," Gr. *deinē theos,* at *Od.* 10.136.) **potentibus herbis:** "powerful herbs"; ablative of means. **terga ferarum:** probably not simply "skins" but the "backs (or bodies) of beasts."

quae ne monstra pii paterentur talia Troës
delati in portus neu litora dira subirent,
Neptunus ventis implevit vela secundis,
atque fugam dedit et praeter vada fervida vexit.
    Iamque rubescebat radiis mare et aethere ab alto   25
Aurora in roseis fulgebat lutea bigis,

21-2. **quae...monstra...talia:** "these such monstrous things," referring back to the men transformed by Circe into beasts (15-20) with *quae* serving as a connecting relative. *Monstra* was "originally a religious term used of a supernatural phenomenon which conveys a portent or an omen: so below 81 'sollicitus monstris', 376 'ingentibus excita monstris'" (Fordyce). **ne...pii paterentur:** a negative purpose clause in secondary sequence (thus imperfect subjunctive) with delayed *ne* (cf. 261 n.). Note the alliteration* in *pii paterentur*. Aeneas had been called *pius* at 5; now the Trojans are described with his defining quality. **delati:** from *defero*, "bring," "convey"; a conditional use of the participle ("if brought" or "driven into"), modifying *Troës*. **neu litora dira subirent:** another negative purpose clause, expanding the idea of the first (*ne...in portus*), an example of theme and variation*. The use of *litora dira* might later seem ironic in retrospect, since in Latium Juno and the Fury (or *Dira*, 324 n.) Allecto will start a horrendous war.

23. **Neptunus:** note that the safety of the Trojans results from the sea god's foresight, not (seemingly) Aeneas' (cf. 10-24 n.). Though Neptune had taken part in the destruction of Troy (2.610-12), his overall attitude toward the Trojans is supportive: at 1.142-56 he calms the storm sent against the Trojans by Juno, and at 5.811-15 he ensures the Trojans' arrival in Italy, though with the loss of one man (who will turn out to be Palinurus at 5.854-61). **ventis... secundis:** "favorable winds," ablative of means.

24. **fugam dedit:** supply the dative (indirect object) *eis*, "to them," i.e., the Trojans. The theme of flight, which was so important in Book 2 as Aeneas was continually told to flee Troy (e.g., 2.289, 619, 640) appears again. Here we find a god not just suggesting flight (as in Book 2) but actually bringing it about. **praeter:** preposition with accusative, "beyond," "past." **vada fervida:** note that the shallows (*vada*) are described as *fervida* ("seething," "violent"), and thus potentially dangerous.

25-36. At dawn on the next morning the Trojans arrive at the Tiber river.

25-6. **Iamque... | cum (27):** "Now (25)...when (27)..."; the combination of these two clauses provides a "vivid formula of transition" in "epic style" (Fordyce), as the Trojans reach a significant moment: they are about to enter the Tiber river, which will ultimately lead them to their promised land. Interestingly, a similar construction occurs at 3.521-2 (*iamque rubescebat stellis Aurora fugatis | cum...*), another significant moment, when the Trojans first see Italy (Horsfall). Note the alliteration* and assonance* of *r* and *a* in this vivid description of dawn. **rubescebat radiis:** *rubesco* (3) from "grow red"; *radius, -i, m.*, here "ray" (of the sun). **in roseis...bigis:** *bigae* (feminine plural, from *bi-* + *iuga* = two yokes) was a two-horse "chariot"; *roseus* ("rosy") is here used not of Aurora (in Homer, she is called "rosy-fingered Dawn") but of her chariot. **lutea:** "golden-yellow," modifying Aurora. Again, Vergil emphasizes the beautiful colors of the scene. Note that 26 is a variation on a golden line*.

cum venti posuere omnisque repente resedit
flatus, et in lento luctantur marmore tonsae.
atque hic Aeneas ingentem ex aequore lucum
prospicit. hunc inter fluvio Tiberinus amoeno   30
verticibus rapidis et multa flavus harena
in mare prorumpit. variae circumque supraque
adsuetae ripis volucres et fluminis alveo

27-8. **cum:** 26-7 n. **posuere:** "settled," "abated," intransitive usage (*OLD* s.v. *pono* 9). **omnis... resedit | flatus:** theme and variation* with *venti posuere*; *flatus, -us*, m., "blowing, but here "breeze." **lento...marmore:** *marmor, -oris*, n. means "marble," but the word was also used metaphorically in poetry (as here) to describe the shining surface of the sea, and thus just the "sea"; the sea is called "slow" or "sluggish" (*lento*) because it does not make rowing (and thus movement) easy. **tonsae:** *tonsa, -ae, f.*, "oar," an archaic poetic word used by Ennius (cf. 4 n.; *Annales* fragments 218, 219 in Skutsch and in *FRL* 1).

29. **atque:** "and at that moment"; *atque* can function as a strong connective particle that introduces an event closely associated (here temporally) with the preceding sentence. **hic:** adverb, "then." **ingentem:** "*ingens* is a word of the solemn epic style, already used by Ennius, and a favourite epithet of Vergil's; he uses it 168 times in the *Aeneid*" (Fordyce ad loc.).

30. **prospicit:** note how Vergil enjambs* this verb (i.e., allows the syntactic construction to extend from one line to the next), thus giving it emphasis. **hunc inter:** anastrophe* (i.e., the preposition *inter* follows its object *hunc* instead of preceding it); with *hunc* understand *lucum* ("grove") from 29. **fluvio...amoeno:** ablative of description (regarding the Tiber river, *Tiberinus*, see below); *amoeno* ("pleasant") provides a suggestion of calm in Latium, which will soon be disrupted as a result of Aeneas' arrival (cf. 1-285 n.). **Tiberinus:** adjectival form of the river *Tiberis/Thybris* (cf. notes on 150-1, 797), here used substantively (i.e., like a noun). Creusa foretold that Aeneas would find the Tiber upon arriving in Hesperia (2.781-2), though he does not immediately recognize it as such here (see also 31 n.).

31. **verticibus rapidis:** ablative; *vertex, -icis*, m., "eddy," "whirlpool." It is probably better to construe this phrase as an ablative (together with *multa...harena*, "sand") explaining why the river is *flavus*, though the phrase could also be taken closely with *prorumpit* (32). **flavus:** "yellow," "golden"; the Tiber's sandy color resonates with the Sibyl's prophecy at 6.88-9 that there would be another Trojan river Xanthus in Italy (*non Simois tibi nec Xanthus nec Dorica castra | defuerint*), since Greek *xanthos* can be translated as Latin *flavus*. The prophecy has in some sense been fulfilled, though, again (30 n.), Aeneas is unaware (O'Hara (1996 = 2017) 184; Fletcher (2014) 222).

32. **in mare prorumpit:** note the effective enjambment* of this phrase (cf. 30 n.), perhaps conveying the movement of the river into the sea. **variae:** describing the *volucres* (33), this adjective can mean "various" or "of diverse colors"; here either meaning seems possible. **circumque supraque:** both adverbs.

33. **adsuetae ripis volucres:** *ripis* is dative after the participle *adsuetae* ("accustomed to"), which modifies *volucres* (*volucris, -is,* f.). **alveo:** "river-channel," also dative after *adsuetae*; the final *e* and *o* are collapsed into one syllable by a phenomenon called synizesis*, which thus makes the word disyllabic.

aethera mulcebant cantu lucoque volabant.
flectere iter sociis terraeque advertere proras   35
imperat et laetus fluvio succedit opaco.
   Nunc age, qui reges, Erato, quae tempora, rerum
quis Latio antiquo fuerit status, advena classem

---

34. **aethera:** Greek accusative singular (*aether, -eris*, m.), "upper air." **mulcebant:** "were delighting." Vergil again emphasizes the landscape's beauty, which will stand in contrast to the horror that will soon engulf the region (286-640 n.). **cantu luco:** note that the former is ablative of means with *mulcebant*; the latter, ablative of place with *volabant*.

35-6. **flectere iter......advertere proras | imperat:** "orders (his comrades, *sociis*, dative) to change (*flectere*, "bend") course and to turn the prows to"; the subject is Aeneas. Note the use of infinitives (*flectere* and *advertere*) with *imperat* instead of an *ut*-clause in indirect command. Vergil, like other poets, employs the infinitive to complete or explain the meaning of a verb, where prose might use a different construction. **terrae:** dative governed by *advertere*. **laetus:** modifying Aeneas, though his joy occurs not because he understands that he has finally reached his fated land; this realization happens only at 120-7. Note that he will again be described as *laetus* at 288 (see n.), just as his suffering in Latium is about to start. **fluvio...opaco:** dative after the compound verb *succedit*, "enters."

37-45. Vergil invokes the Muse Erato for aid in describing the war in Latium.
Vergil has deferred the proem to the second ("Iliadic") half of his epic from the beginning of Book 7 to these lines, in which he announces his new and more weighty martial theme (44-5 n.; 1-285 n.). Yet, despite the focus on war, Vergil intriguingly invokes not Calliope, the Muse of epic, but Erato (37), the Muse of love poetry. By doing so, he seemingly alludes to the epic poet Apollonius (third century BCE), who began the second half of his *Argonautica* with an invocation of Erato (3.1) to introduce the story of Medea's love for Jason and his capture of the famous Golden Fleece, an exploit achieved through her assistance. Like Apollonius, Vergil plays with our expectations concerning genre, and looks forward to the importance of love— particularly the engagement of Lavinia—as central to the cause of war in Books 7-12. (Note too, however, that love is also associated with martial passion, e.g., 461 *amor ferri*, 550 *insani Martis amore*).

For the proem in general, see Putnam (1970) 417, Gransden (1984) 35-6, 39-43, Toll (1989), Kyriakidis (1994), O'Hara (1996) 184-5, Mack (1999) 128-34, Nelis (2001) 267-75, Fletcher (2014) 223-4, Stahl (2016) 355-9. For intertextual influences: Fraenkel (1945: 2-3 = 1990: 256) (historiography and Cyclic epic); Ash (2002) 262-3 (historiography); Dekel (2012) 6-8 (Homer's *Odyssey*); Nelis (2001) 267-75 (Apollonius); Thomas (2004) 135-40 (Alexandrian poets); Goldschmidt (2013) 50-61, 131-9 (Ennius).

37-8. **Nunc age...Erato:** for this invocation of the Muse of love poetry, see 37-45 n. *Age* is the imperative of *agere* ("lead," "drive") and conveys encouragement, "come on"; in conjunction with *Nunc* (thus "come now"), the phrase is modeled on the opening words of Book 3 of Apollonius' *Argonautica* (Gr. *ei d'age nun, Erato*). The phrase *nunc age* is also associated with didactic poetry (Horsfall) and used by Vergil at *Georgics* 4.149 and *Aeneid* 6.756, both places where something is being explained. **qui reges...quae tempora:** *qui* and *quae* are both interrogatives; supply *fuerint* in both clauses, which are indirect questions (like *quis...fuerit*

cum primum Ausoniis exercitus appulit oris,
expediam, et primae revocabo exordia pugnae.   40
tu vatem, tu, diva, mone. dicam horrida bella,
dicam acies actosque animis in funera reges,
Tyrrhenamque manum totamque sub arma coactam

---

status in the next line) governed by *expediam*, which is delayed until (and emphatically enjambed at) the beginning of line 40; *tempora* here means "the times," "circumstances." **rerum:** perhaps better construed with *status*, thus "state of affairs," a phrase found in Livy 8.13.2, though *tempora rerum* is also possible ("timing of events," Lucretius 5.1276; cf. Stahl (2016) 355-9). **advena:** this noun (*advena, -ae*, m. or f., "stranger," "foreigner") is used adjectivally; construe with *exercitus* (39), "foreign army."

39. **cum:** temporal. **primum:** adverbial. **Ausoniis...oris:** dative governed by the compound verb *appulit* (from *appello* (3), "drive" or "bring to"), which takes *classem* (38) as accusative object. The adjective *Ausonii* is formed from Gr. *Ausones*, the Greek name for the people originally inhabiting Campania (they were called *Aurunci* in early Latin). In poetry, *Ausonii* came to refer to Italians more generally, and *Ausonia* to Italy.

40. **expediam:** enjambed* for emphasis (cf. 37-8 n.); "will relate" or "narrate." For this meaning, cf. *Georgics* 4.286 *expediam prima repetens ab origine famam* and *Aen.* 3.379 *expediam dictis.* **primae...exordia pugnae:** "beginnings of the first battle" (i.e., the events leading to the war's outbreak). **revocabo:** "will recall," "revive memory of" (*OLD* s.v. *revoco* 13b).

41-2. **tu...tu...:** note the (unnecessary) repetition of *tu* (i.e., Erato) for emotional effect, as well as to create the juxtaposition of *tu* with *vatem*, Muse and poet. **vatem:** "seer" (*vates, -is*, m.) but also, as here, an archaic word for "poet" that Vergil and Horace revitalized; notably the poet uses this elevated word to describe himself, as he invokes the Muse. **diva:** "goddess," i.e., the Muse Erato. **mone:** "remind," imperative of *moneo* (2), involving an etymological wordplay. Erato (37) was one of the Muses, whose mother was Gr. *Mnemosyne* ("Memory"); *Musa* (Gr. *Mousa*) is etymologically related to *moneo* and *mens* (cf. 645-6 n. and cf. O'Hara (2017) 192-3). **dicam...| dicam:** note the forceful use of anaphora* (with verbs placed emphatically at the beginning of their clauses) and asyndeton*. **dicam horrida bella:** Vergil here describes the war that he will retell in Books 7-12 in words that recall the Sibyl's prophecy at 6.86 (*bella, horrida bella...*). In both passages, note how the harsh elision* involving *horrida* helps convey the nature of the war. **bella...acies...reges:** these are standard themes of martial epic (cf. *Eclogue* 6.3 *canerem reges et proelia*); *acies* (accusative plural of *acies, -ei*, f.) here means "battle lines." **animis:** ablative of means with the sense of *animose*, "with spirit," "bravely"; construe closely with *actos* ("driven," modifying *reges*). **in funera:** *funus* ("burial") can also mean "corpse" or "death"; here the phrase means "to (their) deaths."

43-4. **Tyrrhenamque manum:** *Tyrrhenus* is an adjective formed from Gr. *Turrhenos*, used especially in poetry as a synonym for *Tuscus*, "Etruscan"; *manus* denotes "hand" but can also mean "squadron" or "armed force," as here. **totamque...Hesperiam:** Vergil expands the scope of the traditional war to include all of Hesperia/Italy (see notes on 4 and 641-817). "A Roman reader...could hardly fail to be reminded of the battle of Actium only twelve years before Vergil's death, when, according to Augustus' own propaganda, *tota Italia*...voluntarily swore

Hesperiam. maior rerum mihi nascitur ordo,
maius opus moveo.
    Rex arva Latinus et urbes   45
iam senior longa placidas in pace regebat.
hunc Fauno et nympha genitum Laurente Marica

---

an oath of allegiance to him against Antony" (Mack (1999) 132; see General Introduction on Actium). See also Wimperis (2020) on the idea of *tota Italia* as a rhetorical construct in Books 7-12, and Toll (1997) on the idea of "Roman-ness" in the *Aeneid*.

44-5. **maior rerum...nascitur ordo:** *ordo* means "succession," "sequence." For the sentence, cf. *Ecl.* 4.5 *magnus ab integro saeclorum nascitur ordo* (on the golden age foreseen with the birth of an unnamed child; the so-called "Messianic Eclogue"). Perhaps ironically, Books 7-12 will be dominated not by golden age ease but by the violence and fury of war. Propertius in 2.34.66 (published in the mid-20s BCE), writing about the *Aeneid*, might allude to an early version of this line: *nescio quid maius nascitur Iliade* (see O'Rourke (2011)). **maior...maius opus moveo:** note the polyptoton* (repetition of a word in its inflected cases) of *maior...maius*, emphasizing the weightiness of the epic's theme. For the overall significance of these lines, see Introduction to Book 7. Note also the important and programmatic use of the verb *moveo* at 312 *Acheronta movebo*, as Juno decides to enlist the aid of the underworld to start the Italian war.

45-80. *The situation in Latium: King Latinus has received divine portents indicating that his daughter Lavinia should marry a foreigner, and that this union would initially bring war but then ultimately an impressive empire.*

Latinus (cf. 1-285 n.) is introduced as a good king, ruling the Latins in peace (though see 45-6 n.). He has several models in important Homeric elder/father figures such as Nestor, Priam, and Laertes (see Knauer (1964a), Cairns (1989) 62-6, and Nelis (2001) 275-89). His daughter Lavinia (52 n.), who never speaks and rarely appears in the epic, is presented as a virtuous figure (see Cairns (1989) 151-76, 162-3).

45-6. **Rex...Latinus...regebat:** cf. 45-80 n. Latinus' ability to rule effectively, however, is precisely what will be thrown into question later in Book 7. **iam senior:** "now old," "now an old man"; the comparative form *senior* is roughly equivalent to *senex* in Vergil (cf. 535, 736). Latinus' age is emphasized from the start. **longa...in pace:** ablative of time or circumstance; an important detail, since the peace of his kingdom is about to be destroyed. However, later in the book (183-4, 423-6) and poem (8.55), there are indications that Latinus' reign has not been thoroughly peaceful (see O'Hara (2007) 96-8).

47. **hunc:** i.e., Latinus. **Fauno et nympha...Laurente Marica:** ablatives of origin governed by *genitum* (from *gigno* (3), "bear," "produce," in the passive "be born"); with *genitum* supply *esse* in an accusative-infinitive construction governed by *accipimus* (48-9 n.). Latinus' father is Faunus, who in turn is identified as the son of Picus and grandson of Saturnus (48-9). Such genealogies connecting kings with gods are important for establishing regal authority (cf. Aeneas at 219). Faunus was a god of agriculture and shepherds, and was associated with the Greek god Pan. Latinus' mother was the nymph Marica, who was connected to the river Liris (e.g., Horace, *Odes* 3.17.6-9) in southern Latium near Campania; however, *Laurens*, here as elsewhere in Vergil, can have the more general meaning of "Latin" (e.g., Turnus, who

accipimus; Fauno Picus pater, isque parentem
te, Saturne, refert, tu sanguinis ultimus auctor.
filius huic fato divum prolesque virilis   50
nulla fuit, primaque oriens erepta iuventa est.
sola domum et tantas servabat filia sedes

---

was from Ardea, is described as *Laurentis Turni* at 650). (Note that, though Latinus' city is often called Laurentum, Vergil never gives it this name, which might have arisen from his use of the genitive plural Laurentum; moreover, the precise location of Latinus' city is unclear. See *VE* s.v. *Laurentum* and *Laurentes*.) For other versions and details of Latinus' genealogy, see Rosivach (1980), Moorton (1988), and Fantham (2009) 46-7.

48-9. **accipimus:** "we accept," "we understand" (see 47 n. for syntax). In the learned style of Alexandrian poetry (see "Vergil and his predecessors" in General Introduction), Vergil points to his engagement with the mythographical tradition. **Fauno Picus pater:** supply *erat*; *Fauno* is dative of reference. Picus (189-91 n.) was the father of Faunus and son of Saturn. **isque:** *is* refers to Picus and is subject of *refert* (see below). **te, Saturne...tu:** note the polyptoton* (*te...tu*) and apostrophe*, which rhetorically enliven Latinus' genealogy. Saturn was an Italian harvest god (cf. *sero, serere, sevi, satum*, "sow," "plant"), later associated with the Greek god Kronos (Zeus' father). After being deposed by his son Zeus, Saturnus/Kronos established a golden age in Latium, where tradition said that he had hidden from Zeus/Jupiter (thus the etymology of *Latium* from *lateo*, "lie hidden"). **refert:** here "reports, "claims"; it takes an accusative (*te*) and infinitive (supply *esse*) construction.

50-1. Difficult but important lines. **filius huic...prolesque virilis | nulla:** with *huic* (i.e., Latinus, dative of possessor) supply *est*; *nulla* modifies *proles* (*-is*, f., "offspring," "child") but in sense should also be understood with *filius*. Thus, "There was no son to this man (Latinus) and no male offspring." The two phrases form a *dicolon abundans** (see 7 n.) strongly emphasizing that Latinus did not have a male heir, and thereby indicating the importance of his daughter Lavinia's prospective marriage (52-4). **divum:** Vergil frequently uses the archaic genitive plural in *-um* (sometimes written *-om* when *v* precedes) with proper names (e.g., *Teucrum, Danaum, Argivum, Achivum, Dardanidum, Graium*), or names describing a class of persons (e.g., *divum, deum, virum, superum, caelicolum*). **primaque...iuventa:** "but in early (lit. 'first') youth"; the phrase *prima iuventa* is ablative of time or circumstance, while *-que* has an adversative meaning, i.e., "but" (a usage often occurring when a preceding clause expressing a similar idea is negative, as here, AG §324d note). **oriens erepta...est:** *oriens*, present participle from *orior* (4), modifies *proles* and here means "(as the child was) growing" (though "rising" is its more typical definition); the participle *erepta* is feminine because *proles*—the subject of *erepta est*—is feminine (see above). In these lines Vergil also foregrounds the important theme throughout Books 7-12 of sons/youthful warriors who die young.

52. **sola...filia:** i.e., Lavinia (not named until 72), over whom the war in Books 7-12 will be fought. **tantas...sedes:** "so great a residence," the phrase conveying a broader sense of Latinus' palace (with its political implications) than would *domum* alone. For the range of meaning of *sedes* ("seat"), cf. notes on 3, 158, 229-30, 324 in Book 7. **servabat:** not simply "was inhabiting" but "preserving" (cf. *servat...sedem* 3).

iam matura viro, iam plenis nubilis annis.
multi illam magno e Latio totaque petebant
Ausonia; petit ante alios pulcherrimus omnis   55
Turnus, avis atavisque potens, quem regia coniunx
adiungi generum miro properabat amore;
sed variis portenta deum terroribus obstant.
laurus erat tecti medio in penetralibus altis

---

53. **iam...iam:** note the anaphora* with asyndeton*, as well as the theme and variation* involved in both clauses indicating that Lavinia is of marriable age. **viro:** dative, i.e., "for a husband" or "marriage" (by metonymy*). **nubilis:** "of an age suitable for marriage," "nubile"; an adjective from *nubo* (3), "cover (with veil)," "marry."

54-5. **multi:** substantive, "many men"; note its juxtaposition with *illam* (Lavinia). **tota... Ausonia:** ablative also governed by the preposition *e*; the phrase expands the geography covered in *magno e Latio* (cf. *totam Hesperiam* in 43-4 with n.) to include "all Ausonia" (i.e., Italy, cf. 39 n.). **petebant:** with sense of "were courting" or "wooing." **petit...Turnus (56):** note the initial placement of the verb *petit* and the enjambment* of the subject *Turnus* into 56, both for emphasis. **ante alios pulcherrimus omnis:** construe *omnis* with *alios* (substantive, i.e., "other men"); interestingly, it is Turnus' beauty that is initially highlighted (perhaps in keeping with the "love theme" and Vergil's invocation of Erato, 37-45 n.), not his military skill (see Reed (2007) 48-9). This phrase is also used of Aeneas at 4.141.

56. **Turnus:** cf. 54-5 n. **avis atavisque:** ablatives; construe closely with *potens* ("powerful," "strong"). *Avus* means "grandfather," *atavus* "great-great-great-grandfather"; both, however, can mean "ancestor" more generally, though *atavus* implies greater distance in time. For Turnus' ancestry, see 371-2 n.; for his role in the Aeneas story, see 1-285 n. **regia coniunx:** a periphrasis* for Amata, King Latinus' wife.

57. **generum:** "son-in-law" (*gener, generi*, m.); predicative usage, "to be joined (to herself) as a son-in-law." **miro...amore:** emphasizes how passionately Amata was advocating (*properabat*, "hurrying to bring it about," cf. *OLD* s.v. *propero* 7b) that Turnus become her son-in-law; for the complex nature of this passion, see notes on 341-72 and 343; for *amor*, see 37-45 n.

58. **variis...terroribus:** ablative of means; *terroribus* here means "things that cause terror," "terrifying things." **deum:** genitive plural (50-1 n.). **obstant:** "stand in the way."

59. **laurus:** the laurel tree was associated with Apollo. "Latinus' consecration to Apollo of a laurel tree in his palace...seems to evoke the laurels prominently ornamenting Augustus' Palatine house adjacent to Apollo's temple" (Miller (2009) 163). Note too that there is a *veterrima laurus* in Priam's palace (2.513). **erat:** "there was." **tecti medio:** understand *in* with *medio*. *Tectum, -i*, n. (from the perfect participle of *tego*, "cover") is a standard word for "house," "dwelling"; here "palace" (cf. *tectis...superbis* 12). The use of neuter participles (like *tecti*) and neuter adjectives (like *medio*, "middle," "center") as nouns is fairly common in Vergil (cf. also 86 *in dubiis*, 749 *vivere rapto* (i.e., theft). **in penetralibus altis:** *penetrale (-is*, n.) means "inner room" or "space"; in this case, *altis* means "deep" not "high," and emphasizes the reverential nature of the laurel tree and its placement deep in the palace.

sacra comam multosque metu servata per annos, 60
quam pater inventam, primas cum conderet arces,
ipse ferebatur Phoebo sacrasse Latinus,
Laurentisque ab ea nomen posuisse colonis.
huius apes summum densae (mirabile dictu)
stridore ingenti liquidum trans aethera vectae 65
obsedere apicem, et pedibus per mutua nexis

60. **sacra:** modifying *laurus* (59 n.), which is feminine (*laurus, -i,* f.). **comam:** here "foliage," accusative of respect; construe closely with *sacra*. **multosque metu servata per annos:** *metu* (ablative) here has the sense of "religious awe" (*OLD* s.v. *metus* 4b); for the verb *servare*, cf. 3 (of Caieta) and 52 (of Lavinia). This tree resembles the cypress tree at Troy, where Aeneas plans for his family and household to meet as they flee the burning city: 2.714-15 *antiqua cupressus | religione patrum multos servata per annos.*

61-2. **quam...ferebatur...sacrasse:** *quam* (antecedent is *laurus* 59) is direct object of *sacrasse* (syncopated* form of *sacravisse* from *sacro*, "dedicate"); *ferebatur* here means "was said" (*OLD* s.v. *fero* 33). The clause can thus be translated: "which (Latinus himself) was said to have dedicated." **inventam:** a participle with temporal/circumstantial force, "when it was found"; modifying *quam* (i.e., the laurel tree). **conderet:** imperfect subjunctive in a *cum*-circumstantial clause in past time (AG §546). **ipse...Latinus:** subject of the passive verb *ferebatur* (see above); the phrase artfully frames the line. **Phoebo:** dative, i.e., Apollo (cf. 59 n.); the laurel was his sacred tree.

63. **Laurentis...nomen posuisse colonis:** *posuisse* (here "to have given") is, like *sacrasse*, governed by *ferebatur* (62). Construe *Laurentis* (accusative plural) in apposition to *nomen* (i.e., "the name Laurentes"), while *colonis* is dative of indirect object after *posuisse*. The more common naming idiom would have *Laurentis* in the dative (i.e., *Laurentibus*) to modify *colonis* (Fordyce). **ab ea:** understand *lauro*, which is feminine (60 n.). Note, however, that the naming claim involves an inconsistency with 171 (see n.).

64-5. **huius...summum...apicem (66):** with *huius*, understand *lauri*, "the highest point of this (laurel tree)." Note the long separation (see hyperbaton*) of *summum* and *apicem*, which form the direct object of *obsedere* ("sat on," "occupied," from *obsideo*, potentially having a military resonance) with the subject *apes...densae* (modified by *vectae*, see below). **mirabile dictu:** *dictu* is the ablative of specification of the supine, normally used in Vergil in combination with such adjectives; "wondrous to say" (lit. "with respect to saying"). **stridore ingenti:** ablative of manner; *stridor, -oris,* m., "harsh sound," "buzzing." **liquidum:** "clear" or "bright," as often used to describe the *aether* (upper) air (cf. 34 n.); *aethera* is a Greek accusative. **vectae:** participle modifying *apes*; *veho* ("convey") in the passive (with middle sense) can also mean "ride," "sail," or here "fly" (*OLD* s.v. *veho* 5). Note the long separation between *apes...vectae* (hyperbaton*). The potential metaphor in *veho* of conveyance by ship might suggest a further connection in the comparison between bees and the Trojans (Horsfall).

66-7. **obsedere apicem:** see 64-5 n. **pedibus...nexis:** ablative; the participle *nexis* is from *nectere* (3), "bind." The bees hang down in chain-like formations "with their feet bound together" (*per mutua,* "through one another," *OLD* s.v. *mutuus* 4b). **examen subitum:** describing the

examen subitum ramo frondente pependit.
continuo vates, 'externum cernimus' inquit
'adventare virum et partis petere agmen easdem
partibus ex isdem et summa dominarier arce.' 70
praeterea, castis adolet dum altaria taedis,
et iuxta genitorem astat Lavinia virgo,
visa, nefas, longis comprendere crinibus ignem

---

apes (64), "a sudden swarm." **ramo frondente:** ablative after *pependit* (from *pendeo* (2), "hang down").

68. **continuo:** "immediately." The adverb conveys excitement, enhanced by the seer's speech beginning mid-line (cf. also 120). **vates:** "seer" (cf. 41-2 n.); not mentioned until now, but his sudden appearance and interpretation of the omen add to the excitement. **externum:** "external," "foreign"; emphatically placed and crucial, it modifies *virum* (69), and its meaning will be contested by Amata (see 367-72 n.). *Externum...virum* (69) forms the direct object of *cernimus* in an accusative-infinitive construction with *adventare* (69) as infinitive.

69-70. **partis petere agmen easdem | partibus ex isdem:** the accusative-infinitive construction continues (68 n.) with *agmen* ("army," see below) accusative subject of the infinitives *petere* and *dominarier* (see below). The meaning of this phrase is difficult, but through polyptoton* it closely associates the movements of the (Trojan) army and of the bees. The Trojan army (like the bees) "seek the same 'parts' or 'quarter of the sky' (*partis...easdem*, i.e., citadel, *arx*) from the same quarter of the sky (*partibus ex isdem*, i.e., the sea)"; the words *partis/partibus* suggest augury, in which priests (augurs) would watch for bird signs in designated quarters (*partes*) of the sky (Horsfall). **agmen:** here (Trojan) "army," a well-chosen word since *agmen* can also mean "swarm" (Horsfall). **dominarier:** "to rule over," an archaic infinitive (deponent), which underscores the solemnity of the declaration; the verb governs the ablative *summa...arce*. **arce:** the "citadel" (cf. 61) of Latinus city (cf. 47 n.) is thus associated with his residence. Note the two elisions in 69.

71. **castis...taedis:** ablative of means. **adolet:** "kindles," here describing a ritual; Lavinia (72) should probably be construed as subject (not the *vates* of 68). The verb originally took the offering being burnt as the direct object, but then also the altar (here *altaria*, n. pl.), where the rite was performed.

72. **iuxta:** "next to," a preposition governing the accusative *genitorem* (i.e., Latinus). **Lavinia virgo:** her first naming in the epic (cf. 52 n.); *virgo* emphasizes that she is unmarried (cf. 53 n).

73-6. The horrifying portent of Lavinia's hair aflame recalls similar stories indicating future political power in the cases of Servius Tullius (Rome's sixth king; see Livy 1.39 and Ovid, *Fasti* 6.636) and Ascanius at 2.682-4. The latter passage could thus link Aeneas' son Ascanius to Aeneas' future spouse Lavinia (see discussion in Rogerson (2017) 108-10). The description of Lavinia's burning hair may also recall Euripides, *Medea* 1186-7, "describing the lethal effects of Medea's 'gift' on Jason's new young bride," which would be a terrifying ill-omen (Mack (1999) 133); cf. Cairns (1989) 175 n. 76, Baraz (2009).

73. **visa:** supply *est* (thus "seemed") with *Lavinia* as subject. **nefas:** an appositive comment on the portent that it describes; literally "unspeakable act," here perhaps "shocking!" **longis**

atque omnem ornatum flamma crepitante cremari,
regalisque accensa comas, accensa coronam   75
insignem gemmis; tum fumida lumine fulvo
involvi ac totis Volcanum spargere tectis.
id vero horrendum ac visu mirabile ferri:
namque fore inlustrem fama fatisque canebant
ipsam, sed populo magnum portendere bellum.   80
   At rex sollicitus monstris oracula Fauni,
fatidici genitoris, adit lucosque sub alta

---

comprendere crinibus: an unusual and therefore striking syntactical inversion (enallage*) is involved, since we would expect *ignis* to be the subject of *compre(he)ndere* ("seize"), not Lavinia.

74. **omnem ornatum**: the ornaments in Lavinia's hair (75); accusative of respect or retained accusative after the infinitive *cremari* ("be consumed by fire"), which continues the *visa (est)* construction from line 73.

75. **regalisque accensa comas, accensa coronam | insignem (76)**: *regalis...comas* and *coronam insignem* are accusatives of respect; the participles (*accensa...accensa*) modify Lavinia. Note the repetition of *accensa* and the asyndeton*, both contributing to the excitement caused by the portent (cf. 327 n.).

76-7. **fumida lumine fulvo | involvi**: "she was enwrapped (*involvi*), smoking (*fumida*), in yellowish light"; *involvi* (like *spargere*, "spread") is a historical infinitive (cf. 15-18 n.). **totis... tectis**: ablative of place (cf. 12 n.). **Volcanum**: the god of fire, but here (by metonymy*) "fire."

78. **id**: i.e., the portent just described. **horrendum ac visu mirabile**: *visu* is ablative of specification (64-5 n.). In Vergil, this construction is usually associated with one adjective; the use of two here underscores the wondrousness of the event. **ferri**: historical infinitive (passive), from *fero*; here "was reported" or "made known."

79-80. **fore:** = *futuram esse* (see below). **fama fatisque**: ablatives; the alliterative* phrase indicates two different aspects of Lavinia's importance (cf. *inlustrem*), with both words being etymologically rooted in *for* (*fari*), "speak." (Cf. *attollens umero famamque et fata nepotum*, Aeneas lifting his shield on his shoulder at 8.731.) **canebant**: governs the accusative (*ipsam*, i.e., Lavinia) and infinitive (*fore*) construction with *vates* (cf. 41-2 n.) understood as plural subject; the verb is regularly used of oracles, which were normally pronounced in hexameters. **ipsam**: i.e., Lavinia; note the emphatic enjambment*. **populo**: dative of reference. **magnum... bellum**: note again *magnum* (cf. 45 *maius opus*, and 54 *magno...Latio* earlier): everything about Italy seems to be "great," as befits the outbreak and fighting of the war about to be described.

81-106. *Latinus learns from the oracle of his father Faunus that his daughter must wed a man from a foreign race who will bring fame and empire to his people.*

81-2. **At**: cf. 5 n. **monstris**: i.e., the portents just described in 59-80 (for *monstra*, see 21-2 n.); ablative dependent on *sollictus*. **oracula Fauni**: *oracula* is accusative after *adit* (82); for Faunus, cf. 47 n. Latinus' consultation of his father's oracle makes him, like Aeneas, a *pius* son and

consulit Albunea, nemorum quae maxima sacro
fonte sonat saevamque exhalat opaca mephitim.
hinc Italae gentes omnisque Oenotria tellus   85
in dubiis responsa petunt; huc dona sacerdos
cum tulit et caesarum ovium sub nocte silenti
pellibus incubuit stratis somnosque petivit,
multa modis simulacra videt volitantia miris
et varias audit voces fruiturque deorum   90

---

ruler. In Dionysius of Halicarnassus, *Antiquitates Romanae* 1.57 (first century BCE, cf. 1-285 n.), the prophecy concerning the Trojans involved in this passage comes from a dream of Latinus, not from the oracle of Faunus. **fatidici:** "fate-speaking," "prophetic," an elevated epic compound form.

83-4. **Albunea:** ablative (with *alta* 82); the name (see below) of a grove, now unidentifiable but somewhere outside of Lavinium. **nemorum quae maxima:** "which, mightiest of groves"; *maxima* is feminine after *Albunea*, though we might have expected the neuter case because *nemorum* (*nemus, -oris*) is neuter. **opaca:** "shady," "shaded," modifying Albunea. **mephitim:** accusative (*mephitis, -is*, f.), a "sulphurous exhalation"; it presumably gave rise to the name *Albunea* (from *alba*, "white").

85. **omnis Oenotria tellus:** *Oenotria* is the farthest southern region (i.e., the toe) of the Italian peninsula, but is used here (as an adjective) to indicate Italy more generally. It is an ancient name, and is found in Herodotus 1.167 (fifth century BCE).

86. **in dubiis:** cf. 59 n. **responsa:** "answers," "oracles." **dona:** i.e., sacrificial offerings, cf. Latinus' *centum lanigeras...bidentis* (93).

87-8. **cum tulit...incubuit...petivit...:** a *cum* "whenever" clause with the perfect indicative conveying a frequentative sense, "when(ever) the priest brings...lies on...seeks...." The practice described here is called *incubatio*, in which an *incubator* ("one who lies down," see below) sacrifices animals (cf. *caesarum ovium*) at a god's shrine, and there sleeps at night on the slain animals' hides (cf. *pellibus...stratis*) in order to consult spirits of the dead in dreams (cf. *simulacra* 89). **incubuit:** from *incumbo* ("lie" or 'recline on"), a compound verb governing *pellibus...stratis* (dative).

89. **modis simulacra...volitantia miris:** *simulacrum* (n.) means "image," "shade"; *modis...miris*, "in astonishing ways." This phrase is used at *Geo.* 1.477 but ultimately modeled on Lucretius 1.123 *quaedam simulacra modis pallentia miris* (where Lucretius rejects the poet Ennius' view of shades in the underworld).

90-1. **fruitur:** "enjoys," governing the ablative *conloquio* ("conversation"). **imis...Avernis:** ablative, "in deepest Avernus," i.e., the underworld; Lake Avernus in Campania was considered an entrance to the underworld. **Acheronta:** a Greek accusative (from *Acheron, -ontis*, m.); the Acheron is a river in the underworld, though here, by metonymy* (as in 312), it indicates the gods in the underworld. Vergil brings out the strong infernal connection involved in *incubatio* (87-8 n.).

conloquio atque imis Acheronta adfatur Avernis.
hic et tum pater ipse petens responsa Latinus
centum lanigeras mactabat rite bidentis,
atque harum effultus tergo stratisque iacebat
velleribus: subita ex alto vox reddita luco est: 95
'ne pete conubiis natam sociare Latinis,
o mea progenies, thalamis neu crede paratis;
externi venient generi, qui sanguine nostrum

---

92. **hic:** adverb, "here" (i.e., in the grove, 82-4). **et tum:** "then as well." The focus switches back to Latinus (*pater ipse*), who is performing the rite that was just described in 85-91.

93. **lanigeras...bidentis:** *lanigerus* is a stylized epic compound adjective from *lana* ("wool") + *gero* ("bear"); a *bidens* is a sacrificial animal (here sheep, f.) that has already developed its two central permanent teeth (thus usually two years old). **mactabat rite:** ritual language (*macto*, "sarifice"; *rite*, 5 n.); Latinus performs the sacrifice properly (cf. Aeneas in 5-6).

94-5. **harum:** genitive, referring to the sheep (*lanigeras...bidentis* 93). **effultus:** describing Latinus; "propped up on" or "supported by" with ablative (from **effulcio*). **tergo stratisque... | velleribus:** ablative; "hide" (*tergum, -i,* n.) "and fleeces" (*vellus, -eris,* n.) or, by hendiadys*, "fleece hides spread out" (*stratis* from *sterno* (3)). **reddita est:** note the use of the perfect tense to contrast with the preceding imperfects.

96-101. Latinus receives an oracle from his father Faunus that is consistent with the interpretation of the bee portent at 68-70. These lines give voice to another important prophecy of Rome's rise to world power that reinforces the revelations of Jupiter in Book 1 and of Anchises in Book 6.

96-7. **ne pete:** a poetic negative imperative, archaic* in tone. **conubiis:** the Roman legal term for marriage. The quantity of the *u* is debated: if it is short, then the first *i* is short and the word has four syllables (*cŏnŭbĭīs*); if it is long, then the first *i* is consonantal and the word has three syllables (*cōnūbjīs*). Either scansion is possible. **sociare:** "join," "unite"; infinitive after *pete*. **mea progenies:** note the emphasis on paternal relations; cf. *natam* (i.e., Latinus' daughter Lavinia). **thalamis...paratis:** dative after *crede*; *thalamis* ("bedchambers") here means "marriages," while *paratis* ("prepared") might be better translated as "available" (see *OLD* s.v. *paratus* 1 and Horsfall ad loc.). At 55-8 Vergil did not quite say (nor do we ever learn for certain) that Turnus and Lavinia were already engaged, even if *thalamis...paratis* and characters later (e.g., Amata at 365-6) may imply or claim an engagement.

98-9. **externi...generi:** *externus* is a key word, echoing the *vates* at 68 (see n.); for *gener*, see 57 n. **qui sanguine nostrum | nomen in astra ferant:** relative clause expressing purpose, equivalent to *ut ii....* Latinus will repeat these words to Ilioneus at 271-2. **sanguine:** "by blood," here means "family line" but perhaps also implies bloodshed (i.e., war) (O'Hara (1990) 63; Horsfall ad loc.).

nomen in astra ferant, quorumque a stirpe nepotes
omnia sub pedibus, qua Sol utrumque recurrens   100
aspicit Oceanum, vertique regique videbunt.'
haec responsa patris Fauni monitusque silenti
nocte datos non ipse suo premit ore Latinus,
sed circum late volitans iam Fama per urbes
Ausonias tulerat, cum Laomedontia pubes   105
gramineo ripae religavit ab aggere classem.
  Aeneas primique duces et pulcher Iulus

99-101. **quorumque a stirpe nepotes…videbunt (101)**: the antecedent of *quorum* is *generi* (98-9 n.). Note the change from subjunctive (*ferant* 99) to the more emphatic future indicative (*videbunt* 101) in these relative clauses, though both foretell the future. **qua**: "where." **utrum… Oceanum**: since Oceanus circles the globe, Sol (the Sun) sees "either Ocean"—in the East, when rising, and in the West, when setting. **recurrens**: "returning," "circling back." **vertique regique videbunt**: "will see all things (*omnia* 100) move (*verti*, with middle sense) and be ruled"; construe *sub pedibus* (100) closely with this phrase.

102-3. **monitus**: "warnings"; fourth declension, accusative plural, modified by *datos*. **silenti | nocte**: ablative of time when. **non ipse suo premit ore**: i.e., Latinus does not keep quiet about the prophecy; *premit* takes *responsa* and *monitus* as objects.

104. **circum…volitans**: tmesis*. **Fama per urbes**: repeated from 4.173 (following Dido and Aeneas' sexual encounter in the cave).

105. **Ausonias**: cf. 39 n. **tulerat**: understand *responsa* and *monitus* (102) as objects; the pluperfect tense describes the action as preceding the arrival of the Trojans (cf. *religavit* in 106, perfect tense). **Laomedontia**: i.e., Trojan. Laomedon (Priam's father) cheated Neptune and Apollo out of their pay for helping him build the walls of Troy. The adjective does not seem to suggest treachery here, though it does when spoken at 3.248 (Celaeno) and 4.542 (Dido) (Mack (1999) 140-1). **pubes**: here, as often, "men," "people."

106. **gramineo…ab aggere**: *agger, -eris*, m., here "bank (of a river)" (*OLD* s.v. *agger* 3c). We now return to the situation at 35-6, when the Trojans entered the Tiber. **religavit**: "bind back," but here specifically "moored" (*OLD* s.v. *religo* 3b); the perfect tense contrasts with *tulerat* (105 n.).

107-34. The Trojans land and, while feasting, eat the spelt-cakes that serve as food plates. After a joke from Ascanius, Aeneas claims that a prophecy he heard from Anchises has just been fulfilled.

The prophecy of the eating of the tables and Aeneas' attribution of it to Anchises create a notorious inconsistency. Earlier in the poem, the prophecy was uttered not by Anchises but by the Harpy Celaeno (3.255-7), and she does so threateningly, after the Trojans have committed violence against the Harpies: *sed non ante datam cingetis moenibus urbem | quam vos dira fames nostraeque iniuria caedis | ambesas subigat malis absumere mensas* ("But you will not surround your promised city with walls until wretched hunger and the wrong of our slaughter (i.e., your attempted slaughter of us) compel you to consume tables devoured by your jaws"). (Later in Book 3 the Trojan seer Helenus tells Aeneas that they do not need to fear Celaeno's words: *nec tu mensarum morsus horresce futuros* (3.394).) The tradition itself varied. According

corpora sub ramis deponunt arboris altae,
instituuntque dapes et adorea liba per herbam
subiciunt epulis (sic Iuppiter ipse monebat)   110
et Cereale solum pomis agrestibus augent.

---

to Dionysius of Halicarnassus (1.55.4, first century BCE), the prophecy was made by the oracle of Jupiter at Dodona (also mentioned in Varro, first century BCE, as Servius *ad* 3.256 notes) and by the Erythraean Sibyl, who told them to sail west until they were to eat their tables. In any case, Vergil's discrepancy here may be a sign of the need for further revision. For more on the prophecy, see O'Hara (1990), Mack (1999) 140-2, Nelis (2001) 32-8, Seider (2013) 28-30, 43-4, Syson (2013) 90-116, Fletcher (2014) 226, and Rogerson (2017) 168-89.

107. **Aeneas:** this line, particularly with its initial placement of *Aeneas*, picks up the story of the Trojans from 35-6, reinforcing the transition already indicated in 105-6. **Iulus:** the *I* is a vowel (not consonant), making the name trisyllabic. *Iulus* is an alternate name for Ascanius, probably invented in the late Republic to associate Ascanius with the Julian *gens* (i.e., the family of Julius Caesar and thus also Augustus; see "The *Aeneid*, Rome, and Augustus" in General Introduction), though the dating of the name is debated (cf. Austin (1964) on 2.563). At 1.267-8, Jupiter creates an ancient connection between Ascanius/Iulus (thus also Aeneas and Venus) and the Julian family, through reference to an early king of Troy (=*Ilium*) named *Ilus*: *at puer Ascanius, cui nunc cognomen Iulo | additur* (*Ilus erat, dum res stetit Ilia regno*).

108. **corpora sub ramis...:** Vergil's description of the Trojans lying down is intertextually reinforced by two Lucretian phrases that also convey relaxation: *corpora deponunt* (of cattle and sheep "laying down their bodies" after storms, Lucretius 1.258) and *sub ramis arboris altae* (of people who live without luxury but still enjoy simple pleasures, like reclining "under the branches of a tall tree" near a stream, Lucretius 2.30).

109. **instituunt:** here "prepare." **dapes:** *daps* (*dapis*, f.) a sacrificial feast, seemingly incongruous with the rustic meal the Trojans actually prepare but perhaps fitting for its ultimate significance. In general, note the elevated language in 109-15 to describe the momentous event, even though the eating of the "plates" is initially treated as a joke by Ascanius (cf. *adludens* 117). **adorea liba:** *adorea* means "consisting of spelt," an archaism*; a *libum* is a "cake," usually employed in offerings to the gods.

110. **epulis:** "feasts" (*epula, -ae*, f.), perhaps here more with the sense of "meals"; dative with the compound verb *subiciunt* ("place under"). **sic...monebat:** the idea more fully expressed is "inspired (them to prepare their meal) in this way." **Iuppiter ipse:** *ipse* emphasizes Jupiter's role.

111. **Cereale solum:** here *solum* means not "ground" but "foundation," "base"; *Cerealis*, "of Ceres," here "of wheat" (cf. 109 n.). The phrase thus has the sense of "platter of Ceres" (i.e., a cake upon which the food was placed for eating). **pomis:** *pomum* (*-i*, n.) means a "fruit" of any kind. **augent:** "increase," "pile high"; the verb has religious resonance (cf. 153 n.). Note how this line elaborates the description of the meal in 109-110.

consumptis hic forte aliis, ut vertere morsus
exiguam in Cererem penuria adegit edendi,
et violare manu malisque audacibus orbem
fatalis crusti patulis nec parcere quadris: 115
'heus, etiam mensas consumimus?' inquit Iulus,
nec plura, adludens. ea vox audita laborum
prima tulit finem, primamque loquentis ab ore

112-15. With the eating of the cakes, the Trojans fulfill what had seemed a dire prophecy by the Harpy Celaeno at 3.255-7 (see 107-34 n.). Note that Vergil describes the eating of the cakes in a variety of ways in these lines, thereby emphasizing the importance of the event.

112-13. **consumptis...aliis:** ablative absolute; *aliis*, "other things," i.e., the fruits, *pomis* (cf. 111 n.). **hic:** temporal, "then." **forte:** adverb, "by chance." **ut:** "when," "as." **vertere morsus:** *morsus* ("bites") is a fourth declension accusative plural; note the physical emphasis of the description. **exiguam in Cererem:** *Cererem* is a metonymy* for "grain" and, here more specifically, "cakes"; *exiguus (-a, -um)* means "small" or perhaps here "thin." **penuria...edendi:** "shortage of eating," i.e., they needed to eat more. Vergil strikingly uses the gerund *edendi* (genitive, from *edo* (3)), when we might have expected a word meaning food (e.g., *cibi*); the act of eating is thereby emphasized. **adegit:** note Vergil's use of an accusative (supply *eos*) and infinitive (*vertere, violare, parcere*) construction with *adegit* ("compelled"), instead of a subjunctive object clause (cf. 35-6 n.).

114-15. **violare:** "defile," "pollute" (for syntax, see 112-13 n.). The suggestion of meal desecration perhaps resonates with the Trojans' problematic slaughter of the Harpies' cattle in Book 3 (see 107-34 n.). **malis:** from *mala, -ae,* f., "cheek," "jaw." **orbem...crusti:** "circle of cake," "circular cake"; *crustum* denotes "anything baked" (cf. 109 *liba*). For the varied descriptions of the cakes, see 112-15 n. **fatalis:** modifying *crusti*; "fated," indicating the importance of the cakes as a sign of fate. **patulis...quadris:** dative after *parcere*. *Patulus* means "flat" (Fordyce) or "outspread" (Horsfall); *quadrae*, here "sections" (the cakes were marked on top for division into four parts or "quadrants").

116. **heus:** "Hey!" A colloquial exclamation that draws attention to something. **etiam:** "even," "also."

117-18. **nec plura:** as often in epic, a verb of speaking is omitted (ellipsis*). **adludens:** "joking," construe closely with *inquit*. **ea vox audita:** "that comment having been heard." **laborum | ... tulit finem:** despite this statement, Aeneas' woes in Italy are just about to begin, not end. The phrasing will be pointedly echoed in 481-2 (see n.) The question of when an end (*finis*) will come to Aeneas' troubles continues until the conclusion of Book 12, when Jupiter asks Juno when she will stop opposing Aeneas: *Quae iam finis erit, coniunx?* (12.793). **prima...primam:** the polyptoton* emphasizes the immediate effect of Ascanius' words; with *primam*, understand *vocem*. Both adjectives can be translated adverbially, "first." **loquentis:** i.e., Ascanius; genitive.

eripuit pater ac stupefactus numine pressit.
continuo 'salve fatis mihi debita tellus   120
vosque' ait 'o fidi Troiae salvete penates:
hic domus, haec patria est. genitor mihi talia namque
(nunc repeto) Anchises fatorum arcana reliquit:
"cum te, nate, fames ignota ad litora vectum
accisis coget dapibus consumere mensas,   125
tum sperare domos defessus, ibique memento
prima locare manu molirique aggere tecta."

---

119. **eripuit...pressit:** "seized...and grasped the comment (*vocem*, cf. 117-18 n.)"; note the enclosing line structure of these verbs. The idea conveyed here is *accipere omen*, to take up or accept something as a good omen before anything else is said to undermine it. **stupefactus numine:** "stunned by (the indication of) divine will"; for *numine*, cf. 385 n.

120-1. **continuo:** cf. 68 n. **salve...salvete:** apostrophes* with polyptoton* to *tellus* and the *penates* add a strong emotional effect; cf. 5.80 *salve, sancte parens, iterum salvete...* (Aeneas, as he pours libations on his father's tomb). **fatis mihi:** construe *fatis* as ablative, *mihi* as dative; both are dependent on *debita*. **fidi Troiae...penates:** the *penates* (household gods, here of Troy) had appeared to Aeneas in a dream and counseled him to seek Hesperia/Italy (3.148-71); Aeneas seemingly acknowledges that they were indeed "trustworthy." (Aeneas brought the *penates* out of burning Troy.)

122. **hic domus, haec patria est:** note the polyptoton* of the demonstratives (*hic, haec*), and the line's compression, which conveys excitement; "this is..., this is...." For the phrase, cf. *hic amor, haec patria est* (4.347, Aeneas speaking of Italy to Dido) and see the excellent discussion of Syson (2013) 103-8. **mihi talia:** construe *talia* with *arcana* (123). Schork (1996) suggests that, taken together, these words offer an "acoustic evocation" of *Italia—mihi talia*—with an echo of 4.408 *cernenti talia* (of Dido seeing the Trojans preparing to leave). **namque:** explanatory, "for."

123. **(nunc repeto) Anchises:** *repeto* (3), "recollect," "recall"; an inconsistency is involved, see 107-34 n. Perhaps the presence of this parenthetic comment implicitly acknowledges that such a prophecy by Anchises had *not* been mentioned earlier in the poem. **fatorum arcana:** *arcana* (n. pl.), "secrets," cf. 1.262 *volvens fatorum arcana movebo*, of Jupiter's revelation of the secrets of fate to Venus.

124. **cum:** temporal, "when"; not the preposition. **fames:** *fames, -is,* f., "hunger." **vectum:** modifying *te*; for its meaning, see 64-5 n.

125. **accisis:** with *dapibus*, ablative absolute. *Accido* ("cut") is first attested in poetry in Vergil (cf. 2.626-7 *ornum...accisam*); here it means "use up," "eat." **coget:** takes an infinitive and accusative construction, *te...consumere*. **mensas:** "tables," perhaps with a pun, since *mensa* can also mean "course" or "dish" (of food, *OLD* s.v. *mensa* 4).

126-7. **defessus:** with concessive sense, "though tired" or "worn out." **memento:** "remember to," future imperative, an archaic* form, also used by Anchises in his famous words to Aeneas regarding Roman empire in the underworld (*tu regere imperio populos, Romane, memento,*

haec erat illa fames, haec nos suprema manebat
exitiis positura modum.
quare agite et primo laeti cum lumine solis   130
quae loca, quive habeant homines, ubi moenia gentis,
vestigemus et a portu diversa petamus.
nunc pateras libate Iovi precibusque vocate
Anchisen genitorem, et vina reponite mensis.'

6.851). The imperative governs a tricolon of infinitives (*sperare, locare, moliri*). **prima:** modifies *tecta*, the phrase framing the line. **manu:** Anchises emphasizes the personal effort that will be involved. **molirique aggere tecta:** somewhat unusual phrasing, "and build up (*moliri*, a verb that conveys a strong sense of effort) your homes (*tecta*, 59 n.) with a rampart (*agger, -eris*, m.)," i.e., enclose your homes with a rampart (cf. *sedes...aggere cingit* 158-9).

128. **haec erat illa fames:** "this hunger (i.e., the eating of the platters, 116) was that hunger (i.e., as foretold in Anchises' prophecy, 125)"; *hic...ille* is also used at 255 and 272 to associate something present with something past. **suprema:** "final," modifying *haec* (*fames*). **manebat:** "was awaiting," transitive usage with *nos* as object.

129. **exitiis:** dative, here with sense of "miseries," "woes," not "destruction." **positura modum:** *positura*, future active participle; *modus* (*-i*, m.) here means "end." Line 129 perhaps contains some dramatic irony*, since the reader knows that a war is about to begin (cf. 117-18 n.). This line was left unfinished at the time of Vergil's death. Donatus (fourth century CE), in his *Life of Vergil*, says that on his deathbed Vergil asked that the *Aeneid* be burnt, but he ultimately left it in the hands of Varius and Tucca to edit *ea conditione, ne quid adderent quod a se editum non esset, et versus etiam imperfectos, si qui erant, relinquerent*. There are roughly fifty-eight such verses in the entire *Aeneid* (the number is disputed because some original "half lines" may have been completed by scribes). There are five other incomplete verses in Book 7 (248, 439, 455, 702, 760). For more on half lines, see Sparrow (1931) and O'Hara (2010). As Gould (1970: 152 = 1990: 111) writes, "The conclusion is inescapable: Virgil had no intention of leaving half-lines in the *Aeneid*."

130-1. **quare:** "therefore." **agite:** "come now!" (cf. 37-8 n.). **primo...cum lumine:** i.e., at daybreak; *cum* + ablative can indicate the time or circumstances when an event occurs. **laeti:** better to construe as a nominative plural modifying the understood subject "we" rather than as a genitive singular with *solis*. **quae...qui...ubi:** note the compression achieved with this tricolon* of indirect questions (*quae* and *qui* are interrogative adjectives). In the *quae* and *ubi* clauses, supply *sint*; in the *qui* clause, understand *loca* as object of *habeant*.

132. **vestigemus...petamus:** enclosing hortatory subjunctives; *vestigemus* governs the indirect questions in 131; *petamus* governs *diversa* ("different places" or "directions"), an accusative neuter plural adjective used as a noun (cf. 59 n.).

133-4. **pateras libate:** a *patera* is a shallow bowl used for libations; "pour out the (libation) bowls" (cf. 3.354 *libabat pocula*). **Anchisen:** Greek accusative. **reponite:** perhaps "place," not "replace," since we are not told that wine had been removed. The tricolon* of imperatives (*libate, vocate, reponite*) adds solemnity.

Sic deinde effatus frondenti tempora ramo 135
implicat et geniumque loci primamque deorum
Tellurem Nymphasque et adhuc ignota precatur
flumina, tum Noctem Noctisque orientia signa
Idaeumque Iovem Phrygiamque ex ordine matrem
invocat, et duplicis caeloque Ereboque parentis. 140
hic pater omnipotens ter caelo clarus ab alto
intonuit, radiisque ardentem lucis et auro
ipse manu quatiens ostendit ab aethere nubem.

135-147. Aeneas prays to the gods, and Jupiter thunders in support. The Trojans continue their meal.

135. **Sic deinde effatus:** *deinde* is usually placed after the participle, the force of which it sums up, but Vergil often places it in other places, perhaps to create a more poetic (or less prosaic) tone. **frondenti...ramo:** "leafy bough" (*frondeo* (2), "have leaves"); a wreath is usually worn during the performance of a religious rite. **tempora:** neuter plural; here not "times" but "temples" (of the head).

136-8. **implicat:** "encircles," "enwraps." **genium:** a *genius* is the "protective spirit" of a person or place. **primamque deorum | Tellurem:** Tellus was the Roman earth goddess who was associated with Terra Mater and the Greek goddess Gaia. **ignota...flumina:** presumably the rivers Tiber and Numicus (cf. 150-1 n.), though their names are of course "unknown" to Aeneas. (For Aeneas' death on the shore of the Numicus, see 797 n.). **Noctem Noctisque orientia signa:** the invocation of Night (note the polyptoton*) and the inclusion of rising stars (*orientia signa*) stars suggest that it is evening moving toward night.

139. **Idaeumque Iovem:** *Idaeus* is an epithet of Jupiter that goes back to Homer; here it refers to Mt. Ida at Troy (cf. *Phrygiam...Matrem*) rather than Mt. Ida in Crete. **Phrygiam...matrem:** i.e., Cybele (also called *Magna Mater*), whose cult was brought from Phrygia to Rome in 204 BCE (Livy 29.10-14). In Book 9, when Turnus is about to torch the Trojan fleet, we learn of Cybele's request to Jupiter to protect the fleet, which was made of wood from Mount Ida (9.69-117). **ex ordine:** "in order."

140. **duplicis:** accusative plural modifying *parentis*. Here, as often, *duplex* means "both" (cf. Lucretius 6.1146 *duplices oculi*); it is a more elevated word than *ambo* or *duo*. **caeloque Ereboque parentis:** i.e., Venus (in heaven, *caelum*) and Anchises (in the underworld, *Erebus*, a primordial god, here = underworld). *Caelo* and *Erebo* are ablatives of place; note the antithesis* (cf. 312 n.).

141. **hic:** temporal adverb, "then." **omnipotens:** a standard epithet for Jupiter (*pater*), cf. 427-8 n. **clarus:** adjective, though construe adverbially ("clearly," "loudly") with *intonuit*, which is emphatically enjambed* into 142. Adjectives that refer to a subject or object of a verb sometimes qualify that verb and can thus be translated adverbially (cf. note on 10 n.; AG §290).

142-3. **radiisque...lucis et auro:** *lūcīs*, genitive from *lūx, lūcīs* ("light") (not *lūcŭs, lūcī*, "grove"); cf. 763 n.; probably hendiadys*, "with rays of golden light." **ardentem...nubem:** note the long separation of these two words (hyperbaton*) and the strong signs of support sent by Jupiter.

diditur hic subito Troiana per agmina rumor
advenisse diem quo debita moenia condant. 145
certatim instaurant epulas atque omine magno
crateras laeti statuunt et vina coronant.
    Postera cum prima lustrabat lampade terras
orta dies, urbem et finis et litora gentis
diversi explorant: haec fontis stagna Numici, 150
hunc Thybrim fluvium, hic fortis habitare Latinos.

144-5. **diditur:** "is spread abroad" with *rumor* as subject; the verb *dido* (3) is relatively rare, though used at 8.132 and by Lucretius. **hic:** cf. 141 n. **advenisse diem:** an accusative and infinitive construction governed by *diditur...rumor*. **quo...condant:** "on which they may found," i.e., "on which to found," a relative clause of purpose; cf. 98-9 n. The differing meanings of *condere* are central to the epic: cf. 1.33 *tantae molis erat Romanam condere gentem* (of founding the Roman race) and 12.950 *ferrum adverso sub pectore condit* (of Aeneas stabbing Turnus). See James (1995) for discussion of Vergil's thematic use of this verb, as well as Lowrie (2010) on violence and foundation.

146. **instaurant:** "renew," a verb that is often used in ritual contexts, as here. **omine magno:** ablative; construe closely with *laeti*.

147. **crateras...statuunt:** *crateras* ("mixing-bowls") is accusative plural; *statuunt* means "set up." The line is nearly identical to 1.724 *crateras magnos statuunt et vina coronant* (during Dido's banquet for Aeneas and the Trojans). **vina coronant:** probably "crown the wine (with wreathes)," as in 3.525-6 *magnum cratera corona | induit*; it is based, however, on a Homeric phrase that actually means "fill bowls brimming high with wine" (e.g., *Iliad* 1.470). See Thomas (1988) on *Georgics* 2.528, who argues that Vergil was aware of and perhaps playing with the scholarly debate on the meaning of the Homeric phrase.

148-91. *The Trojans explore the region on the following morning, as Aeneas sends ambassadors to King Latinus and starts building a city.*

148. **Postera:** "next"; construe with *orta dies* (149). **cum:** temporal, "when." **prima...lampade:** ablative. **lustrabat:** conveys the idea both of "traverse" and "illuminate." Note the effective alliterations*. The line is almost identical to 4.6, describing the morning after Aeneas has told his tale to Dido.

149. **orta:** from *orior* (see 50-1 n.), "rise." **urbem et finis et litora gentis:** tricolon* of accusative objects. Aeneas and his comrades will quickly discover these in 150-1.

150-1. **diversi:** "in different places," cf. 132 n. **haec...:** implied indirect discourse with an accusative and infinitive construction (AG §580a); "(they discover) that these (are) the waters of Numicus...." The use of tricolon*, polyptoton* and asyndeton* effectively conveys the Trojans' excitement as they seemingly point out what they have found. **fontis...Numici:** cf. notes on 136-8 and 797. **Thybrim:** the river Tiber. Vergil uses *Thybris* (derived from the Greek spelling of the river) eighteen times in the epic, whereas *Tiberis* occurs only once (715). **fortis...Latinos:** the Latins are the people ruled by Latinus.

tum satus Anchisa delectos ordine ab omni
centum oratores augusta ad moenia regis
ire iubet, ramis velatos Palladis omnis,
donaque ferre viro pacemque exposcere Teucris.   155
haud mora, festinant iussi rapidisque feruntur
passibus. ipse humili designat moenia fossa
moliturque locum, primasque in litore sedes
castrorum in morem pinnis atque aggere cingit.

---

152. **satus Anchisa:** *Anchisa* (from *Anchises, -ae*, m.) is ablative of source; the phrase is a patronymic periphrasis* for Aeneas (also at 5.244, 424; 6.331). **delectos:** from *deligo* (3), "select"; modifies *oratores* (153).

153. **centum oratores...ire iubet (154):** accusative and infinitive construction after *iubet*. *Centum* is probably not to be taken literally but is an indication of a large, impressive group; *oratores*, here meaning "ambassadors," is an archaic (and thus stylistically elevated) usage. **augusta:** "venerable," "worthy of honor." This word has strong religious connotations. It is derived from the verb *augere*, meaning "increase" or "exalt," and indicates something which is given divine support or approval. Augustus carefully chose this to be his name in 27 BCE for such reasons (see "Vergil's lifetime and poetry" in General Introduction). The adjective *augustus* appears only one other time in the *Aeneid*—at line 170 (*tectum augustum*, see n.). Note the heavily spondaic nature of this line.

154-5. **ire...ferre...exposcere:** tricolon* of infinitives dependent upon *iubet* (cf. 153 n.). **ramis velatos Palladis omnis:** in apposition to *centum oratores*; this difficult phrase (literally "all (of them) covered with branches of Pallas") seems to mean that they carried *velamenta*, "olive-branches wrapped in wool," emblems of peace and supplication. The olive tree was sacred to Pallas/Minerva (see Horsfall for further discussion). **viro:** dative, i.e., *regi* (Latinus).

156. **haud mora:** note the ellipsis* of a verb (e.g., *est*) and the asyndeton* that follows, both contributing to the idea of speed. Vergil employs this phrase also at 3.207, 548; 5.140, 749; 6.177; 11.713. **feruntur:** Vergil often uses the passive of *fero* to describe rapid (at times even frenzied) action.

157. **passibus:** *passus, -us*, m., "(foot)step"; the enjambment* helps convey the motion and speed of the *oratores*. **ipse:** Aeneas, in contrast to the *oratores* he sent to Latinus. **humili...fossa:** perhaps alluding to the Roman foundation rite for designating city-wall boundaries with a "shallow furrow." Rossi (2004) 175 points to the "shifting status" of the settlement as *castra* (157-9) and as *urbs* later in the epic. Hardie (1994) 10-12 demonstrates that this ambiguity allows, among other things, for the settlement to be treated both as another Troy besieged by "Greeks" (i.e., the Latins) and as the Homeric Greeks' beach camp, which in the *Iliad* is attacked by Hector and the Trojans.

158. **molitur:** cf. 126-7 n. **sedes:** here "settlement" or "camp" (cf. 52 n.); it was known as *Troia* (Servius), and is here called *primas* presumably because Aeneas will later found the city Lavinium.

159. **castrorum in morem:** "after the fashion of (military) camps," cf. 157 n. **pinnis:** here "battlements" (their precise nature is disputed). **aggere cingit:** cf. 126-7 n.

iamque iter emensi turris ac tecta Latinorum   160
ardua cernebant iuvenes muroque subibant.
ante urbem pueri et primaevo flore iuventus
exercentur equis domitantque in pulvere currus,
aut acris tendunt arcus aut lenta lacertis
spicula contorquent, cursuque ictuque lacessunt: 165
cum praevectus equo longaevi regis ad auris
nuntius ingentis ignota in veste reportat
advenisse viros. ille intra tecta vocari
imperat et solio medius consedit avito.

160-1. **iamque iter emensi...iuvenes:** *emensi* (*emetior, -iri, emensus sum*) means "passed through," "traversed"; *iter* is accusative object. Vergil now turns back to the *iuvenes* (*centum oratores* 153) sent by Aeneas to seek out the Latin king. **turris ac tecta:** objects of *cernebat*; *turris* is accusative plural (*turris, -is,* f., "tower"). **Latinorum:** the extra final syllable is elided with the initial vowel of *ardua* (161), creating a hypermetric* line (cf. 470 n.) that perhaps creates the sense of Latinus' city coming into view to the Trojan ambassadors. **muro:** dative with the compound verb *subibat* ("were approaching").

162. **pueri...iuventus:** in contrast to *pueri* ("boys," "non-adult males"), *iuventus* here describes young men of military age. **primaevo flore:** ablative of description, "in youthful blossom," "in the prime of youth."

163. **exercentur:** with middle force, "they train," "exercise." **currus:** "chariots" (accusative plural) but here with the sense of "horses drawing chariots," since *currus* is object of *domitant*.

164-5. **aut acris...:** note the heavily spondaic opening of this line, as well as the alliteration* and consonance* throughout. The meaning of *acer* is unclear; it may refer, e.g., to the "sharp" action (Fordyce) of the bow (*arcus, -us,* m.) or be transferred from the bow to the "sharp" arrows it shoots (Horsfall). **tendunt:** "stretch," cf. 7 n. **lenta:** means "tough" or "pliant," probably in contrast to *acris*. **cursu:** *cursus, -us,* m., "running." **ictu:** "a blow," here "boxing." **lacessunt:** "challenge (each other) to a contest."

166-7. **cum...:** picks up the action from 160-1. **praevectus...nuntius:** note the separation (hyperbaton*); *praevectus,* from *praevehor* ("travel" or "ride ahead"). **longaevi regis:** i.e., Latinus, whose age is again emphasized (cf. 45-6 n.). **ingentis:** accusative plural. The heroic size of the Trojans (*viros* 168) is quickly noticed by the Latin scout; cf. 6.413 *ingentem Aenean*. **ignota in veste:** note how the Latin messenger comments on the Trojans' unusual clothing, thus suggesting a difference between Trojan and Latin culture. At the end of the epic (12.823-5), Juno will extract from Jupiter the promise that the Latins will not have to change their names, language, or dress (*vestem* 825), when they join with the Trojans.

168-9. **advenisse viros:** an accusative and infinitive construction after *reportat*. **ille:** i.e., Latinus. **vocari | imperat:** understand *viros* or *eos* (i.e., the Trojans) as direct object of *imperat* and accusative subject of *vocari*. Note how decisively the aged (*longaevi* 166) king acts. **avito:** "of a grandfather," "ancestral" (cf. *avus,* 56 n.). The adjective brings back to mind Latinus' descent from Faunus and Picus (47-8) and serves as a transition to the following lines on his kingly residence, the "palace of Picus," *regia Pici* (171).

Tectum augustum, ingens, centum sublime columnis   170
urbe fuit summa, Laurentis regia Pici,
horrendum silvis et religione parentum.
hic sceptra accipere et primos attollere fascis
regibus omen erat; hoc illis curia templum,
hae sacris sedes epulis; hic ariete caeso   175
perpetuis soliti patres considere mensis.
quin etiam veterum effigies ex ordine avorum

170-91. A description of Latinus' palace with its images of the gods, heroes, and victories of his people.

170. **Tectum...**: the spondees*, elisions*, asyndeton*, and tricolon* of adjectives (*augustum, ingens, sublime*) elevate the tone of the description of Latinus' house; cf. *regia* ("palace") in 171 and 59 n. **augustum:** see 153 n. and Zetzel (1997) 195-6 on the potential connection here to Augustus' building program. For analysis of Latinus' palace, see Bleisch (2003). **centum... columnis:** cf. 153 n.

171. **urbe...summa:** i.e., the citadel or *arx*; supply *in*. **Laurentis regia Pici:** a slight inconsistency, since at 61-3 (see notes) Picus' grandson Latinus is the one who calls his people the Laurentes. On Picus, see 48-9 n.

172. **horrendum silvis et religione:** *horrendum*, "inspiring terror" or "wonder," modifying *Tectum* (170); *silvis* and *religione* ("religious awe" or "reverence") are ablatives (of cause) after *horrendum*.

173-5. **hic...hoc...hae...hic:** polyptoton* (cf. 150-1 n.); *hic...hic* are adverbs ("here"), while *hoc... hae* are demonstrative adjectives. **fascis...:** accusative plural; *fasces* (*-ium*, m. pl.) were bundles containing rods with an ax, probably of Etruscan origin and in this passage anachronistic. Lictors (in differing numbers) carried *fasces* when attending the kings, and later (during the Republic) when attending consuls and certain other magistrates. With *fascis*, a connection is suggested between Latinus' kingdom and Rome. **omen erat:** "it was a good omen (i.e., auspicious)...." The final syllable of *erat* is lengthened in arsis*. (Note that the *h* in *hoc* is a breathing, not a consonant, so it does not count as a consonant in making a short syllable long by position; see Appendix 1.) **hoc illis curia templum:** *hoc...templum* elaborates on the description of Latinus' *tectum* (170 n.); supply *erat*. *Curia* ("senate house") is a predicate noun; *illis* is dative of reference. Originally, *templum* meant a "sacred precinct" created by priests called augurs, though it could describe such a space consecrated to a god or gods, thus "temple." **ariete:** "ram"; the *i* must be construed as consonantal, so that the word forms a dactyl (*ārjĕtĕ*); cf. 9.674 *abietibus*.

176. **perpetuis...mensis:** ablative after *considere* ("sit at"); *perpetuis* ("having an unbroken extent or expanse," *OLD* s.v. *perpetuus 1*) is an elevated way to say that the tables were very long. **soliti:** supply *sunt*. **patres:** "elders."

177. **quin etiam:** "moreover." **effigies...avorum:** note that *effigies* is here plural; supply *erant*. Vergil "may hint at *imagines maiorum* [ancestral images] in a Roman *atrium*, and even at the historical statues in the Temple of Jupiter Capitolinus" (Horsfall). For the nature and importance of such ancestral representations, see Flower (1996). **ex ordine:** "in order."

antiqua e cedro, Italusque paterque Sabinus
vitisator curvam servans sub imagine falcem,
Saturnusque senex Ianique bifrontis imago   180
vestibulo astabant, aliique ab origine reges,
Martiaque ob patriam pugnando vulnera passi.
multaque praeterea sacris in postibus arma,
captivi pendent currus curvaeque secures
et cristae capitum et portarum ingentia claustra   185
spiculaque clipeique ereptaque rostra carinis.

---

178. **cedro, Italusque:** between these words note the hiatus*, i.e., the "gap" created when two syllables, which would normally be elided, are not, usually when the preceding syllable receives a special emphasis (here *cedro* ends on the ictus* and is followed by a strong caesura*); cf. 226 *Oceano et* and 631 *turrigerae Antemnae* with notes, and see the discussion of hiatus in Vergil in Trappes-Lomax (2004) 143-54. **Italus…Sabinus:** Vergil seemingly implies that these were the eponymous forefathers of the Italian and Sabine peoples.

179. **vitisator:** "vine-planter," an elevated, compound epithet (*vitis* + *sero/satus*). The early Latin tragic poet Accius (fragment 205 in Warmington 2) used it of Dionysus. (Interestingly, however, Sabine wine was not particularly celebrated; Horace refers to it as "cheap" (*vile… Sabinum, Carm.* 1.20.1).) **servans:** here perhaps "keeping," "retaining." **sub imagine:** an unusual usage that must mean something like "in the representation."

180-1. **Saturnusque senex:** cf. 49 n. **Ianique bifrontis… | vestibulo astabant:** Janus was a two-headed god who protected doors and gates; here he (with Saturnus) is placed at the *vestibulum* (the enclosed area between the street and house entrance, or forecourt; *vestibulo* is dative after *astabant*). Their importance is further explained at 8.357-8 (for Janus, see also 607 n.). **ab origine:** "from the beginning." Vergil here suggests "the Aborigines, the name given to original inhabitants of Italy in Cato, Varro, Livy, and other—mostly Republican—authors" (O'Hara (1996 = 2017) 188).

182. **Martiaque ob patriam pugnando vulnera passi:** *passi*, not modifying *reges* (181), but acting as a substantive ("men having suffered…"); the people's martial valor is emphasized. The line (without *Martia*) is used at 6.660 to describe heroes in the groves of the blessed, a resonance perhaps enhancing the figures mentioned here.

183-4. **multaque praeterea sacris in postibus arma…:** spoils taken from conquered enemies were normally hung in temples and palaces in dedication to the gods (cf. 2.504 *barbarico postes auro spoliisque superbi*, of Priam's palace), though these details might conflict with the characterization of Latinus' reign as peaceful (cf. 45-6 n.). **pendent currus:** Conington (ad loc.) notes that "ancient chariots were so light that Diomedes (*Il.* 10.505) thinks of carrying off that of Rhesus on his shoulder." **secures:** from *securis, -is*, f., "ax."

185. **cristae capitum:** "crests of heads," i.e., crested helmets. **claustra:** the "bolts" or "bars" taken from captured city-gates.

186. **spĭcŭlăquē clĭpĕīquĕ:** note that the first *-que* is lengthened in arsis* (the combination of *cl* following *-que* does not cause lengthening by position (Horsfall)); cf. *ĭngēntĭă clāustră* in the

ipse Quirinali lituo parvaque sedebat
succinctus trabea laevaque ancile gerebat
Picus, equum domitor, quem capta cupidine coniunx
aurea percussum virga versumque venenis   190
fecit avem Circe sparsitque coloribus alas.
   Tali intus templo divum patriaque Latinus
sede sedens Teucros ad sese in tecta vocavit,

---

preceding line. The *-que...-que* construction is in imitation of the Homeric Greek *-te...-te...* (see Wills (1996) 376). Youths were just seen hurling *spicula* ("javelins") at 164-5. **erepta...rostra carinis:** "beaks torn from ships." Such *rostra* decorated columns commemorating naval victories (*columnae rostratae*) as well as the main speaker's platform (*Rostra*) in the Roman Forum.

187-8. **ipse...:** modifying *Picus* (189), on whom see 48-9 n. **lituo...trabea:** ablatives (see below); the *lituus* was a curved staff carried by augurs (cf. 173-5 n.), and *trabea* a mantle worn by the king but later by consuls and various priests at ceremonies. Both were particularly associated with Quirinus (the deified Romulus; adjective *Quirinalis*). **succinctus:** "girt with," governing the ablatives *trabea* and *lituo*, though with the latter, it must be construed differently (see syllepsis*) as "equipped" or "fitted out with," since the *lituus* was a staff, not clothing. **laeva:** ablative; sc. *manu*. **ancile:** *ancile, -is,* n., a small oval shield, traditionally with origins in the time of Numa, was carried by priests called the Salii in their celebration of Mars (as on the shield of Aeneas at 8.664).

189-91. **equum domitor:** "tamer of horses"; for the genitive *equum*, see 50-1 n. The phrase translates the Homeric Gr. *hippodamos*, and is also used of Lausus (651) and Messapus (691; 9.523; 12.128, 550). **quem capta cupidine coniunx:** Circe was smitten with Picus, but he did not fully return her passion. Circe ultimately transformed him into a woodpecker (cf. Ovid, *Metamorphoses* 14.320-96) by striking him with her golden wand (thus *aurea percussum virga*) and transforming him with potions (*versum...venenis*). Vergil, however, suggests a version of the myth in which Circe and Picus were married (thus *coniunx*) at least for a time before the transformation, and Faunus was their son. Circe would thus seem to be Latinus' grandmother. (See Fordyce and Horsfall ad loc. on the issue.) The Trojans avoid her potential metamorphic menace at 10-24 (see n.). **aurea:** scan as two syllables by synizesis* (33 n.). **virga:** "wand"; ablative. **versum:** "altered," "transformed." **fecit:** governs the two accusatives *quem* (189, i.e., Picus) and *avem* (functioning as a predicate), "whom she made (i.e., turned into) a bird."

192-211. Latinus welcomes the Trojans and asks why they have come.

192-3. **Tali...templo:** ablative of place. **intus:** adverb, "within." The action from 168-9 resumes here, following the intervening description of the *templum* (170-91, cf. 173-5 n.), where Latinus receives the Trojans. **patria... | sede sedens:** *sede sedens* is a kind of *figura etymologica*, an archaic figure of speech wherein two words of the same etymological origin are used; it adds stylistic elevation to this scene. *Patria* modifies *sede*, and thus once again Latinus' ancestry, which was just described, is stressed.

atque haec ingressis placido prior edidit ore:
'dicite, Dardanidae (neque enim nescimus et urbem   195
et genus, auditique advertitis aequore cursum),
quid petitis? quae causa rates aut cuius egentis
litus ad Ausonium tot per vada caerula vexit?
sive errore viae seu tempestatibus acti,
qualia multa mari nautae patiuntur in alto,   200
fluminis intrastis ripas portuque sedetis,
ne fugite hospitium, neve ignorate Latinos
Saturni gentem haud vinclo nec legibus aequam,
sponte sua veterisque dei se more tenentem.

---

194. **ingressis:** dative; i.e., the Trojans. **placido...ore:** note that Latinus' calm and control will soon be lost. **prior:** can be translated adverbially, "first." (cf. 141 n.).

195-6. **ne...nescimus:** note the understatement through litotes* with which Latinus begins his speech ("we are not ignorant of," i.e., we know well). **enim:** explains Latinus' greeting of the Trojans as *Dardanidae*. **et... | et:** "both...and...." **auditi:** here "heard of," "known about."

197-8. **quid...quae...cuius:** tricolon crescendo* with polyptoton*. **quae causa rates aut cuius egentis...:** *egentis* can modify *rates* or an understood *vos*, and takes a genitive of need (here *cuius*). In either case, we might see an example of anacolouthon, whereby the initial syntactic construction (*quae causa rates vexit*) is not completed but supplanted by another: *quae causa* (supply *vos/ratis*) *cuius egentis vexit*, "what cause has brought you/your ships in need of what."

199. **sive...seu...:** "whether...or...." **tempestatibus:** *tempestas, -atis, f.*, "season"; here "stormy weather."

200. An appositive line characterizing the types of mishaps mentioned in 199: "such many things as sailors...."

201. **intrastis:** syncopated* form of *intra(vi)stis*. **portuque sedetis:** with this phrase, Latinus emphasizes that the Trojans are in port and now safe from the potential setbacks that can occur on the sea (200).

202-4. **neve ignorate:** litotes*, "don't be unaware," i.e., "recognize," "be assured" (Fordyce); understand *esse* in an accusative and infinitive construction after *ignorate*. For the negative imperative, see 96-7 n. **Saturni gentem:** a predicate noun phrase after an understood *esse*. **haud...aequam, | sua sponte...se...tenentem:** *aequam* and *tenentem* both modify *gentem*; note the asyndeton*, which has an adversative effect (i.e., "but"). **vinclo...legibus:** ablatives of means or cause explaining *aequum* and joined by *nec*. **veteris...dei:** i.e., Saturn. For the Saturnian golden age under Latinus, see Perkell (2002), Adler (2003) 151-66. Evander offers a somewhat conflicting view of the golden age at 8.319-27 (see Lowrie (2010) 393 and O'Hara (2018) 63). **more:** indicating that the Latins' "nature" comes from Saturn. Note the antitheses* at play: *sponte sua* vs. *se vindo* and *legibus* vs. *more*. This passage, however, seemingly undermines the idea in 173 (see n.) of Latin rulers accepting the *fasces* and thus political rule.

atque equidem memini (fama est obscurior annis)   205
Auruncos ita ferre senes, his ortus ut agris
Dardanus Idaeas Phrygiae penetrarit ad urbes
Threïciamque Samum, quae nunc Samothracia fertur.
hinc illum Corythi Tyrrhena ab sede profectum
aurea nunc solio stellantis regia caeli   210
accipit et numerum divorum altaribus auget.'
  Dixerat, et dicta Ilioneus sic voce secutus:

---

205. **atque:** cf. 29 n. **fama:** "story," "tradition." **annis:** ablative.
206. **Auruncos...senes:** object of *memini* (205) in an accusative and infinitive (*ferre*) construction. *Auruncos* is the adjectival form of *Aurunca* (see 39 n.), a town in Campania. **ita ferre...ut:** construe *ita* closely with *ut*, "report (*ferre*) thus...how...." **his...agris:** "in these fields," but not precisely indicating Latinus' kingdom, since Dardanus came from Etruria (207 n.). **ortus:** from *orior* ("rise," "be born"; cf. 50-1 n.), modifying Dardanus.
207. **Dardanus:** Jupiter's son by Electra. He was born in the Etruscan town of Corythus but emigrated to Samothrace, and then to Phrygia (where he founded the city of Troy); he ultimately became a god. The connection between Dardanus and Etruria seems a Vergilian innovation. Other authors say that Dardanus came from Greece. For more on Dardanus in the *Aeneid*, see 3.94-9, 147-91; 8.134-42; in the larger tradition, see Horsfall (1971) and *ad* 206-11, and Perkell (2010) *ad* 3.84-120. **Idaeas:** adjectival form of *Ida*, a mountain near Troy (cf. 139 n.); modifying *urbes*. **penetrarit:**, a syncopated* perfect subjunctive for *penetra(ve)rit*) in a substantive *ut*-clause governed by *memini*.
208. **Threïciamque Samum...Samothracia:** the island of Samos lies off the coast of Asia Minor, but Samothrace (*Threiciam Samum*) is to the west, off the coast of Thrace. Traveling from Italy to the East, Dardanus would have reached Samothrace before Phrygia, though the reverse is stated here (hysteron proteron*) (cf. Horsfall). A wordplay, however, might also be involved. An earlier name for Samothrace seems to have been "Dardania." "Vergil might be...by the mention of Dardanus alluding to the name Dardania and its origin" (O'Hara (2017) 189).
209. **hinc:** "from here." **illum:** i.e., Dardanus. **Corythi:** see 207 n. **Tyrrhena:** cf. 43-4 n.
210. **solio:** *solium, -i*, n., "throne." **stellantis:** from *stello* (1), "be covered with stars."
211. **et numerum divorum...auget:** better to understand Dardanus as subject (not *regia*); for *auget*, cf. 153 n.; construe *divorum* as dependent on *numerum*. **altaribus:** i.e., the altars that are dedicated to Dardanus as a new god; ablative of means.

212-48. Ilioneus' response to Latinus.

Ilioneus provides the Trojans' reply to Latinus. He had also led the Trojan delegation to Dido at 1.520-60, which thus becomes an important intratext. Iloneus' language is at times overly difficult and overblown (cf. especially 222-30 with notes), perhaps in his attempt to impress Latinus. For this passage, see Knauer (1964a) 229-31, Gransden (1984) 60-1, Cairns (1989) 64-5, Nelis (2001) 285-6, Nakata (2012) 346-8, Fletcher (2014) 229-32, and Horsfall ad loc.

'rex, genus egregium Fauni, nec fluctibus actos
atra subegit hiems vestris succedere terris,
nec sidus regione viae litusve fefellit; 215
consilio hanc omnes animisque volentibus urbem
adferimur pulsi regnis, quae maxima quondam
extremo veniens sol aspiciebat Olympo.
ab Iove principium generis, Iove Dardana pubes
gaudet avo, rex ipse Iovis de gente suprema: 220
Troïus Aeneas tua nos ad limina misit.

---

212. **Dixerat:** pluperfect, Latinus had finished his speech; then Ilionius followed, *secutus (est)*, perfect tense. **dicta:** i.e., the "words" or "speech" just given by Latinus. **Ilioneus:** cf. 212-48 n. **secutus:** supply *est*.

213-14. **rex:** vocative. **genus:** here "descendent," in apposition to *rex*; cf. 556. **Fauni:** cf. 47 n. **nec...subegit...succedere:** supply *nos*, "did not compel (us) to come to"; for the infinitive, cf. 35-6 n. **actos:** modifying an understood *nos*. **hiems:** *hiems, -emis,* f., "winter," but here "stormy weather." **vestris...terris:** dative with the compound verb *succedere*.

215. **nec sidus...litusve fefellit:** "neither star...nor shore deceived"; again understand *nos* as accusative object. Ilioneus explains that it was not faulty navigation (i.e., by misreading the stars or various landmarks) that led the Trojans to Latinus' realm. **regione viae:** *regio (-onis,* f.) is a noun formed from the verb *rego* (originally, "direct," "keep straight"; later, "rule," "govern"); the phrase here means "direction of our course."

216. **consilio...animisque volentibus:** ablatives of manner (AG §412). Note the emphasis on the Trojans' deliberate choice to reach Latium. **hanc...urbem:** accusative of direction after *adferimur* (217).

217-18. **pulsi:** modifying the subject (we, Trojans) of *adferimur*. **regnis:** i.e., Troy; ablative of separation. **quae maxima quondam...:** antecedent is *regnis*; object of *aspiciebat*; "which, once the greatest, the sun used to look upon...." **extremo...Olympo:** "from the outermost (i.e., eastern) part of Olympus (i.e., heaven)." The enclosing adjective-noun phrase may help suggest Troy's greatness.

219-20. The Trojans' and, in particular, Aeneas' impressive descent from Jupiter is expressed concisely in a tricolon* construction with asyndeton*. **ab Iove principium generis:** supply *est*. **Dardana pubes:** perhaps "the sons of Dardanus" (cf. 207 n.), though with special reference to the Trojan warriors who have come to Latinus' kingdom. **Iove...avo:** ablatives after *gaudet* ("rejoice in"); here *avo* means "forefather," i.e., not technically "grandfather," cf. 56 n. **rex ipse...:** i.e., Aeneas himself; again, supply *est*. This clause emphasizes Aeneas' special connection to Jupiter, since he was Venus' son, and thus literally Jupiter's grandson. **suprema:** "highest," "most exalted," modifying *gente*.

221. **Troïus Aeneas:** note the delay of and buildup to the naming of Aeneas.

quanta per Idaeos saevis effusa Mycenis
tempestas ierit campos, quibus actus uterque
Europae atque Asiae fatis concurrerit orbis,
audiit et si quem tellus extrema refuso   225
submovet Oceano et si quem extenta plagarum
quattuor in medio dirimit plaga solis iniqui.

222-27. To describe how well known the story of the Trojan War is throughout the world, Ilioneus uses two complicated indirect questions (222-4) governed by the verb *audit*, which has *si quem* clauses as subjects (225-7). The resulting lines are complex and are perhaps meant to convey grandiosely (perhaps excessively so) the world upheaval caused by the Trojan War (cf. 212-48 n.).

222-4. **quanta... | tempestas ierit..., quibus actus uterque...fatis concurrerit orbis:** two indirect questions in primary sequence dependent on *audiit* ("has heard," a present perfect) in line 225, with *ierit* and *concurrerit* being perfect subjunctives, which in primary sequence express past action. Roughly: everyone (see 225-7 n. for the precise subject) "has heard 1) how great a storm went forth..., 2) driven by what fates the two worlds clashed...." **saevis effusa Mycenis:** the *tempestas* originated from "fierce Mycenae," the city ruled by Agamemnon. **uterque | Europae atque Asiae...orbis:** *orbis* ("world" or "continent") is modified by *uterque* ("each of two"; together with *orbis*, essentially "the two worlds"); the genitives *Europae atque Asiae* then indicate the worlds of the West (Europe) and East (Asia), a cultural opposition that developed as a result of the Persian Wars in the fifth century BCE; it is not found in Homer (Fordyce).

225-7. **audiit et si quem...et si quem...:** these difficult lines identify people in two different remote parts of the world who (according to Iloneus) are familiar with the Trojan War. The two *si quem* ("anyone") clauses, joined by *et...et*, function as the subjects of *audiit* (for which the *quanta* and *quibus* clauses serve as objects in indirect questions (cf. 222-4 n.): "Both anyone whom...and anyone whom...has heard" (*audiit*). Ilioneus emphasizes how well known are the struggle and losses of Troy. **refuso...Oceano:** "where Ocean is hurled back," a difficult phrase. Horsfall explains that the idea is "the Ocean is hurled back by those rugged, distant islands which have heard of the fame of Troy" (see his detailed discussion). **submovet:** "separates," "keeps away." **Oceano et:** for the hiatus, see 178 n. **et si quem extenta...:** "and someone whom the zone (*plaga*) of the unjust sun (i.e., the torrid zone), extending in the middle of the four zones (*plagarum quattuor in medio*) divides (from us)." Vergil refers here to the five zones on earth that relate to those in the heavens (see *Geo.* 1.233-9 with Thomas ad loc.): the torrid zone is in the middle (here *in medio...plaga solis iniqui*), with a temperate and then frigid zone both to the north and to the south. Europe and Asia are in the temperate zone to the north of the torrid zone, while lines 226-7 describe those living in the temperate zone to the south of the torrid zone (a distant, unknown region). **dirimit:** "divides," i.e., from us (in the northern temperate zone, see above).

diluvio ex illo tot vasta per aequora vecti
dis sedem exiguam patriis litusque rogamus
innocuum et cunctis undamque auramque patentem.   230
non erimus regno indecores, nec vestra feretur
fama levis tantique abolescet gratia facti,
nec Troiam Ausonios gremio excepisse pigebit.
fata per Aeneae iuro dextramque potentem,
sive fide seu quis bello est expertus et armis: 235
multi nos populi, multae (ne temne, quod ultro
praeferimus manibus vittas ac verba precantia)
et petiere sibi et voluere adiungere gentes;

---

228. **diluvio**: "flood," i.e., the disaster of the Trojan War; cf. the use of *tempestas* in 223. **vasta per aequora vecti**: for *veho*, cf. 64-5 n.; for the line, cf. Cat. 101.1 *multa per aequora vectus* (of Catullus' journey to pay last respects to his deceased brother near Troy); and *Aen.* 1.524 *maria omnia vecti* (in Ilioneus' speech to Dido).

229-30. **dis...patriis**: dative. **sedem...patentem**: note the tricolon crescendo* of accusative object phrases (*sedem exiguam, litus innocuum, undamque auramque patentem*, with the third element doubled); *sedem*, here "home" (cf. 52 n.). **innocuum**: "harmless," i.e., in a passive sense, a place where the Trojans will not be harmed, or, in an active sense, a place from which the Trojans will cause no harm. **undamque auramque patentem**: i.e., water and air are free (*patentem*, "lying open" or "accessible") to all (*cunctis*).

231-3. A tricolon* of negative clauses expressing (through litotes*) ways in which Latinus' realm will not suffer from helping the Trojan refugees. **regno**: dative of reference; construe with *indecores* ("dishonorable," "unseemly"). **nec...-que**: *-que* (here "nor") continues the negative *nec*. **abolescet**: from *abolesco* (3), "vanish," "cease." **Troiam Ausonios...excepisse pigebit**: whether *Troiam* or *Ausonios* is subject accusative of *excepisse* is grammatically unclear, though the latter makes more historical sense (see discussion in Reed (2007) 92). On the Ausonians, see 39 n.

234. **fata per**: *per* ("by," a usage common in oaths and entreaties) follows its (initial) object (*fata*, i.e., anastrophe*) but precedes *dextram potentem*. **Aeneae**: genitive. The forms of *Aeneas* are nom. *Aeneas*, gen. *Aeneae*, dat. *Aeneae*, acc. *Aenean*, abl. *Aenea*.

235. **sive...seu quis...est expertus...**: "if anyone has put it (i.e., *dextram potentem*) to the test either (in trustworthiness)...or (in war and arms)..." **fide**: "honesty," "trustworthiness."

236-8. **multae...gentes**: note the hyperbaton* created by the insertion of a long parenthetic comment. **quod...**: a *quod* "the fact that" clause (AG §572), serving as object of *temne*; "the fact that we...." **ultro**: "of our own accord," "willingly." **manibus**: ablative of means. **vittas**: cf. 154-5 n. **precantia**: trisyllabic; the *i* is treated as a consonant (*prĕcăntjă*, cf. 173-5 n.). **petiere**: = *petierunt*; sc. *nos* as object of this verb (and of *voluere adiungere*).

sed nos fata deum vestras exquirere terras
imperiis egere suis. hinc Dardanus ortus, 240
huc repetit iussisque ingentibus urguet Apollo
Tyrrhenum ad Thybrim et fontis vada sacra Numici.
dat tibi praeterea fortunae parva prioris
munera, reliquias Troia ex ardente receptas.
hoc pater Anchises auro libabat ad aras, 245
hoc Priami gestamen erat cum iura vocatis
more daret populis, sceptrumque sacerque tiaras
Iliadumque labor vestes.'

239-40. **fata deum...imperiis egere suis:** *nos* is the understood object of *egere* (=*egerunt*); cf. Aeneas' claim to Dido in the underworld, *sed me iussa divum...imperiis egere suis* 6.461-3); for *deum*, see 50-1 n. **exquirere:** for the use of the infinitive after *egere*, see 35-6 n. **hinc:** "from here," in a general sense, since Dardanus was actually from the Etruscan town Corythus, cf. 207 n. **ortus:** supply *est*.

241. **huc:** "to this place," "hither"; note asyndeton* and polyptoton* with *hinc* (240). **repetit:** "brings back"; better to construe Apollo (rather than Dardanus) as subject with *nos* as implied object. **iussisque ingentibus urguet Apollo:** there is some debate as to whether the role attributed to Apollo in leading Aeneas to Latium is a Vergilian innovation; see Miller (2009) 99-101 for potential hints of such an earlier tradition, and 95-184 for discussion of Apollo more generally in the *Aeneid*.

242. **Tyrrhenum:** cf. 43-4 n. The Tiber is called "Etruscan," since its source is in Etruria. **Thybrim...Numici:** see 150-1 n. **vada:** "shallows."

243. **dat:** the implied subject is Aeneas. **fortunae...prioris:** note how Ilioneus is very careful to emphasize Troy's former greatness.

244. **munera, reliquias Troia ex ardente receptas:** the first syllable of *reliquias* is lengthened by metrical necessity (it is sometimes written *relliquias*); *reliquias* stands in apposition to *munera*. Dido was also given gifts from Troy (cf. 1.647 *munera praeterea Iliacis erepta ruinis*).

245. **auro:** here a "golden bowl" (synecdoche*), modified by *hoc* (ablative).

246-8. **gestamen:** modified by *hoc* (nominative); "something that is carried or worn"; here probably a collective noun (e.g., "ornaments") looking forward to the *sceptrum*, *tiaras*, and *vestes* described in 247-8. **cum iura... daret:** circumstantial clause, describing the occasions when Priam would bear the *gestamen* just mentioned. **sacer...tiaras:** *tiaras* (nominative, Gr. *tiaras* or *tiara*) is an Eastern (particularly Persian) conical headdress, appropriate for Priam as ruler of Troy in the East. Note the irony* in these gifts, however, since Priam will be a defining model for Latinus, particularly at the beginning of Book 12, where he, like Priam in *Iliad* 22, will try unsuccessfully to prevent his potential son-in-law (son in Priam's case) from meeting death (cf. Coffee (2009) 54). **Iliadum...labor:** *labor* here means not quite "work," but "something produced by work" (metonymy*); the phrase stands in apposition to *vestes* (from *vestis*, -*is*, f., "clothing," "attire").

Talibus Ilionei dictis defixa Latinus
obtutu tenet ora soloque inmobilis haeret, 250
intentos volvens oculos. nec purpura regem
picta movet nec sceptra movent Priameïa tantum
quantum in conubio natae thalamoque moratur,
et veteris Fauni volvit sub pectore sortem:
hunc illum fatis externa ab sede profectum 255
portendi generum paribusque in regna vocari
auspiciis, huic progeniem virtute futuram

249-85. *Understanding that Aeneas is the husband prophesied for his daughter, Latinus welcomes the Trojans, offers an alliance, and asks that Aeneas come to him in person.*

249. **Talibus...dictis:** ablative absolute expressing attendant circumstance. **Ilionei:** four syllables, with the final *e* and *i* pronounced as one syllable by synizesis*. **defixa:** construe with *ora* (250); from *defigo* (3), "fix" or "fasten down."

250. **obtutu:** "gazing," *obtutus, -us*, m.; ablative. **solo:** dative with *haeret*.

251-3. **intentos volvens oculos:** i.e., a detail conveying Latinus' intense thought, in contrast to what we will see as Amata's frenzied eyes in line 399 *sanguineam torquens aciem*. **nec... movet...nec...movent:** *moveo*, "move," "affect"; anaphora* with polyptoton* helps provide contrast with what Latinus is thinking of most—the issue of his daughter's marriage and thus also of Faunus' oracle. **purpura:** nominative singular; "purple cloth" or "garment," the color having royal associations. **picta:** "embroidered" (*OLD* s.v. *pingo* 3b); cf. 277. **tantum | quantum:** "so much as." **natae:** genitive; i.e., Lavinia. This is the first mention of her since the oracular episode at 81-106. Vergil emphasizes Latinus' preoccupation with the issue of his daughter Lavinia's marriage, a concern that trumps the symbols of Trojan kingship and wealth (*purpura, sceptra...Priameia*) being offered. **moratur:** "delays," but here "dwells (on)"; construe with *in conubio...thalamoque*.

254. **volvit:** from *volvo* (3), here "turn over," "ponder." **sortem:** the "oracle" reported at 96-101.

255. **hunc illum...portendi generum (256):** indirect statement dependent on the idea of Latinus' thought process in 254, "this man (i.e., Aeneas) is that son-in-law portended..."; cf. 128 n. **externa ab sede:** the meaning of *externa* will be debated, see 68, 98, 367-72 with notes. Latinus cannot refer to Aeneas simply as *externus*, "foreigner," because the Trojans' genealogical connection to the Etruscan Dardanus has just been acknowledged by him at 205-11 (see 207 n.; Cairns (1989) 120). His emphasis on the geographical distance of Troy from Latium with this phrase (cf. also *externis...ab oris* in 270) is thus significant because it suggests an interpretation of *externus* in the prophecies (68, 98) that would still include Aeneas/the Trojans (see Nakata (2012) 343-51).

256-7. **portendi:** passive infinitive (see 255 n.). **paribus...auspiciis:** "with equal power," i.e., Aeneas and Latinus would share power. **huic:** Aeneas; note the polyptoton* (cf. 255 *hunc*). **virtute...viribus:** perhaps a (false) etymological wordplay, since *virtus* is from *vĭr* ("man") not *vīs* ("strength"). **futuram:** supply *esse*.

egregiam et totum quae viribus occupet orbem.
tandem laetus ait: 'di nostra incepta secundent
auguriumque suum! dabitur, Troiane, quod optas.   260
munera nec sperno: non vobis rege Latino
divitis uber agri Troiaeve opulentia deerit.
ipse modo Aeneas, nostri si tanta cupido est,
si iungi hospitio properat sociusque vocari,
adveniat, vultus neve exhorrescat amicos: 265
pars mihi pacis erit dextram tetigisse tyranni.
vos contra regi mea nunc mandata referte.

---

258. **egregiam et...quae:** the adjective and the relative clause both describe *progeniam* (257). **occupet:** subjunctive in a relative clause of purpose.

259-60. **laetus:** as with Aeneas (35-6 n.), Latinus' happiness is perhaps premature, since war will soon follow. **incepta:** lit. "beginnings," "plans" (Williams), which Latinus will go on to explain. **secundent:** optative subjunctive (AG §441). **augurium:** referring to the portents Latinus had earlier received (cf. 58). **dabitur:** *quod optas* is subject. **Troiane:** vocative; the emphasis on Trojan identity is again significant (cf. 255 n.).

261. **munera nec sperno:** note the litotes* ("I do not spurn your gifts," which suggests "I am happy to accept your gifts"), and the delay of the connective *nec*; such postponements represent a stylistic device providing metrical flexibility that the neoteric poets of the mid-first century BCE (e.g., Catullus) took over from the Hellenistic poets (e.g., Callimachus and Theocritus, third century BCE). **vobis:** dative governed by *deerit* (262). **rege Latino:** ablative absolute (AG §419a); the phrase adds emphasis and formality, particularly since Latinus himself is the speaker.

262. **divitis uber agri:** here *uber* is the noun ("fruitfulness"), not adjective; *uber agri* translates a Homeric phrase, "richest land" (*Il.* 9.141). Ilioneus described *Hesperia* (cf. 4 n.) as *terra antiqua, potens armis atque ubere glebae* at 1.531. **deerit:** scans as disyllabic through synizesis*.

263. **ipse modo Aeneas...adveniat (265):** the long separation of the verb from the subject gives greater emphasis to Aeneas' role, as does *ipse* ("Aeneas himself"). *Modo* here means "only" construed closely with *adveniat* (265-6 n.).

264. **iungi hospitio properat:** note that in line 57 similar phrasing was used of Amata's desire for Turnus to become her son-in-law (*adiungi generum miro properabat amore*, see n.).

265-6. **adveniat...exhorrescat:** jussive subjunctives; *exhorrescat* ("tremble at") governs the accusative phrase *voltus...amicos*. **pars...pacis:** "an (essential) component of peace"; Latinus requires that he forge his agreement in person with Aeneas, though this will not in fact occur. For more on *pax*, see 467 n. **tyranni:** "monarch" (i.e., Aeneas) without connotations of despotism (cf. 342, of Latinus); for seemingly negative usages, cf. 1.361 (Pygmalion), 8.483 (Mezentius), 10.448 (Turnus), 12.75 (Aeneas, from Turnus' perspective), and Cairns (1989) 4 n. 6. Note that 265-6 state a similar idea in three different forms (theme and variation*).

267. **contra:** "in turn." **regi:** i.e., Aeneas.

est mihi nata, viro gentis quam iungere nostrae
non patrio ex adyto sortes, non plurima caelo
monstra sinunt; generos externis adfore ab oris,　　　270
hoc Latio restare canunt, qui sanguine nostrum
nomen in astra ferant. hunc illum poscere fata
et reor et, si quid veri mens augurat, opto.'
haec effatus equos numero pater eligit omni
(stabant ter centum nitidi in praesepibus altis):　　　275
omnibus extemplo Teucris iubet ordine duci
instratos ostro alipedes pictisque tapetis
(aurea pectoribus demissa monilia pendent,

268-70: **mihi:** dative of possessor. **viro gentis...nostrae:** *viro* is dative after *iungere*. **quam:** *quam* has *nata* (i.e., Lavinia) as its antecedent and is the object of *iungere*. **iungere...sinunt (270):** an accusative and infinitive construction; understand *me* as accusative object of *sinunt* but accusative subject of *iungere* ("permit me to join..."). See AG §563c. **non...non...:** construe with *sinunt*, whose subjects are *sortes* ("oracles") and *plurima...monstra*. **patrio ex adyto sortes:** for the oracle of Faunus, Latinus' father, see 96-101 with notes. **monstra:** "portents," i.e., those of the bees (64-7) and of the flames in Lavinia's hair (73-7).

270. **generos...:** the construction depends on *canunt* (271, "prophets" understood as subject); for *generos*, see 98-9 n. **externis...ab oris:** cf. 255 n. **adfore:** = *adfuturos esse*.

271-2. **hoc:** "this" (referring to the prophecy mentioned in 270 but originally reported in 96-101); subject accusative of *restare* ("remain for"). **Latio:** dative. **qui...ferant:** relative clause of purpose; the antecedent of *qui* is *generos*. Note that this clause repeats the exact wording of the prophecy in 98-9 (see n.). **in astra:** note hyperbole*.

272-3. **hunc illum...:** "this man (i.e., Aeneas) is that man (i.e., the husband foretold in Faunus' prophecy) (whom) I both think and hope that fate demands..."; cf. notes on 128 and 255. **veri:** partitive genitive after *quid* (indefinite pronoun, "anything"). **augurat:** an archaic active form instead of the deponent *auguratur*; "foretells," "surmises."

274. **numero...omni:** "from the whole number," explained in the next line.

275. **ter centum:** cf. 153 n. **praesepibus:** *praesepe, -is,* n., "stable," "stall."

276. **omnibus...Teucris:** dative; i.e., the ambassadors (cf. 153 n.). With *omnibus*, Latinus' generosity is implied. **ordine:** "in order" or "succession."

277. **instratos:** "covered" or "adorned," modifying *alipedes*. **ostro...pictisque tapetis:** probably hendiadys* for "purple embroidered horse-cloths" or "housings". **alipedes:** "wing-footed" (singular *alipes*), an elevated and rare compound adjective used here to mean horses (also in 12.484).

278. **monilia:** "chains" or "collars."

tecti auro fulvum mandunt sub dentibus aurum),
absenti Aeneae currum geminosque iugalis   280
semine ab aetherio spirantis naribus ignem,
illorum de gente patri quos daedala Circe
supposita de matre nothos furata creavit.
talibus Aeneadae donis dictisque Latini
sublimes in equis redeunt pacemque reportant.   285

---

279. **tecti auro:** "adorned with gold," perhaps referring to the *tapetis* (277); with *tecti* understand *alipedes* (277 n.). **fulvum...aurum:** "yellow gold," though here "a bit made of yellow gold" (cf. 245 n.).

280-1. **absenti Aeneae currum:** continues the construction after *eligit* (274); *absenti Aeneae* is dative (cf. 234 n.). **iugalis:** lit. "belonging to a yoke," here used substantively (first such usage attested) to mean a team of horses (with *geminos*). **semine ab aetherio:** see 282-3 n. **spirantis:** accusative plural, modifying *iugalis* (280) and governing the accusative *ignem*. These are fire-breathing horses.

282-3. **illorum...:** i.e., the horses of the Sun, the father of Latinus' grandmother Circe. **patri:** dative of separation (AG §381) after *furata* (from *furor*, "steal"). **quos:** antecedent is *illorum* ("those horses"). **daedala:** "clever," "skillful" (lit. relating to Daedalus). **supposita de matre:** "from a mare placed underneath." **nothos:** "of mixed breed." Circe (cf. 10-24 n.) secretly bred the two horses that Latinus gives to Aeneas by mating a mortal mare with a divine horse (cf. *semine ab aetherio* 281) belonging to her father, the Sun. The phrasing is modeled on *Iliad* 5.268-9, describing Aeneas' horses, which Anchises had secretly bred from Laomedon's horses, also of divine lineage.

284. **talibus...donis dictisque:** ablatives of attendant circumstance. **Aeneadae:** nominative, "sons of Aeneas," "Trojans." **Latini:** genitive.

285. **sublimes in equis:** emphatically placed, underscoring the success and changed circumstances of the Trojan envoys, who, adorned as suppliants, had approached Latinus (cf. 154-5 n.) but now return in pomp to their ships and people. **pacem...reportant:** with some irony*, since the Trojans' initial success proves to be only temporary; the phrase stands in contrast to the reentry of Juno in the next line and her orchestration of the Italian war.

286-640: Juno, Allecto and the outbreak of war

When Juno returns from Argos, she observes Aeneas and the Trojans in the process of settling in Latium. She is outraged, and, realizing that her earlier attempts at hindering the Trojans' fate have failed, she calls up the Fury Allecto from the underworld to incite the Latins and Italian peoples to war against the Trojans. Allecto acts with great speed and efficiency: 1) she infects Amata, who is already angered that her daughter will now be married to Aeneas instead of Turnus (341-405); 2) she enrages Turnus, who risks losing Lavinia, whom he regards as his fiancée, though he is initially slow to react to Aeneas' arrival (406-74); and 3) she brings about Ascanius' killing of Silvia's stag, the event that ultimately throws the Trojans and Latins against one another in strife (475-539).

As we have already seen (Introduction to Book 7), Vergil has skillfully transformed the literary tradition here, developing important features that make this section particularly enthralling. First, Allecto is masterfully depicted as a figure of evil, but her actions are often presented in an impressionistic manner that challenges the reader to grapple with her status as a character. Is Allecto to be understood as a physical actor, a representation of the psychological states of Amata and Turnus, or a figure hovering somewhere in between? Such possibilities are central to ongoing discussions about the nature of divinity in the epic and the cosmic tension (often figured in terms of gender) that threatens Jupiter's reign. Second, Vergil's treatment of Allecto allows human actions potentially to have double motivations—both human and divine. For example, Turnus seems infected by the Fury Allecto, but his concerns are also ones that a warrior and prospective husband in his heroic world might naturally have. Making sense of such complexity has important consequences about causation and responsibility. It is perhaps easy to lay blame at the feet of Allecto and Juno (if we see them as physical agents and not simply as sublimations of human psychological states); however, the epic's insistence on human motivation suggests that the war may have developed without divine support. Thus is Turnus responsible for his downfall or is he ultimately a tragic victim of the gods? And in a more general sense, we are left to ponder why Vergil has once again (cf. the ambiguity concerning Dido and Aeneas' marriage, or the status of Turnus' "engagement" to Lavinia) complicated fundamental issues so thoroughly and skillfully. (Feeney (1991) is essential reading for such questions.)

Finally, at the heart of this episode stands Vergil's horrifying Fury Allecto. She has a number of important models: foremost among them are the goddess Eris (Strife) from Homer's *Iliad* and Hesiod's *Theogony*, the Furies (e.g., Eumenides, Erinyes) from tragedy (particularly Aeschylus' *Eumenides* and Euripides' *Herakles*), and the goddess Discordia from Ennius' *Annales*. But Vergil has created his Furies as something even more blood-curdling. He has fully transformed them from goddesses presiding over revenge (usually involving blood guilt) into enthusiastic promoters of violence without concern for justice or morality. This conception of the Furies will have a profound influence on the future epic tradition.

On the outbreak of war, see Heinze (1915: 182-92 = 1993: 148-55), Fraenkel (1945: 4-7 = 1990: 258-63), Gransden (1984) 67-80, Feeney (1991), Horsfall (1995) 155-61, Hershkowitz (1998) 95-105, Mack (1999) 142-6, Anderson (2005), Fratantuono (2007) 213-22, Kamimura (2008), Stahl (2016) 390-430. On the nature of Allecto and the gods, see Heinze (1915: 182-4 = 1993: 148-50, 85-108), G. W. Williams (1983) 22-4, Cairns (1989) 100-1, Feeney (1991), and O'Hara (1990) 62-9, Syson (2013) 18-28. On the Italian war as civil war, see Pogorzelski (2009), Marincola (2010), Fletcher (2014) 243-7. On Juno, Allecto, and the subsequent epic tradition, see Hardie (1993) and Ganiban (2007).

> Ecce autem Inachiis sese referebat ab Argis
> saeva Iovis coniunx aurasque invecta tenebat,
> et laetum Aenean classemque ex aethere longe

286-322. Juno observes the Trojans settling in Latium, is enraged, and calls on the powers of Hell to start a war and delay their fate.

For Vergil's diction in this passage, see especially Lyne (1987) 49-53, 56-60, who points to the contrast between Juno's grand language and her crude hatred of Aeneas. For connections with Juno's actions in *Aeneid* 1, see Hershkowitz (1998) 95-105, Nelis (2001), Cowan (2015), and Quint (2018) 21-2.

286. **Ecce autem:** "but look!" This phrase is used to introduce dramatic and unexpected incidents. **Inachiis...ab Argis:** *Inachius* ("Inachian") is the adjectival form of Inachus (see 371-2 n.); *Argis* is ablative masculine plural, though in Greek the city's name *Argos* is neuter singular. Juno had a special connection to the city, with which Turnus is also closely associated (cf. 371-2 n.). Her most famous temple was there, and in Homer she is given the epithet "Argive" (e.g., *Iliad* 4.8, 5.907). For intertextual (Homeric) and intratextual models, see Introduction to Book 7 and 286-640 n. **sese referebat...:** i.e., "was bringing herself back," "was returning" (*OLD* s.v. *refero* 3a).

287. **saeva Iovis coniunx:** a periphrasis* for Juno. **aurasque...tenebat:** "she was holding (her course through) the winds." **invecta:** *inveho* in the passive can mean "ride," "drive," "sail" (cf. 64-5 n.). **tenebat, | et...prospexit (289):** note the parataxis*, the sequential ordering of independent clauses (as opposed to hypotaxis*, the subordination of one clause to another). Though the two clauses are independent, in sense one (*aurasque...tenebat*, "(as) she was holding her course through the winds") is subordinated to the other (*Aenean...prospexit*, "she saw Aeneas...").

288. **laetum Aenean:** *Aenean* is a Greek accusative (for other forms, see 234 n.). Aeneas' happiness creates dramatic irony* since we know that Juno is about to take violent action against him (cf. also Latinus in 259-60 with n.). The Trojans were likewise *laeti* at 1.35, when Juno sees them leaving Sicily and heading toward Italy; as a result, she shipwrecks them with a storm. (See Introduction to Book 7.)

Dardaniam Siculo prospexit ab usque Pachyno.
moliri iam tecta videt, iam fidere terrae,   290
deseruisse rates: stetit acri fixa dolore.
tum quassans caput haec effundit pectore dicta:
'heu stirpem invisam et fatis contraria nostris
fata Phrygum! num Sigeïs occumbere campis,
num capti potuere capi? num incensa cremavit   295

---

289. **Dardaniam:** adjectival form of Dardanus (cf. 207 n.), which modifies *classem* (288). **Siculo...ab usque Pachyno:** *ab usque* with the ablative means "all the way from." *Pachynus* is the SE promontory of Sicily (*Siculus* is an adjectival form, "Sicilian"). If Juno is traveling from Argos (see 286 with n.) to Carthage (another of her cult centers), she would pass over Sicily (see, e.g., Horsfall).

290-1. **moliri...tecta videt...:** cf. 126-7 n. This is an accusative and infinitive construction following *videt*; understand Aeneas or the Trojans as object of *videt* and accusative subject of the tricolon* of infinitives *moliri...fidere...deseruisse*. **iam...iam:** the repetition helps convey Juno's incipient anger. **terrae:** dative with *fidere*. **stetit...:** the emphatic initial placement of *stetit* perhaps emphasizes the goddess' shock at seeing Aeneas and the Trojans flourishing in Italy. **fixa:** "pierced," "transfixed."

292. **quassans caput:** *quasso* ("shake"), when used of shaking the head, conveys sorrow, anger, or another emotion (*OLD* s.v. *quasso* 1b). **effundit:** "pours forth," originally of liquids, but the verb could be used of other objects as well (here *voces*), cf. 522. Vergil particularly favors this verb over, e.g., *fundit*, and uses it (in some form) forty-five times. **pectore:** ablative of separation after *effundit*.

293-322. Juno's speech must be compared to her words at 1.37-49 (cf. 288 n.).

293-4. **heu stirpem...!:** "Alas, the hated race...!" *Stirpem invisam* and *contraria...fata* are accusatives of exclamation, a syntactic construction that also begins Juno's speech at 1.37-8. **invisam:** with *stirpem* (*stirps, stirpis*, f. "root" or, as here, "race"); *invisam*, here "hated," not "unseen." **fatis contraria nostris | fata Phrygum:** *fata Phrygum* (see below) refers to the fates of the Trojans and Romans, while *fatis...nostris* (dative of reference after *contraria*) refers to the fates regarding Juno's favorite city, though the latter phrase comes close to meaning Juno's will (see Horsfall). Cf. 1.239 *fatis contraria fata rependens* (Venus, as she voices her concern to Jupiter about Aeneas' fate and Juno's actions). **Phrygum:** i.e., Trojans; genitive plural (50-1 n.). The word Phrygian is often used by Troy's enemies when voicing disdain (cf. Turnus at 579); here the word's emphatic position as the last word of the exclamation helps underscore Juno's scorn.

294-5. **num...num...num...:** the interrogative *num* expects a negative answer ("Were they not able to (*potuere*)...?"); note the tricolon* with asyndeton*. These rhetorical questions* convey Juno's heightened indignation and are modeled on Ennius' lines describing *Pergama* (i.e., the citadel of Troy): *quae neque Dardaniis campis potuere perire, | nec, cum capta, capi, nec, cum combusta, cremari* (*Annales* fr. 344-5 in Skutsch and in *FRL* 1). **Sigeis:** "Sigean," adjectival form (modifying *campis*) of *Sigeum*, a promontory in the Troad. The word scans as three long syllables (*Sīgēīs*). **occumbere...capi:** complementary infinitives (present active and present

Troia viros? medias acies mediosque per ignis
invenere viam. at, credo, mea numina tandem
fessa iacent, odiis aut exsaturata quievi.
quin etiam patria excussos infesta per undas
ausa sequi et profugis toto me opponere ponto.　　　300
absumptae in Teucros vires caelique marisque.
quid Syrtes aut Scylla mihi, quid vasta Charybdis
profuit? optato conduntur Thybridis alveo

---

passive respectively) with *potuere*. **num capti...**: "(Though) captured, were they not able (in fact) to be captured...?" **num incensa cremavit**: note the unusual and emotionally evocative elision* in *n(um) incensa*. Juno indignantly emphasizes that Troy, even after it was set ablaze, was not fully consumed by fire (with the metaphor* of cremation strongly present).

296. **medias acies mediosque per ignis**: like *medios...ignis*, the phrase *medias acies* is governed by *per* (anastrophe*). The use of the adjective *medius, -a, -um* here is intensifying (i.e., through "the middle of..."); its repetition underscores Juno's disbelief that the Trojans were able to escape death at Troy and reach Italy.

297-8. **invenere viam**: emphatically enjambed*; *invenere = invenerunt*. **at, credo...**: "but, I suppose..."; with self-conscious irony Juno opines that she has lost her power or has had enough of harming the Trojans. **odiis...exsaturata**: construe the ablative *odiis* as governed by the nominative *exsaturata* (describing the speaker Juno), from *exsaturo* (1), "satisfy completely," "sate."

299. **quin etiam**: the sense is, "No, (I) even...." Juno thus immediately rejects her suggestion in 297-8. **patria**: ablative of separation governed by *excussos* (with which understand "Trojans"). **infesta**: nominative describing Juno, the speaker.

300. **ausa**: supply *sum*. **profugis**: dative after *me opponere*; "fugitives," here used pejoratively, though cf. 1.2 *fato profugus*, where the word, describing Aeneas, does not have this disdainful nuance. **toto...ponto**: ablative of place where (AG §429b), "throughout the entire sea."

301. **absumptae**: from *absumo*, "used up"; supply *sunt* with *vires* ("power," from *vis, vis*, f.) as subject. **in Teucros**: *in* here means "against." **caelique marisque**: genitives after *vires*; these are two of the three main realms of the world—the sky and the sea. By 312, Juno will resort to the third realm, the underworld.

302-3. **quid...mihi, quid... | profuit**: What (use to me were)..., what use was...? These indignant rhetorical questions* are made more powerful by anaphora*, asyndeton*, a tricolon* of subjects (*Syrtes, Scylla, Charybdis*), and the emphatic enjambment* of *profuit*. For the entire line, cf. Cat. 64.156 *quae Syrtis, quae Scylla rapax, quae vasta Charybdis* (Ariadne suggesting that Theseus must be the child of a monster since he has treated her so badly). **Syrtes**: the shallows on the North African coast. At 1.110-1, Juno shipwrecked the Trojans on the Syrtes (though the word there might also be interpreted as *syrtes*, "shallows"). **Scylla...Charybdis**: two female monsters situated across from each other somewhere in the straits between Sicily and southern Italy, cf. 3.420-32; *Odyssey* 12.73-126, 234-259 (where Scylla and Charybdis are devastating to

securi pelagi atque mei. Mars perdere gentem
immanem Lapithum valuit, concessit in iras   305
ipse deum antiquam genitor Calydona Dianae,
quod scelus aut Lapithas tantum aut Calydona merentem?

Odysseus' crew). **profuit:** from *prosum* ("be of use") with dative *mihi*; see above. **optato... alveo:** ablative of place; *optato* means "desired," "hoped for" (i.e., from the perspective of the Trojans); *alveo* (*alveus, -i*, m., "bed" or "channel" of a river) is scanned as two syllables (synizesis*, see 33 n.). **conduntur:** here, "are hidden" or "settled"; an important verb for the epic, cf. 144-5 n. **Thybridis:** see notes on 30 and 150-1.

304-5. **securi pelagi atque mei:** "untroubled by the ocean and by me," describing the Trojans, the understood subject of *conduntur*. *Securus* ("without care") is formed from *sine* + *cura* and followed by the objective genitive. The phrase resonates with Latinus' words at 199-201, where he assures Ilioneus and the Trojan ambassadors that they have escaped the difficulties of the sea and are now in safe harbor. **Mars...:** Juno refers to the Centauromachy, the famous battle between the Lapiths and Centaurs. Mars was not invited to or was not given sacrifice at the wedding celebration of Perithous, king of the Lapiths (a Greek tribe in Thessaly); the god therefore incited the battle between the Centaurs and the Lapiths. The role that Vergil attributes to Mars is first found here. For the full story of the Centauromachy, see Gantz (1993) 277-81; for the role later attributed to Mars, see Horsfall ad loc. **gentem | immanem Lapithum:** the race (*gentem*) of the Lapiths (*Lapithum* is genitive plural from *Lapithae, -arum*, m. pl., cf. 50-1 n.) is called *immanem* ("enormous") in part to emphasize that Mars was able to punish such great heroes, while Juno laments that she cannot stop the Trojans.

305-6. **concessit:** note the emphatic initial placement of this verb with asyndeton*, helping to convey Juno's outrage. **in iras:** *in* + accusative can express purpose; here, "for the sake of (Diana's) wrath," i.e., to sate her wrath. The goddess Artemis/Diana sent a boar to wreak havoc in Calydon because its King Oeneus would not sacrifice to her (see Homer, *Iliad* 9.533-42). **ipse deum...genitor:** emphatic and elevated periphrasis* for Jupiter; on *deum* (50-1 n.). **antiquam...Calydona:** *Calydona* (*Calydon, -onis*, f.) is a Greek accusative. **Dianae:** dative after *concessit*.

307. **quod scelus aut Lapithas tantum aut Calydona merentem:** a difficult clause that asks a question but that, instead of standing independently, is syntactically placed in apposition to what precedes (see below). Translation: "(Either) the Lapiths or Centaurs committing what such great crime?" (i.e., What such great crime did either the Lapiths or Centaurs commit?) *Quod* is the interrogative adjective modifying *scelus...tantum*; *Lapithas* and *Calydona* are accusatives (see listings in notes on 304-6) and stand in apposition to the accusatives *gentem Lapithum* and *Calydona* in 304-6. **merentem:** modifies both *Lapithas* and *Calydona* in 307 but is singular because it is placed closer to the singular form *Calydona* (cf. AG §286). *Mereo* usually means "merit," "earn" but was also used with the sense of "commit" a crime or wrong, as here with *scelus* as direct object (see Horsfall). Some editors (e.g., Hirtzel) accept the manuscript variant *Lapithis...Calydone merente*, but this variant might have arisen from a misreading of *merentem* as *merente* (see, e.g., Fordyce).

ast ego, magna Iovis coniunx, nil linquere inausum
quae potui infelix, quae memet in omnia verti,
vincor ab Aenea. quod si mea numina non sunt   310
magna satis, dubitem haud equidem implorare quod usquam est:
flectere si nequeo superos, Acheronta movebo.
non dabitur regnis, esto, prohibere Latinis,

---

308. **ast ego, magna Iovis coniunx:** Juno points to the humiliating nature of her failure. While lesser gods, such as Mars and Diana (304-6) can fulfill their revenge, Juno—the wife of Jupiter (note the grand periphrasis* that enhances her indignation)—cannot. **inausum:** "undared" (from *in + audeo*), a Vergilian neologism*, also used of the monster Cacus (8.205); modifies *nil*.

309. **quae...quae:** i.e., Juno; note the emotional effect of the asyndeton*. **infelix:** used only here of a divinity; employed most memorably of Dido (4.68, 450, 529, 596; cf. 376 n.), who suffered as a result Juno's (and Venus') actions. **memet in omnia verti:** "turned myself to all things (i.e., resources)"; *-met* is an intensifying suffix, and *verti* perfect indicative active. The phrase should probably not be construed with the metamorphoric force that the verb has in 328 describing the Fury Allecto (*tot sese vertit in ora*, see n.): while Allecto does change forms in the *Aeneid*, Juno does not.

310. **vincor:** emphatic enjambment*. **ab Aenea:** ablative of personal agent; note the emphatic positioning of the phrase at the sentence's conclusion. **quod:** "but." **sunt:** note the double monosyllabic verse ending (cf. 592 n.).

311. **magna:** in 308, Juno called herself *magna Iovis coniunx*. Now she questions whether her powers (*numina* 310) are great enough (*magna satis*), signaling her move to the infernal powers for help in the next line. **dubitem haud equidem:** future less vivid apodosis of a mixed condition (cf. the present general protasis *si mea numina non sunt...*), "I should not, indeed, hesitate to..." (for these conditions, see AG §514-16). **quod usquam est:** "what (help) exists anywhere"; the clause serves as object of *implorare* ("invoke"). Note the triple elision* in the line that helps to convey Juno's indignant anger.

312. **flectere...movebo:** a meaningful contrast between trying to persuade the heavenly gods (*flectere* literally means "bend" (cf. 35-6 n.) but metaphorically "persuade") and taking purposeful action (*movebo*), i.e., "rouse" the infernal powers. Note how the verbs frame the line. For the programmatic sense of *moveo*, see 44-5 n. **Acheronta:** see 90-1 n. Note its emphatic juxtaposition with *superos* (antithesis*). "By stirring the forces of the underworld, by unleashing *furor* in and on the epic, [Juno] opens up the possibility for further poetic expansion of the *Aeneid* after the potential closure offered by the poem by the Trojans' successful arrival in Italy, in a sense beginning the epic anew" (Hershkowitz (1998) 100). Line 312 is quoted by Sigmund Freud on the title page of *The Interpretation of Dreams*.

313. **non dabitur...prohibere...:** "it will not be granted (to me; understand *mihi*) to debar (them; understand *eos*)...." Juno acknowledges that her ability to act is circumscribed by Jupiter and Fate. **regnis...Latinis:** ablative of separation after *prohibere*. *Regnis*, here, "rule" or "kingdom";

atque immota manet fatis Lavinia coniunx:
at trahere atque moras tantis licet addere rebus,   315
at licet amborum populos exscindere regum.
hac gener atque socer coëant mercede suorum:
sanguine Troiano et Rutulo dotabere, virgo,

Latinis can either mean "of Latinus" or "of the Latins." **esto:** "so be it"; third person singular future imperative, here conveying Juno's bitter resignation; cf. 12.821 *esto* (Juno replying to Jupiter's resolution of the Italian war).

314. **immota manet fatis Lavinia coniunx:** *coniunx* here functions as a predicate noun; "Lavinia remains by fate unshaken as (Aeneas') bride." This line involves an intratextual reference to Jupiter's revelation of fate to Venus at 1.257-8: *manent immota tuorum | fata*. Lavinia is first named at 6.764, where she is called *Lavinia coniunx*.

315-16. **at...licet... | at licet:** with *licet* ("it is permitted"), understand *mihi*. The anaphora* and tricolon crescendo* of infinitives (dependent on *licet*) give rhetorical force to Juno's impassioned reassertion of her powers. **trahere:** "drag along"; supply *res* (from *tantis...rebus*) as object, or construe *moras* as object (as well as of *addere*); cf. 10.888 *traxisse moras*. **moras:** Juno introduces the theme of *mora* ("delay") that will dominate particularly in Book 12 (e.g., 12.676-80). **exscindere:** "destroy."

317. **hac...mercede suorum:** "at this cost of (or 'to') their own peoples"; the phrase *hac...mercede* is ablative of price (AG §416) and looks forward to the claim in 318. **gener...socer:** "son-in-law...father-in-law" (i.e., Aeneas...Latinus). The combination resonantly recalls the use of these words at 6.830-1 (*aggeribus <u>socer</u> Alpinis atque are Monoeci | descendens, <u>gener</u> adversis instructus Eois!*) to describe Caesar, his son-in-law Pompey, and their civil war—thus perhaps intimating that the war Juno stirs up in Italy will be something like a civil war among the peoples there (cf. Introduction to Book 7; Rebeggiani (2020) 101-6). **coëant:** jussive subjunctive.

318-19. **sanguine Troiano et Rutulo:** ablative of means. *Troiano* of course refers to the *gener* (Aeneas) in 317 (see n.), while *Rutulo* is used of the *socer* (Latinus) because he will be allied with Turnus and the Rutulians in the ensuing war against Aeneas. Juno makes clear that the blood of both peoples will be spilled as a result of Aeneas' prospective marriage to Lavinia. **dotabere:** second person singular future passive of *doto* ("provide with a dowry"). **virgo...te:** the apostrophe* to Lavinia, over whom the war will be fought, is powerful, especially since she is given no direct speech in the epic. **manet:** with transitive force ("await") with *te* as object, pointedly contrasting with the intransitive use of *manet* (in the same metrical position) at 314. **pronuba:** a woman who helped the bride with wedding arrangements, a "bride's-maid"; Juno (goddess of marriage) was the *pronuba* (4.166) at the controversial "wedding" of Dido and Aeneas in the cave. Here, Juno perversely describes Bellona (goddess of war) as Lavinia's *pronuba*. (Note that Bellona will also be present overseeing the battle of Actium—a civil war—on Aeneas' shield at 8.703 along with *Mavors*, the *Dirae*, and *Discordia*.)

et Bellona manet te pronuba. nec face tantum
Cisseïs praegnas ignis enixa iugalis;   320
quin idem Veneri partus suus et Paris alter,
funestaeque iterum recidiva in Pergama taedae.'
    Haec ubi dicta dedit, terras horrenda petivit;
luctificam Allecto dirarum ab sede dearum

319-20. **nec...tantum...:** "not only..."; setting up a comparison in 321-2 (see notes) of Hecuba and Venus. **face... | Cisseïs praegnas:** *"Cisseïs* pregnant with a torch," also at 10.704-5; *praegnas* is a coarsely precise word for the epic genre (Lyne (1987) 53). When pregnant with Paris, Hecuba (=*Cisseïs*, "daughter of Cisseus," king of Thrace) had a dream that she was pregnant with a firebrand (*fax, facis*, f.) that would bring about Troy's destruction; indeed, according to Juno, Hecuba metaphorically gave birth to the wedding-fires (i.e., wedding-torches, *ignis...iugalis*) of Paris' marriage to Helen that would doom Troy. **enixa:** from *enitor* (3), here "give birth to"; supply *est*.

321. **quin:** "indeed." **idem:** supply *est*, "(is the same," describing *suus partus* (i.e., the birth of Venus' son Aeneas will have just as destructive consequences as the birth of Hecuba's son Paris had). **Veneri partus suus:** *partus* (-*ūs*, m.), "birth," "offspring" from *pario* (3), "bear," "bring forth"; *suus*, reflexive adjective referring to Venus (*Veneri*, dative); "Venus own child" (lit. "her own offspring to Venus"). **Paris alter:** again, understand *est*. Aeneas is "another Paris," because his marriage to Lavinia (stolen from Turnus, from the perspective of Turnus and Amata) will also bring destruction to Troy reborn in Italy (322 n.); Venus would thus be another Hecuba. This phrase expands the idea in the first half of the sentence (an example of *dicolon abundans**). The interpretation of Aeneas as a second Paris will be a powerful one for Aeneas' enemies throughout Books 7-12. See, e.g., Lyne (1987) 109-10 and Dekel (2012) 109-15.

322. **funestae...taedae:** cf. *ignis...iugalis* in 320 with n. This line elaborates and sums up the meaning of the comparison involved in 319-22. **recidiva in Pergama:** see 321 n. *Recidiva* means "recurring," "reborn"; *Pergama, -orum,* n. pl. is "(the citadel of) Troy"; *in* with accusative, "against" or "for."

323-40. Juno calls up the horrifying Fury Allecto from the underworld and enlists her help to start a war in Italy.

Compare this passage with Juno's descent to the wind god Aeolus' kingdom at 1.50-64. Note also that the skills Juno attributes to Allecto at 335-40 are largely borne out by her subsequent actions. For more on Allecto, see 286-640 n.

323. **Haec ubi dicta dedit:** a formulaic phrase marking a speech's conclusion (cf. also 471). **terras...petivit:** whereas in Book 1 Juno comes to earth to rouse the wind god Aeolus, here she comes to earth to call up a Fury from the underworld. **horrenda:** "horrible," describing Juno.

324. **luctificam:** stylized epic compound adjective meaning "grief-making," "causing sorrow." **Allecto:** Greek accusative (same as the nominative form; only these two cases are used in the epic). Allecto is one of the Furies; her name in Greek means "the Unceasing One." **dirarum ab sede dearum:** *ab sede* means "from the home" (for *sedes*, cf. 52 n.); note the sense of rhyming in the genitive phrase *dirarum...dearum*. There are three sister Furies (here described with reference to another name Vergil uses for them, *Dirae*—see Mackie (1992)): Tisiphone, Allecto, and

infernisque ciet tenebris, cui tristia bella 325
iraeque insidiaeque et crimina noxia cordi.
odit et ipse pater Pluton, odere sorores
Tartareae monstrum: tot sese vertit in ora,
tam saevae facies, tot pullulat atra colubris.
quam Iuno his acuit verbis ac talia fatur: 330

Megaera. Tisiphone also appears in the epic (6.555, 571; 10.761), while Megaera is mentioned only at 12.846. An unnamed *Dira* takes action on Jupiter's request at 12.845-68. However, as Syson (2013) 95 notes: "It is never entirely clear whether or to what extent specific members of the groups *Dirae, Erinyes, Eumenides, Furiae, Harpyiae* share an identity in the poem."

325-6. **cui tristia bella...cordi:** supply *sunt*; construe *cui* as a dative of reference with Allecto as antecedent, and understand *cordi* as a dative of purpose (AG §382), "to whom grim wars...are desirable (lit. 'for the purpose of her heart')." **-que...-que et:** note the polysyndeton* in this brief but effective catalogue of things dear to the Fury.

327. **odit...odere:** *odere = oderunt*; note that the polyptoton* (with emphatic initial placement of both words) rhetorically increases the goddess' horrendousness, as does the asyndeton* between the two clauses. **Pluton:** a Greek nominative form; king of the underworld and father of the Furies. **odere sorores:** Vergil intensifies Allecto's horror by claiming that she is hated not only by her father but also by her sister Furies; in Aeschylus (*Eumenides* 73) the Furies are hateful to gods (in general) and mortals.

328. **Tartareae:** adjective modifying *sorores*. *Tartarus* is the region of hell where the most vicious criminals are punished by the Furies (6.548-627); the Fury Tisiphone (324 n.) is specifically described there (6.555, 570-2). **monstrum:** here, "monster," "monstrosity," describing Allecto. **tot sese vertit in ora...:** *ora*, here "faces," "appearances"; cf. 309 *quae memet in omnia verti* (of Juno, see n.). We witness Allecto's metamorphic abilities at 415-19, where she becomes the aged priestess Calybe and subsequently infuriates Turnus, while at 12.862, an unnamed *Dira* (cf. 324 n.) turns into a small bird to terrify Turnus. Note that divine metamorphic abilities had already posed a threat to (though one avoided by) the Trojans, when they sailed by Circe's realm (see 10-24 n.).

329. **tam saevae facies:** supply *ei sunt* (*ei* being dative of possessor); *facies, -ei*, f., "face," "figure," "visage." Note the change in construction from the surrounding clauses, as well as the asyndeton* and anaphora* (*tot...tam...tot...*). **tot pullulat...colubris:** "sprouts forth (with) so many snakes." *Pullulat* is an agricultural word that is here used metaphorically; it appears one other time in Vergil—at *Georgics* 2.17, describing the growth of trees. *Coluber, -bri*, m. is a poetic word for "snake," often used to describe the hair of the Furies (for other references to Allecto's snakes, see 346, 447, 450). **atra:** nominative, modifying Allecto; the adjective could describe the Fury's overall appearance, but it might also be construed as an instance of transferred epithet* or enallage*, whereby the traditional black (here *atra*) color of snakes is used of Allecto instead of the snakes (i.e., *colubris*) on her head.

330. **quam:** a connecting relative pronoun, i.e., Allecto. **acuit:** "sharpens," but the verb could be used, as here, of rousing a person or an emotion, i.e., "excites," "incites" (cf. 406 and 12.108 *acuit Martem*).

'hunc mihi da proprium, virgo sata Nocte, laborem,
hanc operam, ne noster honos infractave cedat
fama loco, neu conubiis ambire Latinum
Aeneadae possint Italosve obsidere fines.
tu potes unanimos armare in proelia fratres   335
atque odiis versare domos, tu verbera tectis
funereasque inferre faces, tibi nomina mille,
mille nocendi artes. fecundum concute pectus,
disice compositam pacem, sere crimina belli;

331. **hunc...proprium...laborem:** note the hyperbaton* involved in this phrase, which frames the line; *proprium*, "proper," i.e., for you to give to me. **sata Nocte:** *sata* (from *sero* (3), "beget," "bring forth") is vocative (cf. also 338-9 n.); *Nocte*, ablative of origin. The phrase is a periphrasis* for Allecto/Fury, also at 12.860 (cf. 328 n.). The Furies are the children of Night and Pluto (327 n.).

332-3. **operam:** "service," "work" (*opera, -ae*, f.). **ne...neu...:** negative purpose clauses. **noster honos...:** as in 1.46-9, Juno is concerned about the slight to her honor caused by Aeneas' actions; for the form *honos*, cf. 3 n. **infracta:** "broken," but it can also mean "diminished" or "weakened"; modifying *fama*. **cedat | ...loco:** *loco* is ablative with *cedat* (subjunctive), "withdraw from"; a military idiom. **ambire:** "go around," "canvass for votes," but here with the sense "inveigle" or "cajole" (Goold).

334. **Aeneadae:** see 284 n. **possint:** governs the infinitives *ambire* (333) and *obsidere*; subjunctive in a negative purpose clause (332-3 n.). **obsidere:** "occupy" (343 n.).

335-7. **unanimos armare...fratres:** *unanimus*, "of one mind," the addition of the compound adjective underscores the Fury's evil talent for fraternal/civil war. (Joseph (2009) argues for a pointed allusion here to Catullus 9.) **armare...versare...inferre:** note the tricolon* of infinitive phrases, describing the types of crimes in which the Fury specializes. Later poets such as Seneca in the *Thyestes* and Statius in the *Thebaid* will focus on these aspects of the Furies. **in proelia:** here *in* conveys purpose. **versare:** "agitate." **verbera...faces:** we will see Allecto actually using such implements when she infuriates Turnus later in the book (451 *verbera*, 457 *taedas*). **tectis:** dative governed by the compound verb *inferre*.

337-8. **tibi nomina mille:** supply *sunt*; *tibi* is dative of possessor. A deity could have countless powers and therefore countless special names. **nomina mille, | mille...artes:** note the effective chiastic* structure, repetition of *mille*, and asyndeton*. Juno generously flatters Allecto and then states her requests in the lines that follow.

338-9. **fecundum:** "fertile," in the sense that Allecto (by means of her *fecundum pectus*) can produce the type of violence that Juno needs. **concute:** imperative, "arouse to action" (*OLD* s.v. *concutio* 5), though the verb originally and more usually means "shake" or "shake something (e.g., a garment) out" to see if anything is in it (cf. Fordyce). **disice:** imperative of *disicio* (3), "break up." **compositam pacem:** "arranged peace"; the nature of the *pax* meant is unclear, cf. notes on 45-6 and 467. **sere:** imperative of *sero* (3), "sow," "plant." **crimina belli:** here "causes of war" or "accusations that lead to war" (Horsfall). Again (cf. 335-7 n.), a tricolon* of actions (three imperatives emphatically placed) and asyndeton*.

arma velit poscatque simul rapiatque iuventus.' 340
Exim Gorgoneïs Allecto infecta venenis
principio Latium et Laurentis tecta tyranni
celsa petit, tacitumque obsedit limen Amatae,
quam super adventu Teucrum Turnique hymenaeis

---

340. **velit poscatque simul rapiatque:** *simul* and a tricolon* (once again) of jussive subjunctives (all in one line) help convey the fury that Juno tells Allecto to use in inspiring young men/warriors (*iuventus*) to start the war.

341-72. *Allecto infuriates Amata, who urges her husband Latinus to accept Turnus as their fated son-in-law.*

On this passage, see especially the discussions in Lyne (1987) 13-27, Feeney (1991) 162-8, and Panoussi (2009) 124-33. Lyne argues for the erotic nature of Amata's infuriation and attachment/relationship to Turnus, while Panoussi examines the Bacchic and maenadic elements in Amata's characterization. Feeney uses this passage to explore how the "symbiosis of the concrete and the hallucinatory fantastic" lies at the center of Vergil's representation of the incomprehensibility of madness (168). Ovid imitates this passage in *Metamorphoses* 4.490-511, when he relates the Fury Tisiphone's infuriation of Ino.

341. **Exim:** = *exinde*, "then," "thereupon." **Gorgoneïs...venenis:** *Gorgoneïs* is an adjective; the heads of the Gorgons (in some versions just Medusa's) were covered with poisonous snakes; hence the use of *venenum* ("poison," "venom") here.

342. **principio:** adverbial, "at first," "first." This will be the first of Allecto's three acts of incitement. She will later go to the Rutulians and infect Turnus (cf. 409), and finally to the Trojans hunting on the shore (cf. 477-8), where she will orchestrate the death of Silvia's stag and the consequent outbreak of war. See 286-640 n. **Laurentis...tyranni:** genitive; a periphrasis* for Latinus (see notes on 47 and 265-6). Observe the interlocking word order* of this phrase with *tecta...celsa*. **tecta:** 59 n.

343. **tacitum...limen:** *tacitum* is probably a transferred epithet* (or enallage*); it grammatically modifies Amata's threshold (*limen*) but really conveys the silence with which the Fury herself acts, as she is about to inspire Amata's madness. **obsedit:** from *obsideo* (2), "sit at" or "on," probably here with a military metaphor*, "besiege" (cf. 334). **Amatae:** the name and its significance are disputed. In Dionysius of Halicarnassus (1.64.2) the queen is Amita; new Vestal Virgins are called Amata (reason unclear) in their admission ceremony (Fordyce); and the name construed as a past participle might resonate with her almost erotic attachment to Turnus that is metaphorically hinted at elsewhere (e.g., 57; see Lyne (1987) 13-18).

344. **quam:** object of *coquebant* (345); antecedent is Amata. **super:** "about," "concerning," preposition governing the ablatives *adventu...hymenaeis*. **adventu Teucrum Turnique hymenaeis:** ; *Teucrum* is genitive plural (50-1 n.); *hymenaeus (-i,* m.) is a wedding song; in plural, often "nuptials" or "wedding." Note the chiastic* phrasing.

femineae ardentem curaeque iraeque coquebant. 345
huic dea caeruleis unum de crinibus anguem
conicit, inque sinum praecordia ad intima subdit,
quo furibunda domum monstro permisceat omnem.
ille inter vestis et levia pectora lapsus
volvitur attactu nullo, fallitque furentem 350

---

345. **femineae...curaeque iraeque**: the violent sound of this line with two elisions*, consonance* (*c/q, r*), and assonance* (*a/ae*) perhaps reflects the Amata's anxious state. **coquebant**: "were boiling," a metaphorical usage that is found in Ennius, *Annales* fragment 338 in Skutsch and in *FRL* 1 *curam...quae nunc te coquit*, and in Plautus, *Trinummus* 225 *egomet me coquo*. On this line, Feeney (1991) 164 writes: "Vergil's presentation here, with its artfully condescending *femineae*, and colloquial *coquebant*, caters to the culture's expectation of what is natural in a woman in such a circumstance." Strong human and gendered motivations are suggested for the queen's subsequent actions that work in tandem with the divine influence of the Fury.

346. **huic dea**: note the pointed juxtaposition of the mortal Amata (*huic*) and the goddess Allecto (*dea*). The dative *huic* is equivalent to *in hanc* (a frequent usage in Vergil) and should be taken closely with *conicit* in 347 (cf. 456 *iuveni coniecit*). **caeruleis**: "greenish blue," a traditional color of serpents that goes back to the poet Ennius; here it is applied to Amata's hair (*de crinibus*) which is made of snakes from which she plucks one (*unum...anguem*). Note the interlocking word order* of *caeruleis...crinibus* and *unum...anguem* (cf. 342 n.).

347. **conicit...subdit**: note the effective enjambment* of *conicit*, and the enclosing of the line with verbs describing the Fury's violent actions. **praecordia ad intima**: gives more specificity to *in...sinum* ("breast"); *ad* + accusative with the sense of "near," "about the area of"; *praecordia*, "diaphragm" or "lungs," though it is more generally understood in poetry as "heart" and even "mind." Allecto's "assault is therefore aimed precisely enough at Amata's passions and reason" (Horsfall).

348. **quo...monstro**: "with this monstrous thing," i.e., the snake. *Anguem* (346) is antecedent of *quo*; *monstro* is technically unnecessary, but its addition represents "a development of the idiom, common in Early Latin and occasionally found in classical prose, especially with *locus* and *dies*, by which the antecedent is repeated in a relative clause," though "here the repeated antecedent is replaced by a word of similar sense" (Fordyce ad 477). **furibunda**: "raging," "furious," describing the state into which Amata will be incited by the Fury's snake; also used of Dido at 4.646. **permisceat**: "mix together," here with the sense of "throw into confusion," "embroil"; subjunctive in a relative clause of purpose (cf. 98-9 n.).

349. **ille**: i.e., the *anguis* (346). **inter vestis et levia pectora**: this picture of the snake sliding (i.e., *lapsus*) between Amata's clothes and chest is somewhat at odds with the details of line 347. What results is an impressionistic view of the snake's movements. See 353 n.

350-1. **volvitur**: passive of *volvo* (3, "roll," "turn round") with middle sense, "roll along," "move with sinuous motion" (*OLD* s.v. *volvo* 1d). **attactu nullo**: the sense must be "with no touch (felt)," i.e., Amata is unaware of the snake's presence and actions. **fallit...furentem**: construe the participle as proleptic*, "tricks her (into) raging," as also in the description of Dido infected

vipeream inspirans animam; fit tortile collo
aurum ingens coluber, fit longae taenia vittae,
innectitque comas et membris lubricus errat.
ac dum prima lues udo sublapsa veneno
pertemptat sensus atque ossibus implicat ignem   355
necdum animus toto percepit pectore flammam,

---

by Venus/Cupid at 1.659-60 *furentem | incendat reginam*. (Note again the parallels between the two queens—Dido and Amata—as a result of divine scheming.)

351-2. **fit..., fit...**: *anguis* (= *ille* in 349) is still the subject. Note the anaphora* of *fit* ("becomes") and the asyndeton* that perhaps help convey the snake's metamorphic ability. **tortile...aurum:** "twisted gold," i.e., a gold necklace. **coluber:** cf. 329 n.; modified by *ingens*. **longae taenia vittae:** a difficult phrase. A *vitta* is a "headband," "fillet"; *taenia* (from a Greek word) can mean the same thing but might be translated here as "ribbon," part of the overall *vitta*—and perhaps the ends dangling down (cf. Servius *taenia est vittarum extremitas*). Horsfall argues that *longae...vittae* is a *genitivus inhaerentiae* or synonymous genitive, "by which a synonym (in the gen.) intensifies the noun upon which it depends"; Lyne (1989) 20-2 suggests that a different meaning of *taenia* might apply here, that of "tape-worm" (see *OLD* s.v. *taenia* 4), in which case the snake, having turned into a twisted gold necklace, then transforms into a tape-worm, a metamorphosis that suggests another perspective on the snake's harmfulness.

353. **membris lubricus errat:** *membris* is ablative of place, but with a sense closer to *per membra* "over her limbs." The impressionistic picture continues, as the snake form suddenly returns: Is this a snake? Was it actually a hairband? In what sense does it not touch Amata? See, especially, Feeney (1991) 164-6.

354. **prima lues:** the adjective *prima* can be construed adverbially, "at first"; *lues, -is*, f., "infection." **udo...veneno:** ablative of means, construed with *pertemptat*; *udus* here means "moist" or "clammy" (Fordyce). Vergil suggests the physicality of the snake's poison (and thus again of Allecto) without making clear how it gets into Amata's body. **sublapsa:** modifying *lues*; "having slid down" with sense of "advanced stealthily" (*OLD* s.v. *sublabor* 3) (cf. *lapsus* 349, of the snake itself). Again, a physical detail is provided, yet Amata seems completely unaware of the snake's presence.

355. **pertemptat:** here "assails," a Vergilian usage found also at *Geo.* 3.250; *Aen.* 1.502, 5.828, but "nowhere else in classical Latin" (Fordyce ad loc.). **sensūs:** accusative plural (fourth declension). **ossibus:** "bones"; it was in bone marrow that emotions and strength were thought to reside. **implicat:** "entangles," "enfolds." **ignem:** fire is used as a metaphor* for fury. The phrase *ossibus implicat ignem* is repeated from 1.660 (the intended effect of Venus'/Cupid's infection of Dido; a passage already echoed in 350, see n.).

356. **animus:** Amata's "mind," the *animus* being located in the chest (cf. 347 n.). **toto percepit pectore flammam:** the phrase recalls Ariadne's passion when she first saw Theseus in Catullus 64.92 *cuncto concepit pectore flammam*. Note how the metaphors* of madness and love overlap.

mollius et solito matrum de more locuta est,
multa super natae lacrimans Phrygiisque hymenaeis:
'exsulibusne datur ducenda Lavinia Teucris,
o genitor, nec te miseret nataeque tuique?   360
nec matris miseret, quam primo aquilone relinquet
perfidus alta petens abducta virgine praedo?
at non sic Phrygius penetrat Lacedaemona pastor,
Ledaeamque Helenam Troianas vexit ad urbes?

357. **et:** combines the adverbial phrases *mollius* and *solito matrum de more*, which are both to be construed with *locuta est*. Amata speaks gently and like a mother, but is her manner caused by the snake/Fury, by natural, human motivation, or by both? On gender roles, cf. 345 n.

358. **multa:** adverbial accusative, "much." **super natae...Phrygiisque hymenaeis:** *super* governs the ablative *hymenaeis* (see 344 n.), which is modified by the adjective *Phrygiis* (i.e., indicating Aeneas) but also by the genitive *natae* ("of her daughter").

359. **exsulibus...Teucris:** dative of indirect object after *datur*. Note Amata's derogatory description of the Trojans as exiles. **datur:** the indicative instead of a deliberative subjunctive; "is Lavinia (to be) given?" **ducenda:** "to be married"; *duco* can idiomatically mean (with man as the subject) "bring home as a wife," i.e., "marry" (*OLD* s.v. *duco* 5a).

360-1. **o genitor:** Latinus' sudden presence contributes to the impressionistic or surreal nature of this episode. Note the powerful emphasis on the family relationship here (and with *natae... matris*) in contrast to *exsulibus* (359). **miseret...miseret...:** impersonal usages with the accusative of person affected (*te*) and genitive of the cause of pity (*natae, tui, matris*). Note the emphatic and syntactically unnecessary repetition of *miseret*, reinforcing Amata's claim that Latinus is giving little thought to his responsibility to his family in betrothing their daughter to Aeneas. **primo aquilone:** *aquilo* is the "North wind"; "with the first North wind" (i.e., Aeneas will leave as soon as the wind blows that will allow him to travel south, the direction from which he arrived at Latium, see Horsfall).

362. **perfidus:** used especially of treacherous lovers; of Aeneas (4.305, 366, 421), and of Theseus (Catullus 64.132, 133, 174)—both in situations where the heroic lover abandons a woman. Interestingly here, however, Amata (mother) imagines *herself* abandoned, as Aeneas takes her daughter Lavinia on the high seas away from her (cf. 341-72 n.). **alta:** "the high (seas)"; neuter plural. **praedo:** "robber," prosaic and derogatory in tone; used of Aeneas by his enemies at 10.774 and 11.484.

363-4. **at non sic...:** Amata draws a parallel between Aeneas' treachery and Paris', as Juno had done in 319-22 (see notes). **Phrygius...pastor:** the "Phrygian shepherd," i.e., Paris. Phrygia was the region east of the Troad, though the Trojans are often called Phrygian in the *Aeneid*. Paris was indeed raised as a shepherd, after he was unsuccessfully left out to die as an infant on Mount Ida to prevent him from fulfilling Hecuba's dream (see 319-20 n.). As a shepherd, he judged the beauty contest between Juno, Minerva, and Venus (i.e., the famous Judgment of Paris). **penetrat:** the present tense (instead of past) vividly brings Paris' action (and its current relevance) to mind. **Lacedaemona:** Greek accusative; *Lacedaemon (-onis,* f.) was an older name

> quid tua sancta fides? quid cura antiqua tuorum 365
> et consanguineo totiens data dextera Turno?
> si gener externa petitur de gente Latinis,
> idque sedet, Faunique premunt te iussa parentis,
> omnem equidem sceptris terram quae libera nostris
> dissidet externam reor et sic dicere divos. 370
> et Turno, si prima domus repetatur origo,
> Inachus Acrisiusque patres mediaeque Mycenae.'

---

for Sparta, where Helen and Menelaus lived and ruled. **Ledaeam:** "of" or "belonging to Leda," an adjective seemingly coined* by Vergil and here modifying *Helenam*. Helen's mother was Leda. She lost Helen to Trojan treachery, as Amata fears will happen with her own daughter Lavinia. This Trojan War/Paris analogy will be crucial for Aeneas' opponents throughout Books 7-12 (cf. 321 n.). See Hardie (1993) 14-18 and Seo (2013) 58-60.

365-6. **quid tua sancta fides…?:** "What (of)" or "What (do you say about) your sacred pledge…?" This is an elliptical usage of the interrogative *quid* followed by the nominative (*OLD* s.v. *quis*[1] 12); the construction is continued with *cura antiqua* and *data dextera*. Amata suggests that a formal pledge had been made to Turnus. **tuorum:** objective genitive after *cura*. Amata again emphasizes the duty Latinus should feel to his people. **consanguineo:** "related by blood," adjective modifying *Turno*; Turnus' mother Venilia (10.76) was Amata's sister (Servius). **totiens:** "so many times," probably an exaggeration. Indeed, nowhere do we objectively learn that Lavinia and Turnus had been formally engaged. **dextera:** "right (hand)." **Turno:** dative.

367-72. Amata offers two arguments for why Turnus should be considered *externus* and thus the son-in-law foretold in Faunus' oracle at 96-101: 1) every region (including Turnus' Ardea) outside of Latinus' political control is "foreign" (*externam* 370); 2) Turnus' ancestry can in fact be traced back to Greece (371-2). For Latinus' usage of *externus*, see 255 n.

367. **gener:** see 317 n. **externa…de gente:** cf. notes on 68, 98-9, 255. **Latinis:** dative. The plural is used since Turnus "will become not only Lavinia's husband but eventually king of the Latins" (Horsfall).

368. **idque sedet:** "and this is settled" or "decided"; cf. 611. **Fauni…iussa parentis:** referring to the oracle Latinus received from his father Faunus, see 96-101 with notes. **premunt:** "press hard upon."

369-70. **omnem…terram…externam reor:** accusative and infinitive statement after *reor* ("think," "judge"); supply *esse* and construe *externam* as a predicate adjective after *esse*. **sceptris…nostris:** ablative of separation. **dissidet:** "sits apart from," "is separate from." **sic dicere divos:** construe with *reor*, i.e., this is what I think the gods mean. For the argument, see 367-72 n.; for its tendentiousness, see Anderson (1957) 21 or (1990) 243 and Cairns (1989) 121-2, though Horsfall finds it technically feasible.

371-2. **Turno:** dative of possessor. **si…repetatur:** present subjunctive in the protasis of a future less vivid condition; in the apodosis in 372, *sunt* must be understood, creating a mixed condition. **domus:** genitive singular. **Inachus:** river-god and first king of Argos (depicted on Turnus' shield at 792). **Acrisius:** an early Argive king, cf. 409-10 n. Turnus' Argive ancestry

His ubi nequiquam dictis experta Latinum
contra stare videt, penitusque in viscera lapsum
serpentis furiale malum totamque pererrat, 375
tum vero infelix ingentibus excita monstris
immensam sine more furit lymphata per urbem:
ceu quondam torto volitans sub verbere turbo,

thus draws him closer to Juno, whose favorite city is Argos (cf. 286 n.). **mediaeque Mycenae:** "the middle" or "center of Mycenae" (cf. 296 n.), i.e., Turnus has undeniably Greek roots (cf. also *prima* in 371). For the complexity of Turnus' genealogy, see Hannah (2004) and Reed (2007) 69-70.

373-405. *Latinus resists the appeals of Amata, who then, in a state of seeming Bacchic madness, rouses all the city's women to join her, while she rages in the woods.*

373-4. **His...dictis:** ablative of means after *experta* (from *experior*, "make trial of," "test"); she "made trial of Latinus with these words" to convince him of her views, but to no avail. **Latinum:** object of both *videt* and the participle *experta*. **contra stare:** "stand against," "oppose." We are not told explicitly how Latinus responded to Amata's powerful, if sophistic, arguments. Rather, the focus stays on Amata's impassioned and increasingly infuriated state, as the influence of Allecto gradually takes over. Note that Latinus "departs" the scene as suddenly as he had entered it (360-1 n.), adding further to the impressionistic nature of the episode. **in viscera lapsum:** with *lapsum* understand *est*; the subject is *furiale malum* (375 n.). The phrase echoes *inter...pectora lapsus* in line 349 (describing the snake, also at line end).

375. **furiale malum:** here "furious" or "Fury's poison" (cf. *Gorgoneis...venenis* 341). **totam:** sc. *Amatam.* **pererrat:** once again, the physicality of the event is suggested.

376. **tum vero infelix:** the same phrasing is used at 4.450 of Dido, whom the poet also calls *infelix* (cf. 309 n.). **ingentibus...monstris:** i.e., the monstrous things experienced by Amata, when she has been infected by the Fury.

377. **immensam...per urbem:** *immensam* hyperbolically* expands the amount of space over which Amata wanders in her crazed state (note too how *immensam...urbem* encloses the verse). For the line, compare Dido's raging in the grip of divine fury at 4.68-9: *totaque vagatur | urbe furens*. **sine more:** "without custom," here "wildly" (*OLD* s.v. *mos* 3c). **furit lymphata:** *lympho* (1) means "make crazy." (Vergil's contemporary Horace describes Cleopatra as *lymphata* in the famous "Cleopatra Ode," *Carmina* 1.37.14.) Note the immediate effect of the Fury Allecto on Amata.

378-83. One of the most memorable and terrifying similes* in the poem, comparing boys playing with a top to a god tormenting a human. Homer included toys in similes, as at *Iliad* 14.413 (Hector, hit by Ajax with a stone, spins like a top), but Callimachus, *Epigram* 1.9-10 (boys spinning a top) is a closer potential Greek influence (Horsfall). In addition, the Roman love elegist Tibullus (contemporary of Vergil) uses a top simile to describe a lover: *namque agor, ut per plana citus sola verbere turben, | quem celer assueta versat ab arte puer* (1.5.3-4, "I am driven like a top, whirled around a level field | That a swift boy has lashed with his usual skill," Putnam and Gaisser (2012). For discussion of the simile, see Rabel (1981), Lyne (1987) 24-7, Feeney (1991) 167, and Bleisch (1996).

quem pueri magno in gyro vacua atria circum
intenti ludo exercent—ille actus habena 380
curvatis fertur spatiis; stupet inscia supra
impubesque manus mirata volubile buxum;
dant animos plagae—non cursu segnior illo
per medias urbes agitur populosque ferocis.

378. **ceu quondam:** *ceu,* "as"; the archaic *quondam* means "sometimes," "at times." Vergil begins similes with these words in three other places (2.416, 6.492, 7.699). **torto...sub verbere:** "under a twirled lash"; *verbere* is ablative (*verber, -eris,* n.) and resonates with Juno's description of Allecto at 336-7 (*tu verbera tectis...inferre*). **turbo:** *turbo (-inis,* m.), a "spinning top" (378-83 n.).

379. **pueri:** the only reference to children in everyday life in the epic. **magno in gyro:** "in a great circle"; this phrase is better construed as describing the movement of the top (*quem,* 380 n.), not the positioning of the *pueri.* **vacua atria circum:** the preposition *circum* is placed after its object *vacua atria* (anastrophe*). The detail echoes *immensam...urbem* (377), and thus the power of the boys to drive the top over a broad distance. Cf. 2.528 *vacua atria lustrat,* describing the wounded Polites, as he frantically scans the *vacua atria* for help.

380. **ludo:** dative after *intenti.* Vergil emphasizes that the boys are playing a game, making the parallel to Amata's situation still more terrifying. **exercent:** "drive on," with *quem* (379, i.e., the *turbo*) as object. **ille:** i.e., the *turbo* (378 n.). **habena:** "strap"; ablative.

381-2. **curvatis...spatiis:** "in circling courses," i.e., describing the top's circular movement on the ground. **inscia...impubesque manus:** *inscia* and *impubes* both modify *manus;* here *inscia* means not "ignorant" but "inexperienced" (i.e., not having seen the top move like this before); *impubes, -is,* adj., "youthful"; *manus,* here "band," "throng," not "hand." **supra:** adverb. **volubile:** "spinning." **buxum:** "boxwood," here standing by metonymy* for the (boxwood) top.

383. **dant animos plagae:** "strokes (*plagae,* from the *habena,* 380) give energy" (if *animos* is taken with respect to the top), or perhaps "enthusiasm" (if with respect to the boys). Both meanings may be suggested. Note the emphasis given to the boys' reaction in 381-3, because it must somehow affect how we view Allecto's reaction to her infuriation of Amata. **non cursu segnior illo:** Vergil now returns to Amata, who is described as *non...segnior* ("not slower") with the ablative of comparison *cursu...illo* referring to the top (i.e., than the course of that top). For *cursu,* cf. *curvatis...spatiis* (381).

384. **medias urbes...:** *medias* means "middle of," cf. 371-2 n.; *urbes* is better taken as a plural for singular referring to Latinus' city (rather than as a plural indicating multiple cities). **agitur:** "she is driven," the passive conveys Amata's lack of control as a result of her Fury-inspired madness. **populosque ferocis:** *ferocis* would seem to have a positive meaning here, "brave" or "courageous." Note the chiastic* arrangement of *medias urbes* and *populosque ferocis,* both governed by the preposition *per.*

quin etiam in silvas simulato numine Bacchi 385
maius adorta nefas maioremque orsa furorem
evolat et natam frondosis montibus abdit,
quo thalamum eripiat Teucris taedasque moretur,
"euhoe Bacche" fremens, solum te virgine dignum
vociferans: etenim mollis tibi sumere thyrsos, 390
te lustrare choro, sacrum tibi pascere crinem.

---

385. **quin etiam:** cf. 177 n. **simulato numine Bacchi:** ablative absolute phrase; *numen* is the power, will, or influence of a divinity. The women are acting as if in the grip of Bacchic frenzy. Vergil does not make clear whether Allecto or Amata contrives this deception (*simulato*, "simulated," "feigned"), presumably to mask the real character of the madness (cf. 405 n.).

386. **maius...maiorem:** note the effective polyptoton*; cf. *maior...maius* in 44-5 (see n.), important programmatic lines for the second half of the epic. **adorta...orsa:** note the wordplay between *adorta* from *adorior* ("undertake") and *orsa* from *ordior* ("begin"). **nefas...furorem:** here, if *furor* ("fury," "rage," "madness") is taken (by metonymy*) as a deed resulting from *furor*, it would then be close in meaning to *nefas*, an "unspeakable act" or "crime." However, if it means "fury," then Amata would seemingly now be able to enhance her crazed state without Allecto's instigation.

Furor is a central theme of the epic. On the human level it describes excessive and overwhelming passion (often destabilizing or destructive) that includes erotic madness, martial rage, and divine possession, though it is also applied to inanimate phenomena such as storm winds (1.51, *furentibus*) and boiling water (7.464, *furit*). *Furor* is personified among the gods by the Furies (cf. 324 n.) and in the *Aeneid* is particularly associated with and employed by the goddess Juno. Throughout the epic, we see figures of *pietas* attempting to control *furor*, both their own and that of other characters. The opposition grows increasingly complex, as Vergil depicts characters of *pietas* also acting with fury. Most significantly, Aeneas, the poem's main symbol of *pietas*, is *furiis accensus* (12.946) when he slays Turnus. (See General Introduction.)

387. **natam:** Lavinia. **frondosis montibus:** ablative of place without preposition. **abdit:** "hides."

388. **quo...:** "by which act (i.e., hiding Lavinia in 387)..."; relative clause of purpose, cf. 98-9 n. **thalamum...taedas:** "(marriage) bedroom...(marriage) torches," though both essentially mean "wedding" (metonymy*). **Teucris:** dative of separation, "from the Trojans." **moretur:** cf. 315-16 n.

389-91. Note the repeated apostrophes* with polyptoton* to Bacchus. **euhoe:** *euhoe!* (the joyful cry of Bacchic worshippers). **Bacche:** vocative. **fremens:** see 460 n. **te virgine dignum | vociferans:** *vociferans* ("shouting," "exclaiming") takes an accusative (*te*) and infinitive (supply *esse*) construction; *dignum* governs the ablative *virgine*. **mollis...thyrsos:** the *thyrsus* was a staff covered with ivy and used in the celebration of Bacchus. **tibi...te...tibi:** i.e., Bacchus. **sumere... lustrare...pascere:** the indirect statement dependent on *vociferans* (Amata) continues; supply *Laviniam* as accusative subject of these infinitives, "(shouting) that Lavinia takes up...dances around...grows." **te lustrare:** "move around you"; *lustro* (a religious word) here means "move

fama volat, furiisque accensas pectore matres
idem omnis simul ardor agit nova quaerere tecta:
deseruere domos, ventis dant colla comasque;
ast aliae tremulis ululatibus aethera complent   395
pampineasque gerunt incinctae pellibus hastas.
ipsa inter medias flagrantem fervida pinum
sustinet ac natae Turnique canit hymenaeos

---

around" in a solemn procession or dance (here *choro*), suggesting that Lavinia is performing a Bacchic rite. **pascere:** "let grow"; the grown hair would ultimately be given as an offering to the god.

392-6. The powerful influence of Amata on the other women is described. Panoussi (2009) 138 notes the similarities between the effect of the "Fury-like and maenadic" elements of Fama on the Carthaginian women in the Dido episode (4.173-95) and the effect of Allecto on the Latin women here.

392. **fama volat:** see 549 n.; cf. *volitans...Fama per urbes* at 104 (of the spreading news of Faunus' oracle). **furiis...accensas...matres:** note that, like the *matres*, Aeneas will also be "inflamed with fury" as he kills Turnus at the end of the epic, *furiis accensus* (12.946; cf. 386 n.). **pectore:** cf. 356 n.

393. **idem omnis simul ardor:** *idem*, "the same" (cf. notes on 69-70, 321), modifying *ardor*. The phrase also occurs at 4.581 (of Aeneas and his men as they rush to prepare to depart Carthage after Mercury's second appearance). **ardor:** note the metaphor* of fire, cf. *accensas* in 392. **omnis...agit...quaerere:** "impels them all to seek" (see 35-6 n.); *omnis* is accusative feminine plural describing the women. **nova...tecta:** "new dwellings," i.e., the woods/mountains, where they will rage for Bacchus.

394. **deseruere:** note the use of the perfect "expressing instantaneous action" (Fordyce). **domos:** in contrast to *nova...tecta* (393). The alliteration* and asyndeton* help convey the women's fury-driven abandon. **ventis:** dative.

395. **ast aliae...:** *ast* is an archaic form (cf. *at*). Note the heavily dactylic character of the line that helps convey the women's Bacchic frenzy. **aethera:** 34 n.

396. **pampineas...hastas:** "spears covered with vine-tendrils," describing the *thyrsus* (389-91 n.), the staff carried by Bacchants; cf. Euripides, *Bacchae* 25, where the thyrsus is called an "ivy missile." **incinctae pellibus:** *incingo* (3), "wrap in"; *pellis, -is,* f., "hide," here fawnskins, typically worn by Bacchants.

397. **ipsa inter medias:** the focus returns to Amata (*ipsa...fervida*) in the middle of the women. **flagrantem fervida:** note the alliteration* and evocative juxtaposition of *flagrantem* modifying *pinum*, and *fervida* modifying *ipsa* (Amata). **pinum:** here a torch made of pine, an instrument in both marriage and Bacchic ritual (Panoussi (2009) 129).

398. **canit:** the final syllable is lengthened in arsis* (see 173-5 n.), creating a clash of ictus and word accent in the fifth foot, which is normally avoided. **hymenaeos:** see 344 and 358 with notes.

sanguineam torquens aciem, torvumque repente
clamat: 'io matres, audite, ubi quaeque, Latinae: 400
si qua piis animis manet infelicis Amatae
gratia, si iuris materni cura remordet,
solvite crinalis vittas, capite orgia mecum.'
talem inter silvas, inter deserta ferarum
reginam Allecto stimulis agit undique Bacchi. 405

399. **sanguineam torquens aciem:** a manifestation of Amata's madness; *acies, -ei*, f., here "sight," or better "eyes"; *torquens* ("turning") here has sense of "rolling" (her eyes). Later at 448-9, Allecto, as she infects Turnus, is described as *flammea torquens | lumina*. Cf. also Dido at 4.643: *sanguineam volvens aciem*. **torvum:** adverbial, "wildly."

400. **io:** Vergil's only use of this exclamation (Gr. *io!*) expressing joy. **ubi quaeque:** a terse phrase, "wherever each one of you is," i.e., "wherever you are."

401-2. **si qua...gratia:** "if any affection" or "favor." **piis animis:** ablative indicating location, "in your pious hearts"; with *piis* Amata draws on the women's connection to her (their queen) and especially to their understanding of her concern for her daughter. **infelicis Amatae:** objective genitive after *gratia* (402); for *infelicis*, cf. 376 n. **iuris materni:** objective genitive after *cura*, "concern for a mother's right"; the phrase here describes family obligations (not legal rights in Roman law). **remordet:** the compound verb (lit. "bite again") here means "vexes" and is mainly a poetic word. Cf. 1.261 *quando haec te cura remordet* (Jupiter to Venus about her concern for her son Aeneas).

403. **crinalis:** adjective from *crinis* ("hair"); the first attested usage of this adjective (also at 11.576), perhaps a Vergilian invention. **vittas:** cf. 351-2 n. **orgia:** neuter plural; here the word can indicate either the nocturnal rites of Bacchus or the implements used in his worship.

404. **talem:** perhaps "in such a state"; emphatically placed, describing *reginam* in 405 (note the hyperbaton*). **inter silvas, inter deserta:** the repetition of *inter* and the asyndeton* help convey Amata's frenzy, as she is driven by the Fury Allecto. **deserta ferarum:** *deserta* here means "deserted places," "haunts." Cf. *nova tecta* with 393 n.

405. **reginam Allecto stimulis agit undique Bacchi:** attention turns back to Allecto's infuriation of Amata. The metaphor* here is from taming horses (Panoussi (2009) 140). Note the pointed juxtaposition of *reginam* and *Allecto* (cf. *huic dea* in 346 with n.), as well as the use of *agit*, which perhaps resonates with *actus* (380) and *agitur* (384) in the spinning top simile at 378-83. In 385 (see n.) it was unclear whether Allecto or Amata had devised the plan for Amata to feign Bacchic madness; here the phrase *stimulis Bacchi* might suggest that Allecto was the motivator—in which case the passive *agitur* in 384 (describing Amata) might pointedly contrast with the active *agit* here (used of Allecto). Still, there is enough ambiguity to allow that Amata and Allecto are in some sense working interdependently (see Lyne (1987) 26 n. 50, 67-8).

Postquam visa satis primos acuisse furores
consiliumque omnemque domum vertisse Latini,
protinus hinc fuscis tristis dea tollitur alis
audacis Rutuli ad muros, quam dicitur urbem
Acrisioneïs Danaë fundasse colonis 410
praecipiti delata Noto. locus Ardea quondam
dictus avis, et nunc magnum manet Ardea nomen,

406-34. *Allecto now goes to Turnus in Ardea. In the guise of the old priestess Calybe, she enrages him to protect his rights and fight the Trojans.*

For Turnus' representation in the *Aeneid* thus far, see notes on 1-285, 54-5, 96-7, 286-640, 367-72. For the representation of Turnus as a problematic warrior and ruler in this episode, see Cairns (1989) 66-77 and Stahl (2016) especially 412-30. For a more complicated view of Turnus, see Gaskin (1992) and Thomas (1998). For Hellenistic influences, see Hollis (1992) 270-2.

406. **visa:** supply *est*. Allecto is subject (*dea* in 408). **primos...furores:** i.e., in Amata and the Latin women; *primos*, however, also suggests that there will be more madness to come. **acuisse:** see 330 with n.

407. **vertisse:** Allecto has "overturned" or "confounded" Latinus' plan and entire household.

408. **protinus:** Allecto "immediately" turns her attention to Turnus. **fuscis...alis:** *fuscus, -a, -um* means "dark," "dusky"; the phrase is also used of *nox* (8.369), the mother of the Furies (12.846). Allecto's "wings" had not been mentioned earlier, but the *Dirae* are winged at 12.848. **tristis:** nominative, "harsh"; note that Allecto specializes in *tristia bella* (325).

409-10. **audacis Rutuli ad muros:** the *audax Rutulus* is Turnus (cf. 9.3, 126; 10.276); the entire phrase is a periphrasis* for Turnus' city, Ardea, named explicitly in 411-12. *Audacis* might contain some irony, since Turnus, though he will scorn Calybe's/Allecto's initial attempt at rousing him, will ultimately be terrified by her. **quam...urbem:** "which city," referring back to Ardea (the city just described, though not yet named); object of *fundasse*. **Acrisioneïs... colonis:** ablative, "with Acrisian colonists." Acrisius (372) was an Argive king and father of Danaë, who is said to have founded Ardea. See 371-2 n. Vergil's version of Danaë's arrival in Italy and her founding of Ardea differ somewhat from the more traditional story: Danaë's father Acrisius, fearing (on account of a prophecy) that he would be killed by her infant son Perseus, enclosed both mother and son in a chest, which was cast into the sea; the chest made it to the island of Seriphus, where Danaë was tormented by the king. Servius (ad 7.372) explains a variant—that the chest floated to Italy, where Danaë married the king, and together they founded Ardea. **fundasse:** "to have founded," syncopated* form of *funda(vi)sse*; governed by *dicitur*, whose subject is the Argive princess *Danaë*. Note that Danaë, "like Dido and like Camilla, plays a man's role in a man's world" (Mack (1999) 134-5). For (neoteric) references in 408-14 connecting Danaë to Turnus, see Reed (2007) 62-4.

411-12. **delata:** "brought," "conveyed" (to Latium); modifying *Danaë*. **Noto:** the "South wind," modified by *praecipiti*; ablative of means. **dictus:** supply *est*. **avis:** 56 n.; dative of personal agent after *dictus* (we would more usually expect *a/ab* + ablative, cf. AG §375). The use of *avis* might involve a wordplay, because of the story that the burnt city of Ardea turned into a bird/

sed fortuna fuit. tectis hic Turnus in altis
iam mediam nigra carpebat nocte quietem.
Allecto torvam faciem et furialia membra   415
exuit, in vultus sese transformat anilis
et frontem obscenam rugis arat, induit albos
cum vitta crinis, tum ramum innectit olivae;
fit Calybe Iunonis anus templique sacerdos,
et iuveni ante oculos his se cum vocibus offert: 420

---

avis (also *ardea* = the heron) (see Ovid, *Metamorphoses* 14.573-80; O'Hara (2017) 190).
nunc...Ardea: cf. 409-10 n. Note that here the poet contrasts his contemporary perspective on Ardea (*fortuna fuit* 413 n.) with Turnus' Ardea.

413. **fuit:** "was," i.e., "no longer exists" (cf. 10.60 *Troia fuit*). **tectis...altis:** *altis* may be an etymological wordplay* on *Ardea*, if the name is derived from *arduus*, "steep"; cf. Servius ad 412, O'Hara (1996 = 2017) 190.

414. **mediam...carpebat...quietem:** *mediam...quietem* "the middle of sleep," i.e., "deep sleep" (Goold), the phrase being a variation on *mediam noctem*; *carpebat* here means "was enjoying" (cf. 4.522 *nox erat et placidum carpebant...soporem*). Turnus is fast asleep, unlike Amata (344-5), whom *curae* were consuming before Allecto came (see O'Hara (1990) 67-9). Cf. 2.268-97, where Aeneas is asleep when a vision of Hector visits him (see Mackie (1991a)). **nigra...nocte:** ablative of time; the adjective naturally describes night, but it may also be used to portend the destructive nature of the visitation about to occur. Cf. the use of *ater* in line 456 (with n.) and 466.

415-16. **torvam:** cf. 399 n. **faciem:** cf. 329 n. **furialia membra | exuit:** *exuo* (3), "cast off" (cf. *induit* in 417). For the phrase, cf. 1.689-90 *alas | exuit*, describing Cupid as he sheds his wings to assume Ascanius' appearance and to infuriate Dido with love for Aeneas. **anilis:** adjective of *anus*, f., "old woman" (419 n.); accusative plural, modifying *vultus*.

417. **obscenam:** "ill-boding," but also with sense of "hateful"; used of the *Dirae* at 12.876. **rugis:** ablative; "creases," "wrinkles." **arat:** "furrows." **induit:** cf. *exuit* 416.

418. **vitta:** ablative; "headband," "fillet" (cf. 351-2 n.), a token of Calybe's status as priestess, *sacerdos* (419). **ramum...olivae:** cf. 751 n.

419. **fit:** "becomes"; used of Allecto's transformations also at 351-2 (see n.). **Calybe:** a Greek name, not appearing in other epics. **Iunonis anus templique sacerdos:** *anus* here the adjective, "old," not the noun; "old priestess of Juno's temple" (i.e., probably hendiadys*, cf. 2.319 *arcis Phoebique sacerdos*). For *anus*, cf. 415-16 n.

420. **iuveni:** Turnus; dative after *se...offert*. Note the emphasis on Turnus' youth, though he is an older, more experienced warrior than most other *iuvenes* slain in the epic. A *iuvenis* is a young man roughly between 20-40 years of age (Lewis and Short ad loc.). **ante oculos:** this phrase can be used of someone receiving a vision when asleep (as in 2.270 of Aeneas), and we are told that Turnus wakes up only at 458. However, the potential suggestion that Turnus is awake here resonates with his vivid response to Allecto at 436-44, and with the way his eyes react to Allecto's appearance and words at 447 (*deriguere oculi*). As with the infection of Amata, the

'Turne, tot incassum fusos patiere labores,
et tua Dardaniis transcribi sceptra colonis?
rex tibi coniugium et quaesitas sanguine dotes
abnegat, externusque in regnum quaeritur heres.
i nunc, ingratis offer te, inrise, periclis;   425
Tyrrhenas, i, sterne acies, tege pace Latinos.
haec adeo tibi me, placida cum nocte iaceres,
ipsa palam fari omnipotens Saturnia iussit.

---

details of Turnus' infuriation are somewhat unclear and impressionistic (cf. 353 n.). **his... vocibus:** *vocibus* here "words," not "voices"; construe with *cum*.

421. **incassum:** adverb, "in vain." **fusos...labores:** supply *esse* with *fusos* ("poured," i.e., expended) to form the perfect passive infinitive. *Labores* would suggest that Turnus had fought in battle for Latinus, a detail that plays against the peaceful description of his reign (cf. 423 n.). For the phrase, cf. *Geo.* 4.491-2 *ibi omnis | effusus labor* (of Orpheus' failed attempt to bring Eurydice back from the underworld). **patiere:** from *patior* (3), "suffer," "endure"; second person future indicative, governing an accusative and infinitive construction.

422. **tua...sceptra:** another object of *patiere* (421); *tua sceptra* (i.e., your rule) refers to the Latin kingdom that would be transferred to Turnus on the death of Latinus, if Turnus and Lavinia were married (cf. 424 *heres*). Allecto/Calybe exaggerates by suggesting that Aeneas would take away something that Turnus already has. **transcribi:** "be transferred," "surrendered," a financial metaphor*. Note the juxtaposition of *tua* (i.e., Turnus) and *Dardaniis* (i.e., Aeneas/Trojans), the potentially scornful tone of *colonis*, and the artful arrangement of the adjective/noun phrases, creating a golden line* variation.

423. **rex:** Latinus. **quaesitas sanguine dotes:** "dowry sought by blood." Again Turnus seems to have aided Latinus in war, another detail (cf. 421 n.) that might contradict the peaceful characterization of Latinus' reign earlier in the book (cf. 45-6 n.; for Latinus' hostility toward the Etruscans, cf. 426 n.). Is Latinus' kingdom at war or peace? Note also that *quaesitas* (if meaning "sought") could suggest that Turnus is not yet engaged to Lavinia (cf. also *petit* 55).

424. **abnegat:** emphatic enjambment*. **externus:** see 255, 367-72 with notes. **quaeritur:** perhaps suggesting further (cf. *quaesitas* in 423 with n.) that Turnus and Lavinia are not engaged. **in regnum:** *in* with accusative here describes purpose. **heres:** cf. 422 n.

425. **ingratis:** with sense of "unrewarded"; dative. **inrise:** vocative, "ridiculed," i.e., because of Latinus' actions.

426. **Tyrrhenas:** "Etruscan," cf. 423 n. **sterne:** from *sterno* (3), "throw down," "lay low." **tege pace Latinos:** i.e., by defeating the Latins' Etruscan enemies; *tege* (lit. "cover"), here "protect" (imperative).

427-8. **haec adeo...me...fari...iussit:** an accusative and infinitive construction, "ordered me to say these very things" with *Saturnia* as subject (see below); note that *adeo* emphasizes the word it follows (*haec*), as often in Vergil. **cum...iaceres:** a *cum*-circumstantial clause. It is a bit odd that Calybe/Allecto tells Turnus that she is speaking to him, as ordered, while he is sleeping, but it is well within the conventions of epic (Fordyce). For this scene, cf. 2.268-95, where a

quare age et armari pubem portisque moveri
laetus in arma para, et Phrygios qui flumine pulchro   430
consedere duces pictasque exure carinas.
caelestum vis magna iubet. rex ipse Latinus,
ni dare coniugium et dicto parere fatetur,
sentiat et tandem Turnum experiatur in armis.'
    Hic iuvenis vatem inridens sic orsa vicissim   435
ore refert: 'classis invectas Thybridis undam
non, ut rere, meas effugit nuntius auris;

---

sleeping Aeneas is visited by a vision of Hector, as the Greeks pour out of the wooden horse. Aeneas will also have a dream vision of the river-god Tiberinus in the next book at 8.26-65. **palam:** "openly," "in person." **omnipotens Saturnia:** i.e., Juno, daughter of Saturn (48-9 n.); *omnipotens* ("all-powerful") is a grand epithet normally used of Jupiter, but also twice of Juno, here and at 4.693 (when Juno sends Iris down to the dying Dido).

429-30. **quare age:** cf. 130-1 n. **armari pubem...moveri:** an accusative (*pubem*) and infinitive (*armari...moveri*) construction after the imperative *para*, cf. 35-6 n. **portis:** *e portis*. **qui flumine pulchro | consedere (431):** relative clause describing *Phrygios...duces*; *flumine pulchro*, i.e., the Tiber. Perhaps the adjective *pulchro* is used to contrast with what may be a derogatory use of *Phrygios* (cf. 293-4 n.).

431. **consedere:** from *consido* (3), "settle," "encamp." **pictas...carinas:** the Trojan ships (*carinas*, "keels," is a synecdoche* for ships) are so described at 5.663 and 8.93. **exure:** "burn up"; governs both *Phrygios...duces* and *pictas...carinas*, though with the former it has a figurative sense ("destroy") (see syllepsis*).

432. **caelestum:** genitive plural of the adjective *caelestis, -e*, "heavenly"; here as noun, "gods."

433. **ni...fatetur:** "if he does not agree to" (*OLD* s.v. *fateor* 3). This line must be read in connection with 423-4. **dicto:** dative after *parere* (2), "obey," "comply with"; note that Allecto describes Latinus' pledge not as a formalized agreement but more vaguely as *dictum*.

434. **sentiat:** jussive subjunctive; construe *sentio* in the sense of "let him feel to his cost" (Fordyce).

435-44. Turnus ridicules the disguised Allecto.

435. **Hic:** temporal adverb, "then." **iuvenis:** cf. 420 n. **vatem:** here "seer," as 427-8 made clear, and as Turnus calls her at 442 (cf. 41-2 n.). **inridens:** "mocking," with *vatem* as object. Interestingly, Turnus treats Calybe/Allecto in the way she said Turnus has been treated at 425. **orsa:** "beginnings" but also, as here, "words" (*OLD* s.v. *orsa* 2) from *ordior* ("begin"), cf. 386 n.; *orsa* is direct object of *refert* ("gives back," i.e., "says in response," "replies").

436-7. **classis invectas Thybridis undam...nuntius:** an accusative-infinitive phrase governed by the idea of reporting in *nuntius* (437), "the news that...." The infinitive *invectas esse* (*esse* must be supplied) has *classis* as accusative subject, governs the object *undam*, and means "have sailed into" (cf. notes on 64-5, 287). The entire phrase ("the news that...") then becomes the subject of *non...effugit*. **rere:** second person singular present indicative deponent; see 369-70 n. **meas... auris:** object of *non...effugit*.

ne tantos mihi finge metus. nec regia Iuno
immemor est nostri.
sed te victa situ verique effeta senectus, 440
o mater, curis nequiquam exercet, et arma
regum inter falsa vatem formidine ludit.
cura tibi divum effigies et templa tueri;
bella viri pacemque gerent quis bella gerenda.'
    Talibus Allecto dictis exarsit in iras. 445
at iuveni oranti subitus tremor occupat artus,

438-9. **ne...finge:** "don't fashion" or "contrive." **nec...Iuno | immemor:** one of Juno's prime characteristics is that she does not forget (cf. 1.4 *saevae memorem Iunonis...iram*; 1.23 *veterisque memor Saturnia belli*); nonetheless Turnus' trust in her protection is ultimately belied by the unwinnable war she incites and her abandonment of him by the end of the epic. **nostri:** objective genitive after *immemor*. Line 439 is an unfinished line, cf. 129 n. Note Turnus' disrespectfulness to Calybe/Allecto in these lines.

440. **te:** object of *exercet* in 442. **victa situ:** *victa*, like *effeta*, modifies *senectus*, the subject of the sentence; *situs* (*-ūs*, m.) here means "decay," "deterioration." **veri...effeta:** *veri* is genitive of lack after *effetus*, "unproductive of" or "barren of" (Goold). Note how Allecto will use Turnus' language caustically against him when she responds at 452-3.

441. **exercet:** "troubles" (*OLD* s.v. *exerceo* 2b). **arma:** object of the preposition *inter* (442) that follows (anastrophe*).

442. **falsa:** ablative with *formidine*. **vatem:** in apposition to an understood *te* (i.e., Calybe/Allecto). **ludit:** here "deceives," "mocks" with *senectus* (440) still subject.

443. **cura tibi... tueri:** supply *est*; "it is a concern for you (i.e., your concern is) to watch over," i.e., "preserve," "protect." **divum:** genitive plural (cf. 50-1 n).

444. **viri:** subject of *gerent*; *viri* is contrasted with *tibi* in 443 (i.e., you, an old woman), both words occupying the same metrical position in their respective lines. **quis bella gerenda:** = *quibus bella gerenda sunt*; *quīs* (AG §150c) is here dative of agent (plural). For the idea expressed in this line, cf. Homer, *Iliad* 6.492-3 "War will be of concern to all men who live in Troy but particularly to me" (Hector's words to his wife Andromache, who has just tried to give him military advice).

445-74. *Allecto is outraged by Turnus, reveals her true appearance, and infuriates him to call for war.*

445. **exarsit:** note the continuing association of fire and fury, cf. 355 n., 393 n.

446. **iuveni oranti:** dative of reference. For *iuveni*, cf. 420 n.; *oranti*, "as he speaks," is perhaps an archaic usage. **artus:** *artus, -ūs*, m., "joint," "limb"; *artus* is found in Ennius, used frequently by Lucretius, and has an especially poetic tone.

deriguere oculi: tot Erinys sibilat hydris
tantaque se facies aperit; tum flammea torquens
lumina cunctantem et quaerentem dicere plura
reppulit, et geminos erexit crinibus anguis,   450
verberaque insonuit rabidoque haec addidit ore:
'en ego victa situ, quam veri effeta senectus
arma inter regum falsa formidine ludit;
respice ad haec: adsum dirarum ab sede sororum,
bella manu letumque gero.'   455
sic effata facem iuveni coniecit et atro
lumine fumantis fixit sub pectore taedas.

447-8. **deriguere oculi:** *derigesco* (3), first found in Vergil, means "grow stiff." For the phrase, cf. 3.259-60 *formidine sanguis | deriguit* (the reaction of Aeneas' men to Celaeno's dire prophecy). **tot...sibilat hydris | tantaque se facies:** Erinys *(Allecto)* is subject of *sibilat, tanta facies* of *aperit*; the Fury lives up to the description in 329 *tam saevae facies, tot pullulat...colubris* (see n.). Note how suddenly Allecto transforms her appearance. **Erinys:** another name for a Fury (also at 2.337, 573; 7.570; cf. 324 n.), though not used frequently before Vergil.

448-9. **flammea torquens | lumina:** describing Allecto, see 399 with n. (of Amata); for *flammea*, cf. 445 n. **cunctantem et quaerentem...:** accusative objects of *reppulit* (450), describing Turnus, as he reacts to Allecto. Cf. Aeneas' reaction to Dido's departure in 4.390-1 *multa metu cunctantem et multa parantem | dicere* (see Segal (1990) 1-12).

450. **reppulit:** emphatically enjambed; subject is Allecto. **geminos...anguis:** cf. the *gemini angues* that attack Laocoön and his sons (2.203-4) and the *geminos anguis* (8.697) that follow Cleopatra (on Aeneas' shield), ominous portents in both passages. **erexit:** "raised up." **crinibus:** ablative; cf. 329 n.

451. **verberaque insonuit:** "and made her whips sound loudly." For *verbera*, cf. 335-7 n.; *insonuit* does not appear before Vergil, and is here, unusually, transitive; cf. 5.579 *insonuitque flagello*.

452-3. **en:** interjection, "behold!" These lines respond directly to Turnus' insulting reply at 440-2 (see notes) to Calybe's/Allecto's initial speech. Note how Allecto uses Turnus' own language against him. **quam:** antecedent *ego* (Allecto).

454. **haec:** neuter plural; presumably referring to the *anguis* and *verbera* just mentioned, as well as to Allecto's general appearance. **dirarum ab sede sororum:** see 324 n.

455. **bella...:** the Fury's concluding words mimic Turnus' scornful language at 444. Note again the close connection between war and the Fury. This is another half line (cf. 129 n.).

456-7. **effata:** participle from *effor* (1), "speak out." **facem...taedas:** the former is the direct object of *coniecit*, the latter of *fixit*; *facem* means "torch," as does *taeda*, "(pine) torch" (here poetic plural for singular), though *taedas* adds variation, while *fumantis* contributes more detail: "she cast the torch at him, and thrust the smoking pine (in his chest)." Note that, since *fax* and *taeda* can more specifically mean "marriage torch," they are especially resonant vehicles by which to infuriate Turnus over the issue of his "stolen" fiancée. See, e.g., Lyne (1987) 69.

olli somnum ingens rumpit pavor, ossaque et artus
perfundit toto proruptus corpore sudor.
arma amens fremit, arma toro tectisque requirit: 460
saevit amor ferri et scelerata insania belli,
ira super: magno veluti cum flamma sonore
virgea suggeritur costis undantis aëni

---

iuveni: dative after *coniecit* (cf. 346 n.); for *iuvenis*, cf. 420 n. **atro**: describing the torch's smoke, but perhaps with infernal and unlucky associations too. Cf. 466 n. and 4.384, where Dido says that she will pursue Aeneas *atris ignibus* (i.e., like those of a Fury).

458. **olli**: archaic* form of *illi* (i.e., Turnus); dative of reference. **somnum...rumpit**: despite the preceding dialogue, we are here reminded that Turnus has been asleep (cf. 413-14); *ingens... pavor* now awakens him. **ossaque et...**: an archaic construction; here the *-que* joins the two halves of the sentence, while *et* joins *ossa* and *artus*. **artus**: accusative plural, cf. 446 n.

459. **toto...corpore**: ablative of separation after *proruptus*, from *prorumpo* (3), "burst out," "send forth." For the line, cf. Aeneas reacting, at 3.175, to the visitation of the Penates as he slept: *gelidus toto manabat corpore sudor.*

460. **arma amens..., arma...**: the anaphora* and asyndeton* of *arma* help convey Turnus' sudden frenzy. Note again the important connection between war (*arma*) and madness/the Fury (*amens*); cf. 2.314 *arma amens capio* (of Aeneas). *Amens* is also used of Turnus at 10.681; 12.622, 742, 776. **fremit**: "roars," growls," here with an internal accusative, *arma*; *fremens* is used of Amata raging like a Bacchant after she has been infected by Allecto (389), and of the Chimaera depicted on Turnus' helmet (787). **arma...requirit**: cf. Ennius, *Annales*, fragment 169 in Skutsch and in *FRH* 2 *omnes arma requirunt*. **toro**: here "bed"; Turnus seemingly stores a sword under his pillow, as had Deiphobus (6.524).

461-2. **saevit amor ferri**: cf. 4.532 *saevit amor*, explaining why Dido cannot sleep. **super**: adverbial, "in addition," or perhaps "above all."

462-6. In another simile* drawn from everyday life (cf. Amata's spinning-top simile, 378-83), Vergil likens Allecto's effect on Turnus to that of a flame on a pot of boiling water (see 462-3 n.). Like the earlier simile, this one describes, in equally terrifying terms, the overwhelming power of fury/the Fury over a mortal. In both cases the mortal is compared to an inanimate object (spinning-top vs. pot of water) that is in some sense "animated" by the frenzy of the goddess. Though Turnus' simile describes a mundane thing (a pot of boiling water), it is imbued with elevated, poetic language (see notes.) The simile is usually compared to *Iliad* 21.362-4 (of the river Xanthus): "And as a cauldron boils within when a large flame forces it, while it melts the lard of a fatted hog, and it bubbles in every part, and dry kindling is set beneath it" (Wyatt).

462-3. **veluti cum**: "just as when"; this phrase also initiates similes at 2.304, 9.435 and 12.103. **magno...sonore**: *sonor* is a poetic form for *sonitus* or *sonus*; the ablative phrase describes the crackling noise made by the *flamma virgea*, as it is placed under the cauldron. **flamma... virgea**: subject; *virgeus* ("made of twigs") is the adjectival form of *virga*; the phrase means "flame produced from twigs," cf. 8.694 *stuppea flamma*. **suggeritur**: "is piled up under,"

exsultantque aestu latices, furit intus aquai
fumidus atque alte spumis exuberat amnis,   465
nec iam se capit unda, volat vapor ater ad auras.
ergo iter ad regem polluta pace Latinum
indicit primis iuvenum et iubet arma parari,
tutari Italiam, detrudere finibus hostem;

---

another largely poetic usage. **costis:** lit. "ribs," here "sides" (*costa, -ae,* f.); construe with *suggeritur*. **undantis aëni:** genitive; *aënum*, "bronze (vessel)," poetic for *vas*. It is best to take *undantis* as "simmering" in contrast to the roiling boil that will occur once the kindling is added; *undantis* might then resonate with Turnus' excited state once Allecto reveals her true appearance (446-55) but before she plunges the torch into his chest (456-62).

464-5 **exsultant:** lit. "jump up" or "vigorously," though also used of inanimate things. Here, it adds power to the picture of inanimate water described as coming alive, which is paralleled by the inexorable effect of Allecto on Turnus (Cf. 462-6 n.). **aestu:** ablative of cause or means; *aestus, -us,* m., "fire," "heat." **latices:** *latex, -icis,* m., poetic for *aqua*. **intus:** adverb, "within," "inside." **aquai | fumidus...amnis:** subject of *furit* and *exuberat* (words that *atque* joins); "smoking stream of water," an elaborately grand periphrasis* with complex hyperbaton* that allows *aquai* (genitive, see below) and *amnis* (nominative) to stand at their line ends. *Aquai* is an archaic* genitive (cf. 3.354 *aulai* and 9.26 *pictai*); *amnis* is a poetic word that usually denotes a "stream" or "river", not water in a cauldron (cf. 466 n.). **spumis:** "with foam," from *spuma, -ae,* f., a word of epic heritage (Ennius and Lucretius). Horsfall (ad loc.) wonders "whether V. thought also of 'foaming at the mouth' (Lucretius 5.985; *Aen.* 1.324, 4.158f.)," a nuance that would enhance the sense of madness. **exuberat:** "surges up."

466. **nec iam se capit unda:** a striking periphrasis* with litotes* indicating that the water (*unda*) does not contain itself, i.e., it bubbles over the edges of the pot; note that with *unda* Vergil's language again (cf. *amnis* 465) elevates the nature of the boiling water. **vapor ater:** cf. *atro lumine* (456-7) of Allecto's torch.

467. **iter:** a "march" (to King Latinus), object of *indicit* (468-9 n.). **polluta pace:** the "violated" *pax* (here "agreement," "peaceful relations") presumably between Latinus and Turnus. However, it is not entirely clear whether Turnus is claiming that the violation was caused by Latinus (for his embrace of Aeneas after supposed agreements with Turnus) or whether Turnus is now breaking the *pax* (because he is rousing his men against Latinus). For *pax*, cf. also 45-6 n.

468-9. **indicit:** "announces," "orders," often used of declaring war. **primis iuvenum:** *primis* is dative after *indicit*. **iubet:** governs a tricolon* of infinitives (*parari, tutari,* and *detrudere*) with asyndeton*. Note, however, the change from passive (*parari*) to active (*tutari*-deponent, *detrudere*) infinitives, and from *arma* as the accusative subject of *parari* in 468 to an understood *primos iuvenum* (understood from *primis iuvenum*) as the accusative subject of both *tutari* and *detrudere*. **Italiam:** again, note the expanded nature of Vergil's war to include all of Italy (cf. 43-4 n.). **detrudere finibus:** *detrudo* (3) means "force from" (cf. 773); *finibus*, "boundaries." Both words are often used in military settings.

se satis ambobus Teucrisque venire Latinisque.   470
haec ubi dicta dedit divosque in vota vocavit,
certatim sese Rutuli exhortantur in arma.
hunc decus egregium formae movet atque iuventae,
hunc atavi reges, hunc claris dextera factis.
    Dum Turnus Rutulos animis audacibus implet,   475

470. **se satis...**: indirect discourse, with a verb of speaking understood; Turnus says that "he comes enough (i.e., a match) for both Trojans and Latins." Note that *Latinisque* is hypermetric* (i.e., the *-que* is an extra syllable but elides with *haec* at the beginning of the next line), a metrical effect that perhaps helps convey Turnus' rage.

471. **haec ubi dicta dedit**: cf. 323 n. **in vota**: i.e., to listen to his vows.

472. **certatim**: "eagerly," "in competition." **exhortantur**: deponent; a poetic word, not appearing before Vergil; its elision* helps convey the frantic call to arms (cf. also 473-4 n.). **in arma**: note the echo of *in vota* (471).

473-4. **hunc...hunc...hunc**: note the anaphora* of *hunc* with asyndeton* in a tricolon* construction that describes how different aspects of Turnus motivate different men (*hunc... hunc...hunc*) to fight for him. **decus egregium formae...iuventae**: again, Turnus' beauty and youth are emphasized, a combination often found in descriptions of those who die tragically young, e.g., Euryalus (5.295), Marcellus (6.861), Pallas and Lausus (10.434-5); Ascanius (*pulcher* at 477; 5.570) is an important exception. (Cf. 54-5 n., 420 n., and Reed (2007) 44-72.) **claris dextera factis**: *claris...factis* can be construed as an ablative of cause, Turnus' "right hand because of its/his famous deeds" ("inspires," *movet*).

475-510. *As Iulus is hunting, Allecto incites his dogs to pursue a pet stag belonging to Silvia, daughter of Tyrrhus, the royal herdsman. Iulus strikes the stag with an arrow.*

This episode represents a Vergilian innovation on the tradition (cf. 1-285 n.) by attributing the outbreak of the war to the killing of a stag. To many readers, this *casus belli* has seemed odd— perhaps even more so since the poet may be adapting a Hellenistic story about a youth named Cyparissus, which presumably was told in a source that does not survive but that perhaps also influenced Ovid's later retelling in *Metamorphoses* 10: Cyparissus, a youth loved by Apollo, accidentally kills a sacred stag, is chided by the god because of his (Cyparissus') excessive grief, and is turned into the cypress tree (a symbol of mourning in the classical world). In fact, some readers take Apollo's criticism of Cyparissus' grief for the stag in *Metamorphoses* 10.132-4 (*quae non solacia Phoebus | dixit et, ut leviter pro materiaque doleret, | admonuit!*) as Ovid's way of faulting Vergil for inappropriately using a stag's death to spark the outbreak of the Italian war in the *Aeneid*. On the death of Sylvia's stag and its sources, see Heinze (1915: 190-2 = 1993: 153-5), Vance (1981), Connors (1992) 8-11, Starr (1992), and Putnam (1995a), (1998) 98-117, Jenkyns (1998), Horsfall ad loc., Fratantuono (2007) 217, and Rogerson (2017) 147-54. For the criticism of this episode in Macrobius' *Saturnalia* 5.17.1-3 (fourth century CE) and in other commentators, see especially Clément-Tarantino (2016).

475. **Dum Turnus Rutulos...**: this line indicates that Allecto's work has been completed among the Rutulians with her successful infection of Turnus; the narrative now pivots to her machinations against the Trojans. **audacibus**: cf. 409-10 n.

Allecto in Teucros Stygiis se concitat alis,
arte nova speculata locum, quo litore pulcher
insidiis cursuque feras agitabat Iulus.
hic subitam canibus rabiem Cocytia virgo
obicit et noto naris contingit odore,   480
ut cervum ardentes agerent; quae prima laborum
causa fuit belloque animos accendit agrestis.
cervus erat forma praestanti et cornibus ingens,
Tyrrhidae pueri quem matris ab ubere raptum

---

476. **in Teucros:** cf. 301 n. **Stygiis...alis:** for Allecto's wings, see 408 n.

477-8. **arte nova:** "with new cunning"; cf. Juno's description of Allecto as having *mille nocendi artes* (338). **speculata:** from *speculor* (1), "spy out." **locum, quo litore:** *litore* is technically unnecessary in this relative clause but adds greater specificity to *locum*. **pulcher...Iulus:** note the hyperbaton* of *pulcher...Iulus*, allowing the adjective and noun to fall at their respective line ends (cf. 464-5 n.). **insidiis cursuque...agitabat:** note the slight syllepsis*, since *agitabat* (from *agito*, "drive," "impel") is used literally with *cursu* ("chasing") but not quite so with *insidiis* (here "snares" or "traps") for which "were hunting" would work better, a definition that could in fact be used with both ablatives. **feras:** from *fera, ae,* f., "wild animals."

479. **hic...:** temporal, "then." **canibus:** dative governed by *obicit*. **Cocytia virgo:** *Cocytius* means "of the Cocytus," a river in the underworld, and thus also "of the underworld" or "infernal"; the phrase is a periphrasis* for Allecto.

480. **obicit:** "throws to" or "upon"; cf. 6.419-21, where the Sybil throws (*obicit* 421) a drugged cake to Cerberus. **noto...odore:** i.e., the "familiar smell" of a stag; ablative of means. **naris:** accusative plural from *naris, -is,* f., "nostril," "nose."

481-2. **ut...agerent:** purpose clause in secondary sequence; an imperfect subjunctive (*agerent*) is used because *obicit* and *contingit* are historic presents that describe actions in the past. **quae prima laborum | causa fuit:** *quae* has the sense of *illa*. The phrase programmatically resonates with the wording in 117-18 (see n.), and thus signals a new stage in Aeneas' *labores* (Putnam (1970) 422-3 and Goins (1993)). Vergil also evokes Homer, *Iliad* 22.116: "this was the beginning of strife" (referring to Paris' abduction of Helen). **laborum:** "hardships," "troubles"; genitive. **bello:** dative of purpose. **accendit:** another fire metaphor*, now afflicting *animos... agrestis* ("rustic") (=*animos agrestium*).

483. **cervus erat:** "there was a stag" (for this usage of the verb *esse*, see AG §284b). **forma praestanti:** "of extraordinary beauty," ablative of description (AG §415). The stag is another beautiful figure to die when caught up in Rome's fate; see 473-4 n. **cornibus:** ablative of specification (AG §418) after *ingens*.

484. **Tyrrhidae:** nominative plural, "sons of Tyrrhus," who is described in the relative clause that follows. The patronymic of *Tyrrhus* would normally be formed as *Tyrrhĭdae*, but the short *i* is lengthened here for metrical purposes. **quem:** antecedent is the *cervus* (483).

nutribant Tyrrhusque pater, cui regia parent 485
armenta et late custodia credita campi.
adsuetum imperiis soror omni Silvia cura
mollibus intexens ornabat cornua sertis,
pectebatque ferum puroque in fonte lavabat.
ille manum patiens mensaeque adsuetus erili 490
errabat silvis rursusque ad limina nota
ipse domum sera quamvis se nocte ferebat.
hunc procul errantem rabidae venantis Iuli

485-6. **nutribant:** for *nutriebant*, cf. 790 *insignibat*. **cui:** dative after both *parent* and *credita (est)*. **regia...armenta:** subject of *parent*; *regia* is an adjective ("royal"), not a noun. **credita:** supply *est*, "was entrusted," with *custodia* ("protection," "care") as subject. Note the elevated description of Tyrrhus' duties.

487. **adsuetum:** i.e., *cervum*; it is the object of *ornabat* with *adsuetum* governing the dative *imperiis*. **soror:** i.e., the sister of the *Tyrrhidae pueri* (484). **omni...cura:** ablative of manner. **Silvia:** the daughter is given a name of good rustic character (Servius), but it also appears in Aeneas' and Rome's ancestry, e.g., Silvius (6.763), his son Silvius Aeneas (6.769), and Romulus' mother Rhea Silvia (though she is called *Ilia* at 1.274 and 6.778).

488. **mollibus intexens...cornua sertis:** construe *cornua* as object of *intexens* (from *intexo* (3), "enwrap," "envelop") and *mollibus...sertis* as ablative of means. Note the artful hyperbaton* creating an enclosing adjective + noun construction. **ornabat:** object is *adsuetum* (sc. *cervum*) in 487.

489. **pectebat ferum:** *pectere* ("to comb") is mainly a poetic word, and contrasts with *ferum* ("wild animal"), a somewhat surprising word, given the stag's description, e.g., as *adsuetum imperiis* (487). Note the use of the imperfects *pectebat* and *levabat* to convey the idea of repeated past action, "she used to..." or "was accustomed to." **puroque in fonte:** another detail indicating the stag's special treatment by Silvia (cf. *omni cura* 487).

490. **manum patiens:** "enduring the hand," i.e., tame (cf. *mansuetus*, "used to the hand," "tame"); describing *ille* (i.e., *cervus*). **mensae...adsuetus erili:** *mensae...erili* is dative after *adsuetus* (cf. 487 n.); *erilis* ("of the master") is a more humble word than, e.g., *dominus*. We are given another sign of the stag's domestication, cf. 487.

492. **ipse...:** the stag always made its way home, however late at night (*sera quamvis...nocte*), a detail redolent of the golden age, cf. *Eclogues* 4.21-2 *ipsae lacte domum referent distenta capellae | ubera, nec magnos metuent armenta leones*. **domum:** accusative of place to which without preposition (AG §427.2). **sera quamvis...nocte:** ablative of time; *quamvis*, "however," "although."

493. **hunc:** *cervum*; we are now returned to the narrative action, as the dogs pursue a stag (481), which will end up being Sylvia's stag (483-92). **errantem:** while *errabat* in 491 expressed the stag's habit, now we see an unfortunate instance of its wanderings. Note that Ascanius' hand will be described as *dextrae erranti* in 498 (see n.). **rabidae:** modifying *canes* (494), the adjective is juxtaposed against the tame deer's wandering (*errantem*), a sign of its calm, secure, and domesticated state.

> commovere canes, fluvio cum forte secundo
> deflueret ripaque aestus viridante levaret. 495
> ipse etiam eximiae laudis succensus amore
> Ascanius curvo derexit spicula cornu;
> nec dextrae erranti deus afuit, actaque multo
> perque uterum sonitu perque ilia venit harundo.
> saucius at quadripes nota intra tecta refugit 500

494-5. **commovere:** = *commoverunt*, "frightened" (*OLD* s.v. *commoveo* 12). Note how the perfect tense pointedly contrasts with the imperfects used in 487-93 to describe the peaceful and safe life that the stag was living before Ascanius arrives on the scene. **fluvio...secundo:** "on a favorable stream," which essentially means "downstream" here. **cum...:** a *cum*-circumstantial clause in secondary sequence with imperfect subjunctives. **deflueret:** "was floating down." **ripaque aestus viridante levaret:** *aestūs* is a fourth declension accusative plural (though it can be translated as a singular); the stag "was alleviating the heat (i.e., cooling) on the verdant bank." Vergil amplifies the description of what the stag was doing in order to emphasize the idea of its complete sense of security.

496. **ipse:** Ascanius. **eximiae laudis succensus amore:** once again a fire metaphor*; just as the Fury presents the hounds with the deer's scent that sets them metaphorically aflame (*ardentes* 481), so the possibility of *laus* that is presented to Ascanius causes him to "burn" (*succensus*). (As we have already seen, Ascanius' natural enthusiasm for hunting was established at 4.156-9.) That Ascanius is driven by love for *eximiae laudis* ("extraordinary praise") might be taken with some irony*, since what results is a horrific, Fury-inspired war.

497. **curvo...cornu:** *cornu* here, by metonymy*, means "bow." **derexit:** from *derigo* (3), "direct," "aim."

498. **nec...afuit:** litotes*, "nor was (the god) absent," i.e., the god was present to help. **dextrae erranti:** dative of reference after *afuit*. Interestingly, note that, because of his "erring right hand," Ascanius seemingly would have missed the deer without the aid of the *deus*. (Fordyce, however, argues that *erranti* is proleptic, i.e., "so that it missed," while Horsfall argues that the *nec* should be construed with both *erranti* and *afuit*.) **deus:** the identity of the divinity is not clear, though it is presumably Allecto. (*Deus* can be used of a goddess, cf. 2.632 *ducente deo*, describing Venus.) **acta:** modifies *harundo* at the end of the next line (hyperbaton*).

499. **perque uterum...perque ilia:** *uterus, -i*, m., here "belly"; *ilia, -orum*, n., "groin." The anaphora* underscores the physical violence done to the stag. **harundo:** nominative, "reed," but also "shaft" of an arrow and thus "arrow" by metonymy*, as here.

500. **saucius:** "wounded." Cf. Dido in 4.1 who is metaphorically *saucia* by her love for Aeneas, and is compared in a famous simile to a *cerva* (deer) wounded unwittingly by a hunter (cf. Aeneas, 4.69-73). The two passages would thus suggest some kind of connection or parallel between Aeneas and Ascanius: "By shooting the stag of the young Latin girl Silvia after Allecto fills his hounds with fury, Ascanius as hunter figuratively repeats his father's actions with Dido" (Pavlock (1992) 75). Putnam (1970: 418 = 1995b: 107) 418 notes that in the simile at 12.749-55, Aeneas is compared to a hunting dog (*venator canis*) and Turnus to a stag

successitque gemens stabulis, questuque cruentus
atque imploranti similis tectum omne replebat.
Silvia prima soror palmis percussa lacertos
auxilium vocat et duros conclamat agrestis.
olli (pestis enim tacitis latet aspera silvis)   505
improvisi adsunt, hic torre armatus obusto,
stipitis hic gravidi nodis; quod cuique repertum
rimanti telum ira facit. vocat agmina Tyrrhus,
quadrifidam quercum cuneis ut forte coactis

(*cervus*). **quadripes:** "four-footed (animal)," an archaic compound that adds dignity to the wounded stag. **nota...tecta:** "familiar dwellings" (cf. *stabulis* in next line). The domesticated nature and psychological perspective of the *cervus* are again emphasized (cf. 491 *ad limina nota*). **refugit:** perfect tense (long *u*).

501-2. **gemens:** again, emphasis on the stag's psychological state. **stabulis:** dative after the compound verb *successit* (here "entered"). **questu...tectum omne replebat:** cf. 2.679 *gemitu tectum omne replebat* (as Creusa tried to prevent Aeneas from going back to fight the Greeks as Troy was being taken). **imploranti similis:** "like one appealing for aid"; *imploranti* is dative after *similis*. Note the human nature of the stag's description in these lines.

503. **Silvia...soror:** cf. 487. **prima:** "first," can be construed adverbially, cf. 141 n. **percussa lacertos:** *lacertus* is the upper part of the arm; the passive participle is used in an active or "middle" sense and takes a direct object (cf. 1.481 *tunsae pectora palmis*, of Trojan women, as they supplicate Minerva).

504. **duros conclamat agrestis:** the transitive use of *conclamat* ("calls together to one's help") is rare; for *agrestis*, cf. *animos agrestis* 482. The phrase represents a variation on *auxilium vocat*; the two phrases thus form a *dicolon abundans**.

505-6. **olli:** i.e., *duri agrestes* (504); nominative plural, cf. 458 n. (**pestis enim...**): this clause looks forward to and elucidates *improvisi adsunt*. The *pestis aspera* ("savage plague") presumably refers to Allecto. **improvisi:** "appearing without warning," "unexpected"; cf. 2.182 *improvisi aderunt* (Sinon speaking of the Greeks). **torre:** from *torris, -is*, m. ("firebrand"), a mainly poetic word. **obusto:** "burnt around"; from *oburo* (3), a word first appearing in (and perhaps coined by) Vergil. The fact that the burnt firebrand is to be used as an implement of war suggests the improvised nature of this weapon (cf. 507-8 n.).

507-8. **stipitis...gravidi nodis:** an unusual locution; we might have expected *stipitis gravidi* (genitive) to be in the ablative ("with a heavy stick" or "club"). As the phrase stands, the emphasis on the stick's *nodis* ("knots," the hardest parts of any piece of wood) seemingly conveys the rustic nature of these homemade weapons. **quod cuique repertum:** supply *est*; *cuique* is dative of agent. The clause functions as the object of *facit*; "what is found by each man, anger makes (into) a weapon (*telum*)." **rimanti:** "groping about" (Conington), modifying *cuique*. **telum:** this accusative functions as a predicate accusative.

509. **quadrifidam:** proleptic* (350-1 n.), "(to be) split into four." **cuneis:** *cuneus* is a "wedge." At the moment, Tyrrhus happens to be chopping wood.

scindebat rapta spirans immane securi. 510
At saeva e speculis tempus dea nacta nocendi
ardua tecta petit stabuli et de culmine summo
pastorale canit signum cornuque recurvo
Tartaream intendit vocem, qua protinus omne
contremuit nemus et silvae insonuere profundae; 515
audiit et Triviae longe lacus, audiit amnis
sulpurea Nar albus aqua fontesque Velini,
et trepidae matres pressere ad pectora natos.

---

510. **rapta...securi:** ablative absolute. **immane:** construe adverbially ("fiercely") with *spirans*.

511-39. With Allecto's continued direction, strife breaks out between the Latins and Trojans with Almo (Tyrrhus' son) and aged Galaesus the first casualties.

511-12. **saeva:** of Allecto at 329 as well; also used of Circe (19) and Juno (287, 592) with Vergil being the first poet to describe the queen of the gods thus. For the use of *saeva* in the epic, see Knox (1997). **speculis:** plural for singular (*specula, -ae,* f.); a "watchtower" or (especially in poetry) "a high place"; cf. *speculata* 477. **nacta:** from *nanciscor* (3), "obtain," "find." **ardua tecta petit stabuli:** Allecto had apparently been in the woods at 505; she now seeks the top of the *stabuli*, here an unspecified "farm building." **de culmine summo:** expands the preceding phrase, emphasizing that Allecto reached the highest point of the farm building.

513. **pastorale canit signum:** "sounds the herdsmen's sign (for action)"; *signum canere* is a military phrase. **cornu...recurvo:** *cornu* here is a military "trumpet" (cf. 519 *bucina*); it is "curved back."

514. **Tartaream...vocem:** *vocem* here means the trumpet's "sound," not Allecto's voice. For *Tartareus*, see notes on 15 and 328. **intendit:** "strains," "exerts" (*OLD* s.v. *intendo* 4a).

515. **contremuit:** "trembled all over"; a rare word, used in Vergil only here. **insonuere:** cf. 451 n.

516. **audiit et...audiit:** *et* = "even"; note the emphatic placement of the *audiit* at the opening of line, as well as the anaphora* with asyndeton*, emphasizing the strength of the horn's *vox*. **Triviae...lacus.** i.e., *lacus Nemorensis* (modern Lake Nemi) in the Alban Hills, near Aricia (cf. 761-82 n). *Trivia* ("of the meeting place of three roads") was an epithet of the goddess Diana, who had a famous cult at the grove along the lake's bank (*nemus Dianae*). **longe:** the distance from the lake to Latinus' city (cf. 47 n.) cannot be determined because the city's location is unknown; the lake is nineteen miles south of Rome.

517. **sulpurea Nar albus aqua:** the river *Nar* flows through Umbria (in central Italy) to the Tiber (see Map 2). For its color, cf. 83-4 n. The phrase *sulpurea...aqua* is ablative of cause. On the name *Nar*, Servius tells us that in Sabine it meant "sulfur," so there may be an etymological wordplay* with *sulpurea* (O'Hara (1996) 190-1). Cf. Ennius' *sulpureas posuit spiramina Naris ad undas* (*Annales* fragment 222 in *FRL* 1). **fontesque Velini:** the *lacus Velinus*, located in the Sabine region by the city Reate.

518. The line seems modeled on Apollonius Rhodius 4.136-7, describing the effect of the hiss of the dragon protecting the Golden Fleece (Nelis (2001) 296-7): "Young mothers awoke in fear and anxiously clasped their newborn babies, who...were trembling at the hissing" (Race).

tum vero ad vocem celeres, qua bucina signum
dira dedit, raptis concurrunt undique telis					520
indomiti agricolae, nec non et Troïa pubes
Ascanio auxilium castris effundit apertis.
derexere acies. non iam certamine agresti
stipitibus duris agitur sudibusve praeustis,
sed ferro ancipiti decernunt atraque late					525
horrescit strictis seges ensibus, aeraque fulgent
sole lacessita et lucem sub nubila iactant:

---

519. **celeres:** modifies *indomiti agricolae* two lines later (hyperbaton*). **bucina:** "(war) trumpet"; more generally it is a summoning instrument, cf. Propertius 4.1.14 *bucina cogebat priscos ad verba Quirites.*

520. **dira:** describing *bucina* (519), but *Dira* is another name for Fury and therefore resonates with Allecto. **raptis...telis:** ablative absolute; makeshift weapons were described in 505-10 (see notes). For the line, cf. Ennius, *Annales* fr. 144 in Skutsch and in *FRL* 1 *hastis ansatis, concurrunt undique telis.*

521. **indomiti:** here "unrestrained," "fierce" (cf. *duros agrestis* 504, cf. 519 n.); modifies *agricolae*. **nec non et:** a formulaic combination that Vergil introduces and uses ten times in the *Aeneid*; literally "nor not as well," i.e., "(the Trojan youth) as well...."

522. **Ascanio:** dative. **castris...apertis:** the participle ("opened") indicates the willingness of the Trojans to fight; ablative after *effundit*. **effundit:** cf. 292 n.

523-4. **derexere acies:** *derexere* = *derexerunt*; "they formed their battle lines," a military phrase. **non iam certamine agresti:** in contrast to the Latins' makeshift and frenzied preparations for the war (cf. 505-10), the Trojans (who spent ten years fighting the Greeks) seemingly use more traditional weapons, as described in 525-7. **stipitibus:** cf. 507-8 n. **agitur:** impersonal passive, "it is done," i.e., "there is fighting" (cf. *bellum agere*). Such impersonal passives are often used in historical/military contexts. **sudibus:** "stakes" (*sudis, -is,* f.). **prăūstīs:** participle from *praeuro* (3), "burn at the end" or "point"; the diphthong *ae* is shortened before a vowel only here and at 5.186 in Vergil.

525-6. **ferro ancipiti:** ablative of means; the sword is "two-edged" (*anceps, ancipitis,* adjective) in contrast to the rustic weapons in 524. **decernunt:** a military usage, "decide by combat"; cf. *derexere* 523 (with n.). **strictis...ensibus:** ablative of means after *horrescit* or ablative of quality used to describe the *atra...seges*, a "black crop of drawn swords." Note the synchysis* in *atra... strictis seges ensibus.*

527. **sole lacessita:** "assailed repeatedly by the sun," with *laessita* (from *lacesso* (3)) modifying *aera* ("bronze (weapons)"), which consequently gleam (526). **sub nubila:** *sub* plus accusative, here "up (from under) to."

fluctus uti primo coepit cum albescere vento,
paulatim sese tollit mare et altius undas
erigit, inde imo consurgit ad aethera fundo.   530
hic iuvenis primam ante aciem stridente sagitta,
natorum Tyrrhi fuerat qui maximus, Almo
sternitur; haesit enim sub gutture vulnus et udae
vocis iter tenuemque inclusit sanguine vitam.
corpora multa virum circa seniorque Galaesus,   535

528-30. **fluctus...**: this is the third simile describing the immediate effects of Allecto's actions. While the first were taken from everyday life, almost domestic scenes (boys playing with a top, 378-83 n.; a boiling pot of water, 462-6 n.), this simile returns us to a more traditional epic context (that of nature) and in particular a rising sea, in order to describe how the rustic fighting gradually turns into a full battle. Some compare the simile at Homer, *Iliad* 4.422-6: "As when the thundering beach the surf of the sea strikes | beat upon beat as the west wind drives it onward; far out | cresting first on the open water, it drives thereafter | to smash roaring along the dry land, and against the rock jut | bending breaks itself into crests spewing back the salt wash" (Lattimore (1951)).

528. **uti...cum:** "just as when." **albescere:** "become white," a largely poetic word in Vergil's time.

529-30. **sese tollit...undas | erigit:** note the theme and variation* describing the swelling of the sea. **imo...fundo:** understand *ab*; *fundus, -i*, m., "bottom," "depth." **consurgit ad aethera:** note the hyperbole*; for *aethera*, cf. 34 n.

531-2. **hic:** adverbial. **iuvenis...Almo:** the name of the youth is delayed; Vergil has given him the name of a small river that runs into the Tiber. **primam ante aciem:** i.e., among the first rank of fighters; cf. 673. **stridente sagitta:** *strideo* means "hiss," "whizz," "creak" (cf. 613); the phrase is ablative of means to be construed closely with *sternitur* (see 533 n.); note the effective alliteration*. **natorum Tyrrhi...maximus:** the focus remains on Tyrrhus' family. The oldest son (cf. *Tyrrhidae pueri* 484) dies first; he is also the first of many young casualties in this fury-inspired war. (See the detailed discussion of 531-4 in Joseph (2012).) **fuerat:** pointedly, "had been," i.e., before he was slain (533). **qui:** note the strong delay (hyperbaton*) of *qui*, giving greater emphasis to both *maximus* and *Almo*.

533-4. **sternitur:** the enjambment* of the verb adds suspense to the death of the *iuvenis*. **haesit:** note the emphatic placement of the verb at the beginning of the clause. **vulnus:** the startling subject of *haesit*, for which we might have expected the subject to be some kind of weapon/arrow (cf. *sagitta* 531). **udae:** with *vocis* but a transferred epithet* really belonging to *iter* ("path," "passage"). **vocis:** the blocked *vox* of this exemplary youth contrasts with the *Tartaream vocem* (514) of the Fury that incites the war and Almo's death. **inclusit sanguine:** i.e., Almo choked on his blood. Note how the praiseworthy description of the youth (531-2) is followed by a graphically physical description of his death wound.

535. **corpora multa virum:** understand *sternuntur* (from *sternitur* 533); *virum* is genitive plural (50-1 n.). **circa:** adverbial. **seniorque Galaesus:** : the *-que* serves to introduce a specific example after a more general word/idea (here *corpora*). The old man Galaesus (cf. Almo with

dum paci medium se offert, iustissimus unus
qui fuit Ausoniisque olim ditissimus arvis:
quinque greges illi balantum, quina redibant
armenta, et terram centum vertebat aratris.
    Atque ea per campos aequo dum Marte geruntur,   540
promissi dea facta potens, ubi sanguine bellum
imbuit et primae commisit funera pugnae,
deserit Hesperiam et caeli conversa per auras
Iunonem victrix adfatur voce superba:
'en, perfecta tibi bello discordia tristi;   545

531-2 n.) shares his name with a river near Tarentum. Note the pointed contrast between the ages of the two men Vergil describes as dying: Almo is *iuvenis*; Galaesus, *senior* (cf. 45-6 n.)

536-7. **iustissimus unus:** *unus* strengthens the superlative, "most just man of all." **olim:** "at one time," "once." Galaesus was both the wealthiest (further described in 538-9) and most just Latin; the poet thus suggests once again the savage nature of this war (cf. G. W. Williams (1983) 197), a moral component lacking in Homer that reveals how the Italian conflict causes "the destruction of values." Cairns (1989) 101 argues that this scene looks forward to Aeneas' wounding as he tries to stop the renewed outbreak of war at 12.311-23.

538-9. **quinque...quina:** for this artful combination of cardinal and distributive numbers, cf. 10.329 *septem...septenaque*. **illi:** dative of possessor or reference (i.e., *Galaeso*). **balantum:** genitive plural (50-1 n.); the participle is used as a substantive, "of bleating ones" (i.e., sheep). **quina:** = *quinque*, with *armenta*. **centum...aratris:** ablative of means; this detail shows that *ditissimus* (537) was an apt description of Galaesus.

540-71. *Allecto announces her deeds to Juno and her willingness to do more, but Juno sends her back to the underworld.*

540. **ea:** neuter plural, referring generally to the preceding details. **aequo...Marte:** *Marte* is a standard metonymy* for "war."

541-2. **promissi...facta potens:** *facta*, "having become" or "been made"; *potens*, "master of," takes the genitive (*promissi*), the phrase essentially meaning that Allecto has fulfilled her promised actions. **imbuit:** perfect, "stained." **primae commisit funera pugnae:** a startling variation on the phrase *committere pugnam* ("join battle"); *funera* refers to the "deaths" particularly of Almo and Galaesus.

543. **conversa:** "turned back," i.e., returning to the heavens.

544. **voce superba:** for *superba*, cf. 12 n. In contrast to her initial meeting with Juno, in which she did not say a word in response (cf. 341-5), Allecto now voices satisfaction in her rapid accomplishments.

545. **en:** "lo!" "behold!" **perfecta tibi:** supply *est*. **bello...tristi:** ablative. **discordia:** a thematically significant word, since it implies the criminality of the proto–civil war that will take place among the peoples in Italy. It may make us think of Ennius' famous lines describing Discordia's role in the outbreak of the first or second Punic wars (which one is debated): see notes on 286-640 and 622.

dic in amicitiam coëant et foedera iungant.
quandoquidem Ausonio respersi sanguine Teucros,
hoc etiam his addam, tua si mihi certa voluntas:
finitimas in bella feram rumoribus urbes,
accendamque animos insani Martis amore   550
undique ut auxilio veniant; spargam arma per agros.'
tum contra Iuno: 'terrorum et fraudis abunde est:
stant belli causae, pugnatur comminus armis,

---

546. **dic...coëant...iungant:** primary sequence indirect commands after *dic* (without *ut*). Compare Juno's use of *coëant* at 317, and note again (cf. 544 n.) Allecto's seeming haughtiness toward Juno.

547. **quandoquidem:** "since indeed"; the *o* is shortened. Vergil uses this word four times, all in speeches, to convey a higher emotional register. **Ausonio:** cf. 39 n.; modifying *sanguine*. **respersi:** perfect from *respergo* (3), "sprinkle," "spatter."

548. **hoc...his:** polyptoton*; *hoc* refers to what Allecto is about to propose, *his* to the things she has already done (545-7). **tua si mihi certa voluntas:** construe *certa* as a predicate adjective. Juno uses this phrase at 4.125, when telling Venus her plan to have Dido and Aeneas seek refuge together in a cave during a storm.

549. **finitimas:** "neighboring"; until Vergil's time, this adjective is largely found in prose. **rumoribus:** with her use of rumors to inflame strife and her ability to change her form (cf. 328-9), Allecto resembles Fama in Book 4.173-92 (see 392 n.; Panoussi (2009) 138 and Hardie (2012) 101-2).

550. **accendam:** again, characteristic fire imagery to describe the Fury's power, cf. 445 n. **insani Martis amore:** note the potential oxymoron* (Horsfall); the opposing nature of love/Venus and Mars is seen, e.g., at the opening of Lucretius' epic, though the two overlap elsewhere in Book 7 (e.g., 461 *amor ferri* and see 37-45 n.).

551. **auxilio:** dative of purpose. **spargam arma per agros:** perhaps *spargo* (3), "scatter," conveys an agricultural metaphor; cf. 339 *sere crimina belli* (Horsfall). The verb is often used of throwing weapons.

552-60. Juno responds to Allecto somewhat dismissively. Allecto's "officiousness is rejected by Juno, who, without a word of thanks, tells the goddess...rather ungraciously 'that will do'...and curtly bids her be off" (Fraenkel (1945: 6 = 1990: 262)).

552. **tum contra Iuno:** note the ellipsis* of a verb of speaking, Juno's somewhat curt tone (552-60 n.), and the beginning of her speech mid-line. **terrorum et fraudis:** partitive genitives after *abunde*. Juno refers to Allecto's actions with Amata, Turnus, and Iulus/Silvia's stag that have just been described. **abunde est:** i.e., "there is more than enough of" (cf. *satis est*).

553. **stant belli causae:** *stant* suggests fixity, "the causes of war stand firm." **pugnatur:** impersonal passive, cf. *agitur* 523-4 (with n.). **comminus:** adverb, "hand-to-hand."

quae fors prima dedit sanguis novus inbuit arma.
talia coniugia et talis celebrent hymenaeos 555
egregium Veneris genus et rex ipse Latinus.
te super aetherias errare licentius auras
haud pater ille velit, summi regnator Olympi.
cede locis. ego, si qua super fortuna laborum est,
ipsa regam.' talis dederat Saturnia voces, 560
illa autem attollit stridentis anguibus alas

---

554. **quae fors prima dedit:** a relative clause, which describes *arma* at the end of the line (thus *arma* is the postcedent of the relative pronoun *quae*—not antecedent—because *arma* comes after (*post*) the relative pronoun, not before (*ante*), cf. 738 n.). *Prima* could modify *fors* with adverbial force ("first," cf. 503 n.), or *prima* could be taken with *arma*.

555. **talia...talis:** effective polyptoton*, underscoring the theme and variation* involved in the line. Note the clash of ictus* and word accent* in *talis* as opposed to their coincidence in *talia*; the clash adds dynamic tension and emphasis to the second use of *talis* and thus also to the movement of the line. **hymenaeos:** cf. 398 n.

556. **egregium Veneris genus:** periphrasis* for Aeneas; *egregium* ("excellent") is surely sarcastic; for *genus*, see 213-14 n.

557-8. **te:** emphatically placed. **super:** not so much "over" as "through" or "in the air above" (Fordyce). **errare:** Allecto's destruction as she wanders on earth contrasts with the case of the stag, whose wandering was a sign of its domestication and ultimate vulnerability, cf. 491, 493 n. **haud...velit:** note the litotes* (conveying understatement) and the politeness of *velit*, calculated to dissuade the Fury from further action. **pater ille:** a respectful use of *ille* (employed particularly in prayers to Jupiter, *OLD* s.v. *ille* 4b), here perhaps with the sense of "the mighty father." **regnator:** "ruler," a poetic word, going back to Naevius (later third century BCE). Juno's concern about Jupiter's wishes must be taken as disingenuous, since Juno has acted with little concern for them, and she herself desires to direct the course of the conflict from here on out—without further assistance from Allecto (cf. 559-60).

559. **cede locis:** "leave (from) the scene" (Horsfall); the plural *locis* avoids the suggestion of the regular military idiom *cedere loco*, "abandon one's place" (see 332-3 n.). **si qua...:** lit. "if any chance of toils is left," i.e., if any problems happen to arise, I will take care them (cf. *ipsa regam*). **super...est:** *superest* (tmesis*).

560. **regam:** Juno will take control from Allecto (cf. 557-8 n.), but with this verb she must also be playing with her description of Jupiter as *regnator* in 558. **dederat...voces:** i.e., "spoke," "a Virgilian coinage apparently" (Horsfall). **Saturnia:** cf. 428 n. The patronymic is used of Juno, perhaps adding to the seriousness of the claim in *regam*.

561. **illa:** i.e., Allecto. **stridentis anguibus alas:** for *stridentis*, cf. 531-2 n. This is the first mention anywhere of snakes in the Fury's wings, not simply on her head or held in her hands, as when she infects Amata and Turnus; the detail increases the Fury's horrifying appearance.

Cocytique petit sedem supera ardua linquens.
est locus Italiae medio sub montibus altis,
nobilis et fama multis memoratus in oris,
Amsancti valles; densis hunc frondibus atrum   565
urguet utrimque latus nemoris, medioque fragosus
dat sonitum saxis et torto vertice torrens.
hic specus horrendum et saevi spiracula Ditis
monstrantur, ruptoque ingens Acheronte vorago
pestiferas aperit fauces, quis condita Erinys,   570
invisum numen, terras caelumque levabat.

---

562. **Cocyti**: cf. 479 n. **supera ardua**: "the heights above." This neuter plural noun phrase is created by two adjectives that overlap in their meaning of "high," though *superus* often describes the upper regions of the world, with *superi* frequently used as "the gods above."

563. **est locus...**: "there is a place...." Such geographical descriptions are part of the epic tradition going back to Homer and Ennius' *Annales* (cf. *est locus, Hesperiam Grai cognomine dicunt*, *Aen.* 1.530, 3.163). **Italiae medio**: supply *in* "in the heart of Italy"; cf. 566 *medio*, "in the midst" and 59 n.

564. **fama**: ablative. **memoratus**: "celebrated," "renowned"; a word found mainly in poetry by Vergil's day.

565. **Amsancti valles**: Amsanctus was a sulphurous lake and valley (*valles*) in Samnium; here an entrance to the underworld. *Valles* is the older nominative singular form of *vallis* (-is, f.) and thus may suggest an elevated tone. **hunc**: i.e., *locus* (563).

566-7. **urguet**: "closes in." **utrimque**: "on both sides." **medio**: substantival usage, "in the middle" (cf. 563 n.). **fragosus...torrens**: "crashing torrent"; note the separation of the words in the phrase (hyperbaton*) and their placement at their respective line ends, cf. 477-8 n. **torto vertice**: "whirling eddy"; ablative of means (like *saxis*).

568. **hic**: adverbial, "here." **spiracula**: "breathing-holes." **Ditis**: *Dis, Ditis*, m. is another name for Pluto, the king of the underworld.

569. **rupto...Acheronte**: *rupto* has a middle sense, "where the river Acheron (90-1 n.) bursts forth." **vorago**: "chasm" (*vorago, -inis*, f.).

570. **pestiferas**: appropriate because the *fauces* (see below) emit "noxious" fumes and provide a passage for Allecto, who is also referred to as *pestis*, cf. 505-6 n. (Horsfall). **fauces**: *fauces, -ium*, f. pl.; "throat," but also "entrance," as here (cf. 6.201 *ad fauces...Averni*). **quis**: = *quibus* (ablative) with *fauces* as antecedent; take *quibus* closely with *condita* ("hidden" from *condo*).

571. **invisum numen**: describing *Erinys*. **levabat**: the imperfect tense conveys the gradual relief resulting from the Fury's departure. The remarkable detail of the relief felt by the upper world at the Fury's departure will be expanded later in such poets as Seneca and Statius (see, e.g., Hardie (1993), Schiesaro (2003) 26-69, Ganiban (2007) 24-43).

Nec minus interea extremam Saturnia bello
imponit regina manum. ruit omnis in urbem
pastorum ex acie numerus, caesosque reportant
Almonem puerum foedatique ora Galaesi, 575
implorantque deos obtestanturque Latinum.
Turnus adest medioque in crimine caedis et igni
terrorem ingeminat: Teucros in regna vocari,
stirpem admisceri Phrygiam, se limine pelli.
tum quorum attonitae Baccho nemora avia matres 580
insultant thiasis (neque enim leve nomen Amatae)

572-600. *The Latins frantically call on Latinus to declare war. He steadfastly refuses, but ultimately gives up and retreats inside his palace.*

572-82. Note that the people earlier infected by Allecto appear in reverse order—the shepherds (573-6), Turnus (577-9), and the Latin women roused by Amata (581-2) (Fraenkel (1945: 7 = 1990: 263)).

572-3. **Nec minus:** "No less"; occurs ten times in the *Aeneid*, all but once at a line beginning. **extremam...manum:** "last hand," i.e., final touch, a metaphor* from the arts and crafts. **Saturnia:** cf. 560 n. **bello:** dative after *imponit*. **ruit:** emphatic positioning.

574-6. **pastorum:** emphatically placed; note the contrast with *urbem* (573). **ex acie:** "from the line of battle." It would seem as if the Latins have lost the initial skirmish, leave their military formation (*ex acie*), and retreat to the city. **caesos:** from *caedo* (3), "cut down," "slay"; note that the descriptions of Almo and Galaesus in 575 stand in apposition to *caesos*. **reportant... implorant...obtestantur:** tricolon*. The verbs now switch to a general plural subject from the initial collective noun *numerus*. **puerum:** important theme, cf. notes on 50-1, 473-4. **foedatique ora Galaesi:** *foedati* really describes *ora* but grammatically modifies *Galaesi* (enallage*); *ora* is plural for singular, though the plural may place the focus on the physical wounds inflicted on Galaesus' face.

577. **medioque in crimine caedis et igni:** *crimine* here means "accusation," "outcry"; *caedis* (genitive), i.e., the first killings of the skirmish (574-6 n.). *Igni* is a bit unusual here since fire has not been employed in the fighting; it might be taken metaphorically* of passion. The entire phrase, if understood as a hendiadys*: "and amid the fiery outcry of murder."

578-9. **ingeminat:** *ingemino* ("utter a second time" or "repeatedly," "re-echo," *OLD* s.v. *ingemino* 1b) is first found in Vergil. **Teucros...vocari...admisceri...pelli:** indirect discourse after the idea of speaking in *ingeminat*, the tricolon* of infinitives perhaps showing what Turnus says to foment the Latins' *terror*; note the effective terseness and asyndeton*. **in regna:** i.e., to (share) rule. **stirpem:** 293-4 n. **Phrygiam:** cf. 293-4 n. **se:** reflexive pronoun, i.e., Turnus.

580-1. **quorum:** its antecedent (or, in this case, postcedent, 554 n.) is the group of men described as *undique collecti* in 582, "gathered from every quarter, the men, whose mothers leap..., assemble and...." **insultant:** "leap" or "dance through," unusually taking an accusative (*nemora avia*). **thiasis:** *thiasus, -i,* m. (Gr. *thiasos*), the dance performed in celebration of Bacchus.

undique collecti coëunt Martemque fatigant.
ilicet infandum cuncti contra omina bellum,
contra fata deum perverso numine poscunt.
certatim regis circumstant tecta Latini;   585
ille velut pelago rupes immota resistit,
ut pelagi rupes magno veniente fragore,

---

582. **Martemque fatigant:** "tire Mars," i.e., by calling for war.
583. **ilicet:** an archaic word (originally from *i/ire* + *licet*, "it is permitted to go"), used by Vergil here in the sense of "straightaway," "immediately." **infandum…bellum…poscunt (584):** Vergil makes clear the immoral nature of the war (cf. 12.804 *infandum accendere bellum*, Jupiter to Juno). **contra omina:** presumably those portents involving Lavinia described at 64-7, 71-7, 268-70.
584. **contra fata deum:** *fata*, perhaps referring, e.g., to Faunus' oracle (96-101). Vergil makes clear that the war demanded by the Latins is contrary (*contra*) to the gods' will. The ramifications are important. Lyne (1987) 79: "If what Jupiter forbids happens, it means (simply) that Fateful Jupiter, Jupiter 'omnipotens', has in fact *incomplete* power over the other gods, in particular Juno, even in such a grave matter as peace and war." **perverso numine:** "with the gods' will subverted" or "under an evil divinity" (i.e., Allecto), an expansion of *contra fata deum*. For *numine*, cf. notes on 385 and 592.
585. **certatim:** adverb, "in rivalry" or "competition." **circumstant:** "surround" but often used of hostile intent, perhaps "besiege" here.
586-90. This simile has a Homeric model in *Iliad* 15.618-21, where the Greeks at their ships are attacked by the Trojans/Hector and compared to a cliff resisting stormy waters: "But even so [Hector] could not break [the Greeks], for all his fury, | for they closed into a wall and held him, like some towering | huge sea-cliff that lies close along the gray salt water | and stands up against the screaming winds and their sudden directions | and against the waves that grow to bigness and burst up against it" (Lattimore).

Vergil also has an intratextual model: the epic's first simile comparing Neptune's calming of Aeolus' raging winds to a pious leader who calms a raging crowd (1.148-53). Cowan (2015) 118 sees them as "reciprocal similes which compare Aeolus' winds to rioters, and Latinus' rioters to winds," and argues that Latinus and Aeolus are both portrayed as weak kings with respect to Hellenistic kingship theory. (For other interpretations, see S. Harrison (1985) 101-2 and Oliensis (2004) 36.) Later, Mezentius (cf. 647-54 n.) will be compared to a resolute cliff battered by raging winds at 10.693-6.
586. **pelago rupes:** this manuscript reading (from the fifth century CE) is accepted by most modern editors, though more manuscripts (of equal age) have *pelagi*, which would create an exact repetition of *pelagi rupes* that occurs in the following line. However, the phrase *pelago rupes* (with *pelago* construed as dative after *resistit*) makes good sense, and it would be easy to see how it could have become *pelagi rupes* from 587 through scribal error.
587. **ut pelagi rupes:** cf. 586 n.

quae sese multis circum latrantibus undis
mole tenet; scopuli nequiquam et spumea circum
saxa fremunt laterique inlisa refunditur alga. 590
verum ubi nulla datur caecum exsuperare potestas
consilium, et saevae nutu Iunonis eunt res,
multa deos aurasque pater testatus inanis:
'frangimur heu fatis' inquit 'ferimurque procella!
ipsi has sacrilego pendetis sanguine poenas, 595

---

588. **quae:** antecedent is *rupes* ("cliff," 587). **circum:** adverb. **latrantibus:** "barking," a dog metaphor* applied to the waves (*undis*), perhaps influenced by the myth of Scylla, the monster with barking dogs around her waist (cf. 3.424, 432).

589-90. **mole:** ablative of means, "by its heavy mass." **circum...fremunt:** perhaps tmesis*. **lateri:** dative after *inlisa* (from *inlido* (3), "smash against"), which modifies *alga* ("seaweed"). **refunditur:** "is poured back."

591-600. The poet now describes Latinus' feelings as his people cry out for war. For the change in perspective and possible Homeric influence, see 586-90 n. and G. W. Williams (1983) 177-9.

592. **saevae...Iunonis:** cf. notes on 287, 511-12. In Book 1, Juno had sent a storm that shipwrecked Aeneas and the Trojans, and in this way she motivated the action of the first half of the epic; now she uses a Fury to start a war that is metaphorically like a storm that besets King Latinus and that initiates the second half of the epic. Cf. 312 n. **nutu:** "nod," from *nutus, -us*, m. (cf. *numine* 584), "nod of the head," "divine will"; *nutus* and *numen* are etymologically related. **eunt res:** such final monosyllables create metrical tension (often reflecting what is being described, as here) by preventing the word accent* from coinciding with the verse accent (ictus*) in the sixth foot. Since the preceding word will normally be of two or more syllables (here éunt) and will not have an accent on the ultima, the word acent will not coincide with the ictus of the sixth foot, and thus a clash of word accent and ictus results. Such clashes in the sixth foot occur infrequently in Vergil, but are more common in Ennius and early Latin poetry and thus can be interpreted as archaic in tone, contributing resonant effects within the context of an individual line.

593. **multa:** adverbial, "much." **auras...inanis:** Latinus (*pater*) invokes the breezes, which are described as *inanis* ("worthless"), because they will not convey his prayer to the gods.

594. **frangimur...:** Latinus metaphorically describes himself as if on a ship in stormy weather, continuing the metaphor* from the sea simile at 586-90.

595. **ipsi...pendetis:** Latinus' words are addressed to his people; *pendetis* (future) is from *pendo* (3), "weigh," here "pay"; not from *pendeo* (2), "hang." **has...poenas:** "these penalties," i.e., "the penalties for this" (i.e., starting this war). **sacrilego...sanguine:** *sacrilego*, because Latinus knows that the war is inconsistent with what he understands to be the will of the gods.

o miseri. te, Turne, nefas, te triste manebit
supplicium, votisque deos venerabere seris.
nam mihi parta quies, omnisque in limine portus
funere felici spolior.' nec plura locutus
saepsit se tectis rerumque reliquit habenas.   600
  Mos erat Hesperio in Latio, quem protinus urbes
Albanae coluere sacrum, nunc maxima rerum
Roma colit, cum prima movent in proelia Martem,

596-7. **o miseri:** cf. 2.42 *o miseri, quae tanta insania, cives* (Laocoön to the Trojans, as they debate what to do with the Trojan Horse). **te...te...manebit:** notice the emphatic repetition of *te*, in contrast to *mihi* (598); for *maneo* ("wait for") with accusative, cf. 318-9 n. **nefas...triste... supplicium:** Latinus is clear about his view of the war, though he is ultimately helpless to stop it. *Nefas* strongly reinforces the idea of *sacrilego* (595).

598-9. **nam:** refers to a suppressed thought and explains why Latinus' own situation differs from that of his people (595-6) and of Turnus (596-7). **omnis:** nominative, describing the speaker Latinus; translate adverbially, "completely," "wholly." **in limine portus:** a difficult phrase, perhaps "at the entrance of the haven." The metaphor* in *portus* ("haven") carries on the metaphor of a ship on a stormy sea (594), while Latinus adds the idea of death (*funere* 599). Latinus has reached the end of his life (which should be a haven or refuge) but "is deprived of a happy death."

600. **rerum...reliquit habenas:** Latinus gives up the (metaphorical*) reins of the affairs of state (*rerum*; *OLD* s.v. *res* 16), retreating into his palace. With this action, resistance to the Italian war is overwhelmed. For *rerum*, cf. 592 *saevae nutu Iunonis eunt res*. Juno has taken charge.

601-40. *The people urge Latinus to open the Gates of War, but he refuses. As a result, Juno breaks through the doors. Throughout the five major cities of Latium, preparations are made for battle.*
  For Vergil's creative (and anachronistic) use of the Roman ritual of opening the Gates of War, see G. W. Williams (1983) 136-8, C. D. Small (1986), D. Fowler (1998), and Nelis (2001) 305.

601-3. **Mos erat Hesperio in Latio:** *Hesperio* (cf. 4 n.) makes clear that the custom to be described was established in prehistorical Latium, thus adding heroic elevation to it. (Livy 1.19, however, attributes it to the reign of the second Roman king, Numa.) **protinus urbes | Albanae coluere sacrum:** the custom passes without interruption (*protinus*) from Latium to Alba, and from Alba to Rome (603). *Sacrum* is predicative, describing *mos...quem* in 601: "a custom which the *urbes Albanae* cherished as sacred." **nunc maxima rerum:** with *nunc* Vergil points to his contemporary times. *Rerum* is partitive genitive and here means "states," i.e., "the greatest of states" (cf. 600 n.). **Martem:** here, metonymy* for "army" or "martial valor" (cf. 582 n.). Note that lines 601-4 form an acrostic that spells the name MARS (see Horsfall ad loc. and Feeney and Nelis (2005)).

sive Getis inferre manu lacrimabile bellum
Hyrcanisve Arabisve parant, seu tendere ad Indos   605
Auroramque sequi Parthosque reposcere signa:
sunt geminae Belli portae (sic nomine dicunt)
religione sacrae et saevi formidine Martis;

604-6. Note the tricolon* of datives (*Getis...Hyrcanis...Arabis*) in 604-5 governed by *inferre* (infinitive dependent on *parant*, "prepare to"), and the tricolon of infinitives (*tendere...sequi... reposcere*) structuring the *seu* clause in 605-6. The conflicts mentioned actually occurred under Augustus or were in some sense aspirational at that time. See, e.g., 6.794-7, *Georgics* 2.170-2, Horace, *Carmina* 1.12.53-6.

604. **Getis**: dative, cf. 604-7 n. The Getae on the lower Danube were defeated by M. Licinius Crassus (29/28 BCE).

605. **Hyrcanis**: the Hyrcani lived south of the Caspian Sea; the campaign envisaged here is unknown and probably meant aspirationally. **Arabis**: Aelius Gallus led an unsuccessful campaign in Arabia (Yemen) in 24 BCE. **tendere ad Indos**: *tendere* (cf. 7 n.) is here used in an intransitive sense, "aim for" or "head toward." For the phrase, cf. 2.205 *ad litora tendunt* (of the two serpents that attack Laocoön and his children). *Indi* are "inhabitants of India."

606. **Auroram...sequi**: by metonymy*, the goddess of dawn means the "East"; for *sequi* (here "pursue," "go after"), cf. 4.361 *Italiam non sponte sequor* (Aeneas to Dido). **Parthosque reposcere signa**: *reposcere* ("demand back") takes a double accusative. Here there is a historical reference to 20 BCE, when Augustus recovered through negotiation the military standards (*signa*) lost by Crassus during his disastrous battle at Carrhae (Parthia) in 53 BCE.

607-15. The custom, introduced in 601, is now explained.

607. **sunt geminae Belli portae**: the *Belli portae* are part of the temple (now lost) associated with Janus (cf. 180-1 n.). During peacetime, its gates were closed, thereby preventing *Bellum* from getting out; during wartime, its gates were open. Livy (1.19; cf. 601-3 n.) relates that the temple was only so closed three times—by Numa (Rome's second king), by T. Manlius after the First Punic War, and by Augustus in 29 BCE, though Augustus himself refers to his closing of the gates three times (*Res Gestae* 13; the exact number is disputed, see Cooley (2009) 158-61). The gates are described by Jupiter at the end of his revelation to Venus at 1.293-6 (cf. notes on 609 and 622), in lines whose significance must be contrasted with Juno's actions in the present passage (cf. 609 n.). For the overall phrase, cf. 6.893 *sunt geminae Somni portae* (see Putnam (1970) 411 = (1995b) 102-3). (**sic nomine dicunt**): this naming formulation indicates that Janus' temple (see above) was also known by its association with *Bellum*, though the nature of the connection between Janus and Bellum is unclear. In Book 1, Furor is bound within this area—are we to picture *Bellum* there as well? Such a combination would be suggestive, since we are told by other sources that Augustus placed a painting of Bellum and Furor in the Augustan Forum, thereby creating an important association between the two. See Servius *auctus*, and Pliny, *Natural History* 35.27; cf. O'Hara (2017) 191-2.

608. **religione**: here means "awe" or "reverence" of a god. The first syllable of *religio* is short, but from Augustan poetry on, it is usually scanned long, as if *relligione*. Cf. 172.

centum aerei claudunt vectes aeternaque ferri
robora, nec custos absistit limine Ianus: 610
has, ubi certa sedet patribus sententia pugnae,
ipse Quirinali trabea cinctuque Gabino
insignis reserat stridentia limina consul,
ipse vocat pugnas; sequitur tum cetera pubes,
aereaque adsensu conspirant cornua rauco.   615
hoc et tum Aeneadis indicere bella Latinus

---

609. **centum aerei vectes:** *aerei* forms a disyllable by synizesis* (see 33 n.); *vectes* (*vectis, -is*, m.) are "bolts" or "bars," the only occurrence of this word in Vergil. In addition to these one hundred bronze bolts, the gates are fortified by "the everlasting strength of iron." At 1.294-6 (cf. 607 n.), the gates are closed with *ferro et compagibus artis*, while *Furor* is confined within (*centum vinctus aënis | post tergum nodis*). The close connection between these two passages emphasizes the essential difference in context: whereas Augustus is prophesied by Jupiter to close the gates of *Bellum/Janus* that confine *impius Furor* in Book 1, here in Book 7 Latinus will fail to keep the gates shut—at 620-2 Juno (closely associated with *furor* and the Fury Allecto) will break them open.

610. **nec...absistit:** litotes*, underscoring Janus' constant role. Cf. Horace, *Epistulae* 2.1.255 *claustraque custodem pacis cohibentia Ianum*, where Janus is the protector of peace.

611. **has:** i.e., *portas* (cf. 607). **sedet:** cf. 368 n. **patribus:** "fathers," i.e., senators. **pugnae:** probably a dative of purpose ("for war") rather than a genitive after *sententia* ("decision").

612. **ipse:** modifies *consul* at the end of the next line (hyperbaton*). **Quirinali:** adjectival form of *Quirinus*, often used as a name for Romulus but also given to Janus (*Ianus Quirinus*, cf. *Res Gestae* 13). **trabea:** "robe of state," "mantle" (see 187-8 n.); like *cinctu,* ablative after *insignis*. **cinctuque Gabino:** a ceremonial style of wearing the *toga* with part wrapped around the waist like a belt (thus *cinctus*); this style was said to have originated during a war with the Gabii (thus *Gabino*).

613. **insignis:** see notes on 655-7. **reserat:** from *resero* (1), "unlock." **stridentia limina:** stands in apposition to *has* (i.e., *portas*) in 611; *stridentia* ("creaking," 531-2 n.) adds a note of antiquity to the gates' opening during the start of war. **consul:** looks forward to Republican/Augustan Rome.

614. **vocat pugnas:** "i.e., calls out the war that is imprisoned behind the gates" (Fordyce). **sequitur:** note its emphatic position at the beginning of its clause. **pubes:** at line end, it stands in contrast/responsion to *consul* at the end of 613.

615. **adsensu...rauco:** "harsh accord," perhaps an oxymoron*. **conspirant:** "sound together." **cornua:** just as "horn" in English indicates the shape of the instrument and not its material, so *cornua* in Latin also can just indicate the instrument because of its shape (cf. 497 n.). Note that this is a golden line*.

616-17. **hoc...more:** note the hyperbaton*; the phrase picks up from *Mos erat* in 601, and returns us to the narrative context of Latinus and the war in Italy. **et tum:** "even then." **Aeneadis:** dative plural (284 n.). **indicere bella:** cf. 468-9 n. **iubebatur:** i.e., Latinus was presumably

more iubebatur tristisque recludere portas.
abstinuit tactu pater aversusque refugit
foeda ministeria, et caecis se condidit umbris.
tum regina deum caelo delapsa morantis 620
impulit ipsa manu portas, et cardine verso
belli ferratos rumpit Saturnia postis.
ardet inexcita Ausonia atque immobilis ante;

---

ordered by the *patres* (611), though, earlier, Latinus seemed to act on his own in allying with the Trojans. **recludere:** "open."

618. **tactu:** ablative after *abstinuit*. **refugit:** perfect tense, here with transitive meaning ("fled from," "avoided"). Compare its intransitive usage in 500 of the wounded stag; both stag and king retreat as a result of the fury created by Juno/Allecto. (Cairns (1989) 66, however, still sees strength in Latinus' principled and pious resistance to the war.)

619. **foeda ministeria:** "foul duties"; *foeda* seemingly reflects Latinus' view of the war he was bidden (616-17 n.) to initiate. **et caecis se condidit umbris:** for *condidit*, see 144-5 n.; for the phrase, compare 2.621 *et spissis noctis se condidit umbris* (of Venus disappearing after revealing to Aeneas the divine dimension of Troy's fall).

620-1. **regina deum:** for *deum*, cf. 50-1 n.; this periphrasis* for Juno also occurs at 1.9. **morantis...portas:** the gates are described as "delaying," seemingly in resistance to Juno's rush to war; for the theme of delay, see 315-16 n. **impulit:** "struck." **ipsa manu:** *ipsa* is nominative, *manu* ablative; note the emphasis on Juno's physical effort. **cardine verso:** ancient doors were not hung on hinges but turned on two pivots with one socket in the *limen* or sill, the other in the *limen superum* or lintel. The term *cardo* can be used either of the pivot or of the socket in which it moves. Juno would seem not to have completely broken down the doors but to have thrust them open, since *verso cardine* suggests that the pivots are still in place but have been swung open with the bars/bolts broken (cf. 609-10 *centum aerei...vectes aeternaque ferri | robora*).

622. **belli...:** as in 1.294-6 (cf. 607 n.), there seems to be a recall here of the description of *Discordia* (a model for Allecto) breaking open the gates of war in Ennius (cf. 545 n.): *Postquam Discordia taetra | belli ferratos postes portasque refregit* (fragment 225-6 in Skutsch and in *FRL* 1). See Horsfall ad loc. and Goldschmidt (2013) 133-9. **ferratos...postis:** *ferratus*, "made of iron" (cf. 609 *ferri*); *postis, -is,* m., "door-post." **rumpit:** a historical present; here "burst through." **Saturnia:** cf. 560 n. The patronymic here is somewhat ironic, since Saturn was associated with peace and abundance in Latium/Italy (cf. 48-9 n.), not frenzied war.

623. **ardet:** note the emphatic placement and use of fire imagery (cf. notes on 445, 462-6) and fury (*furit* 625) to convey the immediate effects of Juno's action. **inexcita:** "unroused," a word seemingly coined by Vergil and used only here in his poetry; pointedly contrasted with *ardet*. **Ausonia:** cf. 39 n. **immobilis:** note that Latinus was *immobilis* at 250, as he considered Ilioneus' speech (cf. also Aeneas, who is *lacrimis immobilis* at 12.400). **ante:** adverb; construe with both *inexcitata* and *immobilis*. Note the elisions and that each word starts in a vowel. This is an unusually resonant line.

pars pedes ire parat campis, pars arduus altis
pulverulentus equis furit; omnes arma requirunt.   625
pars levis clipeos et spicula lucida tergent
arvina pingui subiguntque in cote securis;
signaque ferre iuvat sonitusque audire tubarum.
quinque adeo magnae positis incudibus urbes
tela novant, Atina potens, Tiburque superbum,   630
Ardea Crustumerique et turrigerae Antemnae.
tegmina tuta cavant capitum, flectuntque salignas
umbonum cratis; alii thoracas aënos

---

624. **pars pedes:** "part" or "some as infantry"; *pedes, -itis*, m., here, "foot-soldier". **pars arduus:** "some high (on tall horses)," i.e., mounted. Though *pars* is feminine, the use of *pedes* (m.) earlier with *pars* seemingly influences Vergil's use of *arduus* (not *ardua*) for balance.

625. **pulverulentus:** "covered with dust"; note that there is no connective between *arduus* (624) and this adjective, the asyndeton* perhaps conveying the sense of martial frenzy. **omnes arma requirunt:** cf. Ennius' *balantum pecudes quatit, omnes arma requirunt* (*Annales*, fragment 169 in Skutsch and in *FRL* 1).

626-7. **levis clipeos et spicula lucida tergent:** both *levis* (cf. 789 n.) and *lucida* are proleptic*, "burnish their shields (so that they become) smooth and their spears (so that they become) shiny," cf. 509 n. **clipeos:** round shields, made of bronze (with other material as well). **arvina:** "grease," "fat"; a rare word, found in Plautus, *Poenulus* 1016, used only here in Vergil. **subigunt:** "sharpen" (by grinding down), "whet." **cote:** from *cos, cotis*, f., "sharpening stone," "whetstone."

629. **quinque...urbes:** named in 630-1. **adeo:** construe with *quinque*; cf. 427 n. **positis:** "set up." The metalwork done in these cities to make the weapons is described in 632-6.

630. **tela novant:** "make new spears," i.e., weapons. **Atina:** a Volscian town in Latium. **Tibur:** i.e., modern Tivoli, cf. 670-7 n.; *superbum* may refer to the town's position on a hill, thus making it "lofty" (*OLD* s.v. *superbus* 1c).

631. **Ardea:** see 411-12 n. **Crustumeri:** probably a poetic plural form. *Crustumerium* was a Sabine town north of Rome. **Antemnae:** another Sabine town north of Rome. For locations, see Map 2. Note the hiatus* between *turrigerae* ("having turrets," "turreted") and *Antemnae* (see 178 n.), as well as the rare spondaic fifth foot (see Appendix 1). Spondaic lines* were favored by the Hellenistic poets (cf. 261 n.) but used more sparingly by Vergil. There are only two such lines in Book 7 (see also 634) and thirty-three overall in the *Aeneid*.

632-3. **tegmina tuta cavant capitum:** an elevated periphrasis* for "helmets." Note the onomatopoetic alliteration*. **salignas | umbonum cratis:** "willow frameworks of shields," with *umbo* ("the boss of a shield") a synecdoche* for "shield." **thoracas:** from *thorax, -acis*, f., "chest," but here "breastplate."

aut levis ocreas lento ducunt argento;
vomeris huc et falcis honos, huc omnis aratri   635
cessit amor; recoquunt patrios fornacibus ensis.
classica iamque sonant, it bello tessera signum.
hic galeam tectis trepidus rapit, ille frementis
ad iuga cogit equos, clipeumque auroque trilicem
loricam induitur fidoque accingitur ense.   640

---

634. **lēvīs:** cf. 789 n.; accusative plural. **ocreas:** "greaves," "shin guards." **lento:** here "pliant," modifying *argento*. **ducunt:** "shape," "beat out," used of bronzesmiths (Fordyce). Note that this is another rare spondaic fifth foot (cf. 631 n.).

635-6. **vomeris...et falcis honos:** *vomer, -eris*, m., "plowshare," "plow"; *falx, falcis*, f., "scythe"; for the form *honos*, see 3 n. **huc:** "to this," i.e., the preparations for war just described. **recoquunt:** "reheat" in order to sharpen (Horsfall).

637. **classica:** a *classicum* (-i, n.) is a "military trumpet call," "battle signal (made by a trumpet)."
bello: dative of purpose. **tessera:** "(a small tablet bearing) the password," a military idiom (*OLD* s.v. *tessera* 3), here functioning as a "mobilization order" (Fordyce).

639. **trilicem:** "having a triple thread," "triply woven" (nominative *trilix*).

640. **loricam:** "cuirass" (a breastplate and backplate linked together). **induitur:** "puts on," a middle usage.

Map 2: The Catalogue of Italian Troops (*Aeneid* 7.641-817): Leaders and Locations

641-817: Catalogue of Italian Troops

After the frenzied outbreak of the Italian war, Vergil pauses to introduce the major heroes and peoples who will fight on the Italian side against the Trojans. Such catalogues of troops are a feature of epic poetry that goes back to *Iliad* 2, where Homer provides a lengthy description of the Greek ships and warriors fighting at Troy (*Iliad* 2.484-759), followed by a shorter catalogue of Trojan troops (*Iliad* 2.816-77). Homer is Vergil's main model here and in 10.163-214, where there is a catalogue of Aeneas' Etruscan allies. The Catalogue of the Argonauts in Apollonius 1.20-233 is also an important influence (Nelis (2001) 305-10).

Vergil presents each Italian contingent, constantly varying the content, length and characterization of the entries. Thirteen contingents are described under the following commanders:

641-646: Introduction/proem	723-732: Halaesus
647-654: Mezentius and Lausus	733-743: Oebalus
655-669: Aventinus	744-749: Ufens
670-677: Catillus and Corus	750-760: Umbro
678-690: Caeculus	761-782: Virbius
691-705: Messapus	783-802: Turnus
706-722: Clausus	803-817: Camilla

Passages range in length from six lines (Ufens) to twenty-two (Virbius). In some, the leader is the prime focus with the army mentioned barely (e.g., Aventinus) or not at all (e.g., Umbro, Virbius); in others a more equal balance is struck (e.g., Turnus). Some heroes will return only briefly in the epic; others never again (e.g., Aventinus, Oebalus, Virbius). The armies are not presented in any geographical order; however, if the major warriors at the beginning and end (Lausus and Mezentius, Turnus and Camilla) are omitted, the remaining heroes are in roughly alphabetical order, with the exception of Messapus (but see O'Hara (1989)). What is clear is that the Catalogue serves not simply to introduce the leaders and armies supporting Turnus; it also gives voice to the epic's conception of ancient Italy and raises thematic ideas that will be important for the second half of the epic.

The Catalogue is enclosed by Turnus and his most prominent allies in the epic, but these warriors strike startling notes. Mezentius and Lausus provide an inauspicious beginning: Mezentius is a *contemptor divum*, and Lausus is tragically devoted to his father (647-54 n.), both details looking forward to their deaths in Book 10. The Catalogue ends not with Turnus, as might have been expected so as to present him as the heroic culmination of the Italian leaders, but with Camilla, the epic's only female warrior, whose description contains foreboding details and intra-textual connections to Penthesilea and Dido (803-17 n.)

In between we are introduced to the other Italian leaders, for many of whom Vergil has seemingly created heroic identities, often employing a thoroughly Alexandrian/neoteric interest in mythology, aetiology, and wordplay. Some are the children of gods: Aventinus (Hercules), Caeculus (Vulcan), Messapus (Neptune), Oebalus (the nymph Sebethis). Others have strong Greek connections, thus suggesting that the Trojans' Italian war will on some level continue the Trojan War (e.g., notes on 672, 723-32, 794). Still others are given important proto-Roman resonances: the warrior named Aventinus is born on what will become the Aventine Hill (655-69 n.); Clausus seems a progenitor of the famous *gens Claudia* (706-22 n.).

Aside from the leaders, the geographical expanse of Turnus' allies in the Catalogue contributes to one of Vergil's most important innovations in the epic: in Books 7-12, Vergil has transformed what had traditionally been a relatively small conflict to one that involves much of Italy; the Catalogue is his most important vehicle for expressing this new scope, one that comes with a significant ramification. Since the Catalogue includes many peoples who will later resist historical Rome in battle but will all be Romans by Vergil's time (see 12.503-4 with discussion in Introduction to Book 7), it allows the reader potentially to view the Italian conflict with Aeneas (Rome's forefather) as a proto–civil war, one that resonates not only with the civil wars of Caesar and then Augustus that tore Rome apart in Vergil's lifetime, but also (and perhaps even more so) with the Social or Marsic War (91-88 BCE) fought by Rome with its Italian allies (*socii*), which took place just a generation before Vergil's birth (see especially Marincola (2010)).

For discussion of the Catalogue, see Horsfall ad loc., W. W. Fowler (1916), Fraenkel (1945: 10-12 = 1990: 268-71), R. D. Williams (1961), Parry (1963) 66-9, C. F. Saylor (1974), Lee (1980), Horsfall (1987, on minor warriors), Courtney (1988), O'Hara (1989), Boyd (1992), Malamud (1998), and Nelis (2001) 305-10. For ethnography, see Thomas (1982) 93-107, and Wimperis (2017, 2020). For Alexandrian elements and etymological wordplay*, see O'Hara (1996 = 2017), Nelis (2001) 305-10, and Ferriss-Hill (2011). For the importance of civil war and of the Social War in Book 7 (and Books 7-12 more generally), see Marincola (2010) and Wimperis (2017, 2020).

Pandite nunc Helicona, deae, cantusque movete,
qui bello exciti reges, quae quemque secutae
complerint campos acies, quibus Itala iam tum
floruerit terra alma viris, quibus arserit armis;
et meministis enim, divae, et memorare potestis;   645
ad nos vix tenuis famae perlabitur aura.

641-6. Muses, help me describe the Italian leaders and armies.

Vergil imitates the invocation of the Muses that introduces the "Catalogue of the Ships" at *Iliad* 2.484–93, particularly its opening: "Tell me now, you Muses who have dwellings on Olympus—for you are goddesses and are present and know all things, but we hear only rumor and know nothing—who were the leaders and lords of the Danaans" (*Iliad* 2.484-7, Wyatt).

641. **Pandite...Helicona, deae:** the poet directly addresses the Muses (*deae*). "Open Helicon, goddesses," i.e., so that I can receive your inspiration. **Helicona:** Greek accusative; Mt. Helicon (in SW Boeotia) was inhabited by the Muses (*deae*). **cantusque movete:** *cantus* (fourth declension) is accusative plural; understand *in me*; for the important resonance of the verb *moveo*, see 44-5 n. This same line at 10.163 introduces the Catalogue of Etruscan Troops; both catalogues have *Iliad* 2 as their main model (see 641-817 n.).

642-4. **qui...quae...quibus...quibus:** polyptoton* of interrogative adjectives in indirect questions after *cantus...movete* in line 641. Such repetition of adjectives and pronouns is characteristic of prayer. Note also how each adjective is paired with a noun, and how each adjective-noun pair encloses its clause: *qui...reges, quae...acies, quibus...viris, quibus...armis*. The subjunctives—*exciti (sint), complerint, floruerit, arserit*—are perfect in primary sequence indirect questions.

642. **bello:** probably dative of purpose, as in 637 (see n.). **exciti:** supply *sint*; cf. 623 *inexcita*. **quemque:** "each one," i.e., each king; object of the participle *secutae*, which modifies *quae... acies*.

643. **complerint:** see 642-4 n. **iam tum:** emphatic. Vergil emphasizes the glorious nature of Italy "already then" in the heroic age.

644. **quibus...armis:** ablative of means (cf. 642-4 n.). Italic weaponry will be a central concern of the Catalogue as a means to distinguish the different peoples, though the unusual weaponry itself is not particularly important throughout Books 8-12. **arserit:** again, the fire metaphor*, here indicating martial passion; cf. notes on 393, 445, 482, 496, 550, 623.

645-6. **meministis...memorare:** "remember...relate"; for the etymological wordplay* involving the Muses (here *divae*), see 41-2 n. **ad nos vix:** Vergil emphasizes the distance between mythological and contemporary time, though that distance can also be collapsed (e.g., 708 n.). Cf. the Homeric passage quoted in 641-6 n.

Primus init bellum Tyrrhenis asper ab oris
contemptor divum Mezentius agminaque armat.
filius huic iuxta Lausus, quo pulchrior alter
non fuit excepto Laurentis corpore Turni;   650

647-54. *The Etruscans led by Mezentius and his son Lausus.*
The Catalogue begins with Mezentius and Lausus, leading an Etruscan contingent. Mezentius is immediately described as *asper* and a *contemptor divum* (647-8), but we (interestingly) do not yet learn that he is the former king of Caere (652 n.), exiled, according to Evander's claims at 8.481-95, because of his inhuman crimes. His beautiful young son Lausus accompanies him and is defined by his tragic devotion to his father (see below). Such details central to the epic's plot are, however, Vergilian innovations. In the historiographical tradition (Cato, Dionysius of Halicarnssus, and Livy, see 1-285 n.), Mezentius is the current (not exiled) king of Caere, has not committed inhuman crimes, and does not exhibit a tragic relationship to his son Lausus. (In Cato, he does, however, exhibit *impietas* by demanding that the Rutulians give their *primitiae*, "first-fruits" of the wine vintage, to him, not to the gods; see fragment 9 in *FRH* 2.)

Vergil's depiction of Mezentius as an evil king, in fact, bears some resemblance to that of Rome's final king, the Etruscan Tarqunius Superbus, a violent autocrat who, after being deposed, went into exile at Caere (Livy 1.60). As we learn later, Caere will send troops seeking to punish Mezentius; they will be described at 10.182-3 in the Catalogue of Aeneas' Etruscan Allies (10.163-214).

For interpretations of Lausus and Mezentius, see Eden (1975), Sullivan (1969), Glenn (1971a and b), Leach (1971), Burke (1974 a and b), Nethercut (1975), J. Jones (1977), Gotoff (1984), Gaskin (1992), E. L. Harrison (1988), Putnam (1995b) 134-51, and Kronenberg (2005). For Caere and Etruria in the epic, see McKay (1970) 81-6.

647. Primus: note the prominence of the problematic Mezentius, as well as the ordered way in which the first three paragraphs of the Catalogue in particular are begun: *Primus*, *Post hos* (656), *Tum* (670). **bellum:** accusative after *init*. **Tyrrhenis...ab oris:** see 43-4 n.; construe the phrase as indicating Mezentius' origin, not (with *init*) the place from which he has come to the war, since he is currently in exile among the Rutulians (cf. 647-54 n.)

648. contemptor divum Mezentius: for *divum*, see 50-1 n. Mezentius' impious nature, however, is not explained until later (see 647-54 n.). That the Catalogue begins with a *contemptor deorum* may resonate with the sacrilegious nature of Turnus' cause, as Latinus had characterized it at 595-7.

649-50. huic iuxta: *huic* (i.e., Mezentius), dative of reference with *iuxta* construed adverbially. **Lausus:** see 647-54 n. **quo...:** ablative of comparison; antecedent is Lausus. **excepto Laurentis corpore Turni:** synthesis*; *excepto...corpore* is an ablative absolute. Notice the focus not only on Lausus' physical beauty but also on Turnus' (54-5 n., 473-4 n.). For *Laurentis*, cf. notes on 47 and 63. The line seems modeled on Homer, *Iliad* 2.673-4, describing the warrior Nireus as "the handsomest man...after the incomparable son of Peleus (i.e., Achilles)" (Wyatt). (Cf. also the description of Aeneas at 1.544-5: *quo iustior alter, | nec pietate fuit, nec bello maior et armis.*)

Lausus, equum domitor debellatorque ferarum,
ducit Agyllina nequiquam ex urbe secutos
mille viros, dignus patriis qui laetior esset
imperiis et cui pater haud Mezentius esset.
    Post hos insignem palma per gramina currum   655
victoresque ostentat equos satus Hercule pulchro
pulcher Aventinus, clipeoque insigne paternum

---

651. **Lausus:** note the repetition* of his name (cf. 649). **equum domitor debellatorque ferarum:** note the assonance*, consonance*, and chiastic* structure. For *equum domitor*, see 189-91 n. *Debellator* ("conqueror," "subduer") was perhaps coined by Vergil, and used only here in his poetry. (The verbal form appears in Anchises' famous words to Aeneas in the underworld: *et debellare superbos* at 6.853.) Overall, this introduction of Lausus is in lofty epic style.

652. **Agyllina:** the adjectival form of *Agylla*, an earlier name for the Etruscan town called Caere (mod. Cerveteri). **nequiquam:** "in vain"; the adverb looks forward to the failure of the troops (one thousand strong, 653), since Lausus will be killed (10.789-832), and their cause defeated.

653-4. **mille viros:** interestingly, despite his exile, Mezentius and his son still have support from Caere (647-54 n.). **dignus…:** "worthy to be happier under his father's rule and not to have Mezentius as father (lit. 'for whom Mezentius not be father')." Note the repetition of *esset* and the polyptoton* of *qui* (i.e., *qui…cui…*) in two relative clauses of characteristic following *dignus* (for the construction, see AG §535 f.).

655-69. Hercules' son Aventinus and his army.

    Aventinus is not attested earlier as a warrior in the Italian war. (In Livy 1.3, there is an Aventinus who is one of the final kings of Alba, not long before Rome's founding.) He seems a Vergilian innovation, appearing only here in the epic and created presumably to provide Turnus with a heroic ally from what will later be Rome (i.e., the Aventine Hill; Aeneas will ally with Evander on the future Palatine in Book 8). The passage focuses almost exclusively on Aventinus' descent from and connections to his father Hercules: Aventinus' conception and birth on the (future) Aventine Hill (659-63) and the various Herculean emblems he bears (655-8, 666-9). Surprisingly, the name of his people is not even given, and his troops are barely mentioned (664 n.). This prideful filial relationship, however, contrasts pointedly with that of Mezentius and Lausus (647-54 n.), while Aventinus' birth, intriguingly, resembles that of Romulus and Remus (659 n.).

655. **Post hos:** *hos* indicates Mezentius, Lausus, and their troops; for the preposition *post*, cf. 647 n. **insignem palma…currum:** *insignem* ("distinguished (by a mark)") modifies *currum* ("chariot") and governs the ablative *palma* (cf. 1.10 *insignem pietate*, of Aeneas). *Palma* ("palm-wreath") really means "victory" by metonymy*.

656-7. **victores:** used as an adjective (cf. *victor equus*, *Georgics* 3.499). **satus Hercule pulchro:** a periphrasis* for Aventinus, cf. 152 n. **Hercule pulchro | pulcher Aventinus:** note the polyptoton* of the adjective with chiasmus*, and the focus on the beauty of both father and son (cf. notes on 54-5, 473-4, 649-50). **insigne:** here the noun form (cf. 655 n.), a "decoration" or "mark of honor" indicating one's family, status, etc.; *insigne paternum* is object of *gerit* (658).

centum anguis cinctamque gerit serpentibus Hydram;
collis Aventini silva quem Rhea sacerdos
furtivum partu sub luminis edidit oras, 660
mixta deo mulier, postquam Laurentia victor
Geryone exstincto Tirynthius attigit arva,
Tyrrhenoque boves in flumine lavit Hiberas.
pila manu saevosque gerunt in bella dolones,
et tereti pugnant mucrone veruque Sabello. 665

658. **centum anguis cinctamque...serpentibus Hydram:** the phrase stands in apposition to *insigne paternum* (657), the line perhaps forming a hendiadys*. Hercules killed the hundred-headed Lyrnaean Hydra as the Second Labor of his canonical Twelve Labors (mentioned at 8.300).

659. **collis Aventini:** genitive after *silva*. **silva:** ablative of place; with *Rhea* (nominative) the name of Aventinus' mother, note the allusion to Rhea Silvia, the mother of Romulus and Remus (cf. 655-69 n.). **quem:** i.e., Aventinus.

660. **partu:** "birth," fourth declension; ablative of specification after *furtivum*. **sub luminis... oras:** "(from under) up to the boundaries of light," a phrase going back to Ennius (*Annales*, fragments 109, 135 in Skutsch and in *FRL* 1). **edidit:** from *edo* (3), "bring forth."

661-2. **mixta deo mulier:** *misceo* (2), "mix," is also used of sexual intercourse. The *mulier* is of course Rhea (659); the *deo* is Hercules. Though Hercules was born mortal, at his death he became a god through his father Jupiter's intervention. (See, e.g., Sophocles, *Trachiniae* and Ovid, *Metamorphoses* 9.134-272.) Notice the juxtaposition of *deo* : *mulier* (i.e., god : mortal; cf. 346 n.). **postquam Laurentia... | Geryone exstincto...attigit arva:** *attigit* is from *attingo* (3), "touch"; for *Laurentia*, cf. 47 n. For his Tenth Labor, Hercules killed the monstrous Geryon (*Geryone exstincto*, ablative absolute) in Spain and stole his cattle. Later, as Hercules passed over the Aventine, he killed Cacus, who had stolen some of these cattle (8.184-279). Hercules apparently conceived Aventinus at this time (see Parkes (2007)). **Tirynthius:** adjective; Hercules was born in Tiryns.

663. **Tyrrheno:** see notes on 43-4 and 647. **boves...lavit Hiberas:** *lavit* is perfect of *lavo* (1), "wash." Could the action of this line correspond to Evander's detail in his story about Hercules and Cacus (*boves amnem...tenebant*, 8.204), just before Cacus stole eight of Hercules' cattle? Cf. 661-2 n. *Hiberas* ("Iberian," "Spanish"), from the Greek name for the region.

664. **pila:** "javelins"; adopted by Roman army in the early Republic, thus anachronistic here. **gerunt:** "bear," "carry"; the subject (Aventinus' troops) is only implied (cf. 655-69 n.). **dolones:** the nature of these weapons is disputed, but they were probably iron-tipped pikes (nominative singular *dolo*).

665. **tereti...mucrone:** a *mucro* is "sharp point" or "edge," thus also "sword"; the phrase perhaps means a "slender sword" (Horsfall). **veru Sabello:** the identity of this weapon is disputed as well; perhaps the *verutum* is meant, a javelin with a metal head (cf. Livy 1.43.6, *Geo.* 2.168). *Sabellus* describes the Italic peoples who spoke Oscan (728-30 n.), though attested usage most often indicates "Samnite." The line might also be taken as describing one weapon by hendiadys*: "a Sabellan javelin with tapering point."

ipse pedes, tegimen torquens immane leonis,
terribili impexum saeta cum dentibus albis
indutus capiti, sic regia tecta subibat,
horridus Herculeoque umeros innexus amictu.
    Tum gemini fratres Tiburtia moenia linquunt,   670
fratris Tiburti dictam cognomine gentem,

666-8. **ipse pedes**: Aventinus, on foot (*pedes*), though at 655-7 he was described on a chariot. **tegimen torquens...indutus capiti**: *indutus* (from *induo*, "put on"), a middle participle that, like *torquens* ("flinging around (himself)"), takes *tegimen* as direct object; *capiti* is dative after *indutus*. **terribili...saeta**: ablative of specification (AG §418) to be construed with *impexum* ("uncombed," "unkempt"); *saeta* is a collective noun, "bristles." **impexum**: modifies *tegimen*. For his First Labor, Hercules killed the Nemean Lion; note that Aventinus sports the Lion and the Hydra (658), perhaps the most famous beasts killed by his father. **sic**: "thus (outfitted)." **regia tecta subibat**: an odd detail (he is entering a palace, not battle) but one that resonates with Hercules' entrance into Evander's home as described at 8.362-2 *haec...limina...Alcides subiit, haec illum regia cepit.* Cf. 655-69 n.

669. **Herculeoque...amictu**: i.e., the attire described in 666-8. **innexus**: middle usage; from *innecto* (3), "enwrap," "cover."

670-7. The twin brothers Catillus and Coras from Tibur.

    Catillus and Coras are twins (*gemini* 670) leading a contingent from Tibur in Latium. Their story survives in a number of earlier sources that give them, variously, Greek, Alban, or Sicel origins with some other differences in detail. Traditionally, they are brothers, not twins (this is Vergil's innovation); together they found a city with a third, older brother Tiburtus, after whom the city is named. Tibur was mentioned at 7.630 (*Tibur superbum*, see n.) as one of the five cities that immediately prepare to take up arms on behalf of the Latins. Despite their prominence in the Catalogue, Catillus and Coras do not play a major role later in the epic, appearing only in the battle that follows the break-up of the Latins' council (11.465, 604-07). As far as we are told, they survive the war.

    In the Republic, Tibur was originally an independent ally of Rome but sided with the Gauls in their attacks in 361-360 BCE. They joined the Latin revolt in 340-338 BCE and were defeated, though they were allowed to retain independent status. Tibur ultimately gained full Roman citizenship in 90 BCE, during the Social War. For Tibur in Vergil, see McKay (1970) 176, 193.

670. **Tum**: see 647 n. **gemini fratres**: i.e., Catillus and Coras, named in 672 (cf. 670-7 n.).
    Tiburtia: the adjectival form of the town name *Tibur*. **moenia**: city walls, here "city" by metonymy*, as often.

671. **fratris Tiburti...gentem**: this line explains how the city got its name with *gentem* in loose apposition to *moenia* (i.e., city) in 670. The city/people (*gentem*) were named after Catillus and Coras' brother Tiburtus.

Catillusque acerque Coras, Argiva iuventus,
et primam ante aciem densa inter tela feruntur:
ceu duo nubigenae cum vertice montis ab alto
descendunt Centauri Homolen Othrymque nivalem 675
linquentes cursu rapido; dat euntibus ingens
silva locum et magno cedunt virgulta fragore.
Nec Praenestinae fundator defuit urbis,

---

672. **Argiva iuventus:** in apposition to Catillus and Corus. Note again the focus on youth and on Argive/Greek descent (641-817 n.); various sources identify the brothers as sons of the Argive seer Amphiaraus.

673. **et primam ante aciem...:** this line conveys the brothers' boldness in battle, fighting in the front lines. **feruntur:** often used of hurried movement (cf. 156).

674-7. In this simile, Catillus and Coras are compared to centaurs racing down from mountains in Thessaly. In the hymn to Hercules at 8.285-305, Hercules' killing of the centaurs Hylaeus and Pholus is a great deed (8.293-4). Centaurs are often portrayed as figures threatening to civilization. How, then, should the simile affect our understanding of Catillus and Coras?

674-5. **ceu...cum:** "as when." **nubigenae:** masculine compound adjective (*nubigena, -ae*, m.), seemingly coined by Vergil and modifying *Centauri* (675). When Ixion tried to rape Juno, Jupiter substituted a cloud in her form; the Centaurs resulted and were thus "cloud-born." **Homolen...Othrym:** Thessalian mountains; Greek accusatives, objects of *linquentes* (676).

676-7. **linquentes:** this word echoes *linquunt* in 670; it is there used of Catillus and Coras, and thus ties the brothers and the centaurs closer together. **dat...silva locum...cedunt virgulta...:** theme and variation*. Notice how nature (*ingens silva, virgulta*) is personified* in its reaction and yielding to the Centaurs (cf. 674-7 n.). **euntibus:** dative of indirect object; i.e., the Centaurs (675).

678-90. Caeculus, the founder of Praeneste.

Caeculus leads an army from Praeneste, a prominent town in Latium. He is the son of Vulcan and thus (like Aventinus) a demigod. His story was known as early as Cato the Elder (fragment 67 in *FRH* 2; cf. Servius ad 7.678); his lineage and name (see *FRH* 3.114-16; O'Hara (1996 = 2017) 193-4) connect him to another son of Vulcan, the monster Cacus. Caeculus appears only one other time—at 10.543-4, where, with Umbro (750-60 n.), he resists Aeneas' furious onslaught following Pallas' death.

Caeculus' Praeneste was a prominent town in Latium. Though allied with Rome by the early fifth century BCE, it resisted Rome in the fourth century and joined the Latin revolt of 340-338 BCE in especially close association with Tibur (cf. 670-7 n.). Praeneste was defeated in 338 BCE and ceded some territories but retained its independent status until it received Roman citizenship as a result of the Social War (91-88 BCE). It played an important role in 82 BCE at the end of Marius and Sulla's civil wars (Appian, *Civil Wars* 1.87-94), and later provided a retreat for Lucius Antony and Fulvia (Marc Antony's brother and wife), as they orchestrated the resistance to Octavian (i.e., Augustus) that ultimately led to the Perusine War (41-40 BCE) (Appian, *Civil Wars* 5.21-9). For Praeneste in Vergil, see McKay (1970) 169-72.

Volcano genitum pecora inter agrestia regem
inventumque focis omnis quem credidit aetas,   680
Caeculus. hunc legio late comitatur agrestis:
quique altum Praeneste viri quique arva Gabinae
Iunonis gelidumque Anienem et roscida rivis
Hernica saxa colunt, quos, dives Anagnia, pascis,
quos, Amasene pater. non illis omnibus arma   685
nec clipei currusve sonant; pars maxima glandes

---

678. **Nec...defuit...Caeculus (681):** note the litotes* (i.e., Caeculus was also present) and the long delay of the warrior's name, which allows us first to learn of his identity as Praeneste's founder and of his divine lineage (879-80). **Praenestinae fundator...urbis:** i.e., Caeculus (681), Vulcan's son. *Praenestinae* is an adjectival form of *Praeneste* (cf. 678-90 n.).

679-80. **Volcano...quem...aetas:** long relative clause with the delay of *quem*, whose antecedent is *fundator* (678 n.); *regem* should be construed closely with *quem*, perhaps "whom, a king,..." *Volcano* is ablative of origin after *genitum* (cf. 152 n.). **genitum...inventum:** sc. *esse*; infinitives in indirect discourse after *credidit*. **focis:** "hearth," ablative of place. Caeculus, found on a hearth, was thus thought to be Vulcan's son. **omnis...aetas:** "every age" or "generation," subject of *credidit*.

681. **Caeculus:** 678-90 n. His name may be a diminutive of *caecus* ("blind") because "he was found at a hearth, and had little eyes because of his exposure to the smoke" (see O'Hara (2017) 194 on Servius and the Scholia Veronensia). **hunc:** i.e., Caeculus.

682-3. **viri:** postcedent of the first *quique* (cf. 554 n.), antecedent of the second *quique* and then of *quos...quos* (684-5); the relative clauses explain the people who make up Caeculus' *legio... agrestis* (681). **altum Praeneste:** *Praeneste* (here neuter, but feminine at 8.561) was an important city (modern Palestrina) southeast of Rome (see 678-90 n.); *altum* is an etymological gloss, since the city sits "high" on a hill (cf. O'Hara (1996 = 2017) 194). **Gabinae | Iunonis:** the town Gabii (adjective *Gabinus*), located between Rome and Praeneste, apparently had a temple to Juno, though no certain remains of it survive. An inconsistency is created here, however, since Gabii is mentioned by Anchises as a city to be founded by the Alban kings (6.773; cf. 712-14 n.). **Anienem:** the river Anio (central Italy). **roscida:** "wet," modifying *saxa* (684). **rivis:** "streams"; ablative after *roscida*.

684. **Hernica saxa:** the Hernici inhabited the area in Latium between the Liris river and the Fucine lake. A bilingual etymological wordplay* might be present, since (according to Servius) *herna* meant "rock" in Sabine (O'Hara (1996 = 2017) 194; Ferriss-Hill (2011) 267-70). **Anagnia:** an important Hernican town. **pascis:** this reading creates a double apostrophe* (to Anagnia and to Amasenus in 685). (Another reading, *pascit*, is attested; however, it would require (perhaps a bit awkwardly) that in the next line we still understand *pascis*, since *Amasene* is vocative and thus in an apostrophe*.)

685-6. **quos, Amasene pater:** an apostrophe*; supply *pascis* from 684. The Amasenus is a small river in Latium that reaches the sea west of Anxur (cf. 799 n.); *pater* is an honorific for river-gods, cf. 8.540 *Thybri pater*. **illis omnibus:** Caeculus' troops; not dative of possessor construed with *arma* (*sunt*), but dative of reference after *sonant*. The phrase *nec clipei currusve* stands in

liventis plumbi spargit, pars spicula gestat
bina manu, fulvosque lupi de pelle galeros
tegmen habent capiti; vestigia nuda sinistri
instituere pedis, crudus tegit altera pero. 690
At Messapus, equum domitor, Neptunia proles,

---

apposition to and elaborates on *arma*. The point is that these warriors do not use standard weaponry. **glandes:** from *glans, glandis*, f., "acorn," but also, as here, an acorn-shaped ball for slingshots.

687-8. **liventis plumbi:** genitive of description after *glandes; liventis* (from *liveo*, (2)), "lead-colored." **spargit:** cf. 551 n. **spicula... | bina:** "two spears (at a time)"; carrying two weapons is a Homeric detail. **galeros:** (helmet-like) caps made of animal hide.

689-90. **tegmen...capiti:** *tegmen = tegimen* ("protection"); *capiti* is dative of reference. The phrase stands in apposition to *fulvos...galeros* in the previous line. **habent:** note the change to a plural verb, whereas the previous two clauses used the collective noun *pars* with singular verbs. **vestigia nuda sinistri | ...pedis:** *vestigia* are "footprints," but here "soles"; the entire phrase, "bare soles of the left foot." **instituere:** gnomic perfect expressing custom, "set down," "plant" (*instituo*). **crudus:** the boot's hide is "raw" or "untanned." **altera:** supply *vestigia*; the "other soles" are those of the right foot, which is covered by a boot (*pero*). This description in 689-90 is difficult, but the left foot is bare, seemingly to provide a grip for slingers (Horsfall). **pero:** *-onis*, m., a leather boot.

691-705. Messapus and his army from southern Etruria.

Messapus is the son of Neptune, a lineage first found in Vergil. He leads the Faliscans and others from southern Etruria (cf. 695-7 with notes; for the Etruscans, cf. 647-54 n.), another Vergilian innovation. Messapus was normally associated with Messapia in southern Italy, which had not earlier been part of the Aeneas tradition. (Cf. Halaesus' geographical transposition: he was originally connected to the Falisci but in Vergil placed in Northern Campania, 723-32 n.) Messapus is a prominent fighter on Turnus' side (here; 8.6; 9.27, 124, 160, 351, 365, 458, 523; 10.354, 749; 11.429, 464, 518, 520, 605; 12.128, 289, 294, 488, 550, 661). His plundered helmet plays an important role in Nisus and Euryalus' story (9.365-74, 9.457-8), in which it reflects moonlight and betrays Euryalus to the enemy.

Messapus' people lived to the north of Rome in Southern Etruria and were often aligned with Etruscan interests in their resistance to Roman domination, supporting Veii in 396 BCE and Tarquinia in 358 BCE. Though there were alternating alliances with and struggles against Rome over the following century, Falerii, the most important Faliscan city, was destroyed by the Romans in 241 BCE. For a description of the geography of the Falisci and in particular the location of Fescennium (695-6 n.), see Tilly (1977). For the placement and interpretation of Messapus' entry, see O'Hara (1989) and Malamud (1998). For southern Etruria in Vergil, see McKay (1970) 90-3.

691. **Messapus:** 691-705 n. According to Servius, the great poet Ennius traced his own ancestry back to Messapus (cf. 699-702 n.), though no such Ennian fragments survive for confirmation. Ennius came from Rudiae, a Messapian city in southern Italy. **equum domitor:** cf. 651 n. **Neptunia proles:** see 691-705 n.; Messapus is also so identified at 9.523, 10.353, 12.128.

quem neque fas igni cuiquam nec sternere ferro,
iam pridem resides populos desuetaque bello
agmina in arma vocat subito ferrumque retractat.
hi Fescenninas acies Aequosque Faliscos,   695
hi Soractis habent arces Flaviniaque arva
et Cimini cum monte lacum lucosque Capenos.
ibant aequati numero regemque canebant:
ceu quondam nivei liquida inter nubila cycni
cum sese e pastu referunt et longa canoros   700

---

692. **neque fas...cuiquam:** supply *est*; impersonal construction. The phrase *neque...nec* connects *igni...ferro* (ablatives of means). With his inability to be harmed by fire and sword, Messapus resembles Ovid's Cycnus, another son of Neptune (*Metamorphoses* 12.64-145), cf. O'Hara (1989).

693. **iam pridem:** "now for a long time." **resides:** "inactive." **desueta:** "unaccustomed." This line reworks 1.722, describing Dido, whom Cupid infects with love for Aeneas.

694. **retractat:** "takes in hand again."

695-6. **hi...hi:** anaphora*. **Fescenninas acies:** *acies* (usually "sharp edge," "battle line," etc.) might be best construed here as "(mountain) ridges" (Horsfall). *Fescennium* is a town in Etruria; cf. Tilly (1977). **Aequos...Faliscos:** probably a variant on Aequum Faliscum, a town in the Tiber valley. **Soractis:** genitive; Soracte is a mountain ca. twenty-eight miles north of Rome, famously mentioned in Horace, *Odes* 1.9.1-2 *Vides ut alta stet nive condidum | Soracte*.... **habent:** i.e., "occupy," "live on." **Flavinia...arva:** an unidentifiable location.

697. **Cimini cum monte lacum:** Lake and Mount *Ciminus* are ca. thirty-eight miles northwest of Rome. **lucos...Capenos:** *Capena* was a town at the foot of Mt. Soracte (695-6 n.), and the phrase is probably a reference to the grove of Feronia located there (see *FRH* 3.116 and Horsfall).

698. **aequati numero:** *aequati*, "distributed equally"; *numero*, "in number" or perhaps "in time," "in rhythm." The latter musical meaning ("made equal in time" or "in equal rhythm") would resonate with *canebant* and the singing swans (700-1) in the ensuing simile. See Horsfall ad loc.

699-702. This simile, describing the sound made by the troops, reworks *Iliad* 2.459-63, where Greek troops, pouring forth from their ships onto the Trojan shore, are compared to swans. This Homeric simile is adapted by Apollonius Rhodius 4.1298-1300 (of maids attending Medea) and by Vergil at *Georgics* 1.383-4 (of natural weather-signs). Malamud (1998) argues that, with this simile and catalogue entry more generally, Vergil provides a "complex assessment" (107) of Messapus' "descendant" the poet Ennius (691 n.).

699. **ceu quondam...:** "as at times," initiating the simile (cf. 378 n.). **nivei...cycni:** "snow-white swans." **liquida...nubila:** "moist clouds" (Goold); *liquida* conveys the ancient idea that "the nature of clouds...stands between those of air and water" (Horsfall).

700-1. **cum:** "when." **pastu:** from *pastus, -us*, m., "feeding." **canoros...modos:** "tuneful melodies" (cf. *canebant* 698).

dant per colla modos; sonat amnis et Asia longe
pulsa palus.
nec quisquam aeratas acies ex agmine tanto
misceri putet, aëriam sed gurgite ab alto
urgeri volucrum raucarum ad litora nubem.   705
Ecce Sabinorum prisco de sanguine magnum

701-2. **sonat...pulsa:** "having been struck, the *palus* (and *amnis*) resound," i.e., "echo." **amnis:** the river Cayster in Lydia (in western Asia Minor), famous for its swans, cf. *Iliad* 2.461 and *Georgics* 1.384 (699-702 n.). **Asia...palus:** "Asian marsh," i.e., the marshes along the Cayster (see above). The half-line (cf. 129 n.) in 702 suggests that future revision would have been made; perhaps one of the two comparisons—699-702 or 703-5—would have been omitted.

703-5. In a potential subjunctive (*putet* 704) statement, now the size of the troops (as opposed to their sound) is compared to another flock of birds (cf. 699-702 n.). For these lines, cf. Apollonius 4.238-40 (of Colchian ships): "You would not think so great a host was a fleet of ships, but that a countless multitude of birds in flocks was clamoring over the waves" (Race). (Cf. also Homer, *Iliad* 4.429-30.)

703. **aeratas acies:** "bronze-clad ranks." **ex agmine:** the oldest manuscripts have *EXAGMINE*. Many modern editors (e.g., Fordyce, Mynors, Conte) construe this as an archaic spelling of *examine*, "swarm" (originally of bees); *examine* could also correspond to Gr. *iladon* ("in a mass"), as in *Ap. Rhod.* 4.240 (703-5 n.). Still, *ex agmine* seems to give reasonable sense (cf. Page, Horsfall) and is printed here: "bronze-clad ranks were gathered from so great a column." (The same issue occurs in 2.727 *adverso glomerati EXAGMINE Grai*.)

704-5. **misceri:** here "gather together"; cf. *glomerati* in 2.727 (703 n.). **putet:** potential subjunctive. **gurgite:** *gurges, -itis*, m, "waters," though it more specifically can mean "whirlpool." **aëriam...urgeri...nubem:** an accusative and infinitive construction after *putet* (704). For *nubes*, cf. 793 *nimbus peditum*; *nubes* describes a swarm of bees at *Georgics* 4.60.

706-22. Clausus and the Sabines.

Clausus is another hero seemingly invented by Vergil. His historical resonance, however, is more important than his role in the epic (he appears again only at 10.345-52). Clausus is rooted in the historical Sabine figure named Attus Clausus (Appius Claudius in Latin), who moved to Rome in 504 BCE and founded the *gens Claudia* to which Augustus' wife Livia belonged, as did Marcus Claudius Marcellus (Augustus' nephew, son-in-law, and would-be heir, cf. 6.868-86) and Tiberius (Augustus' stepson and eventual heir), who was Claudian on both his mother's (i.e., Livia's) and father's side. By inventing a Clausus for Aeneas' war in Italy, Vergil has given the Claudian family a role in Rome's prehistory.

The Sabines inhabited the region northeast of Rome and were important from early on, as seen in the episode of the "Rape of the Sabine Women," the brief Sabine-Roman regency under Romulus (for both, see 709 n.; Livy 1.9-14), and the Sabine descent of the Roman kings Numa and Ancius Marcius. Throughout the regal period and in the Republic, however, strife intermittently broke out: we know that the Sabines fought Rome in the early fifth century, that they were conquered in 290 BCE, but that they received full citizenship by 268 BCE. For the Sabine region in Vergil, see McKay (1970) 175, 237.

agmen agens Clausus magnique ipse agminis instar,
Claudia nunc a quo diffunditur et tribus et gens
per Latium, postquam in partem data Roma Sabinis.
una ingens Amiterna cohors priscique Quirites,   710
Ereti manus omnis oliviferaeque Mutuscae;
qui Nomentum urbem, qui Rosea rura Velini,

706-7. **Ecce:** cf. 286 n.; supply a verb such as *it.* **magnum | agmen agens Clausus magnique ipse agminis:** Clausus (706-22 n.) is grandly described as *magnum agmen agens* and *magnique ipse* ("himself") *agminis instar*; *instar* with genitive ("the likeness of...") essentially means "like..." (though it is a noun in apposition), thus "and himself like a *magnum agmen*." Note the etymological wordplay*, since *agmen* is formed from *ago* + *-men* (a neuter suffix used to create nouns from original verbs), as well as the soundplay in *magniq(ue)ips(e)* and *agminis*.

708. **Claudia:** 706-22 n. **nunc:** interestingly refers to Vergil's time (cf. 706-22 n.). **a quo:** the antecedent is of course Clausus. **diffunditur:** "is spread out," originally used of water; though singular here, it has two subjects, *tribus* and *gens*. **tribus:** "tribe" (*tribus, -us*, f.), here (like *gens*) modified by *Claudia*.

709. **postquam in partem data Roma Sabinis:** sc. *est*; *Sabinis* is dative of indirect object. After the infamous "Rape of the Sabine Women" during Romulus' reign (portrayed on Aeneas' shield at 8.635, *raptas sine more Sabinas*) and the subsequent resolution, the Romans for a time shared rule of the city (i.e., *in partem data Roma*) with the Sabines. See 706-22 n.

710-17. Note that the description of the towns sending troops with Clausus forms three different tricolon* constructions in 710-11, 712-14 and 715-17.

710-11. These lines contain a tricolon* of subjects (*cohors, Quirites, manus*) with partial asyndeton*; a verb meaning "march" is implied (cf. 706-7 n.). **una:** adverb, "together" (i.e., with Clausus). **Amiterna:** adjective (modifying *cohors*), "of Amiternum," a town northeast of Rome. **Quirites:** i.e., inhabitants of Cures, from which the Romans were traditionally (but wrongly) said to have received the name Quirites (cf. O'Hara (1996 = 2017); Kings Numa and Titus Tatius were born there. **omnis:** better to construe with *manus* (not *Ereti*). **Ereti:** Eretum, a town north of Rome. **Mutuscae:** Mutusca (also Trebula Mutusca), a town northeast of Eretum.

712-14. A tricolon crescendo* of relative clauses (*qui...qui...qui*), within each of which a form of *colunt* ("inhabit") from 714 must be understood; each relative clause then forms the subject of an implied verb "march" (cf. 710-11 n.): e.g., "those who inhabit...(march with Clausus)." **Nomentum:** a town northeast of Rome; anachronistic, since Anchises had foretold its foundation by Aeneas' descendants (6.773; cf. 682-3 n.). **Rosea rura Velini:** perhaps the *Rosei Campi* in the valley by the river *Velinus* (517 n.) is meant. **Tetricae horrentis rupes montemque Severum:** characteristic Vergilian wordplay, "*horrentis* is a gloss...on the mountain name *Tetrica* (cf. the adjectives *taeter*, "foul, horrible" and *tetricus*, "frowning, severe")...*montemque Severum* (or *severum*) is either another mountain with a Latin adjective for a name, or a further gloss on *Tetrica*" (O'Hara (1996 = 2017) 195). **Casperiam:** location unidentified. **Forulos:** Foruli, a town near Amiternum (710). **Himellae:** genitive; a river whose location is uncertain.

qui Tetricae horrentis rupes montemque Severum
Casperiamque colunt Forulosque et flumen Himellae,
qui Tiberim Fabarimque bibunt, quos frigida misit   715
Nursia, et Ortinae classes populique Latini,
quosque secans infaustum interluit Allia nomen:
quam multi Libyco volvuntur marmore fluctus
saevus ubi Orion hibernis conditur undis,
vel cum sole novo densae torrentur aristae   720
aut Hermi campo aut Lyciae flaventibus arvis.
scuta sonant pulsuque pedum conterrita tellus.

715-17. Another tricolon* of relative clauses, this time with polyptoton* (*qui...quos...quos*). As in 712-14, each relative clause serves as subject of an understood verb "march," though each clause now contains its own finite verb (*bibunt...misit...interluit*). **Tiberim**: accusative; cf. 150-1 n. **Fabarim**: accusative; the Fabaris (mod. Farfa) is small river flowing into the Tiber. **Nursia**: a mountainous town in the Apennine Mountains (thus *frigida*), north of Amiternum (710-11 n.). **Ortinae**: the town referenced is unclear. **classes**: "(military) divisions." **Latini**: meaning unclear, since Sabine troops are being described. **infaustum...nomen**: in apposition to *Allia*. **Allia**: at the river Allia, eleven miles north of Rome, the Romans were defeated by the Gauls, who went on to sack the city in 390 BCE.

718-21. As in 699-705, a double comparison evoking the East concludes the entry. There are no clear models, though details perhaps resonate with various sources: e.g., *multi fluctus* (cf. *Iliad* 2.459-68; *Aen.* 6.309-12), Orion (cf. Apollonius 1.1201-2), *densae aristae* (cf. Catullus 64.353-4).

718. **quam multi...fluctus**: "as many as the waves that...." **Libyco...marmore**: i.e., the southern part of the Mediterranean from Libya east to Crete; for *marmore*, cf. 27-8 n.

719. **saevus...**: the constellation Orion (cf. 10.763-7) sets (*conditur*) in November, a stormy period (thus *saevus*).

720. **cum**: temporal, "when." **sole novo**: the precise meaning is unclear, though somehow the scorching summer is indicated, not the "new sun" (i.e., early morning); the phrase might refer to Sirius, the Dog Star (see Krasne (2019)).

721. **Hermi**: the Hermus is a Lydian river (cf. 701-2 n.). **Lyciae**: Lycia is a region in southern Asia Minor.

722. **scuta**: oblong shields used by ancient Italic peoples and later by the Romans. **sonant**: the *scuta* "clang" during the march or when struck by spears (cf. 8.3 *impulit arma*, Fordyce). **conterrita**: "greatly terrified," better construed as a participle modifying *tellus* (thus part of the compound subject of *sonant*) than as a finite verb (with *est* supplied). Note the pathetic fallacy*.

Hinc Agamemnonius, Troiani nominis hostis,
curru iungit Halaesus equos, Turnoque ferocis
mille rapit populos, vertunt felicia Baccho 725
Massica qui rastris, et quos de collibus altis

723-32. *Halaesus and the Northern Campanians.*

Halaesus leads troops from northern Campania (see 733-43 for southern Campania), and is given a Greek origin through his connection to Agamemnon, who led the Greeks against Troy (cf. 723 n.). Halaesus and the Aurunci (727-8 n.) will join Messapus in battle at 10.352-4; after a brief aristeia, Halaesus will suffer what seems a mortal wound from the young warrior Pallas at 10.411-25, though his death is not explicitly described. The placement of Halaesus in Campania is strange, since he was traditionally associated with the town Falerii in Etruria. (Cf. the seeming dislocation of Messapus, 691-705 n.)

The region of Campania plays no role in early historiographical accounts of the Italian war. Its inclusion by Vergil is therefore striking and suggestive (see 614-817 n.). Historically, Roman domination of Campania occurred much later and was intermingled with Rome's strife with the Samnites, who sought to increase their domination in Campania and (simultaneously) to counter Rome's growing influence in the region. From the latter half of the fourth century BCE into the beginning of the third, however, Rome ultimately achieved domination in Campania, though various cities wavered during (e.g.) the Second Punic War (218-201 BCE) and the Social War (91-88 BCE). For this region of Campania in Vergil, see McKay (1970) 227-37.

723. **Hinc**: "next." **Agamemnonius**: adjective, probably meaning that Halaesus was a follower of Agamemnon (not an illegitimate son, a possibility reported in Servius) and thus a *Troiani nominis hostis.*

724. **curru**: dative after *iungit...equos.* **Halaesus**: see 723-32 n. **Turno**: dative of advantage (AG §376).

725-32. Note the rhetorical complexity (cf. 710-17 with notes) in these lines that describe the *mille...populos* (725) under Halaesus' command: first, a tricolon* of relative clauses (*qui... quos...qui...*; "those who/whom") in 725-8; then, a tricolon of nominative subjects (*accola... Saticulus...manus*) in 729-30 that in sense (if not grammatically) stand in apposition to *mille populos.* (Note also the use of polysyndeton* that helps convey the vast array of the peoples that Halaesus leads.) The passage concludes in 730-2 with the mention of three types of military equipment: *aclydes, caetra, falcati enses.*

725. **rapit**: "hastens," "sweeps with him" (Fordyce). **felicia**: "fertile," its original meaning. **Baccho**: "wine" (metonymy*), ablative; construe closely with *felicia.*

726. **Massica**: neuter substantive, referring to the region of *Mons Massicus*, the wine of which was celebrated. **qui**: antecedent is *populos* (725), "tribes who...." **rastris**: *rastrum, -i,* n., "hoe," "mattock"; ablative of means.

Aurunci misere patres Sidicinaque iuxta
aequora, quique Cales linquunt, amnisque vadosi
accola Volturni, pariterque Saticulus asper
Oscorumque manus. teretes sunt aclydes illis   730
tela; sed haec lento mos est aptare flagello.
laevas caetra tegit, falcati comminus enses.
  Nec tu carminibus nostris indictus abibis,

727-8. **Aurunci:** cf. notes on 39 and 206. **Sidicina...iuxta | aequora:** the Sidicini were another ancient Campanian people; *aequor* is literally "level surface" but is often used to mean "sea," or, as here, "plain." *Iuxta* is best taken adverbially ("nearby") with *Sidicina...aequora* a second subject of *misere*. **Cales:** accusative plural, a town a little south of the Sidicini.

728-30. **amnisque vadosi | accola Volturni...:** the river Volturnus was south of Cales (727-8 n.). Note that the syntactic construction changes, and now we are given three nominative subjects (*accola, Saticulus, manus*) describing other peoples who joined Halaesus (cf. 725-32 n.). **Saticulus:** a "Saticulan," i.e., an inhabitant of Saticula, a Samnian town, a little south of the river Vulturnus (see above). **Oscorum:** the *Osci* (or *Opici*) were an ancient people, but here the name is used (as usual) to describe their language, which was spoken by the Aurunci, Samnites, and Sidicini (see above).

730-1. **teretes...aclydes:** perhaps "smooth javelins"; *aclys* is probably a transliteration of Greek *agkulis* ("small javelin"), appearing first here in Latin. **illis:** dative of possession or reference. **tela:** here, "weapons" in a general sense. **haec:** understand *tela*, referring to the *teretes aclydes*. **mos est:** impersonal construction, "it is (their) custom to...." **flagello:** a "strap" on the *aclydes* is used for easier throwing.

732. **laevas:** understand *manus*. **caetra:** a round, leather shield, probably Spanish in origin. **falcati comminus enses:** an extremely compressed phrase, "(they had) curved swords (for fighting) hand-to-hand (*comminus*)."

733-43. Oebalus and the Southern Campanians.
  This section continues the description of Campanian forces joining Turnus' cause (cf. 723-32 n.). The leader of the southern Campanian contingent is Oebalus, who is addressed with an apostrophe* (cf. 733 n.) that adds rhetorical variety to the Catalogue. He seems to have been invented by Vergil and given the name of a mythical Spartan king. As with Vergil's geographical placements of Messapus (691-705 n.) and Halaesus (723-32 n.), we might have expected Oebalus—with his Greek name—to be located farther south in Italy (e.g., in Tarentum, a Spartan Greek colony). Despite his prominence in the Catalogue, Oebalus will not appear again in the epic. For this region of Campania in Vergil, see McKay (1970) 225-7.

733. **Nec tu...abibis:** litotes* and apostrophe* (cf. 744-5, 759-60). **carminibus nostris:** ablative of means. Note that here Vergil self-consciously refers to his poetry and his role as poet (see Dinter (2005) 165-6). **indictus:** "unmentioned."

Oebale, quem generasse Telon Sebethide nympha
fertur, Teleboum Capreas cum regna teneret,   735
iam senior; patriis sed non et filius arvis
contentus late iam tum dicione premebat
Sarrastis populos et quae rigat aequora Sarnus,
quique Rufras Batulumque tenent atque arva Celemnae,
et quos maliferae despectant moenia Abellae,   740
Teutonico ritu soliti torquere cateias;
tegmina quis capitum raptus de subere cortex
aerataeque micant peltae, micat aereus ensis.

734-5. **Telon:** likely invented by Vergil, perhaps to suggest an etymology for the name of his people, the Teleboans, who originally came from NW Greece. **Sebethide nympha:** ablative of origin. Sebethis is a nymph named after a stream near Naples. **fertur:** impersonal, "is said to"; notice how Vergil hedges on Oebalus' ancestry. **Teleboum...regna:** in apposition to *Capreas*; *Teleboum* is genitive plural (see above). **Capreas:** Caprae (mod. Capri) is an island off the coast of the Bay of Naples. **cum...teneret:** circumstantial clause; subject is Telon.

736-7. **iam senior:** emphatically enjambed*, describing Telon; cf. 45-6 n. **sed non et filius arvis | contentus:** construe *et* as "also," taken closely with *contentus*; not satisfied with his father Telon's kingdom, Oebalus expands it. **dicione premebat:** ablative, from *dicio, -onis,* f., "rule," "sway"; *premebat* from *premo* (3), "bear down."

738-41. Another tricolon* of relative clauses (cf. 725-32 n.).

738. **Sarrastis:** accusative plural. Precisely where in southern Campania the Sarrastes lived is debated. **rigat:** "waters," "leads water to." **aequora:** "plains" (cf. 727-8 n.), postcedent of *quae* (i.e., construe as *aequora quae rigat Sarnus*; cf. 554 n.). **Sarnus:** a river south of Pompeii.

739. **quique:** supply *illos* as antecedent and another object of *premebat*. **Rufras...Batulum...arva Celemnae:** a tricolon* of locations unknown but clearly on the mainland opposite *Capreae* (734-5 n.).

740. **quos:** again, add *illos* as antecedent and object of *premebat* (cf. 739 n.). **maliferae:** "apple-bearing," a neologism*. **Abellae:** *Abella* is situated on a hill (cf. *despectant*), the name is perhaps an Italic word that means "apple," thus making *maliferae...Abellae* an etymological wordplay*. See Ferriss-Hill (2011) and O'Hara (2017) 197.

741. **Teutonico ritu:** *Teutonicus* is an adjectival form of *Teutones*, a German tribe that Marius destroyed in 102 BCE; *ritus, -us,* m. ("manner") refers to the use of the *cateia* (see below). **soliti:** "accustomed to"; though nominative, *soliti* modifies *quos* in sense. **torquere:** "whirl," "throw." **cateias:** a *cateia* is a weapon of uncertain type, though in Isidore (*Origines* 18.7.7, early seventh century CE) it is something like a boomerang.

742-3. As in 730-2, this Catalogue entry ends with the mention of three types of military equipment: *tegmina capitum/cortex, aeratae peltae, aereus ensis.* **quis:** i.e., *quibus* (dative). **raptus de subere cortex:** *subere* is ablative of *suber, -eris,* n., "cork-tree"; *cortex* means "bark"; the phrase describes *tegmina...capitum.* **aeratae...micant...micat aereus:** note the chiastic* structure, asyndeton* and polyptoton*.

Et te montosae misere in proelia Nersae,
Vfens, insignem fama et felicibus armis, 745
horrida praecipue cui gens adsuetaque multo
venatu nemorum, duris Aequicula glaebis.
armati terram exercent semperque recentis
convectare iuvat praedas et vivere rapto.
   Quin et Marruvia venit de gente sacerdos 750

744-9. Ufens and the Aequiculi.

Ufens hails from the city of Nersae (location unclear) and leads the Aequiculi, an Italic people inhabiting the Apennine Mountains and defined by their banditry (749). We know little for sure about the Aequiculi, though they may be associated with the Aequi, who strongly resisted Roman expansion in central Italy in the early Republic but were defeated by the end of the Second Samnite War (326-304 BCE) (Livy 9.45, 10.1; McKay (1970) 238). Ufens seems to have been invented by Vergil, presumably to provide a leader for troops from a region that was not traditionally part of Aeneas' war in Italy and must not have had a well-established, traditional figurehead. Vergil has named him after a river in Latium (cf. 802), which also stands behind the name of one of Rome's thirty-five tribes: *tribus Ufentina*. Though Ufens is given the shortest Catalogue entry, he is a prominent ally of Turnus (8.1-8). Four of his sons are taken by Aeneas for human sacrifice in the aftermath of Pallas' death (10.518-20), and he is killed quite suddenly and unremarkably at 12.460, eliciting a despairing comment from Turnus (12.641-2).

744. **montosae...Nersae:** see 744-9 n. **te:** note the poet's apostrophe* to Ufens, cf. 733 n.

745. **Vfens:** 744-9 n. **insignem fama et felicibus armis:** *insignem* modifies *te*; see 655 n. for the construction. Despite his heroic description here, Ufens will die in battle (744-9 n.).

746-7. **horrida:** "rough," "frightful"; the adjective suggests the mountainous nature of the *gens*. **cui:** dative of possessor with *Ufens* as antecedent; supply *erat*. **multo | venatu:** ablative after *adsueta*, modifying *gens*. **duris Aequicula glaebis:** the adjective *Aequicula* (cf. 744-9 n.) modifies *gens* (746), with *duris...glaebis* an ablative of quality, "his clan...Aequiculan, of rugged soil").

748-9. **terram exercent:** "work" or "till the land." **semper...rapto:** this line and a half are adapted by Numanus Remulus while boasting about Rutulian virtues (9.612-13); immediately thereafter he is killed by Ascanius. **convectare...vivere:** both infinitives depend on *iuvat*; the verb *convectare*, "carry in abundance," seems to have been coined by Vergil. **iuvat:** impersonal construction with infinitive, "it is pleasing (to them) to...." **rapto:** neuter participle as noun (59 n.); ablative of means.

750-60. Umbro and the Marsi.

The priest Umbro leads the Marsi (cf. 750 n.), who inhabited a mountainous region by the Fucine Lake, east of the Aequiculi (744-9 n.), and were known as formidable warriors. They fought Rome from 308-304 BCE during the Second Samnite War but, in the end, forged a treaty. Thereafter they were generally loyal to Rome until the early first century, when their demand for full Roman citizenship rights helped lead to the Social War of 91-88 BCE, also

fronde super galeam et felici comptus oliva
Archippi regis missu, fortissimus Vmbro,
vipereo generi et graviter spirantibus hydris
spargere qui somnos cantuque manuque solebat,
mulcebatque iras et morsus arte levabat.   755
sed non Dardaniae medicari cuspidis ictum
evaluit neque eum iuvere in vulnera cantus
somniferi et Marsis quaesitae montibus herbae.

---

called the Marsic War (see 641-817 n.). For more on the Marsi in Vergil, see McKay (1970) 238-40.

Umbro seems an invented character (cf. 752 n.), appearing only one other time (and fleetingly) in the epic, with Caeculus (678-90 n.) at 10.543-4. For intertextual models, see notes on 756-60. Despite the powerful lament described at 759-60 (see notes), Umbro's death is not recounted in the epic. In a landmark article, Parry (1963) reads this passage as embodying a poetic voice that conveys the suffering and loss entailed by Aeneas' fate as opposed to the epic's triumphalist, Augustan voice. See also Moorton (1989), Putnam (1982), and Dinter (2005) 166-8; Martindale (1993b) 40-3 offers a forceful critique of Parry's reading.

750. **Quin et:** "and furthermore" (*OLD* s.v. *quin* 3b). **Marruvia:** adjectival form of *Marruvium*, the main town of the *Marsi* (cf. 750-60 n.) on the *Lacus Fucinus* (cf. 684 n.). **sacerdos:** note the emphasis on Umbro's status as priest; he is not named until the end of 752.

751. **fronde...et felici...oliva:** ablative phrase after *comptus* (*como* (3), "adorn," "deck"); probably hendiadys*, "with leaves of the auspicious (or fruitful, cf. 725 n.) olive." Umbro's priestly wreath is placed on top of his helmet (cf. *super galeam*) and thus contrasts with his military role. If *felici* is translated as "auspicious" or "fortunate," then irony* is at play, since he apparently does not meet a happy end in the war (see 750-60 n.).

752. **Archippi:** genitive; an unknown king. **missu:** ablative, fourth declension, "at the dispatching" or "sending." **Umbro:** 750-60 n. Like Ufens (744-9 n.), Umbro shares his name with a river, though the river Umbro was in Etruscan (not Marsic) land.

753. **graviter spirantibus hydris:** like *vipereo generi*, dative after *spargere...somnos*. *Graviter* (here "harmfully") because the breath of a water snake (*hydra*) was thought poisonous (Servius).

754. **spargere...somnos:** "to spread sleep." **cantu...manu:** i.e., with incantation and handling.

756-7. **sed non...:** note the change of subject from Umbro (*evaluit*) to his magic arts (*cantus... herbae...iuvere = iuverunt*), whose futility adumbrates his death (cf. Homer, *Iliad* 2.859 "but not with augury did he keep off black death," of Ennomos). **medicari:** "heal," "cure," deponent. **evaluit:** "had sufficient force to" (*OLD* s.v. *evalesco* 2a). **eum:** "oblique cases of *is* are very rare in high poetry...here almost with the force of *talem*" (Horsfall). **in vulnera:** *in* with accusative here indicates purpose or a goal. **cantus:** nominative plural; cf. 754 n.

758. **somniferi:** "sleep-bringing," an epic compound adjective modifying *cantus* (nominative plural, fourth declension) and perhaps a neologism*. **Marsis...montibus:** ablative, cf. 750-60 n.

te nemus Angitiae, vitrea te Fucinus unda,
te liquidi flevere lacus.   760
   Ibat et Hippolyti proles pulcherrima bello,
Virbius, insignem quem mater Aricia misit,

---

759. **te...te...te (760):** in this apostrophe* (cf. 733-43 n., 744 n.), note the anaphora* with asyndeton*. For potential models for these lines, see Homer, *Iliad* 2.671-4, Theocritus, *Idylls* 1.71-2; Vergil, *Eclogues* 10.13, *Georgics* 4.465-6, and 750-60 n. By including elements resonant of various genres (e.g., epic, pastoral, love poetry), Vergil adds a surprising but effective note of pathos to the description of a character of no prominence later in the epic. **Angitiae:** genitive; a Marsic goddess, perhaps associated with Medea. The name Angitiae derives from *anguis* (snake) or because Medea in Italy was so-called because her spells could throttle (*angere*) snakes; cf. O'Hara (2017) and Umbro's skills (753-5). **vitrea:** "glass-like," perhaps close in meaning to *liquidi*, "flowing" but also "clear." **Fucinus:** i.e., *Lacus Fucinus* (cf. notes on 684 and 750-60).

760. **te liquidi flevere lacus:** a half-line effective by itself (cf. 129 n.). See Parry (1963) who offers an influential interpretation of this passage as part of his arguments about the "two voices" of the *Aeneid* (cf. 750-60 n.).

761-82. Virbius from Aricia.

The Catalogue returns to Latium with the warrior Virbius from Aricia (ca. sixteen miles SE of Rome; see McKay (1970) 164-7). Virbius is the son of Hippolytus (Theseus' son), who became the object of passion for his stepmother Phaedra. After Hippolytus rejected her sexual advances because of his devotion to chastity, Phaedra killed herself but left behind a letter charging him with rape (cf. *arte novercae* 765). Her husband Theseus called on his own father, the god Poseidon, to punish Hippolytus (*patrias...poenas* 766). While Hippolytus, now banished by his father, was riding by the sea, his horses were frightened by a monstrous bull sent from the sea by Poseidon, and they dragged him to his gory death (765-7). Hippolytus was brought back to life by Apollo's son Aesculapius, assumed the identity of Virbius, and was brought to Aricia (516 n.), where he was associated with the goddess Diana (774-7) and somehow managed to have a son, despite his well-known misogyny. The inclusion of Virbius (Hippolytus' son) is the most striking aetiological* and mythological* innovation in the Catalogue; his entry is also the longest but makes no mention of an army under his command. Virbius will not appear again in the *Aeneid*. (For Hippolytus' story, see Euripides' *Hippolytus* and Seneca's *Phaedra*; his transformation into Virbius seemingly figured in Callimachus' *Aetia* (Harder fragment 190 with n.) and was treated by Ovid (*Metamorphoses* 15.497-546; *Fasti* 6.737-56.)

761-2. **et:** also used to introduce Ufens (744) and Umbro (750); for the delayed connective, see 261 n. **Hippolyti proles:** "child of Hippolytus," a striking periphrasis* for Virbius, since Hippolytus' chastity and denunciation of women were central to his downfall (761-82 n.). **pulcherrima:** cf. 473-4 n. **bello:** dative of purpose after *ibat*. **Virbius:** cf. 776-7 n. **insignem:** cf. 655 and 745. **mater Aricia:** see 761-82 n.; the phrase can identify Virbius' mother as from Aricia, her name as Aricia, or Aricia as being his motherland.

eductum Egeriae lucis umentia circum
litora, pinguis ubi et placabilis ara Dianae.
namque ferunt fama Hippolytum, postquam arte novercae   765
occiderit patriasque expleritsanguine poenas
turbatis distractus equis, ad sidera rursus
aetheria et superas caeli venisse sub auras,
Paeoniis revocatum herbis et amore Dianae.
tum pater omnipotens aliquem indignatus ab umbris   770
mortalem infernis ad lumina surgere vitae,

763. **eductum:** "reared," "brought up" (*OLD* s.v. *educo*[1] 10), though it could also mean "bear," "produce" (*OLD* s.v. *educo*[1] 6). **Egeriae:** a nymph who, later, was the consort of Numa (second king of Rome), and advised him (so Numa claimed) on religious reforms (Livy 1.19). **lucis:** *lūcīs*, ablative from *lūcus*, "grove" (not *lux, lūcis*, "light"). **circum:** note that the preposition is surrounded by its object *umentia...litora*. The language here and in 764 echoes the description of Arcens' son at 9.583-5.

764. **pinguis...et placabilis ara Dianae:** referring both to the worship of Diana *Nemorensis* ("of the grove" or "of Lake Nemi," 516 n.) near Aricia (cf. 761-82 n.) and (presumably) to the rite of the *rex nemorensis* (i.e., Diana's priest), which involved human sacrifice (see Dyson (2001)). Note that *pinguis...placabilis* can modify *ara* (nominative) or *Dianae* (genitive), though hypallage* is involved either way, since *placabilis* ("easily appeased," "placable") more naturally describes Diana, while *pinguis* ("rich") her altar, because of blood sacrifices.

765. **ferunt...Hippolytum...venisse (768):** *ferunt* ("they say") governs the indirect statement; note the delay of the infinitive. **fama:** ablative. **arte novercae:** see 761-82; Phaedra was Hippolytus' stepmother (*noverca*).

766. **occiderit...explerit:** Hippolytus is subject; *postquam* clauses usually take the indicative, but here the subjunctive is used in indirect statement. **patriasque...poenas:** cf. 761-82 n. **explerit:** = *expleverit* (syncope*), "satisfied."

767-8. **distractus equis:** *distractus* (from *distraho* (3)) means "torn apart"; the phrase is an etymological wordplay* on Hippolytus' name (Gr. *hippo*-, "horse"; Gr. *lutos*, "destroyed," "broken apart"), cf. O'Hara (2017) 198-9 and the gruesome punishment of Mettus Fufetius (depicted on Aeneas' shield, 8.642-5; Livy 1.24, 28). **superas...sub auras:** cf. 527 n. **venisse:** see 765 n.

769. **Paeoniis:** the Greek Παιώνιος, "healer," used of Apollo in his medical role, but here referring to the powers of his son Aesculapius, who healed Hippolytus (cf. 772-3 n.). The -*o*- in *Paeoniis* is naturally long but shortened for metrical purposes. **Dianae:** cf. 761-82 n., 764 n.

770-1. **pater omnipotens:** cf. 428 n. **aliquem indignatus ab umbris | mortalem infernis... surgere:** i.e., Hippolytus was brought back to life (thus *ab umbris...surgere*), despite the anger of Jupiter (*indignatus* from *indignor*, "be displeased" or "angry at"). Note the juxtaposition of *mortalem* and *infernis* (cf. 312 n.) with interlocking word order* (*aliquem...umbris | mortalem infernis*).

ipse repertorem medicinae talis et artis
fulmine poenigenam Stygias detrusit ad undas.
at Trivia Hippolytum secretis alma recondit
sedibus et nymphae Egeriae nemorique relegat,   775
solus ubi in silvis Italis ignobilis aevum
exigeret versoque ubi nomine Virbius esset.
unde etiam templo Triviae lucisque sacratis
cornipedes arcentur equi, quod litore currum
et iuvenem monstris pavidi effudere marinis.   780
filius ardentis haud setius aequore campi
exercebat equos curruque in bella ruebat.

772-3. **repertorem medicinae talis et artis:** "the inventor of such medicine and skill," i.e., "of such medical art" (hendiadys*). The phrase is a periphrasis* for Aesculapius, who was the son of Coronis and Apollo, whose healing powers he received (769 n.). **poenigenam:** "punishment-born"; the better attested but more difficult reading (forcefully advocated by Horsfall) that refers to Aesculapius' violent 'birth,' which occurred when Apollo or Artemis killed his mother Coronis (pregnant with Aesculapius) as punishment for adultery, but saved the baby, cf. Ovid, *Met.* 2.596-632. (The other possible reading *Phoebigenam*, "born of Apollo," is also effective and is preferred, e.g., by Hirtzel, Mynors, and Conte.) **detrusit:** see 468-9 n.

774. **Trivia:** i.e., Diana, cf. 516 n. Hippolytus was a devotee of Diana/Artemis. **secretis...recondit | sedibus (775):** Diana hides Hippolytus presumably from further punishment before she sends him to Egeria.

775. **nymphae Egeriae nemorique:** for *Egeriae*, see. 763 n. Construe *nymphae...nemorique* both as datives dependent on *relegat*; the phrase might be considered a hendiadys*, "the nymph Egeria's grove" (Horsfall). **relegat:** "sends away."

776-7. **aevum | exigeret:** "spend his life"; subjunctive (like *esset*) expressing purpose. **Virbius:** the name has been etymologized as *vir* and *bis* (Servius), "twice a man."

778. **unde etiam...:** "wherefore too" i.e., because of the nature of Hippolytus' death (766-7). **etiam:** "even now," referring to Vergil's time. **lucis:** 763 n.

779-80. **cornipedes:** "horn-footed," "hoofed." **quod...:** causal clause. **monstris...marinis:** the huge bull sent by Poseidon, see 761-82 n. and Euripides, *Hippolytus* 1194–1247. **pavidi:** understand *equi*. **effudere:** perfect; *effundo* (3), here "throw from" (a horse or vehicle), *OLD* s.v. *effundo* 12.

781-2. **filius:** the focus returns to Hippolytus'/Virbius' son, the warrior Virbius. **ardentis:** construe with *equos* (782). **haud setius:** "none the less" (*OLD* s.v. *setius* 2c); Virbius' enthusiasm for horses is startling, given his father's gruesome death and Trivia's consequent prohibition on horses (779-80). **aequore:** 727-8 n. **curru:** cf. notes on 163 and 655. **ruebat:** "was rushing," perhaps with a heightened sense of impetuosity.

> Ipse inter primos praestanti corpore Turnus
> vertitur arma tenens et toto vertice supra est.
> cui triplici crinita iuba galea alta Chimaeram 785
> sustinet Aetnaeos efflantem faucibus ignis;
> tam magis illa fremens et tristibus effera flammis
> quam magis effuso crudescunt sanguine pugnae.

783-802. Turnus and the Rutulians.

Turnus, Aeneas' main foe and rival for Lavinia, leads the Rutulians. His Catalogue entry focuses not on his background (which was given earlier, see 55-7, 365-72, 406-45 with notes; cf. McKay (1970) 157-9) but on his heroic appearance and his troops. Surprisingly, his entry does not serve as the Catalogue's culmination, nor does it mention his claim on Lavinia's hand in marriage, the main cause for which he fights the Trojans.

In the entry's first half (783-92), Turnus' armor is described in mini-ecphrases* containing images that capture his complex nature (see especially Gale (1997)). His helmet is decorated with a fire-breathing Chimaera, perhaps resonating with Turnus' role in violently opposing Aeneas and thus fate (785-6 n.). Turnus' shield, however, bears a depiction of the Argive princess Io in her cow form (for the story see 789-92 n.), an innocent victim of Jupiter and Juno's passions and thus perhaps symbolic of Turnus, who is infuriated by Juno to fight Aeneas. The second half of the entry (793-802) provides an impressive list of towns that have sent Turnus troops, thereby underscoring his great stature.

For Turnus' ancestry, see especially Mackie (1991b) and Hannah (2004). For his helmet and shield, see S. Small (1959), Putnam (1970: 424-6 = 1995b: 113-15), Breen (1986), Hardie (1986) 118-19, O'Hara (1990) 78-81, M. F. Williams (1993), (especially) Gale (1997), and Thomas (1998) 285-8.

783. **Ipse...Turnus:** note the hyperbaton* and enclosing line structure, giving emphasis to the name. **praestanti corpore:** ablative of description; cf. notes on 473-4 and 649-50.

784. **vertitur:** middle sense, "moves about" (*OLD* s.v. *verto* 3). **et toto vertice supra est:** *supra* is adverbial; *toto vertice*, ablative of degree of difference. Like the best epic heroes, Turnus towers above everyone else. Note the wordplay in *vertitur...vertice* (also in 11.683).

785-8. Turnus' helmet (cf. 783-802 n.) is decorated with the Chimaera, a tri-form monster (lion in front, goat in middle, dragon in back) that, at 6.288, sits by the underworld's entrance.

785-6. **cui:** connecting relative pronoun; antecedent is Turnus. **triplici...iuba:** "triple plume," ablative. **crinita:** literally "covered with hair," but here "bedecked"; modifying *galea*. **Chimaeram:** 785-8 n. **Aetnaeos...ignis:** the Chimaera's "flames" are thus metaphorically connected to the Giants, who were defeated by Jupiter and the Olympians, buried under Aetna, the volcano in Sicily, and thus the source of flaming eruptions there, cf. 3.578-82 and Hardie (1986) 118-10.

787-8. **tam magis illa fremens...effera...quam magis...crudescunt...pugnae:** an archaic construction (according to Quintilian (9.3.15)); "the more she is raging and savage..., the more the fighting grows violent." The vivid depiction almost brings the Chimaera to life. **illa fremens...effera:** i.e., the Chimaera. **tristibus:** here, "harsh." **crudescunt:** "grow worse" or "violent," possibly a Vergilian neologism*.

at levem clipeum sublatis cornibus Io
auro insignibat, iam saetis obsita, iam bos, 790
argumentum ingens, et custos virginis Argus,
caelataque amnem fundens pater Inachus urna.
insequitur nimbus peditum clipeataque totis
agmina densentur campis, Argivaque pubes
Auruncaeque manus, Rutuli veteresque Sicani, 795

789-92. Turnus' shield is adorned with Io's story (783-802 n.). Io was seduced by Jupiter, roused the jealousy of Juno, was turned into a cow (by Jupiter or Juno), and tracked by the hundred-eyed Argus. (See Ovid, *Metamorphoses* 1.588-746; the neoteric poet Calvus wrote an *epyllion* (little epic) called *Io*, but it unfortunately is almost all lost.) Once again, Turnus' Argive ancestry is emphasized (cf. notes on 371-2, 409-10), now with Io, an Argive woman victimized by the gods, cf. 783-802 n. (Note that the sword-belt Turnus strips from Pallas is decorated with the story of the Argive Danaids, 10.497-9.) Quint (2018) 117 points to the strong (and perhaps somewhat humorous) contrast between Turnus' shield (featuring a cow) at the end of Book 7 and the glorious shield of Aeneas at the end of Book 8.

789. **levem:** from *lēvis* ("smooth"), not *lĕvis* ("light").

790. **auro:** Io was represented on the shield "in gold." **insignibat:** "adorned" (with an *insigne*, cf. 656-7 n.), "emblazoned," cf. 485-6 n. **iam saetis obsita, iam bos:** *obsita* (from *obsero* (3), here "cover") modifies Io, depicted as already transformed into a cow (789-92 n.); *saetae* are "bristles." The monosyllabic line ending in *bos* (cf. 592 n.) perhaps gives some emphasis to the metamorphosis.

791. **argumentum:** an artistic "theme" or "subject" (*OLD* s.v. *argumentum* 5b). **Argus:** cf. 789-92 n. There may be wordplay with *argumentum* and *Argus* (see Adkin (2011)).

792: **caelata...urna:** enclosing adjective/noun structure; ablative. *Caelata* is from *caelo* (1), "engrave." **amnem fundens:** river-gods were often depicted spilling water from an urn. **Inachus:** a river-god, Argive king and Io's father (mentioned by Amata in 372).

793. **insequitur:** note the emphatic initial placement, signaling a change of focus toward the troops. **nimbus peditum:** *peditum* is genitive plural from *pedes*, here "foot-soldier"; *nimbus peditum* translates a Homeric phrase (*Il.* 4.274), cf. also 704-5 n. **clipeata:** "armed with a shield," from *clipeo* (1). **totis...campis (794):** ablative of place where (without preposition), "throughout all the fields" (AG §429.2).

794. **densentur:** not *denso* (1), but *denseo* (2) "crowd together"; Vergil emphasizes the large number of Turnus' troops, underscored as well by the polysyndeton* in 794-6. **Argiva:** Turnus is from Ardea, but both his and Ardea's Argive ancestry are again emphasized, cf. notes on 789-92.

795. **Auruncae:** adjective modifying *manūs*, here "troops." The Aurunci (cf. 727-8 n.) had also been mentioned as contributing troops to Halaesus from Northern Campania. **Sicani:** an ancient people of disputed origin but who would later settle in Sicily.

et Sacranae acies et picti scuta Labici;
qui saltus, Tiberine, tuos sacrumque Numici
litus arant Rutulosque exercent vomere collis
Circaeumque iugum, quis Iuppiter Anxurus arvis
praesidet et viridi gaudens Feronia luco; 800
qua Saturae iacet atra palus gelidusque per imas
quaerit iter vallis atque in mare conditur Vfens.
   Hos super advenit Volsca de gente Camilla

---

796. **Sacranae:** modifying *acies*. The identity of the Sacrani is not understood. **picti scuta Labici:** *scuta* is accusative of respect, with the passive participle *picti* transferred (enallage*) from the shields to the Labici themselves, although *picti* might also be construed as middle, taking *scuta* as object. *Labici* is a Vergilian neologism* (cf. *Labicani*) for people from Labicum, a town southeast of Rome in Latium.

797. **qui saltus, Tiberine, tuos:** apostrophe* (cf. notes on 685, 733-43, 750-60) to the god of the Tiber river (cf. 150-1 n.). **sacrumque Numici | litus:** for the river Numicus (also Numicius), cf. notes on 136-8, 150-1; *sacrum* is used proleptically* because on the shore of the Numicus Aeneas would ultimately die while fighting, and become a god (Livy 1.2.6).

798. **exercent:** cf. 748-9 n.

799. **Circaeumque iugum:** cf. 10-24 n. **quis...arvis:** *quis= quibus*; the phrase is dative after *praesidet* ("preside," "reign"). We would, however, have expected *arva* as accusative object of *exercent* and postcedent (554 n.) of *quis* (=*quibus*), but instead *arva* seems attracted to the dative case of *quis*. **Anxurus:** adjectival form of *Anxur*, an ancient town on the coast of Latium, later called Terracina.

800. **praesidet:** "preside" or "reign over" (with dative). **Feronia:** like Iuppiter Anxurus, also a subject of *praesidet*. Feronia was a Sabine goddess and mother of Erulus, a king of Praeneste (678-90 n.), whom Evander killed (8.563-7).

801-2. **qua:** "where." **Saturae:** a corrupt manuscript reading. A small river is indicated, but *Satura* is unknown. A reference to the river Astura in Latium is perhaps meant. **Ufens:** cf. 744-9 n.

803-17. Camilla and the Volsci.

   The Catalogue ends surprisingly—not with Turnus, but with the woman warrior Camilla. She has been created by Vergil and has two important models from earlier in the epic who also embrace traditionally male roles: the Amazonian warrior Penthesilea (1.490-3) and the Carthaginian queen Dido. (Artemisia, appearing last in Herodotus' Catalogue of Persian Forces (7.99), has also been seen as a model.) Both Penthesilea and Dido, however, die tragically and might be read as models suggesting Camilla's ultimate doom.

   Camilla is depicted as a person of wondrous abilities and as a person whose physical presence is an object of wonder. Yet her interest in luxury that draws the gaze of her people (812-15) will lead to her demise in Book 11: there, in the midst of her aristeia, she is distracted by the unusual clothing of the Trojan priest Chloreus and is then fatally wounded by the Etruscan warrior Arruns (11.768-835).

agmen agens equitum et florentis aere catervas,
bellatrix, non illa colo calathisve Minervae   805
femineas adsueta manus, sed proelia virgo
dura pati cursuque pedum praevertere ventos.
illa vel intactae segetis per summa volaret
gramina nec teneras cursu laesisset aristas,

Camilla leads the Volsci, an Italic people who, in the sixth century BCE, migrated from the central Apennines to the southern region of Latium and, by the early fifth century, began to dominate there. Frequently resisting Roman influence, the Volsci were subdued by the end of the fourth century and then fully Romanized.

For more on Camilla, see Courtney (1988), Tarleton (1989), Boyd (1992), Mack (1999) 146-7, Keith (2000) 27-31, Nelis (2001) 308-9, Fratantuono (2007) 226-9 with n. 29, Viparelli (2008) 9-12, and Sharrock (2015) 157-68.

803. **Hos super:** cf. *inter primos* (783, Turnus). The preposition (*super*, here "in addition to") follows its object *hos* (i.e., all the warriors already described; anastrophe*). Camilla is presented as a kind of epilogue to the entire Catalogue. **Volsca de gente:** cf. 803-17 n. **Camilla:**. she was named after her mother Casmilla (11.542-3); *camilla/casmilla*, however, also can mean "an attendant for sacred rites" (Varro, *De Lingua Latina* 7.34), and *Camillus* is Etruscan for Mercury (Callimachus, fr. 723) (Horsfall).

804. **agmen agens:** cf. 706-7 n. **florentis:** unusual for describing troops; here probably "shining" (*OLD* s.v. *floreo* 2a). The line appears again at 11.433 describing Camilla.

805-6. **bellatrix:** "female warrior," a word first found in the *Aeneid*, at 1.493 of Penthesilea (cf. 803-17 n.). **colo:** dative, "distaff" (a staff or spindle on which wool is wrapped). **calathis:** "baskets," like *colo* dative after *adsueta manus* ("having accustomed her hands to"). **Minervae:** one of the goddess' special arts was weaving (cf. her contest with Arachne in Ovid, *Metamorphoses* 6.1-145)—thus the baskets and distaff are connected to her (see above). **virgo:** unnecessary but added to underscore Camilla's rejection of traditionally female pursuits.

807. **pati:** construe with *dura*, "hardy" or "able to endure." This is a mainly poetic usage of the infinitive after an adjective (see AG §461). **cursuque pedum praevertere ventos:** the idea of "out-running the winds" develops Catullus 64.340-1 (Achilles outrunning deer), but the theme is also found in Greek epic and tragedy (see Horsfall).

808-11. Camilla's running speed (807) is elaborated in lines modeled on Homer, *Iliad* 20.227-9, describing half-divine horses that "would pass along the tassels of corn and not break the divine yield, | but again, when they played across the sea's wide ridges | they would run the edge of the wave where it breaks on the gray salt water" (Lattimore). Apollonius, *Argonautica* 1.182-4 is also a source, see Nelis (2001) 309. Camilla's miraculous speed becomes a model for Atalanta's race in Ovid (*Metamorphoses* 10.654-5).

808-9. **intactae:** "untouched," modifying *segetis*. **per:** here "over," not "through," since *nec... laesisset* suggests that Camilla causes no damage. **summa...gramina:** "topmost grass-blades." **volaret...laesisset:** potential subjunctives referring to past time; the pluperfect subjunctive *laesisset* conveys an action prior to that conveyed by the imperfect subjunctive *volaret*.

vel mare per medium fluctu suspensa tumenti, 810
ferret iter celeris nec tingeret aequore plantas.
illam omnis tectis agrisque effusa iuventus
turbaque miratur matrum et prospectat euntem,
attonitis inhians animis ut regius ostro
velet honos levis umeros, ut fibula crinem 815
auro internectat, Lyciam ut gerat ipsa pharetram
et pastoralem praefixa cuspide myrtum.

810-11. **per**: cf. 808-9 n. **fluctu suspensa tumenti**: a miraculous feat. **ferret...tingeret**: for syntax, see 808-9 n. **celeris**: accusative modifying *plantas* (here "soles of the foot," "feet").

812-17. Note the emphasis on how *omnis...iuventus* and *turba...matrum* view Camilla as an object of wonder (*miratur...prospectat*). Cf. 803-17 n.

813. **prospectat**: "gaze out at," "look intently at" (*OLD* s.v. *prospecto* 1).

814-17. **inhians...ut...ut...ut...**: anaphora* of *ut* in three object clauses governed by *inhians*, "gaping (with awestruck minds) at how..." **regius ostro | ...honos**: here *honos* (cf. 3 n.) means a "mark of honor," i.e., a cloak; purple (*ostro*, ablative) had strong regal (cf. *regius*) associations. **fibula**: here "hair-clasp." **internectat**: "bind together"; likely a Vergilian neologism*, used later rarely. (Note that Dido too was shown in a purple cloak and with a golden hair-clasp at 4.136-9, cf. Boyd (1992) 228.) **Lyciam**: Lycia (in Asia Minor) was renowned for archery (cf. 8.166; Herodotus 7.77). **pastoralem...myrtum**: the shepherd's (myrtle) staff is transformed into a weapon of war (cf. *Geo.* 2.447 *at myrtus validis hastilibus*). For possible metaliterary implications, see Putnam (1970) 419. **praefixa cuspide**: "with a tip fastened at the end."

Appendix 1: Vergil's Meter[1]

Dactylic hexameter was the meter of Homer and later Greek epic. Once it was adopted by the influential Latin poet Ennius in his *Annales* (second century BCE),[2] it became the meter of Roman epic as well. The basic rhythm of the dactylic hexameter can be felt in the following line from the opening of Longfellow's *Evangeline*:

This is the fórest primévál. The múrmuring pínes and the hémlocks

Here five dactyls (búm-ba-ba) are followed by a final disyllabic foot. These metrical units (as with English verse more generally) are created through the use of natural word stress to create patterns of stressed and unstressed syllables. Thus a dactyl in English poetry is a stressed syllable followed by two unstressed syllables (e.g., "Thís is the" and "múrmuring"). In classical Latin meter, however, metrical feet are based not on word *stress* but on the *quantity* of individual syllables (i.e., whether they are long or short). Thus, in Latin a dactyl contains one long syllable followed by two short ones (-⏑⏑).

As the name indicates, "dactylic hexameter" literally describes a line that contains six (Gr. *hex*) measures or feet (Gr. *metra*) that are dactylic (-⏑⏑).[3] In actual practice, however, spondees (- -) could substitute for dactyls within the first four feet,[4] and the line's ending was largely regularized as -⏑⏑/ -x. The Latin dactylic hexameter can thus be notated as follows:

---

1   For more on Vergil's meter, see Jackson Knight (1944) 232-42, Duckworth (1969) 46-62, Nussbaum (1986), Ross (2007) 143-52, and *VE* s.v. meter.

2   The earliest Latin epics by Livius Andronicus and Naevius were composed in Saturnian verse, a meter that is not fully understood.

3   The word "dactyl" comes from the Greek word *dactylos*, "finger." A metrical dactyl with its long and two short syllables resembles the structure of a finger: the bone from the main knuckle to the first joint is longer than the two bones leading to the fingertip.

4   More technically the two short syllables of a dactyl are "contracted" into one long, and a spondee is formed.

– ⏑⏑/ – ⏑⏑/ – ⏑⏑/ –⏑⏑/ –⏑⏑/ –x

(Here, "/" separates metrical feet; "–" = a long syllable; "⏑" = a short syllable; and "x" = an *anceps* ("undecided") syllable, one that is either long or short but in an actual line will be one or the other.)

Very rarely a spondee is used in the fifth foot, in which case the line is called "spondaic."[5]

To *scan* a line (i.e., to identify a line's rhythm and meter), long and short syllables must be identified. A syllable can be *long* in two ways: *by nature*, if it contains a vowel that is inherently long or is a diphthong;[6] or *by position*, if it contains a naturally short vowel followed either by a double consonant (*x* or *z*) or, in most cases, by two consonants, even if one or both consonants are in the next word.[7] In general, all other syllables are *short*.[8] If, however, a word ending in a vowel, diphthong, or *-m* is followed by a word that begins with a vowel, diphthong, or *h*, the first vowel or diphthong is *elided* (cf. *tec(tum) augustum* in 170 below; elided syllables are enclosed in parentheses in the examples below). As a result the two syllables merge and are scanned as one—a phenomenon called *elision*. *Elision* occurs frequently in Vergil.[9]

By applying these rules, we may scan hexameter lines as follows:

āt rēx/ sōllĭcĭ/tūs mōn/strīs ō/rācŭlă/ Faūnī   (*Aen.* 7.81)

nē pĕtĕ/ cōnŭbĭ/īs nā/tām sŏcĭ/ārĕ Lă/tīnīs   (*Aen.* 7.96)

---

5   E.g., 634 *āūt lē/vīs ŏcrĕ/ās lēn/tō dū/cūnt ār/gēntō*.
6   One can determine if a vowel is long by nature by looking the word up in a dictionary to see if it has a macron over it or by checking inflected endings in a grammar (for example, some endings, like the first and second declension ablative singular (*-ā, -ō*), are always long; others, like the second declension nominative neuter plural (*-ă*), are always short).
7   An exception to this general rule: if a short vowel is followed by a mute consonant (*b, c, d, g, p, t*) and a liquid (*l* or *r*), the resulting syllable can be either short or long. Cf. 2.663 where the initial syllables of *patris* and *patrem* are short and long respectively: *natum ante ora pătris, pātrem qui obtruncat ad aras*. It should also be noted that *h* is a breathing, not a consonant; it therefore does not help make a vowel long by position.
8   However, at times a short syllable is lengthened in *arsis* (see Appendix 2).
9   Sometimes, however, a final vowel is left unelided in what is called *hiatus* (see Appendix 2).

flēctĕrĕ/ sī nĕquĕ/ō[10] sŭpĕ/rōs, Ăchĕ/rōntă mŏ/vēbō
(*Aen.* 7.312)

tēct(um) āū/gūst(um), īn/gēns, cēnt/ūm sūbl/īmĕ cŏ/lūmnīs
(*Aen.* 7.170)

When a line is read, a long syllable generally takes twice as long to pronounce as a short, and the first syllable of each foot receives a special metrical emphasis known as the *ictus* (see discussion below).

The flow of a line is affected not only by its rhythm but also by the placement of word breaks. A word break between metrical feet is called a *diaeresis*:[11]

rēppŭlĭt, / ēt gĕmĭ/nōs ē/rēxīt/ crīnĭbŭs/ ānguīs   (*Aen.* 7.450)

Here, *diaereses* (plural) occur after *reppulit, erexit,* and *crinibus* (note how the first diaeresis helps reinforce the syntactic pause after *reppulit*). A word break *within* a metrical foot is called a *caesura*. When a caesura falls after the first syllable of a foot, it is called "strong" (as after *ingens* in 7.170 above); if it falls after the second syllable in a dactylic foot, it is called "weak" (as after *sublime* in 7.170). The most important caesura in any given line often coincides with a sense break and is called the *main* or *principal caesura*.[12] It most frequently falls in the third foot, but also occurs not uncommonly in the second or fourth (or sometimes both). Although word breaks are important mainly because they affect the interplay between *ictus* and word accent (see below), the slight pause implied in the *main caesura* may also be seen to shape the movement of each verse by breaking it into two (or more) parts. Here are the first seven lines of the *Aeneid*, scanned and with the *main caesurae* marked ("||"):

---

10   In the combinations *qu, gu, su* (e.g., *-que, sanguis, suesco*), note that the *u* is consonantal but that the combinations themselves count as a single consonant for the purposes of scansion.

11   When a *diaeresis* occurs just before the fifth foot, it is often called a *bucolic diaeresis* because this type of diaeresis was used frequently in pastoral poetry: e.g., *nos patriam fugimus; tu, Tityre,* || *lentus in umbra* (Vergil, *Eclogues* 1.4).

12   Readers may differ on where (or even if) there is a main caesura in a given line.

ārmă vĭ/rūmquĕ că/nō, ‖ Trō/iāē quī / prīmŭs ăb / ōrīs

Ītălĭ/ām fā/tō prŏfŭ/gūs ‖ Lā/vīniăquĕ / vēnĭt

lītŏră, / mūlt(um) īll(e) / ēt tēr/rīs ‖ iāc/tātŭs ĕt / āltō

vī sŭpĕ/rūm, ‖ sāē/vāē mĕmŏ/rēm Iū/nōnĭs ŏb / īrăm,

mūltă quŏ/qu(e) ēt bēl/lō pās/sūs, ‖ dūm / cōndĕrĕt / ūrbĕm

īnfēr/rētquĕ dĕ/ōs Lătĭ/ō, ‖ gĕnŭs / ūndĕ Lă/tīnŭm

Ālbā/nīquĕ pă/trēs ‖ āt/qu(e) āltāē / mōēnĭă / Rōmāē.

(Note that in line 2, *Laviniaque* is pronounced as four (not five) syllables, as if the second *i* were a consonant.)

In addition to metrical length, words also have a natural accent,[13] which may coincide or clash with the metrical stress (*ictus*) that falls on the first syllable of each foot. Coincidence of word accent and metrical stress produces fluidity in the verse; clashing of word accent and metrical stress creates tension. For example:

```
      +      +       +      +       /      /
āētēr/nām mŏrĭ/ēns fā/mām, Cāī/ētă, dĕ/dīstī   (Aen. 7.2)
```

(Naturally accented syllables are in boldface; "/" = ictus that coincides with word accent; "+" = ictus that clashes with word accent.)

In this line, there are clashes in each of the first four feet (wherein the word accent does not coincide with the verse accent, *ictus*) but coincidence in the

---

13 Disyllabic words have their accent on their initial syllable: *cáris, dábant, mólis*. If, however, words are three syllables or longer, the word accent falls: on the penultima (second to last syllable), if it is long (*ruébant, iactátos*) but on the antepenultima (the syllable preceding the penultima), if the penultima is short (*géntibus, mária, pópulum*).

final two.¹⁴ In creating clashes, the placement of *strong caesurae* is particularly important. For example, "if a word of two or more syllables ends after the first long of a foot (that is, producing a strong caesura), there will be a clash between accent and ictus in that foot," because the final syllable of such words is not accented.¹⁵ The *strong caesurae* in 7.2 (above) after *aeternam*, *moriens*, and *famam* all display this principle well.

The metrical features sketched above were masterfully employed by Vergil, and, in the *Aeneid*, the Latin hexameter reached its height of greatness. While there are many elements that contribute to the grandeur of Vergil's use of meter, two are of particular significance.

First, Vergil managed the sequence of clash and coincidence of word accent and verse ictus in such a way as to achieve a rhythmically varied and pleasing line. In general we find that Vergilian hexameters are characterized by a varied clash of ictus and word accent in the first four feet and by the coincidence of ictus and word accent in the last two feet.¹⁶ A pleasing resolution of stress thereby results at line end. For example:

```
  +    +    /    +         /         /
Ālbānāē cŏlŭĕrĕ săcrŭm, nūnc māxĭmă rērŭm   (7.602)

  /       +      +     +      /      /
sūnt gĕmĭnae Bēllī pōrtāē (sīc nōmĭnĕ dīcūnt)   (7.607)
```

By employing such dynamic interplay between *ictus* and word accent, Vergil ensures that successive verses will sound and "feel" somewhat different, and he thereby avoids the potential monotony of the dactylic rhythm (búm-ba-ba, búm-ba-ba) when *ictus* and word accent coincide. Vergil's rhythmic innovation constituted an advance over his predecessors, such as Ennius, who could write:

```
    /      /      /      /       /      /
spārsīs/ hāstīs/ lōngīs/ cāmpūs/ splēndĕt ĕt/ hōrrĕt
```

---

14   Classical Latin speakers would presumably have pronounced the word accents in reading lines, while still maintaining the basic rhythm of hexameter. Otherwise, the ictus would have transformed the basic sound of the word.

15   Ross (2007) 146. For word accentuation, see n. 13 (above).

16   Vergil sometimes avoids such resolution for special effect, though he does so rarely. For example, in the following line, a clash between ictus and word accent occurs in the final foot: *consili(um,)/ et sae/vae nu/tu Iu/nonis é/**unt** res* (592).

This verse exhibits a coincidence of *ictus* and word accent throughout the entire line.

Second, Vergil looked beyond the individual hexameter as a compositional unit.[17] The dactylic hexameter suggests a natural pause at line end, and it was understandable for poets to complete the expression of a thought by the end of a verse (i.e., "end-stopped" verses*). For example, consider the following passage from Ariadne's soliloquy in poem 64 of Catullus, one of Vergil's most important Latin predecessors:

> nunc iam nulla viro iuranti femina credat,
>
> nulla viri speret sermones esse fideles;
>
> quis dum aliquid cupiens animus praegestit apisci,
>
> nil metuunt iurare, nihil promittere parcunt:
>
> sed simul ac cupidae mentis satiata libido est,
>
> dicta nihil metuere, nihil periuria curant.
>
> (Cat. 64.143-8)

Here, each individual hexameter forms a unit for the expression of a thought. This is not to claim that Catullus' lines (or those of Vergil's other predecessors) are all end-stopped in this way, nor that Vergil did not compose such lines. Nonetheless, in the *Aeneid* Vergil displayed a stronger tendency to express ideas beyond the confines of the single hexameter. *Enjambment** (the continuation of the sense or a syntactic unit from one line to the next), for example, takes on an increased importance, and this is related to Vergil's characteristically paragraphic or periodic style[18]—one that develops ideas over several lines, and has the effect of moving the reader through the narrative at a more dynamic pace. The opening of the poem is an excellent example (1.1-7):

> ARMA virumque cano, Troiae qui primus ab oris
>
> Italiam fato profugus Laviniaque venit
>
> litora—multum ille et terris iactatus et alto
>
> vi superum, saevae memorem Iunonis ob iram,

---

17 The hexameters of the *Eclogues* and *Georgics* function much more frequently than those of the *Aeneid* as individual units of thought.

18 See, e.g., the discussion in Gransden (1976) 45.

> multa quoque et bello passus, dum conderet urbem
> inferretque deos Latio—genus unde Latinum
> Albanique patres atque altae moenia Romae.

Here Vergil uses *enjambment**, a variety of sense pauses (*caesurae* and *diaereses*, see above), as well as other stylistic features such as polysyndeton*, alliteration*, and assonance* to create one sentence that reads like a paragraph. What results is a forceful, metrically varied, and memorable introduction to the epic.

In the *Aeneid*, the Latin hexameter attained a state of refinement that would influence all subsequent poets. Vergil's metrical skill is a fundamental part of his artistry, an aspect of the *Aeneid* that only readers of Vergil in Latin can fully appreciate.

Appendix 2: Stylistic Terms

Vergil's skillful use of language is a defining element of his artistry. He often employs rhetorical figures and stylistic devices to reinforce the content of his poetry. Careful attention should therefore be paid both to what Vergil says and to how he says it. The following list defines many of the terms (primarily rhetorical, stylistic, and metrical) that are encountered in studying Vergil and that are used in the commentary. For more information on the terms, see Lanham (1991), Brogan (1994), and Lausberg (1998). Fuller information on Vergilian style can be found in Jackson Knight (1944) 225-341, Camps (1969) 60-74, O'Hara (1997), Conte (2007) 58-122, and Dainotti (2015). Stylistic analyses of Vergilian passages are presented in Horsfall (1995) 237-48 and Hardie (1998) 102-14.

NB: all line references are to Aeneid 7 unless otherwise noted.

Aetiology (Gr. "investigation of causes"): the study of the origin or cause of a name, event, custom, ritual, etc. Explanations of how something came into being are important elements of Hellenistic poetry, represented most significantly by Callimachus' influential *Aetia* ("Causes" or "Origins"), and thus *aetiology* became an important component of Latin poetry as well. The interest in *aetiology* can be seen in numerous passages in the *Aeneid*, where Vergil explains the origin, e.g., of the port of Caieta (1-4 n.), or of the name *Virbius* (776-7 n.). *Aetiology* is also an important component of numerous wordplays through the epic, see O'Hara (1996 = 2017).

Alliteration: the repetition of a letter or sound in neighboring words, though the term today is most often used of the repetition of initial consonants. (For the repetition of vowel sounds, see *assonance*; of consonants more generally, see *consonance*.) *Alliteration* is frequent in Vergil and employed for a variety of purposes: e.g., to emphasize words, to suggest connections between words, to create effects such as *onomatopoeia* and *paronomasia*, or simply to please the ear. Some examples: *fore...fama fatisque* (79, of a prophecy regarding Lavinia), *deseruere domos...dant colla comasque* (394, of the infuriated Latin *matres*), *stridente sagitta* (531, of the first arrow shot in the Latin war).

Anaphora (Gr. "bringing back"): the repetition of a word at the beginning of consecutive sentences or clauses. It is commonly used, among other effects, to convey emphasis, emotion, or stylistic elevation. Consider, e.g., *dicam horrida bella, | dicam acies* (41-2, Vergil's announcement of the subject matter of Books 7-12:); *iam matura viro, iam plenis nubilis annis* (53, the emphatic description of Lavinia as ready for marriage).

Anastrophe (Gr. "turning back"): the inversion of normal word order involving only two words (Quintilian, *Institutio Oratoria* 8.6.65), usually prepositions and their objects, e.g., *fata per* (234) and *Hos super* (803). The preposition is delayed, thereby putting more emphasis on the initial word. As Quintilian notes, we can also see *anastrophe* in everyday phrases involving certain ablative pronouns and the preposition *cum*, which is treated as an enclitic: e.g., *mecum* (403). *Anastrophe* is a type of *hyperbaton* (see below).

Antithesis (Gr. "opposition"): the juxtaposition of contrasting ideas usually within a balanced or parallel construction. In line 312, Juno expresses her decision to rely on the power of the underworld to achieve her will as follows: *flectere si nequeo superos, Acheronta movebo* ("If I am unable to bend the heavenly gods, Acheron I will incite"). The *antithesis* of *superos* (i.e., heaven) and *Acheronta* (i.e., hell) adds clarity, force, and emotion to Juno's decision.

Apostrophe (Gr. "turning away"): a sudden shift of address to a figure (or idea), absent or present. E.g., *etenim mollis tibi sumere thyrsos, | te lustrare choro, sacrum tibi pascere crinem* (390-1). In this line, the narrator suddenly addresses Bacchus *(tibi...te...tibi)* in describing the Bacchic possession that Amata experiences after her infection by the Fury Allecto. Cf. also the emotional apostrophe (with *anaphora* and *asyndeton*) in the description of how the natural world mourns the warrior Umbro: *te nemus Angitiae, vitrea te Fucinus unda, | te liquidi flevere lacus* (759-60). *Apostrophe* occurs as early as Homer, but in the Hellenistic period it became a characteristic feature. Vergil uses it more discerningly, usually to heighten the emotional register or to vary the pace of a passage.

Archaism: the use of a form or expression that is older or no longer current. It can be introduced for a variety of effects. Quintilian (*Institutio Oratoria* 8.3.24) writes that "age confers dignity, because words which not everyone would have used give style a more venerable and distinguished air. Vergil, with his perfect judgment, used this Ornament with unique skill. *Olli, quianam, moerus, pone,* and *pelligerent* produce a sprinkling of that authoritative air of antiquity, which is impressive also in picture, and which no art can reproduce" (Russell (2002) Loeb). Some examples in Book 7: *dominarier* (70), *ast* (395), *olli* (458), *aquai* (464).

Arsis, lengthening in: the lengthening of a final short syllable of a word when it occurs in *arsis* (i.e., at the first long syllable of a hexameter foot, which receives the *ictus*, the metrical stress). E.g., *regibus omen erāt; hoc illis curia templum* (174). (Note that the *h* in *hoc* is a breathing, not a consonant, so it does not count as a consonant in making a short syllable long by position; see Appendix 1).

Assonance (Lat. "answer with the same sound"): the repetition of vowel sounds in neighboring words or phrases. Latin is rich in vowel sounds, making *assonance* a natural and frequent poetic feature. E.g., *formae magnorum ululare luporum* (18), in which the assonance perhaps conveys the moaning of the men transformed into wolfs, with *ululare* an *onomatopoetic* word. See also *alliteration* and *onomatopoeia*, which often makes use of *assonance*.

Asyndeton (Gr. "unconnected"): the omission of conjunctions (e.g., *et, -que, aut, sed*) between words, phrases, or clauses. *Asyndeton* can convey effects such as emphasis, suddenness, and vehemence. One of the most famous Latin examples is Caesar's *veni, vidi, vici*. Vergil uses *asyndeton* frequently both on a small scale with individual words (e.g., *Tectum augustum, ingens, centum sublime columnis* (170), and on a larger scale with clauses, as in the description of Allecto as *odit et ipse pater Pluton, odere sorores | Tartareae monstrum* (327-8), in which the loathsomeness of Allecto is enhanced by the *asyndeton* (and *anaphora*). Cf. also the following description of Saturn's race (i.e., the Latins): *gentem haud vinclo nec legibus aequam, | sponte sua veterisque dei se more tenentem* (203-4). This last example, which lacks a conjunction between *aequam* and *sponte sua*, can be further classified as *adversative asyndeton* because a contrast is implied: "a race, equitable not by bond nor by laws, [but] controlling itself by its own will and the custom of the ancient god (i.e., Saturn)."

Caesura (Lat. "a cutting down"): a word break within a metrical foot. *Caesurae* (plural) are often described as strong or weak: a *strong caesura* is one that falls after the first syllable of a foot; a *weak caesura* is one that falls after the second syllable of a *dactylic* foot. The most important *caesura* in any given line often coincides with a sense break and is called the *main* or *principal caesura* (indicated by "||" below). It most frequently falls in the third foot, but also occurs not uncommonly in the second or fourth (or sometimes both). For example:

> stānt bēl|lī cāu|sāe, || pūg|nātūr | cōmmĭnŭs | ārmīs   (553)
>
> Pāndĭtĕ | nūnc Hĕlĭ|cōnă, dĕ/āe, || cān|tūsquĕ mŏ|vētĕ   (641)

In line 641, there are *strong caesurae* after *nunc* and *deae*; *weak caesurae* occur after *Helicona* and *cantusque*. (*Weak caesurae* are also described as *trochaic*, since the initial two syllables before the word break form a *trochee* (–◡), as with *-cōnă* above in the third foot.) The *main caesura* may be taken as falling after *deae*. For further discussion and additional examples, see Appendix 1.

Chiasmus (Gr. "crossing"): an arrangement of words whereby parallel constructions are expressed in reverse word order. E.g., *equum domitor debellatorque ferarum* (651, *equum = equorum*). The word "chiasmus" is derived from the Greek letter "chi" because if the parallel constructions are split in half and placed one over the other, an X is formed when the syntactically related words are connected:

> equum   domitor
>   X
> debellator   ferarum

Coinage: see **Neologism**.

Consonance (Lat. "concord"): the repetition of consonant sounds in neighboring words or phrases. E.g., *femineae ardentem curaeque iraeque coquebant* (345). Note the use of *c/q* and *r* sounds in this line (and also the *assonance* involving the vowel *a* and diphthong *ae*). See also *alliteration* and *assonance*.

Dactyl: a metrical foot composed of one long syllable followed by two short ones (–◡◡). See Appendix 1.

Diaeresis (Gr. "division"): A word break between metrical feet. For example, in line 81:

> At rex / sollici/tus mon/stris o/racula / Fauni

Diaereses (plural) occur after *rex* and *oracula*. When a *diaeresis* occurs after the fourth foot (i.e., just before the fifth foot), it is often called a *bucolic diaeresis* because this type of *diaeresis* was used frequently in pastoral poetry: e.g., *nos patriam fugimus; tu, Tityre, || lentus in umbra* (*Eclogues* 1.4). For further discussion and additional examples of *diaeresis*, see Appendix 1.

Dicolon Abundans: the restatement of an initial phrase or clause in different language. For example, when Neptune guides the Trojans to sail safely by the island of Circe, who turns men into beasts, Neptune's intention is described: *quae ne monstra pii paterentur talia Troës...neu litora dira subirent* ("in order that the Trojans not suffer such monstrous things...that they not enter such horrific shores," 21-2). The purpose clause *neu litora dira subirent* is a variation on the idea in *ne monstra pii paterentur talia Troes*: in both cases, Neptune acts to save the Trojans from Circe's devastating magic. The variation does not have to simply repeat the initial idea but can also develop it and heighten its intensity and pathos. *Dicolon abundans* is also called *theme and variation*.

Ecphrasis (Gr. "description"): a detailed and vivid description of an object, person, or event, though in a more restricted sense the term *ecphrasis* was applied to a detailed description specifically of a work of art. Consider, e.g., the description of Turnus' helmet and shield at 785-92. The three most elaborate and important ecphrases of art in the *Aeneid* are the paintings Aeneas views at Carthage (1.418-93), the doors on Apollo's temple at Cumae (6.20-33), and Aeneas' shield (8.626-728).

Elision: if a word ending in a vowel, diphthong, or vowel + *-m* is followed by a word that begins with a vowel, diphthong, or *h*, the first vowel or diphthong is *elided*. As a result the two syllables merge and are scanned as one. For example, in the following lines there are two *elided* syllables (enclosed in parentheses):

> Tēct(um) āū/gūst(um), īn/gēns, cēnt/ūm sūbl/īmĕ cŏ/lūmnīs   (170)
> fēmĭnĕ(ae) / ārdēn/tēm cū/rāē (que) ī/rāēquĕ cŏ/quēbānt   (345)

For further discussion and additional examples, see Appendix 1.

Ellipsis (Gr. "leaving out"): the omission of a syntactically necessary word (or words) that can be inferred from the context. For example, when Aeneas sends envoys to king Latinus, we learn that they act without delay: *haud mora* (156). Here a form of *esse* is omitted but easily inferred, and the ellipsis may help convey the envoys' speed (which is also emphasized by the word that follows, *festinant*). *Ellipsis*, however, also can serve to create "the charm of brevity and novelty" (Quintilian, *Institutio Oratoria* 9.3.58, Russell (2002) Loeb).

Enallage (Gr. "interchange"): the distortion of "the syntactic relations among words: one element of the phrase, often the adjective, is referred not to the element to which it belongs by a logical or grammatical connection, but to another one more or less nearby" (Conte (2007) 70). E.g., when Allecto besets Amata's *limen* ("threshold"), it is grammatically modified by *tacitum* (*tacitumque obsedit limen Amatae*, 343), though the adjective, in sense, better describes the manner in which Allecto was acting, i.e., silently. Another example: Galaesus, one of the first Italians wounded after the death of Silvia's stag, is described as *foedatique ora Galaesi* ("the face of disfigured Galaesus," 575). Here *foedati* ("disfigured") modifies *Galaesi* in grammar, but probably better describes *ora* in sense, thereby suggesting that Galaesus dies from a wound to the face or head. Such instances of *enallage* are also referred to as *transferred epithet* or *hypallage*. But other types of syntactic exchanges fall under the category of *enallage* as well. Consider the following phrase: *visa...longis comprendere crinibus ignem* (Lavinia "seemed to take hold of fire with (or in) her long tresses," 73). Here Vergil has reversed the real syntactic relationship between the words that we would more naturally understand (i.e., the fire seemed to take hold of Lavinia's hair, not that Lavinia seemed to take hold of the fire in her hair.) As these examples show, *enallage* forces us to stop momentarily and puzzle out the semantic and syntactic connections. It occurs much more frequently in the *Aeneid* than in Vergil's other works and can thus be construed as an element of stylistic elevation. See the discussion of these examples and of *enallage* as a defining aspect of Vergil's style in Conte (2007) 70-5. The term *hypallage* is often used interchangeably with *enallage*.

End-Stopped Lines: see **Enjambment**.

Enjambment (Fr. "crossing over," "spanning"): the continuation of the sense or a syntactic unit from one line to the next. This feature is frequent in Vergil and plays with our expectations that thoughts and clauses will be contained within the individual hexameter line. As a result, enjambed words are given more emphasis, which can be heightened if some kind of pause follows, as in the inciteful words of Allecto (disguised as the priestess Calybe) to the sleeping Turnus (423-4):

> rex tibi coniugium et quaesitas sanguine dotes
>
> abnegat, externusque in regnum quaeritur heres.

Here, *abnegat* ("refuses") has been enjambed and is followed by a diaeresis, which gives more force to the outrage conveyed by the verb. Such *enjambment* of the main verb for emphasis is particularly characteristic of Vergil. Lines without *enjambment* are called *end-stopped*.

Epic or Compound Adjective: an adjective formed from two (or more) words. Compound adjectives are frequent in Homer and thus become a characteristic element of classical epic poetry, one that conveys elevated style. E.g., *saetigeri* ("bristle-covered," 17), *alipedes* ("wing-footed," 277), *luctificam* ("sorrow-causing," 324), and *nubigenae* ("cloud-born," 674). Vergil employs compound adjectives with reserve, particularly when compared to his Latin epic predecessors such as Lucretius.

Epithet (Gr. "added"): an adjective or descriptive phrase that accompanies or substitutes for a name. The use of epithets goes back to the *Iliad* and *Odyssey* (e.g., "rosy-fingered" Dawn and "gray-eyed" Athena), where they are important compositional elements for oral poetry such as Homeric epic. In Vergil they become literary devices that help create epic tone. Just as Homer's Odysseus is "of many turns" (Gr. *polytropos*), and Achilles "swift-footed" (Gr. *podas okus*), so Aeneas is *pius* (e.g., 1.220, 7.5, etc.), an *epithet* underscoring the importance of *pietas* for his heroic characterization. Some other examples in Vergil: *infelix Dido* (1.749), and *omnipotens*, used of Jupiter (as *pater*, 7.770) and of Juno (as *Saturnia*, 7.428). Vergil's most frequent epithet is *ingens*, which is used 168 times in the *Aeneid*, particularly to convey the grandeur of heroes and of various elements of the heroic age.

Etymology: the (study of the) derivation of a word. The word *etymology* itself, e.g., is from Gr. *etumos* ("true") and *logos* ("word"). *Etymologies* were particularly characteristic of Hellenistic writers and important for Vergil. E.g., at 761-77, Vergil tells the story of the Greek hero Hippolytus, who had been torn apart by his horses, but was brought back to life as *Virbius* and taken to Italy. Vergil implies that his new name comes from *vir* ("man") + *bis* ("twice"), and thus means "twice a man," or "man a second time." Often we can see Vergil engaging in etymological wordplay (cf. *paronomasia**): e.g., at 1.261-2, we find *fabor...fatorum*, perhaps suggesting the etymological connection between the words, or at 7.79, the relationship of cognate words, such as *fama fatisque* (79). But sometimes wordplay can playfully suggest etymologies that are false, such as *virtute...viribus* (257-8), since *virtus* derives from *vir*, not *vis* (abl. *viribus*). In 684 Vergil might be seen as engaging in bilingual etymological wordplay by describing the Latin word *saxa* as *Hernica*, which is an adjective describing the Hernici, a people living among the Apennines. However, *hernica* is also a Sabine word for "rock" (Servius). Thus *saxa* serves as a Latin gloss for the etymology of the Sabine *Hernica*. See O'Hara (2017) for these and countless other examples of etymological wordplay in Vergil.

Golden Line and Variations: in dactylic hexameter, an artful arrangement of two adjective-substantive phrases with a verb in between. It usually takes the form of ABVab, wherein V is a verb/participle, while Aa and Bb are both adjective-noun phrases and interlocking. E.g.

    A   B   V   a   b

proxima Circaeae raduntur litora terrae   (10)

    A   B   V   a   b

arguto tenuis percurrens pectine telas   (14)

The variation ABVba is often called a *silver line*, in which the two adjective-noun phrases are not interlocking; rather one phrase frames the other. E.g.

    A   B   V   b   a

cetera populea velatur fronde iuventus   (5.134)

The term "golden line" is not an ancient one but dates to the seventeenth century, most famously in Dryden's preface to his *Sylvae* (1685).

Hendiadys (Gr. "one through two"): the expression of one idea through two terms joined by a conjunction. E.g., *radiis...lucis et auro* (142-3) "with rays of light and with gold" might be taken as "with rays of golden light"; *fronde... et felici...oliva* (751) "with leafage and fruitful olive tree" really means "with leafage of the fruitful olive tree."

Hiatus (Lat. "gaping," "yawning"): the "gap" created when two syllables, which would normally be elided (see *elision* above), are not, usually when the preceding syllable receives special emphasis. E.g., 631:

> Ardea Crustumerique et turrigerae Antemnae.

Here, *hiatus* occurs between *turrigerae* and *Antemnae* (i.e., there is no elision between the final *-ae* of *turrigerae* and the initial *a* of *Antemnae*.)

Hypallage: see **Enallage**.

Hyperbaton (Gr. "transposed"): any distortion of normal word order. Because Latin is a highly inflected language, there is much latitude in altering word arrangements without sacrificing clarity of meaning. Indeed *hyperbaton* is a central element of Latin poetry. It includes simple distortions, such as *anastrophe* and *tmesis*, but can also involve more formalized patterns such as *synchysis* (or *interlocking word order*, e.g., *Laurentis tecta tyranni | celsa*, 342-3), *chiasmus* (*equum domitor debellatorque ferarum*, 651 with *equum* = *equorum*), enclosing noun-adjective phrases (e.g., *mollibus...sertis* in *mollibus intexens ornabat cornua sertis*, 488), and *golden lines* (e.g., *aereaque adsensu conspirant cornua rauco*, 615).

Hyperbole (Gr. "excess"): exaggeration, used for emphasis or some other effect. E.g., Latinus received an oracle saying that foreign sons-in-law will come "who will raise the name of our people to the stars," *qui sanguine nostrum | nomen in astra ferant* (98-9). See Quintilian (*Institutio Oratoria* 8.6.67-76), who writes that "Hyperbole only has positive value when the thing about which we have to speak transcends the ordinary limits of nature. We are then allowed to amplify, because the real size of the thing cannot be expressed, and it is better to go too far than not to go far enough" (8.6.76, Russell (2002) Loeb).

Hypermetric Line: a line in which an extra final syllable elides with the initial syllable of the following line. E.g. 470-1:

> se satis ambobus Teucrisque venire Latinis(que).
>
> haec ubi dicta dedit divosque in vota vocavit,

The final syllable (*-que*) of *Latinisque* elides with *haec* at the start of the following line, and we might see this hypermetric elision as adding to the poetic texture. Turnus has just been infected with fury by Allecto; the hypermetric line helps convey his frenzied words and actions. Hypermetric lines do not occur in Homer, though Vergil's Latin epic predecessors such as Ennius and Lucretius employed them. In Vergil they most often involve the elision of -*que* at line end, as here (but see 160-1). As Austin (1955) on 4.558 writes: "it was Vergil who first used [hypermetric lines] for artistic purposes."

Hypotaxis: see **Parataxis**.

Hysteron Proteron (Gr. "later earlier"): a kind of syntactic *hyperbaton* by which the chronological order of events is reversed. For example, at 207-8, Dardanus is described traveling first to Troy and then to Samothrace, though geographically he would have arrived at Samothrace first: *Dardanus Ideas Phrygiae penetrarit ad urbes | Threiciamque Samum, quae nunc Samothracia fertur.* (See also 208 n. for wordplay that might be involved.) Individual cases, however, might be disputed. For example in line 7, Aeneas directs his course before he leaves the harbor: *tendit iter velis portumque relinquit.* Here, however, we might treat the two ideas as happening roughly simultaneously and thus perhaps represent an example of *dicolon abundans**, not an instance of chronological reversal.

Ictus (Lat. "stroke," "blow"): the special metrical emphasis that the first syllable of each foot receives. The dynamic interplay between *ictus* and *word accent* is central to Vergil's metrical artistry. See Appendix 1.

Interlocking Word Order: see **Synchysis**.

Irony (Gr. "dissembling"): saying one thing but with its opposite somehow implied or understood. For example, after Allecto has sown the seeds of strife, she says to Juno: *dic in amicitiam coeant et foedera iungant* ("tell them to unite in friendship and to join in treaties," 546). Of course Allecto actually means the reverse, that such an alliance is no longer possible because of the war she has started. *Dramatic irony* results when the reader or spectator possesses information unknown to a character and consequently interprets the character's words or actions in a different light. Thus, when Juno returns from Argos in Book 7 and sees Aeneas flourishing in Italy, Vergil describes the Trojan hero as *laetum Aenean* (288). The adjective *laetum* involves *dramatic irony*, because Aeneas has no idea that at that moment Juno sees him, she is filled with rage at him and is about to set Italy ablaze with war.

Litotes (Gr. "simplicity"): the description of something by negating its opposite. Because it provides emphasis through understatement, *litotes* can be considered the opposite of *hyperbole* and is not unusual in Vergil. So, when

Latinus accepts the gifts Ilioneus has brought, he uses the language *munera nec sperno* (261). He conveys, through *litotes*, that he is actually happy to receive the gifts. Cf. also *non...indecores* ("not unbecoming," i.e., decorous, 231), *nec...absistit* ("does not go away," i.e., remains, 610).

Metaphor (Gr. "transference"): the application of a word or phrase from one field of meaning to another, thereby suggesting new meanings. E.g., *femineae ardentem curaeque iraeque coquebant* (345). Amata's anxieties and anger are described as "cooking" her, and she herself is "ablaze" (*ardentem*) with anger over the Trojans' arrival and the threat to Turnus' marriage to Lavinia.

Metonymy (Gr. "change of name"): the substitution of one word for another somehow closely related. In Vergil, *metonymy* often involves names, qualities, or attributes. For example, *Volcanus* can stand in for "fire" (77), and *Mars* for "war" (582), *thalamus* ("bridal chamber") for "wedding" (388), and *buxus* ("boxwood") for a "spinning top" (made out of boxwood) (382). But *metonymy* can involve other types of relationships, such as those between cause and effect (e.g., *furorem* for "an act produced by *furor*," 386, see n.). See also *synecdoche*, which is a type of *metonymy*.

Neologism (Gr. "new word" or "utterance"): a newly coined word. E.g., 651 *debellator*, 674 *nubigenae*, 758 *somniferi* (see notes on these lines). Because such words would presumably have seemed unusual to a contemporary reader/hearer, they would have had a special poetic resonance. *Neologism* is also referred to as *coinage*.

Onomatopoeia (Gr. "making of a word" or "name"): the use or formation of words that imitate natural sounds. Individual words may be *onomatopoetic*, as *ululare* at 18 (see n.). *Onomatopoetic* effects can be found in phrases as well. For example, the alliteration of *s* in *stridente sagitta* (531) might suggest the whizzing of an arrow; in *tegmina tuta cavant capitum* (632) the use of *t* and *c* might convey the sound of hammers beating out helmets. *Onomatopoeia* often involves devices such as *alliteration, assonance,* and *consonance*.

Oxymoron (Gr. "pointedly foolish"): the juxtaposition of seemingly contradictory words. For example, in *aereaeque adsensu conspirant cornua rauco* ("the bronze horns blow in raucous agreement," 615), the phrase *adsensu...rauco* combines two seemingly contradictory ideas. Cf. also *festina lente* ("hurry slowly," Gr. *speude bradeos*), a proverb, we are told, that Augustus especially liked (Suetonius, *Augustus* 25.4).

Parataxis (Gr. "placing side by side"): the sequential ordering of independent clauses (as opposed to *hypotaxis*, the subordination of one clause to another). A famous example is Caesar's *veni, vidi, vici*. An example from *Aeneid 7*: *sese referebat ab Argis…prospexit* (286-9). Though the two clauses are independent, in sense one (*sese referebat*, "as she was coming back," see n.) is subordinated to the other (*Aenean…prospexit*, "she saw Aeneas…"). Vergil leaves it to the reader to sense such logical relationships. *Parataxis* is particularly characteristic of Vergil and epic more generally.

Paronomasia (Gr. "slight alteration of name"): a wordplay or pun, usually employing words that sound similar. Consider <u>acris</u> tendunt <u>arcus</u> ("bend their bitter bows," 164), *Fauno Picus <u>pater</u>, isque <u>parentem</u> | te, Saturne, refert* ("Faunus' father was Picus, and he (Picus) claims you, Saturn, as parent," 48-9). *Paronomasia* often makes use of word *etymology* and various sound effects such as *alliteration* and *assonance*, and is a feature of Vergilian poetry that has roots going back to Homer but that bears the special influence of the erudite work of the Alexandrian tradition. In 684 *Hernica saxa* (see n.), Vergil might be seen as engaging in bilingual etymological wordplay by combing the Latin word *saxa* ("rocks") with the adjective *Hernica*, from the Sabine word for rock, *herna*. (See the list and discussion of *paronomasia* in O'Hara (2017) 60-3 with n. 316 and passim.)

Pathetic Fallacy: see **Personification**.

Patronymic (Gr. "father's name"): a name formed by attaching a suffix to the name of a father or other ancestor. E.g., 320 *Cisseïs*, "daughter of Cisseus," i.e., Hecuba; 484 *Tyrrhidae*, "sons of Tyrrhus"; 560 *Saturnia*, daughter of Saturn," i.e., Juno. Patronymics are elevated in tone and characteristic of epic poetry.

Periphrasis (Gr. "circumlocution"): the use of many words to express an idea that could be stated more succinctly, if not by just one word. It is an important element of elevated, epic style, one used by Vergil as a stylistic embellishment, particularly to achieve an elevated or erudite tone, such as in *satus Anchisa* ("the one born from Anchises," i.e., Aeneas, 152), *saeva Iovis coniunx* ("the fierce wife of Jove," i.e., Juno, 287), *tegmina tuta…capitum* ("safe coverings of heads," i.e., helmets, 632).

Personification: a metaphorical use of language whereby an inanimate object or abstract idea is given human abilities or qualities. E.g., at 26 Aurora (Dawn) is shown riding in a rosy chariot (*Aurora in roseis fulgebat lutea* *bigis*), or at 629-30 five great cities are said to forge new weapons (*quinque… magnae…urbes | tela novant*). *Pathetic Fallacy* is a specific type of personification whereby human emotions are attributed to inanimate objects in nature. For example, consider how the natural surroundings mourn for Umbro (i.e., *te*): *te nemus Angitiae, vitrea te Fucinus unda, | te liquidi flevere lacus* (759-60).

Polyptoton (Gr. "in many cases"): the repetition of a word in its inflected cases. When Vergil describes Latinus' palace at 173-5, he uses four clauses in *asyndeton*, each of which begins with a form of *hic, haec, hoc* (in adverbial and adjectival forms): *hic…hoc…hae…hic*. Here *polyptoton* creates an artful, but grammatically varied patterning that adds to the grandeur and authority of Latinus' power and palace. *Polyptoton* can create other effects: at 327-8, the repetition of *odit…odere* enhances the revulsion that even Pluto and the other Furies feel for Allecto: *odit et ipse pater Pluton, odere sorores | Tartareae monstrum* (i.e., Allecto).

Polysyndeton (Gr. "much-connected"): the repetition or excessive use of connective particles (especially *et* and *-que*). For example, Allecto is described as *cui tristia bella | iraeque insidiaeque et crimina noxia cordi* (325-6). With respect to possible effects, *polysyndeton* (and its opposite *asyndeton*) make "our words more vigorous, more insistent, and able to display a force that seems to come from repeated outbursts of emotion" (Quintilian, *Institutio Oratoria* 9.3.54, Russell (2002) Loeb).

Prolepsis (Gr. "anticipation"): the use of a word or phrase that anticipates a later event or outcome. For example, when the shore of the river Numicus is described as *sacrum* in 797, the adjective looks forward to the future, when Aeneas will die on this shore and become a god, i.e., the events that will make the river's shore *sacrum* (see n.). Consider also 350 *fallit…furentem*, "tricks her (into) raging" (of the effect of the Fury Allecto's snake on Amata).

Rhetorical Question: a question that is posed not to receive an answer but for some other purpose or effect. E.g., Juno asks several *rhetorical questions* when she sees the Trojans settling in Italy at 294-6: *num Sigeïs occumbere campis, | num capti potuere capi? num incensa cremavit | Troia viros?* Here, the questions help convey Juno's indignation and anger (as they also do at 1.39-41, 48-9).

Silver Line: see **Golden Line and Variations**.

Simile (Lat. "similar"): a figurative comparison between two different things. It is an important component of epic style. E.g., *saevit amor ferri et scelerata insania belli, | ira super: magno veluti cum flamma sonore | virgea suggeritur costis undantis aëni | exsultantque aestu latices, furit intus aquai | fumidus atque alte spumis exuberat amnis, | nec iam se capit unda, volat vapor ater ad auras* (461-6). In this simile (462-6), the raging of Turnus, who has just been infected by the fury Allecto, is compared to a pot of water boiling over.

Spondaic Line: a hexameter line in which the fifth foot is a spondee (- -), not a dactyl (- ◡◡). E.g. 631:

Ardea Crustumerique et turrigerāē Āntēmnāē

Vergil does not employ spondaic lines frequently. Such lines often involve Greek names (e.g., 8.54 *nomine Pallanteum*, 11.659 *flumina Thermodontis*). In the example above (631), we have the name of an ancient town (*Antemnae*; note also the *hiatus* between *Antemnae* and the compound adjective *turrigerae*, and see 631 n.).

Spondee: a metrical foot composed of two long syllables (- -). See Appendix 1.

Syllepsis: see **Zeugma**.

Synchysis (Gr. "mingling," "confusion"): an arrangement of two phrases (here Aa and Bb) that interweave their members in an ABab pattern. It is also called *interlocking word order*. E.g.,

    A   B   a   b

Laurentis tecta tyranni celsa (342-3)

atra ... strictis   seges   ensibus (525-6)

Syncope (Gr. "a cutting short"): the omission of a letter or syllable from the interior of a word. E.g., 62 *sacrasse* for *sacravisse*, 201 *intrastis* for *intravistis*, and 766 *explerit* for *expleverit*.

Synecdoche (Gr. "understanding one thing with another"): a type of *metonymy* that uses the part for the whole (or the reverse). E.g., *flectere si nequeo superos, Acheronta movebo* (312). Here *Acheronta* (a river in the underworld) stands in for the (powers of the) underworld more generally. Other examples include *carinas* ("keels," 431) for "ships," *tectum* ("covering" or "roof," 59, 170) for "house" or "palace," and *umbonum* ("shield bosses," 633) for "shields." Quintilian (*Institutio Oratoria* 8.6.19) says that "*synecdoche* has the power to vary the discourse, enabling the hearer to understand many things from one, the whole from the part, the genus from the species, the consequences from the antecedents, and vice versa" (Russell (2002) Loeb).

Synizesis (Gr. "collapse"): the collapsing of two vowels into one (a diphthong or simple vowel) to allow a word to fit into a poetic meter. For example, in *alveo* (33) the *e* and *o* combine to form one syllable. Cf. also *deerit* at 262 and *aerei* at 609, both of which scan as disyllables.

Theme and Variation: See **Dicolon Abundans**.

Tmesis (Gr. "cutting"): the "cutting" of the elements of a word (usually a compound word) by interjecting a word or words in between. Most often *tmesis* involves the separation of a prefix, as with *circum...volitans* (104) and *super...est* (559). *Tmesis* involving compound verbs often has an archaic flavor, since in Homer such prefixes function as adverbs and can stand independently, though in later usage they formed compound words. However, *tmesis* can also occur for other reasons, such as the creation of emphasis or for metrical purposes.

Transferred Epithet: see **Enallage, Hypallage**.

Tricolon (Gr. "having three limbs"): the grouping of three parallel words, phrases, or clauses. Consider, e.g., *urbem et finis et litora gentis | diversi explorant* (149-50). Here, there are three accusative objects (*urbem, finis, litora*) of the verb *explorant*. Another example: *qui Nomentum urbem, qui Rosea rura Velini, | qui Tetricae horrentis rupes montemque Severum | Casperiamque colunt Forulosque et flumen Himellae* (712-14). Here, three relative clauses, all dependent on the verb *colunt*, are initiated with *qui* and describe peoples under the command of Clausus; the three elements increase in length, and thus the resulting *tricolon* can be described as *abundans, crescens*, or *crescendo*.

Trochee: a metrical foot composed of a long syllable followed by a short one (–◡). In the dactylic hexameter (see Appendix 1) the final foot is disyllabic and can be either a *trochee* or *spondee*. E.g., *aura* in the final foot of 646 (*ad nos vix tenuis famae perlabitur aūră*) is a trochee.

Word Accent: disyllabic words have their accent on their initial syllable: *cáris, dábant, mólis*. If, however, words are three syllables or longer, the word accent falls: on the penultima (second to last syllable), if it is long (*ruébant*, *iactátos*) but on the antepenultima (the syllable preceding the penultima), if the penultima is short (*géntĭbus, márĭa, pópŭlum*). The interplay between (i.e., the clash or coincidence of) *word accent* and *ictus* is a fundamental element of Vergil's artistry. See Appendix 1.

Wordplay: see **Paronomasia.**

Zeugma (Gr. "yoking"): the governing of two (or more) words by one, as in *qui Nomentum urbem, qui Rosea rura Velini, | qui Tetricae horrentis rupes montemque Severum | Casperiamque colunt Forulosque et flumen Himellae* (712-14), wherein all the accusative objects are dependent on *colunt* in the final clause. Sometimes the "yoking" can involve literal and metaphorical senses of a word, in which case the *zeugma* is sometimes referred to as *syllepsis* (Gr. "taking together"): e.g., *Phrygios...duces pictasque exure carinas* (430-1), wherein Allecto (in the guise of the priestess Calybe) appears to Turnus in a dream, exhorting him with the imperative *exure*, which should probably be construed in two ways: 1) literally, "burn the ships" and 2) figuratively, "destroy" the Phrygian leaders.

Bibliography

Adkin, N. (2011) "Etymology and the Shield of Turnus." *Latomus* 70.4: 1118-19.

Adler, E. (2003) *Vergil's Empire: Political Thought in the* Aeneid. Lanham, MD.

Allen, G. (2000) *Intertextuality*. London.

Anderson, W. S. (1957) "Vergil's Second *Iliad*." *Transactions of the American Philological Association* 88: 17-30. Reprinted in *Oxford Readings in Vergil's* Aeneid, ed. S. J. Harrison (1990), 239-52. Oxford.

———. (1969 1st ed.; 2005 2nd ed.) *The Art of the* Aeneid. Wauconda, IL.

Anderson, W. S., and Quartarone, L. N. (eds.) (2002) *Approaches to Teaching Vergil's* Aeneid. New York.

Ando, C. (2002) "Vergil's Italy: Ethnography and Politics in First-Century Rome." In *Clio and the Poets: Augustan Poetry and the Traditions of Ancient Historiography*, eds. D. S. Levene and D. P. Nelis, 123-42. Leiden.

Armstrong, D., J. Fish, P. A. Johnston, and M. Skinner (eds.) (2004) *Vergil, Philodemus, and the Augustans*. Austin, TX.

Ash, R. (2002) "Epic Encounters? Ancient Historical Battle Narratives and the Epic Tradition." In *Clio and the Poets: Augustan Poetry and the Traditions of Ancient Historiography*, eds. D. S. Levene and D. P. Nelis, 253-73. Leiden.

Austin, R. G. (ed.) (1955) *P. Vergili Maronis Aeneidos Liber Quartus*. Oxford.

———. (ed.) (1964) *P. Vergili Maronis Aeneidos Liber Secundus*. Oxford.

Baraz, Y. (2009) "Euripides' Corinthian Princess in the *Aeneid*." *Classical Philology* 104.3: 317-30.

Barchiesi, A. (1984) *La traccia del modello: Effetti omerici nella narrazione virgiliana*. Pisa. Revised edition trans. by I. Marchesi and M. Fox, *Homeric Effects in Vergil's Narrative*. Princeton, 2015.

Basto, R. (1982) "The Grazing of Circe's Shore: A Note on *Aeneid* 7.10." *Classical World* 76: 42-3.

Binder, G. (2019) *P. Vergilius Maro,* Aeneis*: Ein Kommentar*. 3 vols. Trier.

Bleisch, P. R. (1996) "On Choosing a Spouse: *Aeneid* 7.378-384 and Callimachus' Epigram 1." *American Journal of Philology* 117: 453-72.

———. (2003) "The 'regia' of Picus: Ekphrasis, Italian Identity, and Artistic Definition in *Aeneid* 7.152-93." In *Being There Together: Essays in Honor of Michael C. J. Putnam on the Occasion of His Seventieth Birthday*, eds. P. Thibodeau and H. Haskell, 88-109. Afton, MN.

Boas, H. (1938) *Aeneas' Arrival in Latium*. Amsterdam.

Bowman, A., E. Champlin, and A. Lintott (eds.) (1996) *The Augustan Empire: 43 B.C.-A.D. 69*. 2nd. ed. Vol. 10 of *The Cambridge Ancient History*. Cambridge.

Boyd, B. W. (1992) "Virgil's Camilla and the Traditions of Catalogue and Ecphrasis (*Aeneid* 7.803-17)." *American Journal of Philology* 113: 213-34.

Breen, C. (1986) "The Shield of Turnus, the Swordbelt of Pallas, and the Wolf: *Aeneid* 7.789-92, 9.59-66, 10.497-99." *Vergilius* 32: 63-71.

Briggs, W. W., Jr. (1981) "Virgil and the Hellenistic Epic." In *Aufstieg und Niedergang der römischen Welt*. 2.31.2: 948-84.

Brogan, T. V. F. (ed.) (1994) *The New Princeton Handbook of Poetic Terms*. Princeton.

Burke, R. K. (1974a) "Mezentius and the First Fruits." *Vergilius* 20: 28-30.

———. (1974b) "The Role of Mezentius in the *Aeneid*." *Classical Journal* 69.3: 202-9.

Cairns, F. (1989) *Virgil's Augustan Epic*. Cambridge.

———. (2006) "The Nomenclature of the Tiber in Virgil's *Aeneid*." In *What's in a Name? The Significance of Proper Names in Classical Latin Literature*, eds. J. Booth and R. Maltby, 65-82. Swansea.

Camps, W. A. (1969) *An Introduction to Virgil's* Aeneid. Oxford.

Casali, S. (2007) "Killing the Father: Ennius, Naevius and Virgil's Julian Imperialism." In *Ennius Perennis: The Annals and Beyond*, eds. W. Fitzgerald and E. Gowers, 103-28. Cambridge.

———. (2010) "The Development of the Aeneas Legend." In *A Companion to Vergil's* Aeneid *and Its Tradition*, eds. J. Farrell and M. C. J. Putnam, 37-51. Malden, MA.

Clausen, W. (1964a) "Callimachus and Latin Poetry." *Greek, Roman and Byzantine Studies* 5: 181-96.

———. (1964b) "An Interpretation of the *Aeneid*." *Harvard Studies in Classical Philology* 68: 139-47. Reprinted with revisions in *Virgil: A Collection of Critical Essays*, ed. S. Commager (1966), 75-88. Englewood Cliffs, NJ.

———. (1987) *Virgil's* Aeneid *and the Tradition of Hellenistic Poetry*. Berkeley, CA.

———. (1994) *A Commentary on Virgil*, Eclogues. Oxford.

———. (2002) *Virgil's* Aeneid: *Decorum, Allusion, and Ideology*. Munich. A revised and expanded version of Clausen (1987).

Clément-Tarantino, S. (2016) "*Caderent omnes a crinibus hydri*: The Problems of the Irrational in the Juno and Allecto Episode in *Aeneid* 7." In *Augustan Poetry and the Irrational*, ed. P. Hardie, 263-80. Oxford.

Coffee, N. (2009) *The Commerce of War: Exchange and Social Order in Latin Epic*. Chicago.

Coleman, R. (ed.) (1977) *Virgil*: Eclogues. Cambridge.

Commager, S. (ed.) (1966) *Virgil: A Collection of Critical Essays*. Englewood Cliffs, NJ.

Conington, J. (1963) *The Works of Virgil with a Commentary*. Rev. by H. Nettleship. Hildesheim. Repr. of 1883-4 London ed.

Connors, C. (1992) "Seeing Cypresses in Virgil." *Classical Journal* 88: 1-17.

Conte, G. B. (1986) *The Rhetoric of Imitation: Genre and Poetic Memory in Virgil and Other Latin Poets*, trans. C. Segal. Ithaca, NY.

———. (1999) "The Virgilian Paradox: An Epic of Drama and Sentiment." *Proceedings of the Cambridge Philological Society* 45: 17-42. A revised version is included in Conte (2007), 23-57.

———. (2007) *The Poetry of Pathos: Studies in Virgilian Epic*. Oxford.

———. (ed.) (2009) *P. Vergilius Maro: Aeneis*. Berlin.

Cooley, A. E. (2009) *Res Gestae Divi Augusti: Text, Translation and Commentary*. Cambridge.

Cornell, T. J. (2014) *The Fragments of the Roman Historians*. 3 vols. Oxford.

Courtney, E. (1988) "Vergil's Military Catalogues and Their Antecedents." *Vergilius* 34: 3-8.

Cowan, R. (2015) "On the Weak King According to Vergil: Aeolus, Latinus, and Political Allegoresis in the *Aeneid*." *Vergilius* 61: 97-124.

Crook, J. (1996) "Political History: 30 B.C. to A.D. 14." In *The Augustan Empire: 43 B.C.-A.D. 69*. 2nd ed., eds. A. Bowman, E. Champlin, and A. Lintott, 70-112. Vol. 10 of *The Cambridge Ancient History*. Cambridge.

Dainotti, P. (2015) *Word Order and Expressiveness in the* Aeneid. Berlin.

Dekel, E. (2012) *Virgil's Homeric Lens*. New York.

Dinter, M. (2005) "Epic and Epigram: Minor Heroes in Virgil's *Aeneid*." *Classical Quarterly*, n.s., 55.1: 153-69.

Duckworth, G. E. (1957). "The *Aeneid* as a Trilogy." *Transactions of the American Philological Association* 88: 1-10.

———. (1969) *Vergil and Classical Hexameter Poetry: A Study in Metrical Variety*. Ann Arbor, MI.

Dyson, J. (2001) *King of the Wood: The Sacrificial Victim in Vergil's* Aeneid. Norman, OK.

Eden, P. T. (1975) *A Commentary on Virgil:* Aeneid *VIII*. *Mnemosyne*, Supplement 35. Leiden.

Edmunds, L. (2001) *Intertextuality and the Reading of Roman Poetry*. Baltimore.

Fagles, R. (1990) *Homer: The* Iliad. New York.

———. (1996) *Homer: The* Odyssey. New York.

Fantham, E. (1998) "Allecto's First Victim: A Study of Vergil's Amata (*Aen*. 7.341-405 and 12.1-80)." In *Vergil's* Aeneid: *Augustan Epic and Its Political Context*, ed. H-P. Stahl, 135-53. London.

———. (2009). *Latin Poets and Italian Gods*. Toronto.

Farrell, J. (1991) *Vergil's* Georgics *and the Traditions of Ancient Epic: The Art of Allusion in Literary History*. Oxford.

———. (1997) "The Virgilian Intertext." In *The Cambridge Companion to Virgil*, ed. C. Martindale, 222-38. Cambridge.

———. (2005) "The Augustan Period: 40 BC-AD 14." In *A Companion to Latin Literature*, ed. S. J. Harrison, 44-57. Oxford.

———. (2014) *Vergil:* Aeneid *5*. Newburyport, MA.

Farrell, J., and M. C. J. Putnam (eds.) (2010) *A Companion to Vergil's* Aeneid *and Its Tradition*. Malden, MA.

Feeney, D. (1991) *The Gods in Epic: Poets and Critics of the Classical Tradition*. Oxford.

Feeney, D., and D. Nelis (2005) "Two Virgilian Acrostics: *certissima signa*?" *Classical Quarterly*, n.s., 55.2: 644-6.

Ferriss-Hill, J. L. (2011) "Virgil's Program of Sabellic Etymologizing and the Construction of Italic Identity." *Transactions of the American Philological Association* 141.2: 265-84.

Fletcher, K. F. B. (2014) *Finding Italy: Travel, Nation, and Colonization in Vergil's* Aeneid. Ann Arbor, MI.

Flower, H. (1996) *Ancestor Masks and Aristocratic Power in Roman Culture*. Oxford.

Fordyce, C. J. (1977) *P. Vergili Maronis:* Aeneidos *Libri VII-VIII*. Oxford.

Forsythe, G. (2005) *A Critical History of Early Rome: From Prehistory to the First Punic War*. Berkeley, CA.

Foster, J. (1991) "Three Passages in Virgil." *Symbolae Osloenses* 66: 109-13.

Fowler, D. (1983) "An Acrostic in Vergil (*Aeneid* 7.601-4)?" *Classical Quarterly* 33: 298.

———. (1997) "On the Shoulders of Giants: Intertextuality and Classical Studies." *Materiali e discussioni per l'analisi dei testi classici* 39: 13-34.

———. (1998) "Opening the Gates of War: *Aeneid* 7.601-40." In *Vergil's* Aeneid: *Augustan Epic and Its Political Context*, ed. H-P. Stahl, 135-53. London. Reprinted in *Roman Constructions: Readings in Postmodern Latin*, by D. Fowler, 173-92.

Fowler, W. W. (1916) *Virgil's Gathering of the Clans*. Oxford.

Fraenkel, E. (1945) "Some Aspects of the Structure of *Aeneid* 7." *Journal of Roman Studies* 35: 1-14. Reprinted in *Oxford Readings in Vergil's* Aeneid, ed. S. J. Harrison (1990), 253-76. Oxford.

Fratantuono, L. (2007) *Madness Unchained: A Reading of Virgil's* Aeneid. Lanham, MD.

———. (2011) *A Commentary on Vergil,* Aeneid *XI*. Brussels.

Fredericksmeyer, E. A. (1985) "Structural Perspectives in *Aeneid* VII." *Classical Journal* 80.3: 408-30.

Gale, M. R. (1997) "The Shield of Turnus (*Aeneid* 7.783-92)." *Greece and Rome* 44: 176-96.

———. (2000) *Virgil on the Nature of Things: The* Georgics, *Lucretius and the Didactic Tradition*. Cambridge.

Galinsky, G. K. (1988) "The Anger of Aeneas." *American Journal of Philology* 109: 321-48.

———. (1996) *Augustan Culture: An Interpretive Introduction.* Princeton.

———. (2003) "Greek and Roman Drama and the *Aeneid.*" In *Myth, History, and Culture in Republican Rome: Studies in Honour of T. P. Wiseman*, eds. S. Braund and C. Gill, 275-94. Exeter.

———. (ed.) (2005) *The Cambridge Companion to the Age of Augustus.* Cambridge.

Ganiban, R. (2007) *Statius and Virgil: The* Thebaid *and the Reinterpretation of the* Aeneid. Cambridge.

———. (2008) *Vergil:* Aeneid *2.* Newburyport, MA.

———. (2009) *Vergil:* Aeneid *1.* Newburyport, MA.

———. (ed.) (2012) *Vergil:* Aeneid, *Books 1-6.* Newburyport, MA.

Gantz, T. (1993) *Early Greek Myth.* 2 vols. Baltimore.

Gaskin, R. (1992) "Turnus, Mezentius and the Complexity of Virgil's *Aeneid.*" In *Studies in Latin Literature and Roman History VI.* Collection Latomus 217, ed. C. Deroux, 295-316. Brussels.

George, E. V. (1974) Aeneid *VIII and the* Aitia *of Callimachus. Mnemosyne*, Supplement 27. Leiden.

Geymonat, M. (ed.) (2008) *P. Vergili Maronis opera: Post Remigium Sabbadini et Aloisium Castiglioni recensuit Marius Geymonat.* New edition with additions and corrections. Rome.

Glare, P. G. W. (ed.) (2012) *Oxford Latin Dictionary.* 2nd ed. Oxford.

Glenn, J. (1971a) "Mezentius and Polyphemus." *American Journal of Philology* 92: 129-55.

———. (1971b) "Mezentius, *contemptor deorum.*" *Vergilius* 17: 7-8.

Goins, S. (1993) "Two Aspects of Vergil's Use of *labor* in the *Aeneid.*" *Classical Journal* 88.4: 375-84.

Goldberg, S., and G. Manuwald (eds.) (2018) *Fragmentary Republican Latin.* 2 vols. Cambridge, MA.

Goldschmidt, N. (2013) *Shaggy Crowns: Ennius'* Annales *and Virgil's* Aeneid. Oxford.

Goold, G. P. (1970) "Servius and the Helen Episode." *Harvard Studies in Classical Philology* 74: 101-68. Reprinted in *Oxford Readings in Vergil's* Aeneid, ed. S. J. Harrison (1990), 60-126. Oxford.

———. (1999) *Virgil.* 2 vols. Cambridge, MA.

Gotoff, H. C. (1984) "The Transformation of Mezentius." *Transactions of the American Philological Association* 114: 191-218.

Gransden, K. W. (1976) *Virgil.* Aeneid *Book VIII.* Cambridge.

———. (1984) *Virgil's Iliad: An Essay on Epic Narrative.* Cambridge.

Gruen, E. (1992) *Culture and National Identity in Republican Rome.* Ithaca, NY.

Gurval, R. A. (1995) *Actium and Augustus.* Ann Arbor, MI.

Hannah, B. (2004) "Manufacturing Descent: Virgil's Genealogical Engineering." *Arethusa* 37.2: 141-64.

Harder, A. (2012) *Callimachus:* Aetia. 2 vols. Oxford.

Hardie, P. R. (1986) *Virgil's* Aeneid: *Cosmos and Imperium.* Oxford.

———. (1991) "The *Aeneid* and the *Oresteia.*" *Proceedings of the Virgil Society* 20: 29-45.

———. (1992) "Augustan Poets and the Mutability of Power." In *Roman Poetry and Propaganda in the Age of Augustus,* ed. A. Powell, 59-82. London.

———. (1993) *The Epic Successors of Virgil.* Cambridge.

———. (1994) *Virgil,* Aeneid: *Book IX.* Cambridge.

———. (1997) "Virgil and Tragedy." In *The Cambridge Companion to Virgil,* ed. C. Martindale, 312-26. Cambridge.

———. (1998) *Virgil.* Greece and Rome. New Surveys in the Classics 28. Oxford.

———. (2012) *Rumour and Renown: Representations of Fama in Western Literature.* Cambridge.

Harrison, E. L. (1980) "The Structure of the *Aeneid*: Observations on the Links between the Books." In *Aufstieg und Niedergang der römischen Welt* 2.31.1: 359-93.

———. (1988) "Virgil's Introduction of Mezentius: *Aeneid* 7.647-8." *Proceedings of the Virgil Society* 19: 70-7.

Harrison, S. J. (1985) "Vergilian Similes: Some Connections." *Papers of the Liverpool Latin Seminar* 5: 99-107.

———. (ed.) (1990) *Oxford Readings in Vergil's* Aeneid. Oxford.

———. (1991) *Vergil,* Aeneid *10: With Introduction, Translation, and Commentary.* Oxford.

———. (2005) *A Companion to Latin Literature.* Oxford.

Heinze, R. (1903 1st ed.; 1908 2nd ed.; 1915 3rd ed.) *Vergils epische Technik.* Leipzig.

———. (1993) *Virgil's Epic Technique,* trans. H. Harvey, D. Harvey, and F. Robertson. Berkeley, CA.

Hejduk, J. (2009) "Jupiter's *Aeneid: Fama* and *imperium.*" *Classical Antiquity* 28.2: 279-327.

Henkel, J. (2011) "Nighttime Labor: A Metapoetic Vignette Alluding to Aratus at *Georgics* 1.291-296." *Harvard Studies in Classical Philology* 106: 179-98.

Hershkowitz, D. (1998) *The Madness of Epic: Reading Insanity from Homer to Statius.* Oxford.

Heyworth, S. (2005) "Pastoral." In *A Companion to Latin Literature,* ed. S. J. Harrison, 148-58. Oxford.

Hinds, S. (1998) *Allusion and Intertext: Dynamics of Appropriation in Roman Poetry.* Cambridge.

Hirtzel, F. A. (ed.) (1900) *P. Vergili Maronis Opera*. Oxford.

Hollis, A. S. (1992) "Hellenistic Colouring in Vergil's *Aeneid*." *Harvard Studies in Classical Philology* 94: 269-82.

Horsfall, N. (1971) "Numanus Remulus: Ethnography and Propaganda in *Aeneid* 9.598ff." *Latomus* 30: 1108-16. Reprinted in *Oxford Readings in Vergil's* Aeneid, ed. S. Harrison (1990), 305-15.

———. (1973) "Corythus: The Return of Aeneas in Virgil and His Sources." *Journal of Roman Studies* 63: 68-79.

———. (1987) "*Non viribus aequis*: Some Problems in Virgil's Battle-Scenes." *Greece and Rome* 34: 48-55.

———. (1991) "*Externi duces*." *Rivista di Filologia e Istruzione Classica* 119: 188-92.

———. (1995) *A Companion to the Study of Virgil*. Leiden.

———. (2000) *Virgil, Aeneid 7: A Commentary*. Leiden.

———. (2003) *Virgil, Aeneid 11: A Commentary*. Leiden.

———. (2006) *Virgil, Aeneid 3: A Commentary*. Leiden.

———. (2008) *Virgil, Aeneid 2: A Commentary*. Leiden.

———. (2013) *Virgil, Aeneid 6: A Commentary*. Berlin.

Hunter, R. L. (2006) *The Shadow of Callimachus: Studies in the Reception of Hellenistic Poetry at Rome*. Cambridge.

Jackson Knight, W. F. (1944) *Roman Vergil*. London.

James, S. (1995) "Establishing Rome with the Sword: *Condere* in the *Aeneid*." *Transactions of the American Philological Association* 116: 623-37.

Jenkyns, R. (1998) *Virgil's Experience: Nature and History; Times, Names, and Places*. Oxford.

Johnson, W. R. (1976) *Darkness Visible: A Study of Vergil's* Aeneid. Berkeley, CA.

———. (2005) Introduction to *Virgil: Aeneid*, trans. S. Lombardo, xv-lxxi. Indianapolis, IN.

Johnston, P. A. (1980) *Vergil's Agricultural Golden Age: A Study of the* Georgics. Leiden.

———. (2012) *Vergil: Aeneid 6*. Newburyport, MA.

Jones, A. H. M. (1970) *Augustus*. London.

Jones, J. W. (1977) "Mezentius the Isolated Hero." *Vergilius* 23: 50-4.

Joseph, T. (2009) "The Disunion of Catullus' *fratres unanimi* at Virgil, *Aeneid* 7.335-6." *Classical Quarterly*, n.s., 59.1: 274-8.

———. (2012) "The Death of Almo in Virgil's Latin War." *New England Classical Journal* 39.2: 99-112.

Kamimura, K. (2008) "The Outbreak of 'Civil War' in *Aeneid* 7: The Function of Allecto." *Classical Studies* 21: 37-52.

Keith, A. (1991) "Etymological Play on *ingens* in Ovid, Vergil, and Octavia." *American Journal of Philology* 112: 73-6.

——— (2000) *Engendering Rome: Women in Latin Epic*. Cambridge.

Kennedy, D. (1992) "'Augustan' and 'Anti-Augustan': Reflections on Terms of Reference." In *Roman Poetry and Propaganda in the Age of Augustus*, ed. A. Powell, 26-58. Bristol.

———. (1997) "Modern Receptions and Their Interpretive Implications." In *The Cambridge Companion to Virgil*, ed. C. Martindale, 38-55. Cambridge.

Knauer, G. N. (1964a) *Die* Aeneis *und Homer: Studien zur poetischen Technik Vergils mit Listen der Homerzitate in der* Aeneis. Göttingen.

———. (1964b) "Vergil's *Aeneid* and Homer." *Greek, Roman and Byzantine Studies* 5: 61-84. Reprinted in *Oxford Readings in Vergil's* Aeneid, ed. S. J. Harrison (1990), 390-412. Oxford.

Knox, P. (1997) "Savagery in the *Aeneid* and Virgil's Ancient Commentators." *Classical Journal* 92.3: 225-33.

Kraggerud, E. (2012) "The Tragedy of Latinus: A Conjecture on Vergil, *A.* 7.598-9." *Symbolae Osloenses* 86: 111-17.

Krasne, D. (2019) "A New Look at Vergil's New Sun (*Aen.* 7.720-721)." *Vergilius* 65: 43-60.

Kraus, C., J. Marincola, and C. Pelling (eds.) (2010) *Ancient Historiography and Its Contexts: Studies in Honour of A. J. Woodman*. Oxford.

Kronenberg, L. (2005) "Mezentius the Epicurean." *Transactions of the American Philological Association* 135.2: 403-31.

Kyriakidis, S. (1994) "*Invocatio ad Musam* (*Aen.* 7.37)." *Materiali e discussioni per l'analisi dei testi classici* 33: 197-206.

Lanham, R. A. (1991) *A Handlist of Rhetorical Terms*. 2nd ed. Berkeley, CA.

La Penna, A. (1980) "Mezenzio: Una tragedia della tirannia e del titanismo antico." *Maia* 32: 3-30.

———. (1988) "Gli archetipi epici di Camilla." *Maia* 40: 228-50.

Laterza, G. (2015) "*Aeneid* VII 53-57: An Acrostic?" *Maia* 67.3: 515-19.

Lattimore, R. (1951) *Homer: The* Iliad. Chicago.

———. (1965) *Homer: The* Odyssey. New York.

Lausberg, H. (1998) *Handbook of Literary Rhetoric: A Foundation for Literary Study*. Leiden.

Leach, E. W. (1971) "The Blindness of Mezentius (*Aeneid* 10.762-768)." *Arethusa* 4: 83-9.

Lee, M. O. (1980) *Fathers and Sons in Vergil's* Aeneid*: Tum Genitor Natum*. Albany, NY.

Lewis, C. T., and C. Short (eds.) (1879) *A Latin Dictionary*. Oxford.

Lowrie, M. (1999) "Telling Pictures: Ecphrasis in the *Aeneid*." *Vergilius* 45: 111-20.

———. (2010) "Vergil and Founding Violence." In *A Companion to Vergil's* Aeneid *and Its Tradition*, eds. J. Farrell and M. C. J. Putnam, 391-403. Malden, MA.

Lyne, R. O. A. M. (1987) *Further Voices in Vergil's* Aeneid. Oxford.

———. (1989) *Words and the Poet: Characteristic Techniques of Style in Vergil's* Aeneid. Oxford.

Mack, S. (1999) "The Birth of War: A Reading of *Aeneid* 7." In *Reading Vergil's* Aeneid, ed. C. Perkell, 128-47. Norman, OK.

Mackie, C. J. (1991a) "*Nox erat…*: Sleep and Visions in the *Aeneid*." *Greece and Rome* 38.1: 59-61.

———. (1991b) "Turnus and His Ancestors." *Classical Quarterly* 41.1: 261-5.

———. (1992) "Vergil's Dirae, South Italy, and Etruria." *Phoenix* 46.4: 352-61.

Mahoney, A. (2001) *Allen and Greenough's New Latin Grammar.* Newburyport, MA. Reprint (with additional material) of the 1903 edition.

Malamud, M. (1998) "Gnawing at the End of the Rope: Poets on the Field in Two Vergilian Catalogues." *Ramus* 27.2: 95-126.

Marincola, J. (ed.) (2007) *A Companion to Greek and Roman Historiography.* Malden, MA.

———. (2010) "*Eros* and Empire: Virgil and the Historians on Civil War." In *Ancient Historiography and Its Contexts: Studies in Honour of A. J. Woodman*, eds. C. Kraus, J. Marincola, and C. Pelling, 183-204. Oxford.

Martindale, C. (ed.) (1984) *Virgil and His Influence.* Bristol.

———. (1993a) "Descent into Hell: Reading Ambiguity, or Virgil and the Critics." *Proceedings of the Virgil Society* 21: 111-50.

———. (1993b) *Redeeming the Text: Latin Poetry and the Hermeneutics of Reception.* Cambridge.

———. (ed.) (1997) *The Cambridge Companion to Virgil.* Cambridge.

Martindale, C., and R. Thomas (eds.) (2006) *Classics and the Uses of Reception.* Malden, MA.

McKay, G. (1970) *Vergil's Italy.* Greenwich, CT.

Miles, G. (1995) *Livy: Reconstructing Early Rome.* Ithaca, NY.

Miller, J. F. (2009) *Apollo, Augustus and the Poets.* Cambridge.

Moorton, R. (1988) "The Genealogy of Latinus in Vergil's *Aeneid*." *Transactions of the American Philological Association* 118: 253-9.

———. (1989) "The Innocence of Italy in Vergil's *Aeneid*." *American Journal of Philology* 110.1: 105-30.

Murray, A. T. (1924) *Homer:* Iliad. 2 vols. Cambridge, MA.

Mynors, R. A. B. (ed.) (1969) *P. Vergili Maronis Opera.* Oxford.

———. (ed.) (1990) *Virgil.* Georgics. Oxford.

Nakata, S. (2012) "*Egredere o quicumque es*: Genealogical Opportunism and Trojan Identity in the *Aeneid*." *Phoenix* 66: 335-63.

Nappa, C. (2005) *Reading after Actium: Vergil's* Georgics, *Octavian, and Rome*. Ann Arbor, MI.

Nelis, D. (2001) *Vergil's* Aeneid *and the* Argonautica *of Apollonius Rhodius*. Leeds.

Nethercut, W. R. (1975) "The Characterization of Mezentius: *Aeneid* 10: 843-845." *Classical Bulletin* 51: 33-7.

Nussbaum, G. B. (1986) *Vergil's Meter: A Practical Guide for Reading Latin Hexameter Poetry*. Bristol.

O'Hara, J. J. (1989) "Messapus, Cycnus, and the Alphabetical Order of Vergil's Catalogue of Italian Heroes." *Phoenix* 43: 35-8.

———. (1990) *Death and the Optimistic Prophecy in Vergil's* Aeneid. Princeton.

———. (1996) *True Names: Vergil and the Alexandrian Tradition of Aetiological Wordplay*. Ann Arbor, MI.

———. (1997) "Virgil's Style." In *The Cambridge Companion to Virgil*, ed. C. Martindale, 241-58. Cambridge.

———. (2007) *Inconsistency in Roman Epic: Studies in Catullus, Lucretius, Vergil, Ovid, and Lucan*. Cambridge.

———. (2010) "The Unfinished *Aeneid*?" In *A Companion to Vergil's* Aeneid *and Its Tradition*, eds. J. Farrell and M. C. J. Putnam, 96-106. Malden, MA.

———. (2011) *Vergil:* Aeneid 4. Newburyport, MA.

———. (2017) *True Names: Vergil and the Alexandrian Tradition of Aetiological Wordplay*. Expanded from O'Hara (1996). Ann Arbor, MI.

———. (2018) *Vergil:* Aeneid 8. Indianapolis, IN.

Oliensis, E. (2004) "Sybilline Syllables: The Intratextual *Aeneid*." *Proceedings of the Cambridge Philological Society* 50: 29-45.

———. (2009) *Freud's Rome: Psychoanalysis and Latin Poetry*. Cambridge.

O'Rourke, D. (2011) "The Representation and Misrepresentation of Virgilian Poetry in Propertius 2.34." *American Journal of Philology* 132: 457-97.

Osgood, J. (2006) *Caesar's Legacy: Civil War and the Emergence of the Roman Empire*. Cambridge.

Otis, B. (1964) *Virgil: A Study in Civilized Poetry*. Oxford.

Page, T. E. (1894, 1900) *Virgil:* Aeneid. 2 vols. London.

Panoussi, V. (2002) "Vergil's Ajax: Allusion, Tragedy, and Heroic Identity in the *Aeneid*." *Classical Antiquity* 21: 95-134.

———. (2009) *Greek Tragedy in Vergil's* Aeneid: *Ritual, Empire, and Intertext*. Cambridge.

Parkes, R. (2007) "Where Was Hercules? A Note on Vergil, *Aeneid* 8.201-212." *Vergilius* 53: 100-3.

Parry, A. (1963) "The Two Voices of Virgil's *Aeneid.*" *Arion* 2: 66-80. Reprinted in S. Commager (ed.) (1966), 107-23.

Pavlock, B. (1985) "Epic and Tragedy in Vergil's Nisus and Euryalus Episode." *Transactions of the American Philological Association* 115: 207-24.

———. (1992) "The Hero and the Erotic in *Aeneid* 7-12." *Vergilius* 38: 72-87.

Pelling, C. (1996) "The Triumviral Period." In *The Augustan Empire: 43 B.C.-A.D. 69.* 2nd ed., eds. A. Bowman, E. Champlin, and A. Lintott, 1-69. Vol. 10 of *The Cambridge Ancient History.* Cambridge.

Perkell, C. (1989) *The Poet's Truth: A Study of the Poet in Virgil's* Georgics. Berkeley, CA.

———. (1994) "Ambiguity and Irony: The Last Resort?" *Helios* 21: 63-74.

———. (ed.) (1999) *Reading Vergil's* Aeneid: *An Interpretive Guide.* Norman, OK.

———. (2002) "The Golden Age and Its Contradictions in the Poetry of Vergil." *Vergilius* 48: 3-39.

———. (2010) *Vergil:* Aeneid 3. Newburyport, MA.

Petrini, M. (1997) *The Child and the Hero: Coming of Age in Catullus and Vergil.* Ann Arbor, MI.

Pogorzelski, R. J. (2009) "The 'Reassurance of Fratricide' in the *Aeneid.*" *American Journal of Philology* 130.2: 261-89.

Pöschl, V. (1950) *Die Dichtkunst Vergils: Bild und Symbol in der* Aeneis. Innsbruck.

———. (1962) *The Art of Vergil: Image and Symbol in the* Aeneid, trans. G. Seligson. Ann Arbor, MI.

Powell, A. (ed.) (1992) *Roman Poetry and Propaganda in the Age of Augustus.* Bristol.

Putnam, M. (1965) *The Poetry of the* Aeneid: *Four Studies in Imaginative Unity and Design.* Cambridge, MA.

———. (1970) "*Aeneid* VII and the *Aeneid.*" *American Journal of Philology* 91: 408-30. Reprinted in Putnam (1995b), 100-18.

———. (1979) *Virgil's Poem of the Earth: Studies in the* Georgics. Princeton.

———. (1980) "The Third Book of the *Aeneid*: From Homer to Rome." *Ramus* 9: 1-21.

———. (1982) "Umbro, Nereus, and Love's Threnody." *Vergilius* 38: 12-23.

———. (1993) "The Languages of Horace, *Odes* 1.24." *Classical Journal* 88.2: 123-35.

———. (1995a) "Silvia's Stag and Virgilian Ekphrasis." *Materiali e discussioni per l'analisi dei testi classici* 34: 107-33.

———. (1995b) *Virgil's* Aeneid: *Interpretation and Influence.* Chapel Hill, NC.

———. (1998) *Virgil's Epic Designs: Ekphrasis in the* Aeneid. New Haven, CT.

Putnam, M., and J. Gaisser (2012) *The Complete Poems of Tibullus: An En Face Bilingual Edition.* Berkeley, CA.

Quint, D. (1993) *Epic and Empire: Politics and Generic Form from Virgil to Milton.* Princeton.

———. (2011) "Virgil's Double Cross: Chiasmus and the *Aeneid.*" *American Journal of Philology* 132.2: 273-300.

———. (2018) *Virgil's Double Cross: Design and Meaning in the* Aeneid. Princeton.

Rabel, R. (1981) "Vergil, Tops, and the Stoic View of Fate." *Classical Journal* 77.1: 27-32.

Race, W. (2008) *Apollonius Rhodius:* Argonautica. Cambridge, MA.

Rebeggiani, S. (2020) "Theban Myth in Virgil's *Aeneid*: The Brothers at War." *Classical Antiquity* 39.1: 95-125.

Reckford, K. (1961) "Latent Tragedy in *Aeneid* VII, 1-285." *American Journal of Philology* 82: 252-69.

Reed, J. (2007) *Virgil's Gaze.* Princeton.

Rogerson, A. (2017) *Virgil's Ascanius: Imagining the Future in the* Aeneid. Cambridge.

Rosivach, V. J. (1980) "Latinus' Genealogy and the Palace of Picus (*Aeneid* 7.45-9, 170-91)." *Classical Quarterly* 30: 140-52.

Ross, D. O. (1987) *Virgil's Elements: Physics and Poetry in the* Georgics. Princeton.

———. (2007) *Virgil's* Aeneid: *A Reader's Guide.* Oxford.

Rossi, A. (2004) *Contexts of War: Manipulations of Genre in Virgilian Battle Narrative.* Ann Arbor, MI.

Russell, D. A. (2002) *Quintilian: The Orator's Education.* 5 vols. Cambridge, MA.

Saylor, C. F. (1974) "The Magnificent Fifteen: Vergil's Catalogues of the Latin and Etruscan Forces." *Classical Philology* 69: 249-57.

Schiesaro, A. (2003) *The Passions in Play:* Thyestes *and the Dynamics of Senecan Drama.* Cambridge.

Schmidt, E. (2001) "The Meaning of Vergil's *Aeneid*: American and German Approaches." *Classical World* 94.2: 145-71.

Schork, R. (1996) "Acoustic Intratexts in *Aeneid* 7.122 and 4.408." *Classical Philology* 91: 61-2.

Scullard, H. H. (1982) *From the Gracchi to Nero: A History of Rome from 133 B.C. to A.D. 68.* 5th ed. London.

Segal, C. (1990) "Dido's Hesitation in *Aeneid* 4." *Classical World* 84: 1-12.

Seider, A. (2012) "Competing Commemorations: Apostrophes of the Dead in the *Aeneid.*" *American Journal of Philology* 133.2: 241-69.

———. (2013) *Memory in Vergil's* Aeneid: *Creating the Past.* Cambridge.

Seo, J. M. (2013) *Exemplary Traits: Reading Characterization in Roman Poetry.* Oxford.

Sharrock, A. (2015) "Warrior Women in Roman Epic." In *Women and War in Antiquity*, eds. J. Fabre-Serris and A. Keith, 157-78. Baltimore.

Shotter, D. (2005) *Augustus Caesar.* 2nd ed. London.

Skempis, M. (2010) "Caieta's Undying Fame: *Aeneid* 7.1-7." *Museum Helveticum* 67.2: 114-26.

Skutsch, O. (1985) *The* Annals *of Q. Ennius.* Oxford.

Small, C. D. (1986) "Virgil, *Aeneid* 7. 620-2." *Classical Quarterly* 36: 278-80.

Small, S. G. P. (1959) "The Arms of Turnus: *Aeneid* 7.783-92." *Transactions of the American Philological Association* 90: 243-52.

Smith, R. A. (2005) *The Primacy of Vision in Virgil's* Aeneid. Austin, TX.

———. (2011) *Virgil.* West Sussex, UK.

Southern, P. (1998) *Augustus.* New York.

Sparrow, J. (1931) *Half-Lines and Repetitions in Virgil.* Oxford.

Stahl, H.-P. (ed.) (1998) *Vergil's* Aeneid: *Augustan Epic and Political Context.* London.

———. (2016) *Poetry Underpinning Power: Vergil's* Aeneid; *The Epic for the Emperor Augustus.* Wales.

Starr, R. (1992) "Silvia's Deer (Vergil, *Aeneid* 7.479-502): Game Parks and Roman Law." *American Journal of Philology* 113: 435-9.

Sullivan, F. A. (1969) "Mezentius: A Vergilian Creation." *Classical Philology* 64.4: 219-25.

Syme, R. (1939) *The Roman Revolution.* Oxford.

Syson, A. (2013) *Fama and Fiction in Vergil's* Aeneid. Columbus, OH.

Tarleton, N. (1989) "*Pastoralem praefixa cuspide myrtum* (*Aeneid* 7.817)." *Classical Quarterly* 39: 267-70.

Taylor, M. E. (1955) "Primitivism in Virgil." *American Journal of Philology* 76.3: 261-78.

Thibodeau, P. (2011) *Playing the Farmer: Representations of Rural Life in Vergil's* Georgics. Berkeley, CA.

Thomas, R. F. (1982) *Lands and Peoples in Roman Poetry: The Ethnographical Tradition.* Cambridge.

———. (1985) "From *Recusatio* to Commitment: The Evolution of a Vergilian Programme." *Papers of the Liverpool Latin Seminar* 5: 61-73.

———. (1986) "Virgil's *Georgics* and the Art of Reference." *Harvard Studies in Classical Philology* 90: 171-98.

———. (1988) *Virgil:* Georgics. 2 vols. Cambridge.

———. (1998) "The Isolation of Turnus: *Aeneid* Book 12." In H.-P. Stahl (ed.) (1998), 271-302.

———. (1999) *Reading Virgil and His Texts: Studies in Intertextuality.* Ann Arbor, MI.

———. (2001) *Virgil and the Augustan Reception.* Cambridge.

———. (2004) "Stuck in the Middle with You: Virgilian Middles." In *Middles in Latin Poetry*, eds. S. Kyriakidis and F. De Martino, 123-50. Bari.

Thomas, R., and J. Ziolkowski (eds.) (2014) *The Virgil Encyclopedia.* 3 vols. Malden, MA.

Tilly, B. (1977) "Some Excursions into Vergil's Faliscan Country: In Search of Fescennium." *Vergilius* 23: 39-49.

Toll, K. (1989) "What's Love Got to Do with It? The Invocation to Erato, and Patriotism in the *Aeneid*." *Quaderni Urbinati di Cultura Classica* 33.3: 107-18.

———. (1991) "The *Aeneid* as an Epic of National Identity: *Italiam laeto socii clamore salutant*." *Helios* 18:3-14.

———. (1997) "Making Roman-ness and the *Aeneid*." *Classical Antiquity* 16.1: 34-56.

Trappes-Lomax, J. (2004) "Hiatus in Vergil and in Horace's *Odes*." *Proceedings of the Cambridge Philological Society* 50: 141-58.

Vance, E. (1981) "Wildness and Domesticity in Virgil's *Aeneid*." *Arethusa* 14: 127-38.

Van Sickle, J. (1992) *A Reading of Virgil's Messianic Eclogue*. New York.

Vernant, J.-P., and P. Vidal-Naquet (1988) *Myth and Tragedy in Ancient Greece*, trans. J. Lloyd. New York.

Viparelli, V. (2008) "Camilla: A Queen Undefeated, Even in Death." *Vergilius* 54: 9-23.

Volk, K. (ed.) (2008a) *Virgil's* Eclogues. Oxford.

———. (ed.) (2008b) *Virgil's* Georgics. Oxford.

Wallace-Hadrill, A. (1993) *Augustan Rome*. London.

———. (2008) *Rome's Cultural Revolution*. Cambridge.

Warmington, E. H. (1935-40) *Remains of Old Latin*. Rev. ed. 4 vols. Cambridge, MA.

White, P. (1993) *Promised Verse: Poets in the Society of Augustan Rome*. Cambridge, MA.

———. (2005) "Poets in the New Milieu: Realigning." In *The Cambridge Companion to the Age of Augustus*, ed. K. Galinsky, 321-39. Cambridge.

Wigodsky, M. (1972) *Vergil and Early Latin Poetry*. Wiesbaden.

Wilkinson, L. P. (1969) *The Georgics of Virgil: A Critical Survey*. Cambridge.

Williams, G. W. (1983) *Technique and Ideas in the* Aeneid. New Haven.

Williams, M. F. (1993) "Turnus, the Chimaera, and Aeetes: A Note on *Aeneid* 7.785-88." *Vergilius* 39: 31-6.

Williams, R. D. (1961) "The Structure and Function of Virgil's Catalogue in *Aeneid* 7." *Classical Quarterly*, n.s., 11.2: 146-53.

———. (1972-73) *Virgil*: Aeneid. 2 vols. London.

Wills, J. (1996) *Repetition in Latin Poetry: Figures of Allusion*. Oxford.

Wimperis, T. (2017) "Cultural Memory and Constructed Ethnicity in Vergil's *Aeneid*." PhD diss., University of North Carolina–Chapel Hill.

———. (2020) "Turnus's *tota Italia*: Italian Solidarity and Political Rhetoric in *Aeneid* 7-12." *Transactions of the American Philological Association* 150.1: 143-79.

Wlosok, A. (1976) "Vergils Didotragödie: Ein Beitrag zum Problem des Tragischen in der *Aeneis*." In *Studien zum antiken Epos*, eds. H. Görgemanns and E. A. Schmidt, 228-50. Meisenheim.

———. (1999) "The Dido Tragedy in Virgil: A Contribution to the Question of the Tragic in the *Aeneid*." Translation of Wlosok (1976). In *Virgil: Critical Assessments of Classical Authors*. Vol. 4, ed. P. Hardie, 158-81. London.

Wyatt, W. (1999) *Homer*: Iliad. 2 vols. Revision of A. T. Murray (1924). Cambridge, MA.

Zanker, P. (1988) *The Power of Images in the Age of Augustus*, trans. A. Shapiro. Ann Arbor, MI.

Zetzel, J. E. G. (1994) "Looking Backward: Past and Present in the Late Roman Republic." *Pegasus* (Journal of the Exeter University Classics Society) 37: 20-32.

———. (1997) "Rome and Its Traditions." In *The Cambridge Companion to Virgil*, ed. C. Martindale, 188-203. Cambridge.

List of Abbreviations

a.	= active	n.	= neuter
abl.	= ablative	nom.	= nominative
acc.	= accusative	num.	= numeral
adj.	= adjective	opp.	= opposed
adv.	= adverb	orig.	= originally
appos.	= appositive	part.	= participle
cf.	= *confer*, i.e., compare	pass.	= passive
comp.	= comparative	perf.	= perfect
conj.	= conjunction	pers.	= personal
dat.	= dative	pl.	= plural
dep.	= deponent	poet.	= poetic (usage)
dim.	= diminutive	poss.	= possessive
f.	= feminine	prep.	= preposition
fig.	= figurative	pron.	= pronoun
freq.	= frequentive	rel.	= relative
gen.	= genitive	sc.	= *scilicet*, i.e., understand, supply
i.e.	= *id est*, that is		
impers.	= impersonal	sing.	= singular
indecl.	= indeclinable	subst.	= substantive
indef.	= indefinite	sup.	= supine
interj.	= interjection	superl.	= superlative
intr.	= intransitive	s.v.	= *sub verbo*, under the word
interrog.	= interrogative		
intens.	= intensive	tr.	= transitive
m.	= masculine	usu.	= usually
meton.	= metonymy	v.	= verb
mod.	= modern	viz.	= *videlicet*, namely

Vocabulary

(In general, macrons are placed only over long vowels in a metrically indeterminate position, as in the *Oxford Latin Dictionary*.)

A

ā, ab, abs, prep. with abl., *from, by.*
abdō, -ere, -didī, -ditum, *withdraw; conceal.*
abdūcō, -ere, -dūxī, -ductum, *lead or take away.*
Abella, -ae, f., *Abella, a town in Campania, NE of Naples.*
abeō, -īre, -iī, -itum, *go away.*
abnegō, -āre, -āvī, -ātum, *deny, refuse.*
abolēscō, -ēscere, -ēvī, --, *decay; be forgotten.*
absistō, -ere, -stitī, --, *stand off or away from.*
abstineō, -ēre, -stinuī, -stentum, *hold back, keep away from,* followed by the abl. alone or abl. with prep.
absum, abesse, āfuī, āfutūrum, *be away, be absent.*
absūmō, -ere, -sumpsī, -sumptum, *take away, consume, destroy.*
abundē, adv., *sufficiently, enough.*

ac, short form of **atque** (used only before words beginning with a consonant), conj., *and, in addition;* (after words of comparison) *as, than.*
accendō, -ere, -cendī, -cēnsum, *kindle, set on fire.*
accīdō, -ere, -cīdī, -cīsum, *cut into; devour.*
accingō, -ere, -cinxī, -cinctum, *gird on; equip.*
accipiō, -ere, -cēpī, -ceptum, *receive; accept; hear or learn (of).*
accola, -ae, m. or **f.,** *neighbor.*
ācer, ācris, ācre, adj., *sharp, piercing; fierce.*
Acherōn, -ontis, m., *Acheron, a river of Hades; the lower world.*
aciēs, -ēī, f., *edge; line of battle; keenness.*
āclys, -ydis, f., *small javelin with a strap.*
Ācrisiōnēus, -a, -um, adj., *pertaining to Acrisius or his daughter Danaë.*
Ācrisius, -ī, m., *Acrisius, a king of Argos, son of Abas, father of Danaë.*

acuō, -ere, -uī, -ūtum, *make pointed.*
ad, prep. with acc., *to, up to, toward.*
addō, -ere, -didī, -ditum, *add, give to; say in addition; increase.*
adeō, adv., *to such an extent; thus far; so, even.*
adeō, -īre, -īvī or **-iī, -itum,** *approach; visit.*
adferō, -ferre, attulī, adlātum, *bring to, convey; report, allege, announce; produce.*
adfor, -fārī, -fātus sum, *speak to; address; beseech.*
adhūc, adv., *thus far, to this point, still.*
adigō, -ere, -ēgī, -actum, *drive to, force to, compel.*
adiungō, -ere, -iunxī, -iunctum, *join to, connect.*
adlūdō, -ere, -lūsī, -lūsum, *speak playfully, jest; mock.*
admisceō, -ēre, -miscuī, -mixtum, *mingle with.*
adoleō, -ēre, -oluī, -ultum, *cause to increase; worship; burn in sacrifice, offer; kindle.*
adōreus, -a, -um, adj., *of fine wheat.*
adorior, -īrī, adortus sum, *to attack; attempt; begin.*
adsensus, -ūs, m., *an assenting; answering sound.*
adsiduus, -a, -um, adj., *established, steady.*
adsuēscō, -ere, -ēvī, -ētum, *grow accustomed to.*
adsuētus, -a, -um, adj., *usual, customary.*
adsum, -esse, -fuī, --, *be near; be present.*
advena, -ae, m. or **f.,** *newcomer; a stranger, foreigner;* adj., *foreign.*
adveniō, -īre, -vēnī, -ventum, *arrive.*

adventō, -āre, -āvī, -ātum, *come rapidly nearer; approach.*
adventus, -ūs, m., *an arrival, approach; visit; appearance.*
advertō, -ere, -vertī, -versum, *turn toward.*
adytum, -ī, n., *the innermost part of a temple; a shrine, sanctuary, oracle.*
Aeneadēs, -ae, m., *a son of Aeneas.*
Aenēās, -ae, m., *Aeneas.*
aēnus, -a, -um, adj., *of bronze, brazen;* (n. used as subst.) *a bronze vessel; caldron.*
Aequī, -ōrum, m. pl., *The Aequi,* a warlike people of ancient Italy, in the neighborhood of the Latins and Volsci.
Aequīculus, -a, -um, adj., *of the Aequiculi,* a tribe sometimes associated with the Aequi; *Aequiculan.*
aequō, -āre, -āvī, -ātum, *make level, equalize.*
aequor, -oris, n., *level surface; sea; plain.*
aequus, -a, -um, adj., *equal; just; calm.*
aerātus, -a, -um, adj., *furnished with copper, bronze; made of bronze; bronze-covered.*
aereus, -a, -um, adj., *made of copper* or *bronze.*
āerius, -a, -um, adj., *pertaining to the air; lofty.*
aes, aeris, n., *copper, bronze; money.*
aestus, -ūs, m., *heat; agitation, passion, seething; wave, surge, tide.*
aetās, -ātis, f., *age; lifetime; time.*
aeternus, -a, -um, adj., *everlasting, eternal.*
aethēr, -eris, n., *pure upper air, heaven, sky.*

aetherius, -a, -um, adj., *pertaining to the upper air; ethereal, heavenly; airy.*
Aetnaeus, -a, -um, adj., *of Mount Aetna; Aetnaean.*
aevum, -ī, n., *eternity; lifetime, age.*
Agamemnonius, -a, -um, adj., *pertaining to Agamemnon; Agamemnonian, Argive, Greek.*
age, agite, interj., *come on! let's go!*
ager, -grī, m., *field.*
agger, -eris, m., *mound, rampart.*
agitō, -āre, -āvī, -ātum, *drive, shake, move about; revolve; pursue.*
agmen, -inis, n., *line of march, column; army; multitude, throng; swarm.*
agō, -ere, ēgī, actum, *drive, do, act, concern oneself with.*
agrestis, -e, adj., *rural, rustic.*
agricola, -ae, m., *farmer.*
Agyllīnus, -a, -um, adj., *of Agylla,* a town in Etruria, afterward called Caere; *the people of Agylla.*
āiō, defect., *say, affirm, say yes.*
āla, -ae, f., *wing.*
Albānus, -a, -um, adj., *pertaining to Alba Longa* (city in Latium); (m. pl. used as subst.) *the Albans.*
albescō, -ere, --, --, *grow white; to brighten, dawn.*
Albunea, -ae, f., *Albunea,* a fountain at Tibur.
albus, -a, -um, adj., *white.*
alga, -ae, f., *seaweed.*
ālipēs, -edis, adj., *wing-footed;* (m. used as subst.) *wing-footed horse.*
aliquī, aliqua, aliquod, indef. adj., *some.*
aliquis, aliquid, indef. pron., *someone, something; some, any;* **si quis, si quid:** *anyone who, anything that.*
alius, alia, aliud, adj., *other, another.*

Allectō, -ūs, f., *Allecto, one of the Furies.*
Allia, -ae, f., *Allia,* a small stream running into the Tiber, eleven miles above Rome, where the Romans were defeated by the Gauls in 390 BCE.
Almō, -ōnis, m., *Almo,* a Latin youth, son of Tyrrheus.
almus, -a, -um, adj., *giving nourishment; blessed; kindly, propitious.*
altāria, -ium, n. pl., *the upper part of an altar; a high altar; an altar.*
altē, adv., *aloft, on high; deep;* comp. adv., **altius.**
alter, -era, -erum, adj., *other of two.*
altum, -ī, n., *deep sea; height.*
altus, -a, -um, adj., *tall, high; deep.*
alveus, -ī, m., *cavity, hollow; channel* or *bed of a river.*
Amasēnus, -ī, m., *Amasenus,* a river of Latium; the river-god *Amasenus.*
Amāta, -ae, f., *Amata,* the wife of Latinus.
ambiō, -īre, -īvī or **-iī, -ītum,** *go round; strive for, aim at; encompass.*
ambō, ambae, ambō, num. adj., *both.*
āmens, -mentis, adj., *mad, insane.*
amīcitia, -ae, f., *friendship.*
amictus, -ūs, m., *an upper garment; cloak, mantle; veil.*
amīcus, -a, -um, adj., *friendly.*
Amiternus, -a, -um, adj., *of Amiternum,* a Sabine town near the source of the Aternus; *Amiternian.*
amnis, -is, m., *river stream; current.*
amoenus, -a, -um, adj., *charming, delightful, pleasant.*
amor, -ōris, m., *love.*

Amsanctus, -ī, m., *Lake Amsanctus, in the country of the Hirpini, from its noxious exhalations supposed to be one of the entrances to Hades.*
Anagnia, -ae, f., *Anagnia, a town of the Hernici.*
anceps, -cipitis, adj., *two-headed, two-edged; undecided; ambiguous.*
Anchīsēs, -ae, m., *Anchises, father of Aeneas by Venus.*
ancīle, -is, n., *a small oval (curved inward at the sides) shield.*
anguis, -is, m. or f., *snake.*
Angitia, -ae, f., *Angitia.*
anīlis, -e, adj., *old woman.*
anima, -ae, f., *breath; spirit, soul.*
animus, -ī, m., *spirit, mind;* pl., *strong feelings.*
Anien, -ēnis, m., *Anio (Anien), a branch of the Tiber, flowing from the Sabine Mountains through Latium.*
annus, -ī, m., *year.*
ante, adv., *before, earlier, previously;* prep. with acc., *in front of.*
Antemnae, -ārum, f. pl., *Antemnae, a Sabine town on the Anio.*
antīquus, -a, -um, adj., *ancient, old.*
anus, anūs, f., *old woman.*
Anxurus, -a, -um, adj., *of Anxur.*
aperiō, -īre, -eruī, -ertum, *uncover, open; disclose; explain.*
apes, -is, f., *bee.*
apex, -icis, m., *the point of anything; peak; pointed flame; cone of a helmet; a peaked cap.*
Apollō, -inis, m., *Apollo.*
appellō, -ere, -pulī, -pulsum, *drive to; bring; moor on the shore.*
aptō, -āre, -āvī, -ātum, *adapt to, prepare; fit together, join.*
aqua, -ae, f., *water.*

Aquilō, -ōnis, m., *Aquilo, the north wind; wind (in general); wintry, tempestuous wind.*
āra, -ae, f., *altar.*
Arabus, -a, -um, adj., *Arabian.*
arātrum, -ī, n., *plow.*
arbor, -oris, f., *tree; mast; spear shaft.*
arcānus, -a, -um, adj., *secret, mysterious, hidden.*
arceō, -ēre, -cuī, --, *ward off, keep away; confine; protect.*
Archippus, -ī, m., *Archippus, king of the Marsi.*
arcus, -ūs, m., *bow, arch.*
Ardea, -ae, f., *Ardea, the chief town of the Rutulians.*
ardens, -entis, adj., *burning.*
ārdeō, -ēre, -sī, -sum, *burn, glow.*
ardor, -ōris, m., *burning, heat, eagerness.*
arduum, -ī, n., *high place; height.*
arduus, -a, -um, adj., *steep, difficult.*
argentum, -ī, n., *silver.*
Argī, -ōrum, m. pl., *Argives.*
Argīvus, -a, -um, adj., *belonging to Argos, Argive; Greek.*
argūmentum, -ī, n., *proof, evidence, argument.*
Argus, -ī, m., *Argus, the hundred-eyed keeper who was made the guard of Io, after she was changed into a heifer by Juno.*
argūtus, -a, -um, adj., *clear; clever; rustling, whistling.*
Arīcia, -ae, f., *Aricia, a city near Rome, on the Appian Way; a nymph, mother of Virbius.*
ariēs, -etis, m., *ram.*
arista, -ae, f., *the beard or head of wheat.*
arma, -ōrum, n. pl., *arms, weapons.*
armātus, -a, -um, adj., *armed.*

armentum, -ī, n., *herd; animals used for plowing.*
armō, -āre, -āvī, -ātum, *equip, arm.*
arō, -āre, -āvī, -ātum, *plow.*
ars, artis, f., *skill, art; guile, trick.*
artus, -ūs, m., *limb, leg.*
arvīna, -ae, f., *grease.*
arvum, -ī, n., *plowed land, field.*
arx, arcis, f., *summit, citadel.*
Ascanius, -ī, m., *Ascanius,* son of Aeneas, and traditional founder of Alba Longa.
Āsius, -a, -um, adj., orig. *of Asia,* a town in Lydia near the Cayster River; later, *of Asia Minor.*
asper, -era, -erum, adj., *rough, harsh; sharp; savage.*
aspiciō, -ere, -spexī, -spectum, *look at, behold.*
aspīrō, -āre, -āvī, -ātum, *breathe upon; inspire; aid, favor; aspire.*
ast, see *at.*
astō, -stāre, -stitī, --, *stand by* or *near.*
astrum, -ī, n., *star; constellation*
at or **ast,** conj., *but, but on the other hand; on the contrary; while, whereas; but yet; at least.*
atavus, -ī, m, *grandfather; forefather, ancestor.*
āter, ātra, ātrum, adj., *black.*
Ātīna, -ae, f., *Atina,* a town in Latium.
atque (ac is often used instead before words beginning with a consonant), conj., *and, in addition;* (after words of comparison) *as, than.*
attactus, -ūs, m., (only in the abl., **attāctū**), *touching; touch.*
attingō, -ere, -tigī, -tactum, *touch; reach; belong to.*
attollō, -ere, --, --, *raise up.*

attonitus, -a, -um, adj., *astonished.*
auctor, -ōris, m., *author, founder, proposer.*
audax, -ācis, adj., *bold, daring; reckless.*
audeō, -ēre, ausus sum, *dare.*
audiō, -īre, -īvī or **iī, audītum,** *hear, listen (to).*
augeō, -ēre, auxī, auctum, *increase, augment; honor; promote.*
augurium, -ī, n., *augury, prophecy.*
augurō, -āre, -āvī, -ātum, *divine, conjecture.*
augustus, -a, -um, adj., *august, holy.*
aura, -ae, f., *breeze, wine;* (pl.) *upper air, heavens.*
aureus, -a, -um, adj., *golden; gleaming like gold.*
auris, -is, f., *ear.*
aurōra, -ae, f., *dawn, morning;* personified, *Aurora,* the goddess of the dawn, who precedes the horses of the sun-god; *the east; the sun.*
aurum, -ī, n., *gold.*
Auruncus, -a, -um, adj., *Auruncan; of Aurunca,* an ancient town in Campania.
Ausonia, -ae, f., *Ausonia,* an ancient name of middle and lower Italy; *Italy,* in general.
Ausonius, -a, -um, adj., *Ausonian; Italian.*
auspicium, -ī, n., *divination* (by the flight of birds).
aut, conj., *or;* **aut...aut,** *either...or.*
autem, conj., *however; moreover.*
auxilium, -ī, n., *aid, help;* (pl.) *auxiliary troops.*
Aventīnus, -ī, m., *the Aventine mount* in Rome; *Aventinus,* a Latin chief.

Avernus, -a, -um, adj., *of Avernus,* a lake near Naples, between Baiae and Cumae, in Campania, now Lago d'Averno. Near it was one of the entrances to Hades; *Avernian.*
āversus, -a, -um, adj., *turned away, from behind.*
avis, -is, f., *bird.*
avītus, -a, -um, adj., *of a grandfather, ancestral, ancient.*
āvius, -a, -um, adj., *pathless, remote, trackless.*
avus, -ī, m., *grandfather; forefather, ancestor.*

B

Bacchus, -ī, m., *Bacchus.*
bālō, -āre, -āvī, -ātum, *bleat;* (f. part. **balans** used as subst.), *sheep.*
Batulum, -ī, n., *Batulum,* a Samnite town in Campania.
bellatrix, -īcis, f., *female warrior, a warlike heroine;* adj., *warring.*
Bellōna, -ae, f., *Bellona,* Roman goddess of war.
bellum, -ī, n., *war.*
bibō, -ere, bibī, --, *drink; draw off; dwell in region of* (with acc. river name).
bidens, -dentis, adj., *having two teeth or two complete rows of teeth;* (f. used as subst., sc. **victima**), *an animal suitable for sacrifice.*
bifrons, -frontis, adj., *two-faced, double-faced.*
bīgae, -ārum, f. pl., *team of two horses; car* or *chariot drawn by two horses.*
bīnī, -ae, -a, distr. num. adj., *two by two; two to each; two.*
bōs, bovis, m., *ox.*
būcina, -ae, f., *trumpet.*
buxus, -ī, f., *the box tree;* (meton.) *a flute* or *pipe.*

C

Caeculus, -ī, m., *Caeculus,* son of Vulcan, and mythical founder of Praeneste.
caecus, -a, -um, adj., *blind; hidden, secret, dark.*
caedēs, -is, f., *killing, murder.*
caedō, -ere, cecīdī, caesum, *kill, strike, cut.*
caelestis, -e, adj., *from* or *of heaven.*
caelō, -āre, -āvī, -ātum, *cut in relief; carve.*
caelum, -ī, n., *sky, heaven.*
caerulus or **caeruleus, -a, -um,** adj., *dark blue; sea-colored;* (n. pl. used as subst.) *the dark blue waters; the sea.*
caetra, -ae, f., *short Spanish shield.*
Cāiēta, -ae, f., *Caieta,* the nurse of Aeneas; *Caieta,* a town and haven of Latium, named after the nurse of Aeneas (now Gaëta).
calathus, -ī, m., *wicker basket; workbasket.*
Calēs, -ium, f. pl., *Cales,* a town in Campania.
Calybē, -ēs, f., *Calybe,* an aged priestess of Juno.
Calydōn, -ōnis, f., *Calydon,* a town in Aetolia, the home of Meleager.
Camilla, -ae, f., *Camilla,* a Volscian female hero, ally of Turnus.
campus, -ī, m., *plain.*
candidus, -a, -um, adj., *white.*
canis, -is, m. or **f.,** *dog.*
canō, -ere, cecinī, cantum, *sing (of).*
canōrus, -a, -um, adj., *harmonious; resounding.*

cantus, -ūs, m., *singing* or *playing; melody; song; incantation, charm.*
Capēnus, -a, -um, adj., *of Capena,* a town in the southern part of Tuscany.
capiō, -ere, cēpī, captum, *seize; capture; win.*
Capreae, -ārum, f. pl., *Capreae,* now *Capri,* an island in the Bay of Naples.
captīvus, -a, -um, adj., *captured.*
caput, -itis, n., *head, one's life; capital punishment.*
cardō, -inis, m., *hinge.*
carīna, -ae, f., *keel; ship.*
carmen, -inis, n., *song, poem; oracular response, prophecy.*
carpō, -ere, carpsī, carptum, *pluck, seize; criticize.*
Casperia, -ae, f., *Casperia,* a town of the Sabines.
castra, -ōrum, n. pl., *(military) camp.*
castus, -a, -um, adj., *pure, spotless; chaste.*
catēia, -ae, f., *a slender javelin.*
caterva, -ae, f., *band (esp. of soldiers); a crowd.*
Catillus, -ī, m., *Catillus,* with his brothers Coras and Tiburtus, founder of Tibur.
causa, -ae, f., *cause, reason, lawsuit.*
cavō, -āre, -āvī, -ātum, *hollow* or *scoop out.*
cēdō, -ere, cessī, cessum, *to go, move; yield; withdraw.*
cedrus, -ī, f., *cedar.*
celebrō, -āre, -āvī, -ātum, *frequent; celebrate.*
Celemna, -ae, f., *Celemna,* a town of Campania.
celer, -eris, -ere, adj., *swift.*

celsus, -a, -um, adj., *high, lofty.*
Centaurus, -ī, m., *a Centaur,* a fabulous monster, with a human head and neck and the body of a horse.
centum, indecl. num. adj., *hundred.*
Cereālis, -e, adj., *pertaining to Ceres or to grain.*
Cerēs, -eris, f., *wheat; Ceres.*
cernō, -ere, crēvī, crētum, *discern, separate; resolve, determine; see; examine; decide.*
certāmen, -inis, n., *contest, struggle.*
certātim, adv., *with striving* or *contention.*
certus, -a, -um, adj., *sure, fixed; trusty, reliable; resolved.*
cervus, -ī, m., *stag, deer.*
cēterus, -a, -um, adj., *the other, remainder, rest (of), remaining part (of); (pl.) the rest, the others.*
ceu, conj., *as, just as, as if.*
Charybdis, -is, f., *Charybdis,* a whirlpool near the Sicilian coast, in the Straits of Messina, opposite the rock of Scylla; personified as a monster.
Chimaera, -ae, f., *Chimaera,* a monster, said to have infested Lycia, having the head of a lion, the body of a goat, and the tail of a dragon, and breathing out fire.
chorus, -ī, m., *dance in circle; dance; company of singers* or *dancers.*
cieō, -ēre, cīvī, citum, *cause to move; stir; agitate, excite; raise; call upon, invoke.*
Ciminus, -ī, m., *Lake Ciminus,* in Etruria.
cingō, -ere, -nxī, -nctum, *surround, encircle; gird (on oneself).*

circā or **circa**, adv., prep. with acc., *around*.
Circaeus, -a, -um, adj., *of Circe*.
Circē, -ēs or **-ae, f.**, *Circe, a sorceress, daughter of the Sun and Perse*.
circumstō, -stāre, -stetī, --, *stand around, surround*.
Cissēis, -idis, f., *Cisseis, the daughter of Cisseus, Hecuba*.
clāmō, -āre, -āvī, -ātum, *call, shout; proclaim*.
clārus, -a, -um, adj., *clear; famous, distinguished*.
classicum, -ī, n., *the sound of the trumpet; the trumpet*.
classis, -is, f., *division, fleet*.
Claudius, -a, -um, adj., *pertaining to the Claudii*.
claudō, -ere, -sī, -sum, *close; conclude, finish; besiege; confine*.
claustrum, -ī, n., *bolt, bar*.
Clausus, -ī, m., *Clausus, a chief of the Sabines*.
clipeātus, -a, -um, adj., *armed with a shield*.
clipeus, -ī, m., *round shield, shield*.
Cōcȳtius, -a, -um, adj., *of Cocytus (river)*.
Cōcȳtus, -ī, m., *Cocytus, "the river of lamentation," in the underworld*.
coeō, -īre, -īvī or **-iī, -itum**, *come together*.
coepiō, -ere, coepī, coeptum, *begin*.
cognōmen, -inis, n., *surname, family name; name*.
cōgō, -ere, coēgī, coactum, *drive together; compel*.
cohors, -rtis, f., *cohort, band, troop*.
colligō, -ere, -lēgī, -lectum, *collect; amass; rally*.
collis, -is, m., *hill; mound; high ground; mountain*.

colloquium, -ī, n., *conversation, discussion; meeting*.
collum, -ī, n., *neck*.
colō, -ere, coluī, cultum, *inhabit, cultivate; cherish, honor*.
colōnus, -ī, m., *farmer, colonist*.
color, -ōris, m., *color*.
coluber, -ubrī, m., *snake*.
columna, -ae, f., *column*.
colus, -ī or **-ūs, f.**, *distaff*.
coma, -ae, f., *hair*.
comitor, -ārī, -ātus sum, *accompany*.
comminus, adv., *hand to hand*.
committō, -ere, -mīsī, -missum, *bring together, join, entrust; start, bring about*.
commoveō, -ēre, -mōvī, -mōtum, *shake up, agitate; trouble, upset*.
cōmō, -ere, compsī, comptum, *arrange, adorn, embellish*.
compleō, -ēre, -ēvī, -ētum, *fill up*.
compōnō, -ere, -posuī, -positum, *build, arrange, bury, calm down*.
comprendō or **comprehendō, -ere, -endī, -ēnsum**, *unite; seize*.
concēdō, -ere, -cessī, -cessum, *withdraw, allow, concede; pardon; submit*.
concitō, -āre, -āvī, -ātum, *incite*.
conclāmō, -āre, -āvī, -ātum, *cry out together, shout*.
concurrō, -ere, -currī, -cursum, *assemble; concur; coincide; engage in battle*.
concutiō, -cutere, -cussī, -cussum, *shake, beat, strike; terrify; disturb, distract*.
condō, -ere, -didī, -ditum, *put or join together; found; bury; sink; shut (eyes); conceal; compose; sheathe (sword); plunge/bury (weapon in enemy)*.

coniciō, -ere, -iēcī, -iectum, *throw together, unite collect.*
coniugium, -ī, n., *joining together; marriage; husband, wife, consort.*
coniūnx, -iugis, m. or f., *spouse; husband, wife.*
consanguineus, -a, -um, adj., *kindred, related by blood.*
consīdō, -ere, -sēdī, -sessum, *sit down, settle; take up a position.*
consilium, -ī, n., *plan; council; advice; judgment.*
conspīrō, -āre, -āvī, -ātum, *blow or sound together.*
consul, -ulis, m., *consul.*
consulō, -ere, -uī, -sultum, *consult; plan, deliberate.*
consūmō, -ere, -sumpsī, -sumptum, *use up, consume.*
consurgō, -ere, -surrexī, -surrectum, *rise together.*
contemptor, -ōris, m., *despiser, scorner.*
contentus, -a, -um, *content.*
contendō, -ere, -tendī, -tentum, *strain, exert.*
contentus, -a, -um, *content.*
conterreō, -ēre, -terruī, -territum, *frighten greatly; terrify.*
contingō, -ere, -tigī, -tactum, *touch.*
continuō, adv., *immediately, continuously.*
contorqueō, -ēre, -torsī, -tortum, *turn round entirely; hurl, cast.*
contrā, adv., prep. with acc, *against, opposite.*
contrārius, -a, -um, adj., *opposite, contrary, hostile.*
contremiscō, -ere, -uī, --, *tremble all over, shake.*
cōnūbium, -ī, n., *marriage.*

convectō, -āre, -āvī, -ātum, *bring together; convey.*
convertō, -ere, -vertī, -versum, *turn round, change; cause to turn.*
coquō, -ere, coxī, coctum, *cook.*
cor, cordis, n., *heart; mind.*
Corās, -ae, m., *Coras, a hero of Tibur.*
cornipēs, -pedis, adj., *horn-hoofed.*
cornū, -ūs, n., *horn; trumpet. wing of army.*
corōna, -ae, f., *garland; crown.*
corōnō, -āre, -āvī, -ātum, *crown, surround.*
corpus, -oris, n., *body.*
cortex, -icis, m., *bark, shell, cork.*
Corythus, -ī, m., *Corythus, an ancient city of Etruria, later, and now Cortona.*
cōs, cōtis, f., *whetstone; a flint or jagged rock; cliff.*
costa, -ae, f., *rib, side.*
crātēr, -ēris, m. or crātēra, -ae, f., *large mixing bowl.*
crātis, -is, f., *hurdle; wickerwork.*
crēdō, -ere, -didī, -itum, *trust, believe.*
cremō, -āre, -āvī, -ātum, *burn.*
creō, -āre, -āvī, -ātum, *create, produce.*
crepitō, -āre, -āvī, -ātum, *make a rattling noise; crackle.*
crīmen, -inis, n., *crime; verdict, accusation; blame, fault.*
crīnālis, -e, adj., *of the hair.*
crīnis, -is, m., *hair.*
crīnītus, -a, -um, adj., *long-haired.*
crista, -ae, f., *crest, plume; helmet.*
crūdescō, -ere, -duī, --, *become harsh; grow fierce.*
crūdus, -a, -um, adj., *bloody, raw; cruel.*

cruentus, -a, -um, adj., *bloody, bloodstained.*
crustum, -ī, n., *crust.*
Crustumerī, -ōrum, m. pl., *the people of Crustumerium,* a town of the Sabines.
culmen, -inis, n., *top, summit, height; house top, ridge, roof (cf. columna).*
cum, prep. with abl., *with.*
cum, conj., *when; since; although.*
cunctor, -ārī, -ātus sum, *delay.*
cunctus, -a, -um, adj., *all.*
cuneus, -ī, m., *wedge.*
cupīdō, -inis, f., *desire, craving.*
cūra, -ae, f., *care, concern, anxiety.*
cūria, -ae, f., *place of assembly, Roman senate; court.*
currus, -ūs, m., *chariot.*
cursus, -ūs, m., *running; course, advance; race.*
curvō, -āre, -āvī, -ātum, *bend, curve; swell.*
curvus, -a, -um, adj., *curved; winding; crooked.*
cuspis, -idis, f., *sharp point, spear, tip (esp. of a spear).*
custōdia, -ae, f., *custody, protection, prisoner.*
custōs, -ōdis, m., *guardian; custody; protection.*
cycnus, -ī, m., *swan.*

D

daedalus, -a, -um, adj., *artificial, skillful, cunningly wrought.*
Danaē, -ēs, f., *Danaë,* daughter of Acrisius, and mother of Perseus.
daps, dapis, f., *feast, banquet; food; flesh of sacrificial victims;* usually found in the pl.

Dardanidēs, -ae, m., *a son* or *descendant of Dardanus, Aeneas;* (pl.) **Dardanidae, -ārum,** *the Trojans.*
Dardanius, -a, -um, adj., *Dardanian; Trojan.*
Dardanus, -a, -um, adj., *Dardanian, Trojan.*
Dardanus, -ī, m., *Dardanus,* son of Jupiter and Electra, father of the Trojan line of kings, and thus progenitor of the Romans.
dē, prep. with abl., *down from; about, concerning.*
dea, -ae, f., *goddess.*
dēbellātor, -ōris, m., *conqueror.*
dēbeō, -ēre, -uī, -itum, *owe; ought.*
dēcernō, -ere, -crēvī, -crētum, *determine, decide; contend.*
decus, -oris, n., *beauty; ornament; glory.*
dēferō, -ferre, -tulī, -lātum, *carry away; convey; report, confer.*
dēfessus, -a, -um, adj., *weary, exhausted.*
dēfīgō, -ere, -fīxī, -fīxum, *fix, sink, stick.*
dēfluō, -ere, -fluxī, -fluxum, *flow down; sail down; descend.*
deinde or **dein,** adv., *then, next, thenceforth.*
dēlābor, -lābī, -lapsus sum, *glide; slip* or *fall down; descend.*
dēligō, -ere, -lēgī, -lēctum, *choose from; choose.*
dēmissus, -a, -um, adj., *hanging down, modest.*
dens, dentis, m., *tooth.*
denseō, -ēre or **densō, -āre, -āvī, -ātum,** *make thick; thicken; close up; crowd.*

densus, -a, -um, adj., *thick, dense.*
dēpōnō, -ere, -posuī, -positum, *put down.*
dērigescō, -ere, -riguī, --, *grow completely stiff; be cold.*
dērigō, -ere, -rēxī, -rectum, *lay straight; aim, direct.*
descendō, -ere, -dī, -sum, *descend.*
dēserō, -ere, -uī, -tum, *leave, abandon.*
dēserta, -ōrum, n. pl., *haunts, waste places.*
dēsignō, -āre, -āvī, -ātum, *mark out, arrange.*
despectō, -āre, -āvī, -ātum, *look down upon.*
dēsuescō, -ere, -suēvī, -suētum, *become unaccustomed;* part. dēsuētus,- a,- um, *unaccustomed, unused; neglected; dormant.*
dēsum, -esse, -fuī, *be lacking; be away.*
dētrūdō, -ere, -trūsī, -trūsum, *thrust down* or *away; push off from.*
deus, -ī, m., *god.*
dexter, -tra, -trum, adj., *right, on the right side; dexterous; favorable.*
dextera, -ae, f., *right hand.*
Diāna, -ae, f., *Diana* (goddess).
diciō, -ōnis, f., *dominion, power, rule.*
dīcō, -ere, dixī, dictum, *say, speak.*
dictum, -ī, n., *word; saying.*
dīdō, -ere, -didī, -ditum, *spread abroad.*
diēs, diēī, m., sometimes f. in sing., *day.*
diffundō, -ere, -fūdī, -fūsum, *pour round about; spread.*
dīgnus, -a, -um, adj., *worthy; worthy of* (with abl.).
dīluvium, -ī, n., *washing away; flood, deluge, destruction.*

dirimō, -ere, -ēmī, -emptum, *take asunder; separate; break off.*
dīrus, -a, -um, adj., *dire, horrible.*
Dīs, -ītis, m., *Dis,* the ruler of Hades, *Pluto.*
discordia, -ae, f., *disagreement, dissension.*
disiciō, -ere, -iēcī, -iectum, *throw; overthrow, demolish; scatter.*
dissideō, -ēre, -sēdī, -sessum, *be situated apart; disagree with.*
distrahō, -ere, -traxī, -tractum, *pull apart, tear to pieces.*
dīva, -ae, f., *goddess.*
dīversus, -a, -um, adj., *different, diverse, separate.*
dīves, -itis, adj., *rich; fertile, productive.*
dīvus, -a, -um, adj., *divine.*
dīvus, -ī, m., *divine being, god.*
dō, dare, dedī, datum, *give; pay; grant; devote; allow; make; surrender; relate.*
dolō, -ōnis, m., *staff* or *pole with an iron point; pike.*
dolor, -ōris, m., *pain, grief, suffering; resentment, indignation.*
dominor, -ārī, -ātus sum, *be lord* or *master; rule.*
domitō, -āre, -āvī, -ātum, *tame; train, exercise.*
domitor, -ōris, m., *tamer; ruler, sovereign.*
domus, -ūs or -ī, f., *house, home.*
dōnum, -ī, n., *gift.*
dōs, dōtis, f., *gift, endowment; dowry.*
dōtō, -āre, -āvī, -ātum, *endow.*
dubitō, -āre, -āvī, -ātum, *hesitate, doubt.*
dubius, -a, -um, adj., *doubtful.*
dūcō, -ere, dūxī, ductum, *lead; consider.*

dum, conj., *while, until, provided that; since.*
duō, -ae, -o, num. adj., *two.*
duplex, -icis, adj., *double; twofold.*
dūrus, -a, -um, adj., *hard, harsh.*
dux, ducis, m. or f., *leader, general.*

E

ē, ex, prep. with abl., *out of, from.*
ecce, interj., *lo! behold! look!*
ēdō, -ere, -didī, -ditum, *emit, bring forth; exhibit; utter solemnly; make known; declare.*
ēdūcō, -ere, -dūxī, -ductum, *train; educate; rear; lead forth.*
efferus, -a, -um, adj., *savage, frantic; fierce; cruel.*
effētus, -a, -um, adj., *no longer producing; exhausted; incapable.*
effigiēs, -ēī, f., *a portrait, image, effigy.*
efflō, -āre, -āvī, -ātum, *blow or breathe out.*
(effor), effārī, effātus sum, *speak forth; speak, say.*
effugiō, -ere, -fūgī, --, *flee, escape.*
effultus, -a, -um, *propped up; supported.*
effundō, -ere, -fūdī, -fūsum, *pour out.*
effūsus, -a, -um, adj., *poured forth; overflowing; thronging.*
egeō, -ēre, eguī, -- , *want, need, lack; be without.*
Ēgeria, -ae, f., *Egeria,* a nymph of Roman mythology, instructor of Numa.
egō, gen. **meī,** dat. **mihi,** acc. **mē,** abl. **mē,** pers. pron., sing., *I, me.*
ēgregius, -a, -um, adj., *distinguished, uncommon, extraordinary.*
ēligō, -ere, -lēgī, -lectum, *pick out, select.*

ēmētior, -īrī, -mensus sum, *measure out* or *off; pass over, traverse.*
ēn, interj., *look!*
enim, conj., *in fact, for.*
ēnītor, -ī, -nīsus or **-nīxus sum,** *struggle, strive, give birth to.*
ensis, -is, m., *sword.*
eō, īre, iī or **īvī, itum,** *go, walk; march, advance; pass; flow; pass (time).*
epulae, -ārum, f. pl., *banquet, feast.*
eques, -itis, m., *horseman.*
equidem, adv., *indeed, certainly; for my part.*
equus, -ī, m., *horse.*
Eratō, -ūs, f., *Erato,* the muse of love poetry (only in nom.).
Erebus, -ī, m., *Erebus,* the god of darkness, son of Chaos and brother of Night; *darkness; the lower world.*
Ēretum, -ī, n., *Eretum,* an ancient Sabine town.
ergō, conj., *therefore; well, then, now.*
ērigō, -ere, -rēxī, -rectum, *set up, erect; rouse, excite.*
erīlis, -e, adj., *pertaining to an owner, master,* or *mistress; master's.*
Erīnys, -yos, f., *Erinys, a Fury.*
ēripiō, -ere, -uī, -reptum, *tear away, snatch away.*
errō, -āre, -āvī, -ātum, *wander, err.*
error, -ōris, m., *wandering, error.*
et, conj., *and.*
et, adv., *even, also.*
etenim, conj., *and indeed; since.*
etiam, adv., *also, even; still.*
euhoe, interj., *a joyous Bacchanalian shout; evoe! joy!*
Eurōpa, -ae, f., *Europa* (name), the daughter of Agenor, king of Phoenicia, brought by Jupiter over the sea to Crete; *Europe.*

ēvalescō, -ere, -valuī, *grow strong; be able.*
ēvolō, -āre, -āvī, -ātum, *fly away.*
exāmen, -inis, n., *a multitude; swarm.*
exardescō, -ere, -arsī, -arsum, *begin to burn;* (fig.) *be roused to anger; kindle, burn.*
exaudiō, -īre, -īvī, -ītum, *hear.*
excieō or exciō, -īre, -īvī,-ītum or -itum, *summon, rouse up* or *forth; call forth; stir.*
excipiō, -ere, -cēpī, -ceptum, *take out; receive.*
excutiō, -ere, -cussī, -cussum, *shake off.*
exerceō, -ēre, -uī, -itum, *train, exercise, carry on; cultivate, cherish.*
exercitus, -ūs, m., *army.*
exhālō, -āre, -āvī, -ātum, *breathe out.*
exhorrēscō, -ere, -horruī, --, *shudder greatly; shudder at, dread.*
exhortor, -ārī, -ātus sum, *encourage; advise.*
exigō, -ere, -ēgī, -actum, *drive out; collect; achieve, complete.*
exiguus, -a, -um, adj., *small, little.*
eximius, -a, -um, adj., *exceptional, distinguished.*
exinde, (abbrev. exin), adv., *from that place; thereafter, then.*
exitium, -ī, n., *destruction, ruin.*
exordium, -ī, n., *beginning; origin.*
expediō, -īre, -iī or -īvī, -ītum, *set free;* (impersonal) *be useful; relate, narrate.*
experior, -īrī, -pertus sum, *test, try, experience.*
expleō, -ēre, -ēvī, -ētum, *fill up, fulfil.*
explōrō, -āre, -āvī, -ātum, *explore, investigate; reconnoiter.*

exposcō, -ere, -poposcī, --, *ask earnestly; beg, entreat.*
exquīrō, -ere, -quisīvī, -quisītum, *seek out.*
exsaturō, -āre, -āvī, -ātum, *satisfy, glut.*
exscindō, -ere, -scidī, -scissum, *tear out; tear down, destroy; extirpate.*
exsequiae, -ārum, f. pl., *funeral rites.*
exstinguō, -ere, -stinxī, -stinctum, *extinguish, quench; kill, destroy.*
exsul, -ulis, m., *exile.*
exsultō, -āre, -āvī, -ātum, *be ecstatic, exult.*
exsuperō, -āre, -āvī, -ātum, *be completely above; mount upward; overrule.*
extemplō, adv., *immediately.*
extendō, -ere, -tendī, -tentum or -tensum, *extend, stretch forth; stretch.*
exter, -tera, -terum, adj., *outward, foreign.*
externus, -a, -um, adj., *outside, foreign, strange.*
exūberō, -āre, -āvī, -ātum, *abound, overflow.*
exuō, -ere, -uī, -ūtum, *take off, strip.*
exūrō, -ere, -ussī, -ustum, *burn out, consume with fire; purge; destroy.*

F

Fabaris, -is, m., *Fabaris, a small branch of the Tiber.*
faciēs, -ēī, f., *appearance, face, form.*
faciō, -ere, fēcī, factum, *do, make; reckon.*
factum, ī, n., *deed.*
falcātus, -a, -um, adj., *scythe-shaped; hooked, crooked.*

Faliscī, -ōrum, m. pl., adj., *Falisci,* a Tuscan people dwelling in Falerii; perhaps kindred with the Aequicoli.
fallō, -ere, fefellī, falsum, *deceive; be mistaken, beguile; fail; cheat.*
falsus, -a, -um, adj., *deceptive, false.*
falx, falcis, f., *scythe, sickle.*
fāma, -ae, f., *rumor, report; reputation, fame.*
famēs, -is, f., *hunger, famine.*
fās, n., *right* (indecl.); *what is permitted.*
fascis, -is, m., *bundle; burden;* pl., **fasces, -ium,** *the fasces* or *bundle of rods,* a symbol of authority, carried by the lictors in front of the higher magistrates of Rome.
fātālis, -e, adj., *fated, fatal.*
fateor, -ērī, fassus sum, *confess, admit.*
fātidicus, -a, -um, adj., *prophetic.*
fatīgō, -āre, -āvī, -ātum, *tire, wear out.*
fātum, -ī, n., *destiny, fate;* (in pl. often), *death.*
fauces, -ium, f. pl., *throat; entrance.*
Faunus, -ī, m., *Faunus,* the tutelary god of farmers, identified by the Romans with the Greek Pan.
fax, facis, f., *torch, fire.*
fēcundus, -a, -um, adj., *bringing forth, productive, fruitful.*
fēlix, -īcis, adj., *fortunate, happy.*
fēmineus, -a, -um, adj., *feminine.*
fera, -ae, f., *wild animal.*
ferō, ferre, tulī, lātum, *bear, carry; edure; report.*
Fērōnia, -ae, f., *Feronia,* an ancient Italian goddess, presiding over woods and orchards.
ferox, -ōcis, adj., *bold; wild; warlike; cruel.*

ferrātus, -a, -um, adj., *furnished* or *covered with iron.*
ferrum, -ī, n., *iron; sword.*
ferus, -a, -um, adj., *wild, untamed; ruthless.*
fervidus, -a, -um, adj., *intensely hot, blazing.*
Fescennīnus, -a, -um, adj., *of Fescennium,* a Tuscan city on the Tiber.
fessus, -a, -um, adj., *tired, exhausted.*
festīnō, -āre, -āvī, -ātum, *hurry.*
fībula, -ae, f., *clasp, brooch.*
fidēs, -eī, f., *trust, faith; trustworthiness.*
fīdō, -ere, fīsus sum, *trust, believe.*
fīdus, -a, -um, adj., *faithful, trustworthy.*
fīgō, -ere, fīxī, fīxus, *fix, fasten; pierce.*
fīlia, -ae, f., *daughter.*
fīlius, -ī, m., *son.*
fingō, -ere, finxī, fictum, *shape; invent; imagine.*
fīnis, -is, m., *end, boundary;* (pl.) *country, territory, land.*
fīnitimus, -a, -um, adj., *bordering, neighboring.*
fīō, fierī (used as pass. of **faciō**), *become; take place; be made.*
flagellum, -ī, n., *scourge* or *whip; thong* (dim. of **flagrum,** *whip*).
flagrō, -āre, -āvī, -ātum, *burn.*
flamma, -ae, f., *flame; ardor.*
flammeus, -a, -um, adj., *fiery, flaming.*
flātus, -ūs, m., *blowing; wind; blast.*
flāveō, -ēre, --, --, *be yellow.*
Flāvīnius, -a, -um, adj., *of Flavinium* or *Flavina,* in Etruria.
flāvus, -a, -um, adj., *golden, yellow.*
flectō, -ere, flexī, flexum, *bend, curve; persuade, prevail upon.*

fleō, -ēre, -ēvī, -ētum, *cry.*
flōreō, -ēre, -uī, --, *bloom; flourish; be prosperous.*
flōs, -ōris, m., *flower, bloom.*
fluctus, -ūs, m., *wave; flood; tide, surge; turbulence, commotion.*
flūmen, -inis, n., *river.*
fluvius, -ī, m., *river, stream.*
focus, -ī, m., *fireplace, hearth.*
foedō, -āre, -āvī, -ātum, *defile, pollute, dishonor.*
foedus, -eris, n., *contract, treaty, agreement; alliance.*
foedus, -a, -um, adj., *foul.*
fons, fontis, m., *spring, fountain; source.*
for, fārī, fātus sum, *speak, say.*
forma, -ae, f., *shape, form; beauty.*
formīdō, -inis, f., *fear.*
fornax, -ācis, f., *furnace; forge.*
fors, fortis, f., *chance, luck.*
forte, adv., *by chance.*
fortis, -e, adj., *brave; strong.*
fortūna, -ae, f., *fortune, chance.*
Forulī, -ōrum, m. pl., *Foruli,* a Sabine town.
fossa, -ae, f., *ditch, trench.*
fragor, -ōris, m., *breaking, the noise of breaking; a crash.*
fragōsus, -a, -um, adj., *crashing, roaring.*
frangō, -ere, frēgī, fractum, *break, shatter; subdue.*
frāter, -tris, m., *brother.*
fraus, fraudis, f., *fraud, deceit; offense, crime.*
fremō, -ere, -uī, -itum, *roar, groan.*
frīgidus, -a, -um, adj., *cool, cold.*
frondeō, -ēre, --, --, *be leafy; bear* or *put forth leaves;* part., **frondens**, *leafy; green.*

frondōsus, -a, -um, adj., *full of leaves, leafy.*
frons, frondis, f., *leaf; foliage; branch; wreath.*
frons, frontis, f., *forehead; front.*
fruor, -ī, fructus sum, with abl., *enjoy, delight in; profit by.*
Fūcinus, -ī, m., *Fucinus,* a lake in the Apennines, east of Rome.
fuga, -ae, f., *flight.*
fugiō, -ere, fūgī, fugitum, *flee, escape: avoid.*
fulgeō, fulgēre, fulsī, --, *shine.*
fulmen, -inis, n., *lightning, thunderbolt.*
fulvus, -a, -um, adj., *reddish or tawny yellow.*
fūmidus, -a, -um, adj., *smoking, steaming.*
fūmō, -āre, -āvī, -ātum, *smoke, send up vapor; fume.*
fundātor, -ōris, m., *founder.*
fundō, -āre, -āvī, -ātum, *found.*
fundō, -ere, fūdī, fūsum, *pour, scatter; rout.*
fundus, -ī, m., *foundation, base.*
fūnereus, -a, -um, adj., *funereal.*
fūnestus, -a, -um, adj., *deadly.*
fūnus, -eris, n., *funeral; death; dead body.*
furia, -ae, f., *a fury.*
furiālis, -e, adj., *raging.*
furibundus, -a, -um, adj., *raging, frenzied.*
furō, -ere, --, --, *rage, be mad.*
furor, -ōris, m., *madness, rage, fury.*
fūror, -ārī, -ātus sum, *steal.*
furtīvus, -a, -um, adj., *secret, furtive.*
fuscus, -a, -um, adj., *dark, dusky.*

G

Gabīnus, -a, -um, adj., *of Gabii,* an ancient city in Latium.
Galaesus, -ī, m., *Galaesus,* a Latin nobleman; a river near Tarentum.
galea, -ae, f., *helmet.*
galērus, -ī, m. *a cap made of animal skin.*
gaudeō, -ēre, gāvīsus sum, *be glad, rejoice.*
gelidus, -a, -um, adj., *cold, icy.*
geminus, -a, -um, adj., *twin.*
gemitus, -ūs, m., *groan, lamentation; cry; noise.*
gemma, -ae, f., *jewel, gem.*
gemō, -ere, -uī, -itum, *groan, sigh.*
gener, -erī, m., *son-in-law.*
generō, -āre, -āvī, -ātum, *sire, create.*
genitor, -ōris, m., *father.*
genius, -ī, m., *the birth-spirit; a tutelar deity.*
gens, gentis, f., *family, clan; nation.*
genus, -eris, n., *origin; race, stock.*
gerō, -ere, gessī, gestum, *bear; manage; perform.*
Gēryōn, -onis, *Geryon,* a giant with three bodies, dwelling in Gades, slain by Hercules, who carried his herd of cattle to Italy.
gestāmen, -inis, n., *that which is carried; equipment.*
gestō, -āre, -āvī, -ātum, *carry, bear; wear.*
Getae, -ārum, m. pl., *Getae,* a Thracian people dwelling on the Danube.
gignō, -ere, genuī, genitum, *bring forth, beget, bear.*
glaeba, -ae, f., *lump of earth; clod; soil.*
glans, glandis, f., *an acorn; a leaden ball* or *bullet.*
glōria, -ae, f., *renown, glory.*
Gorgoneus, -a, -um, adj., *pertaining to a Gorgon; Gorgonian.*
grāmen, -inis, n., *grass, plant, herb.*
grāmineus, -a, -um, adj., *grassy.*
grātia, -ae, f., *favor, influence, gratitude.*
gravidus, -a, -um, *heavy; pregnant, teeming with.*
graviter, adv., *heavily; deadly; heavily, mournfully.*
gremium, -ī, n., *lap, bosom.*
grex, gregis, m., *herd, flock.*
gurges, -itis, m., *whirlpool; wave; billow; raging sea* or *waters.*
guttur, -uris, n., *windpipe, throat.*
gȳrus, -ī, m., *circle.*

H

habēna, -ae, f., *rein; strap, thong; whip.*
habeō, -ēre, -uī, -itum, *have, hold; consider.*
habitō, -āre, -āvī, -ātum, *inhabit, dwell; live, stay.*
haereō, -ēre, haesī, haesum, *stick to, hang on to.*
Halaesus, -ī, m., *Halaesus,* an ally of Turnus, formerly companion of Agamemnon.
harēna, -ae, f., *sand; arena.*
harundō, -inis, f., *reed, stick.*
hasta, -ae, f., *spear.*
haud, adv., *not at all, by no means.*
Helena, -ae, f., *Helen,* daughter of Jupiter and Leda, sister of Clytemnestra and of Castor, and wife of Menelaus.
Helicōn, -ōnis, m., *Helicon,* mountain in Boeotia, sacred to the Muses and Apollo.
herba, -ae, f., *grass, herb.*

Herculēs, -is, m., *Hercules, the god of strength and labor, son of Jupiter and Alcmena.*
Herculeus, -a, -um, adj., *of Hercules; Herculean.*
hērēs, -ēdis, m. or f., *heir.*
Hermus, -ī, m., *Hermus, a river in Aeolis, depositing gold.*
Hernicus, -a, -um, adj., *of the Hernici, an Italian tribe of Latium; Hernican.*
Hesperia, -ae, f., *Hesperia, the western land; Italy.*
Hesperius, -a, -um, adj., *of the west; western* (in relation to Asia and Greece); *Hesperian, Italian.*
heu, interj., *alas! oh!*
heus, interj., *hi! hey!*
hībernus, -a, -um, adj., *of winter, wintry.*
Hibērus, -a, -um, adj., *of Iberia, Spanish; western.*
hīc, adv., *here, in this place; at this time.*
hic, haec, hoc, dem. pron. or adj., *this, these.*
hiems, -emis, f., *winter; stormy weather.*
Himella, -ae, m., *Himella, a river of the Sabine country.*
hinc, adv., *from here, hence.*
Hippolytus, -ī, m., *Hippolytus, son of Theseus and Hippolyte; father of Virbius.*
homō, -inis, m., *human being, man;* (pl.) *people.*
Homolē, -ēs, f., *Homole, a mountain near Tempe, in Thessaly.*
honor or **honos, -ōris, m.,** *honor, respect; glory.*
horrendus, -a, -um, adj., *be shuddered at; dreadful; wonderful.*
horrens, -entis, adj., *bristling; rough.*
horrescō, -ere, -horruī, --, *become rough; bristle; shudder; dread.*
horridus, -a, -um, adj., *rough, uncouth, shaggy.*
hospitium, -ī, n., *hospitality.*
hostis, -is, m., *(public) enemy.*
hūc, adv., *to here, hither.*
humilis, -e, adj., *humble.*
hydra, -ae, f., *a water-serpent,* any serpent like the Lernaean *Hydra,* a monster with many heads, slain by Hercules.
hydrus, -ī, m., *water-serpent; snake.*
hymenaeus, -ī, m., *the Greek wedding refrain, hymeneal; personified as god of marriage;* (pl.) *marriage.*
Hyrcānus, -a, -um, adj., *belonging to the Hyrcani, a tribe on the Caspian; Hyrcanian.*

I

iaceō, -ēre, iacuī, --, *lie; lie in ruins; be situated.*
iactō, -āre, -āvī, -ātum, *throw (away); disturb; boast; discuss.*
iam, adv., *now, already, by* or *even now; besides.*
iam prīdem, adv., *some time before or since; long ago, long since.*
Iānus, -ī, m., *Janus, an ancient divinity of Latium, represented with two faces.*
ibī, adv., *there; then.*
ictus, -ūs, m., *blow, stroke.*
Īdaeus, -a, -um, adj., *of Mount Ida* (either in Crete or in the Troad), *Idaean.*
īdem, eadem, idem, dem. pron., *the same.*
ignis, -is, m., *fire.*

ignōbilis, -e, adj., *unknown, obscure; undistinguished; ignoble.*
ignōrō, -āre, -āvī, -ātum, *not know; be unfamiliar with; disregard; ignore.*
ignōtus, -a, -um, adj., *unknown, strange; unacquainted with, ignorant of.*
īlia, -ium, n. pl., *the groin; belly.*
Īlias, -adis, f., adj., *daughter of Ilium or Troy;* pl., **Īliades, -um,** *Trojan women.*
īlicet, adv., *immediately, at once, instantly* (< **ire** and **licet**).
Īlioneus, -eī, m., *Ilioneus, commander of one of the ships of Aeneas.*
ille, illa, illud, dem. pron. and adj., *that; those.*
illustris, -e, adj., *bright; clear; distinguished, famous.*
imāgō, -inis, f., *likeness, image; echo; statue; ghost.*
imbuō, -ere, -uī, -ūtum, *drench; permeate; wet; stain.*
immāne, adv., *wildly.*
immānis, -e, adj., *huge, monstrous.*
immemor, -oris, adj., *unmindful, forgetful.*
immēnsus, -a, -um, adj., *immense.*
immōbilis, -e, adj., *unmoved, immovable.*
immōtus, -a, -um, adj., *unmoved, unchanged, unrelenting.*
impellō, -ere, -pulī, -pulsum, *strike against; impel.*
imperium, -ī, n., *command, power; empire.*
imperō, -āre, -āvī, -ātum, *order, command.*
impexus, -a, -um, adj., *uncombed, untrimmed.*

impleō, -ēre, -ēvī, -ētum, *fill up; fulfill.*
implicō, -āre, -āvī, -ātum, *fold in; involve; entwine; bind to.*
implōrō, -āre, -āvī, -ātum, *implore.*
impōnō, -pōnere, -posuī, -positum, *put on, impose; establish; impose upon.*
imprōvīsus, -a, -um, adj., *unforeseen, unexpected.*
impūbēs, -is or **-eris,** adj., *not full grown; youthful.*
īmus, -a, -um, adj. superl. of **inferus,** *deepest, last; of the underworld.*
in, prep. with acc., *into, onto; against;* prep. with abl., *in, on.*
inaccessus, -a, -um, adj., *difficult of approach, perilous to be approached.*
Īnachius, -a, -um, adj., *of Inachus; Inachian; Argive, Greek.*
Īnachus, -ī, m., *Inachus, the first king of Argos, father of Io.*
inānis, -e, adj., *empty, void; vain; inane; foolish.*
inausus, -a, -um, adj., *undared, unattempted.*
incassum, adv., *in vain.*
incendō, -ere, -cendī, -cēnsum, *set fire to, burn.*
inceptum, -ī, n., *a beginning; deliberation; undertaking; purpose.*
incingō, -ere, -cīnxī, -cīnctum, *gird (on); clothe.*
inclūdō, -ere, -sī, -sum, *enclose; include*
incubō, -āre, -uī, -itum, *lie; recline upon* (with abl. or dat.).
incūs, -ūdis, f., *an anvil.*
inde, adv., *from there, from then.*
indecor, -oris or **indecoris, -e,** adj., *disgraceful, bringing disgrace; infamous.*

indīcō, -ere, -dīxī, -dictum, *proclaim, announce.*
indictus, -a, -um, adj., *unmentioned; unsung.*
indignor, -ārī, -ātus sum, *deem unworthy; fret; scorn; be angry or indignant.*
indomitus, -a, -um, adj., *untamed, wild.*
induō, -ere, -duī, -dūtum, *put on, clothe.*
Indus, -a, -um, adj., *belonging India, Indian.*
ineō, -īre, -iī or **-īvī, -itum,** *enter.*
inexcītus, -a, -um, adj., *dormant, quiet.*
infandus, -a, -um, adj., *not be uttered, unspeakable; cruel; accursed.*
infaustus, -a, -um, adj., *unfortunate, ill-omened.*
infectus, -a, -um, adj., *not done; unworked; corrupted.*
infēlix, -īcis, adj., *unfortunate, unhappy.*
infernus, -a, -um, adj., *lower, that which lies beneath; of Hades, infernal.*
inferō, -ferre, -tulī, -lātum, *bring upon* or *against; inflict upon.*
inferus, -a, -um, adj., *low, vile; infernal;* (m. used as subst.) *inhabitant of the underworld.*
infestus, -a, -um, adj., *hostile, aggressive.*
infringō, -ere, -frēgī, -fractum, *break in; break.*
ingeminō, -āre, -āvī, -ātum, *repeat; shout again and again.*
ingens, -ntis, adj., *huge.*
ingrātus, -a, -um, adj., *unpleasant; ungrateful, displeased.*

ingredior, -ī, -gressus sum, *step in, enter.*
inhiō, -āre, -āvī, -ātum, *gape at or over; inspect; gape at.*
inīquus, -a, -um, adj., *uneven; inequitable, unjust.*
inlīdō, -ere, -līsī, -līsum, *dash upon, thrust; dash into.*
innectō, -ere, -nexuī, -nexum, *bind, tie; entwine; link together.*
innocuus, -a, -um, adj., *harmless, involving no danger to anyone; unharmed, safe.*
inquam, inquis, inquit, inquiunt, *say; one says.*
insānia, -ae, f., *madness.*
insānus, -a, -um, adj., *insane.*
inscius, -a, -um, adj., *not knowing; unaware; amazed.*
insequor, -ī, -secūtus sum, *follow after, pursue.*
insidiae, -ārum, f. pl., *ambush.*
insigne, -is, n., *medal, decoration.*
insigniō, -īre, -īvī or **-iī, -ītum,** *decorate with a mark; adorn; decorate.*
insignis, -e, adj., *conspicuous, manifest, distinguished.*
insonō, -āre, -uī, *sound within; resound;* with acc., *sound, crack (as to or with) the lash.*
inspīrō, -āre, -āvī, -ātum, *breathe into; inspire.*
instar, n., (indecl.) *the equivalent, just like* (with gen.).
instaurō, -āre, -āvī, -ātum, *build; perform; celebrate.*
insternō, -ere, -strāvī, -strātum, *spread over; cover.*
instituō, -ere, -uī, -ūtum, *undertake; establish, set down; build.*

insultō, -āre, -āvī, -ātum, *dance; leap upon.*
intactus, -a, -um, adj., *untouched, unbroken.*
intendō, -ere, -tendī, -tentum, *stretch, strain.*
intentus, -a, -um, adj., *earnestly attentive, intent; expectant.*
inter, prep. with acc., *between, among; during.*
intereā, adv., *meanwhile.*
interior, -ōris, adj., *inner, more intimate.*
interluō, -ere, --, --, *wash between; flow between.*
internectō, -ere, --, --, *bind together, bind up.*
intexō, -ere, -uī, -tum, *weave into or in; work in; entwine; cover; frame.*
intonō, -āre, -uī, -ātum, *thunder forth.*
intrā, prep. with acc., *within.*
intrō, -āre, -āvī, -ātum, *enter; reach.*
intus, adv., prep. with abl., *within, inside.*
invehō, -ere, -vexī, -vectum, *carry into* or *forward;* pass., *to ride or drive.*
inveniō, -īre, -vēnī, -ventum, *find, discover.*
invīsus, -a, -um, adj., *hated, hostile.*
invocō, -āre, -āvī, -ātum, *call upon; invoke.*
involvō, -ere, -volvī, -volūtum, *roll on or in; cast upon.*
iō, interj., *hurrah! oh!*
Īō, -ūs, f., *Io,* daughter of Inachus, changed into a cow, watched by Argus, and again restored to her own form, and worshiped by the Egyptians as Isis.

ipse, ipsa, ipsum, intens. pron., *himself, herself, itself*
īra, -ae, f., *anger, wrath.*
irrīdeō, -ēre, -rīsī, -rīsum, *laugh at, ridicule.*
is, ea, id, dem. pron. and adj., *he, she, it; that.*
ita, adv., *thus, so.*
Italia, -ae, f., *Italy.*
Italus, -a, -um, adj., *Italian.*
Italus, -ī, m., *Italus,* the ancient king from whom Italy was supposed to have been named.
iter, itineris, n., *journey; road, path.*
iterum, adv., *again.*
iuba, -ae, f., *mane,* of a horse; *plume, crest,* of a helmet.
iubeō, -ēre, iussī, iussum, *order; request.*
iugālis, -e, adj., *yoked; nuptial;* (n. pl. used as subst.) *yoked* or *harnessed horses; a team.*
iugum, -ī, n., *yoke; ridge; chain of hills.*
Iūlus, -ī, m., *Iulus* or *Ascanius,* son of Aeneas.
iungō, -ere, iunxī, iunctum, *join, bring together; yoke, harness.*
Iūnō, -ōnis, f., *Juno.*
Iuppiter, Iovis, m., *Jupiter.*
iūrō, -āre, -āvī, -ātum, *swear, take an oath.*
iūs, iūris, n., *right, justice, law, oath.*
iussum, -ī, n., *command, order.*
iustus, -a, -um, adj., *just, fair; proper.*
iuvenis, -is, m., *youth.*
iuventa, -ae, f., *youth.*
iuventūs, -ūtis, f., *youth, young man; men of military age.*
iuvō, -āre, iūvī, iūtum, *help, aid; please, delight.*
iūxtā, adv., *near, close.*

L

Labīcī, -ōrum, m. pl., *the Labici,* people of Labicum (or *Labici*), a Latin town near the present Colonna.
lābor, -ī, lapsus sum, *glide, slip.*
labor, -ōris, m., *work; effort, hardship.*
Lacedaemōn, -onis, f., (acc. **-ona**), *Lacedaemon* or *Sparta*, the capital of Laconia.
lacertus, -ī, m., *the arm,* esp. *the upper arm.*
lacessō, -ere, -īvī, -ītum, *provoke, irritate.*
lacrimābilis, -e, adj., *causing tears, piteous, disastrous.*
lacrimō, -āre, -āvī, -ātum, *cry.*
lacus, -cūs, m., *lake, reservoir.*
laedō, -ere, laesī, laesum, *injure by striking, hurt; offend; annoy.*
laetus, -a, -um, adj., *happy.*
laeva, -ae; f., (sc. **manus**) *the left hand; on left side.*
lampas, -adis, f., *light; torch, firebrand.*
lāniger, -era, -erum, adj., *wool-bearing.*
Lāomedontius, -a, -um, adj., *pertaining to Laomedon,* father of Priam; *Laomedontean, Trojan.*
Lapitha, -ae, m. or **f.,** *one of the Lapithae;* pl., **Lapithae, -ārum,** *the Lapithae,* a race of Thessalians, who fought with the Centaurs at the marriage of Pirithous, king of the Lapithae.
lātē, *widely; far and wide; on all sides, far around; all over.*
lateō, -ēre, -uī, --, *lie hidden, be hidden.*
latex, -icis, m., *liquid; liquor; wine; water.*

Latīnī, -ōrum, m. pl., *the Latins,* the *people of Latium.*
Latīnus, -a, -um, adj., *of Latium; Latin.*
Latīnus, -ī, m., *Latinus,* king of the Laurentines, father of Lavinia.
Latium, -ī, n., *Latium,* a country of ancient Italy, extending from the left bank of the lower Tiber to Campania.
lātrō, -āre, -āvī, -ātum, *bark, snarl.*
latus, -eris, n., *side, flank, strength.*
lātus, -a, -um, adj., *broad, wide.*
Laurens, -entis, adj., *Laurentine, Laurentian.*
laurus, -ī, f., *laurel.*
laus, laudis, f., *praise, glory.*
Lausus, -ī, m., *Lausus,* a young Etruscan warrior, son of Mezentius.
Lāvīnia, -ae, f., *Lavinia,* a Latin princess, daughter of King Latinus.
lavō, -āre, -āvī, lautum or **lōtum,** *wash, bathe; soak.*
Lēdaeus, -a, -um, adj., *pertaining to Leda; Ledaean; daughter of Leda.*
legiō, -ōnis, f., *legion.*
lentus, -a, -um, adj., *flexible, pliant; slow.*
leō, -ōnis, m., *lion.*
lētum, -ī, n., *death.*
levis, -e, adj., *light, trivial.*
lēvis, -e, adj., *smooth, slippery; delicate.*
levō, -āre, -āvī, -ātum, *raise; make light; comfort; relieve, alleviate.*
lex, lēgis, f., *law.*
līber, -era, -erum, adj., *free; independent; unimpeded.*
lībō, -āre, -āvī, -ātum, *pour, taste.*
lībum, -ī, n., *cake.*
Libycus, -a, -um, adj., *Libyan.*

licenter, adv., *freely, without restraint;* comp. adv., **licentius**.
licet, licēre, licuit or **licitum est,** *it is permitted.*
līmen, -inis, n., *threshold.*
linquō, -ere, līquī, --, *leave, relinquish.*
liquidus, -a, -um, adj., *clear, liquid, melodious.*
lītus, -oris, n., *seashore.*
lituus, -ī, m., *an augur's staff; trumpet, cornet.*
līveō, ēre, --, --, *be bluish, pallid.*
locō, -āre, -āvī, -ātum, *place, put.*
locus, -ī, m. or **loca, -ōrum, n. pl.,** *place, region.*
longaevus, -a, -um, adj., *aged, of advanced age.*
longus, -a, -um, adj., *long, far; long-standing.*
loquor, -ī, locūtus sum, *speak.*
lōrīca, -ae, f., *leather corselet; corselet of any material; cuirass.*
lūbricus, -a, -um, adj., *smooth, slippery;* (fig.) *cunning, deceitful.*
lūcidus, -a, -um, adj., *bright, shining; clear.*
luctificus, -a, -um, adj., *grief-inducing.*
luctor, -ārī, -ātus sum, *wrestle, struggle, strive.*
lūcus, -ī, m., *grove, wood.*
lūdō, -ere, -sī, -sum, *play; play with; mock.*
lūdus, -ī, m., *game, sport; entertainment.*
luēs, -is, f., *pestilence, contagion.*
lūmen, -inis, n., *light; lamp; eye* (of a person).
lūna, -ae, f., *moon.*
lupus, -ī, m., *wolf.*

lūstrō, -āre, -āvī, -ātum, *purify by atonement; survey, traverse; go or dance around an altar or the image of a god.*
lūteus, -a, -um, adj., *yellowish, saffron-hued.*
lux, lūcis, f., *light, daylight.*
Lycia, -ae, f., *Lycia,* a country on the SW coast of Asia Minor.
Lycius, -a, -um, adj., *Lycian.*
lymphō, -āre, -āvī, -ātum, *dilute with water; craze;* part., **lymphātus, -a, -um,** *mad, distracted, frenzied, furious.*

M

mactō, -āre, -āvī, -ātum, *punish, reward, kill.*
magis or **mage,** adv., *more; to greater extent.*
māgnus, -a, -um, adj., *large, big; great, powerful.*
māla, -ae, f., *cheek.*
mālifer, -fera, -ferum, adj., *fruit-producing.*
malum, -ī, n., *evil, calamity.*
mandātum, -ī, n., *order, commission.*
mandō, -ere, -dī, -sum, *chew, bite, champ.*
maneō, -ēre, mansī, mansum, *remain; await; endure.*
manus, -ūs, f., *hand; band of men.*
mare, -is, n., *sea.*
Marīca, -ae, f., *Marica,* a nymph of the river Liris, supposed to be the mother of the Latins.
marīnus, -a, -um, adj., *of the sea.*
marmor, -oris, n., *marble; (the surface of) the sea.*
Marruvius, -a, -um, adj., *of Marruvium,* the capital of the Marsi.

Mars, Martis, m., *Mars.*
Marsus, -a, -um, adj., *Marsian.*
Massicus, -a, -um, adj., *of Mount Massicus,* in Campania, *Massic;* (n. pl. used as subst., sc. **iuga**) *the Massic hills.*
māter, -tris, f., *mother.*
māternus, -a, -um, adj., *maternal.*
mātūrus, -a, -um, adj., *mature; speedy; ripe; timely.*
Māvortius, -a, -um or Martius, -a, -um, adj., *pertaining to Mavors or Mars; warlike, martial.*
medicīna, -ae, f., *the healing art; medicine.*
medicō, -āre, -āvī, -ātum, *treat, medicate (with); dye (with).*
medium, -i, n., *middle.*
medius, -a, -um, adj., *in the middle, in the middle, in half;* (n. sing. as subst.) *the middle.*
membrum, -ī, n., *limb; part.*
meminī, -isse, defect., *remember, recollect.*
memorō, -āre, -āvī, -ātum, *remember; mention, recount, remind, speak of.*
mens, mentis, f., *mind; intention; attitude.*
mensa, -ae, f., *table; course (of meal); meal.*
mephītis, -is, f., *poisonous vapor or exhalation.*
mercēs, -ēdis, f., *pay, wages; price, cost.*
mereō, -ēre, -uī, -itum, *earn, deserve; serve as a soldier.*
Messāpus, -ī, m., *Messapus,* a Latin chief, allied with Turnus.
metus, -ūs, m., *fear, dread, anxiety.*
meus, -a, -um, poss. adj., *my.*

Mēzentius, -ī, m., *Mezentius,* tyrant of Agylla (also called Caere), and ally of Latinus and Turnus.
micō, -āre, micuī, --, *vibrate; flash, gleam.*
mille, indecl. num. adj., *a thousand.*
Minerva, -ae, f., *Minerva.*
ministerium, -ī, n., *service, ministry.*
minus, adv., *less* (comp. adv. of **parvus**).
mīrābilis, -e, adj., *wonderful, extraordinary.*
mīror, -ārī, -ātus sum, *wonder at, be astonished.*
mīrus, -a, -um, adj., *marvelous, wonderful.*
misceō, -ēre, miscuī, mixtum, *mix, mingle, gather together.*
miser, -era, -erum, adj., *wretched, pitiable.*
miseret, -ēre, -uit, --, *it moves (one) to pity.*
missus, -ūs, m., *a sending away; a throwing, a shot.*
mittō, -ere, mīsī, missum, *send; release, let go.*
modo, adv., *provided that; only; now.*
modus, -ī, m., *measure; rhythm, meter; manner.*
moenia, -ium, n. pl., *(city) walls.*
mōlēs, -is, f., *large mass; rock; bulk; burden; force.*
mōlior, -īrī, ītus sum, *work at, devise.*
mollis, -e, adj., *soft, yielding, gentle.*
molliter, adv., *softly, gently, sweetly;* comp. adv., **mollius.**
moneō, -ēre, -uī, -itum, *warn, advise.*
monīle, -is, n., *necklace.*
monitus, -ūs, m., *an admonition, warning.*
mons, montis, m., *mountain, hill.*
monstrō, -āre, -āvī, -ātum, *show, point out.*

monstrum, -ī, n., *omen; monster.*
montōsus, -a, -um, adj., *mountainous.*
mōra, -ae, f., *delay.*
morior, -ī, mortuus sum, *die.*
moror, -ārī, -ātus sum, *delay, hinder.*
morsus, -ūs, m., *bite.*
mortālis, -e, adj., *mortal, subject to death.*
mōs, mōris, m., *custom, habit; manner;* pl., *character.*
moveō, -ēre, mōvī, mōtum, *set in motion, stir (up), move.*
mūcrō, -ōnis, m., *sharp point* or *edge; blade.*
mulceō, -ēre, mulsī, mulsum, *stroke; lick; soothe, comfort; charm.*
mulier, -eris, f., *woman.*
multa, adv., *much, greatly.*
multus, -a, -um, adj., *much, many.*
mūnus, -eris, n., *gift; duty; public show.*
mūrus, -ī, m., *wall.*
Mutusca, -ae, f., *Mutusca,* a city of the Sabines.
mūtuus, -a, -um, adj., *interchangeable, reciprocal;* **per mūtua,** *mutually, to each other.*
Mycēnae, -ārum, f. pl., *Mycenae,* an ancient city of Argolis, the home of Danaus, Pelops, and Agamemnon.
myrtus, -ī, f., *myrtle.*

N

nam, conj., *for.*
namque, conj., *for in fact.*
nancīscor, -ī, nactus sum, *obtain; meet.*
Nār, Nāris, m., *Nar,* a river of Umbria.
nāris, -is, f., *nostril.*
nāscor, -ī, nātus sum, *be born, come into being.*
nāta, -ae, f., *daughter.*
nātus, -ī, m., *son.*
nauta, -ae, m., *sailor.*
-ne, (added to the first word of a question).
nē, conj.,(introduces negative purpose clause) *in order that...not;* (introduces negative indirect command) *that...not;* (introduces positive fear clause) *that.*
nec, conj., *nor; and not; neither; not even.*
necdum, adv., *nor yet.*
nectō, -ere, nexuī, nexum, *tie, bind, connect, weave.*
nefās (indecl.), n., *unspeakable act, crime, sin.*
negō, -āre, -āvī, -ātum, *deny, refuse.*
nemus, -oris, n., *grove, forest.*
nepōs, -ōtis, m., *grandchild; nephew; descendant.*
Neptūnius, -a, -um, adj., *pertaining to Neptune; Neptunian.*
Neptūnus, -ī, m., *Neptunus,* one of the sons of Saturn, and brother of Jupiter, Juno, and Pluto; identified by the Romans, as god of the sea, with the Greek Poseidon.
neque or **nec,** conj., *and not.*
nequeō, -īre, -iī or **-īvī, -itum,** *be unable.*
nēquīquam, adv., *in vain.*
Nersae, -ārum, f. pl., *Nersae,* a town of the Aequi.
nesciō, -īre, -iī or **-īvī, -itum,** *not know.*
neu or **neve,** conj., *or not, and not, nor, neither.*
niger, -gra, -grum, adj., *black; unlucky, wicked.*
nihil or **nīl, n.,** *nothing.*

nimbus, -ī, m., *rain-cloud, cloudburst, downpour.*
nisi or **nī,** conj., *if...not; unless.*
nitidus, -a, -um, adj., *shining, bright.*
nivālis, -e, adj., *snowy, snow-covered.*
niveus, -a, -um, adj., *snowy, snow-white.*
nōbilis, -e, adj., *illustrious, famous.*
noceō, -ēre, -cuī, -itum, *harm.*
nocturnus, -a, -um, adj., *nocturnal.*
nōdus, -ī, m., *knot; knot or wood of a tree.*
nōmen, -inis, n., *name.*
Nōmentum, -ī, n., *Nomentum,* a town of Latium.
nōn, adv., *not.*
nōs, gen. **nostrum, nostrī,** dat. **nōbīs,** acc. **nōs,** abl. **nōbīs,** pers. pron., pl., *we, us.*
noster, -tra, -trum, poss. adj., *our.*
nothus, -a, -um, adj., *illegitimate; born out of wedlock (of a known father); crossbred.*
nōtus, -a, -um, adj., *well-known, famous; notorious.*
Notus, -ī, m., *the south wind; wind, storm.*
noverca, -ae, f., *stepmother.*
novō, -āre, -āvī, -ātum, *make new, renew.*
novus, -a, -um, adj., *new.*
nox, noctis, f., *night.*
noxius, -a, -um, adj., *guilty, hurtful, destructive.*
nūbēs, -is, f., *cloud.*
nūbigenae, -ārum, m. or **f. pl,** *the cloud-born;* a name of the Centaurs, born of Ixion and a cloud (> **nubes** and **geno**).
nūbilis, -e, adj., *marriageable.*
nūbilum, -ī, n., *darkness; cloud.*
nūdus, -a, -um, adj., *nude, bare.*

nūllus, -a, -um, adj., *not any, no.*
num, adv., *introduces a direct question expecting the answer "no"; (introduces an indirect question) "whether".*
nūmen, -inis, n., *divine will, divine power, divine spirit.*
numerus, -ī, m., *number, amount; measure (of verse).*
Numīcus, -ī, m., *Numicus,* a river of Latium near Lavinium.
nunc, adv., *now.*
nuntius, -ī, m., *messenger; news; report.*
Nursia, -ae, f., *Nursia,* a Sabine town.
nutriō, -īre, -īvī or **-iī, -ītum,** *nourish, rear, train.*
nūtrīx, -īcis, f., *nurse.*
nūtus, -ūs, m., *nod, will.*
nympha, -ae, f., *bride; nymph.*

O

ō, interj., *oh!*
ob, prep. with acc., *on account of.*
obiciō, -ere, -iēcī, -iectum, *throw to, cast; oppose.*
obscēnus, -a, -um, adj., *filthy; ill-boding; foul, loathsome.*
obscūrus, -a, -um, adj., *covered, dark.*
obserō, -ere, -sēvī, -situm, *plant upon* or *over.*
obsideō, -ēre, -ēdī, -essum, *blockade; beset.*
obstō, -āre, -stitī, -stātum, *stand before, stand in the way; hinder.*
obtestor, -ārī, -ātus sum, *call to witness; conjure; swear.*
obtūtus, -ūs, m., *looking at; look; gaze.*
obustus, -a, -um, adj., *burnt, hardened in the fire.*
occidō, -ere, -cidī, -cāsum, *go down; set; fall; die.*

occumbō, -ere, -cubuī, -cubitum, *sink; die; meet.*
occupō, -āre, -āvī, -ātum, *seize; anticipate; attack.*
Ōceanus, -ī, m., the god *Oceanus;* the *waters encompassing the lands;* the *ocean.*
ocrea, -ae, f., *greave,* a covering made of metal for protecting the leg.
oculus, -ī, m., *eye.*
ōdī, -isse, defect., *hate.*
odium, -ī, n., *hatred.*
odor, -ōris, m., *scent, odor; stench.*
odōrātus, -a, -um, adj., *sweet-smelling.*
Oebalus, -ī, m., *Oebalus,* an Italian prince, ally of Turnus; or a king of Sparta, the father of Tyndarus and grandfather of Helen.
Oenōtrius, -a, -um, adj., *of Oenotria,* an ancient name of Southern Italy; *Italian, Oenotrian.*
offerō, offerre, obtulī, oblātum, *offer, present.*
olim, adv., *formerly; once; in the future.*
olīva, -ae, f., *olive.*
olīvifer, -fera, -ferum, adj., *olive-bearing.*
Olympus, -ī, m., *Olympus.*
ōmen, -inis, n., *omen.*
omnipotens, -entis, adj., *all-powerful, supreme.*
omnis, -e, adj., *every; all.*
opācus, -a, -um, adj., *shady, dark.*
opera, -ae, f., *work; aid; service.*
oppōnō, -ere, -posuī, -positum, *place opposite, oppose.*
optātus, -a, -um, adj., *desired.*
optō, -āre, -āvī, -ātum, *desire; choose.*
opulentia, -ae, f., *wealth.*
opus, -eris, n., *work; need.*
ōra, -ae, f., *shore, coast; region.*
ōrāculum, -ī, n., *oracle, prophecy.*
ōrātor, -ōris, m., *speaker.*
orbis, -is, m., *circle, orb.*
ordior, -īrī, orsus sum, *begin.*
ordō, -inis, m., *row; order; series.*
orgia, -ōrum, n. pl, *the rites of Bacchus.*
orīgō, -inis, f., *origin; birth, family, ancestry.*
Orīōn, -ōnis, m., *Orion,* a fabulous giant, celebrated as a hunter; *the constellation Orion.*
orior, -īrī, ortus sum, *rise; be born.*
ōrnātus, -ūs, m., *an equipping; adornment, attire.*
ōrnō, -āre, -āvī, -ātum, *equip, decorate.*
ōrō, -āre, -āvī, -ātum, *pray (for), beg (for).*
Ortīnus, -a, -um, adj., *of Orta,* a Tuscan city.
ōs, ōris, n., *mouth; face.*
os, ossis, n., *bone.*
Oscī, -ōrum, m. pl, *Osci,* an ancient people of Campania.
ostendō, -ere, -tendī, -tentum, *show; reveal; point out.*
ostentō, -āre, -āvī, -ātum, *display; exhibit.*
ostrum, -ī, n., *the purple fluid of the murex; purple dye; purple cloth.*
Ōthrys, -yos, m., *Othrys,* a mountain in Thessaly.
ovis, -is, n., *sheep.*

P

Pachȳnum, -ī, n., *Pachynum* or *Pachynus,* the southeastern promontory of Sicily.
Paeonius, -a, -um, adj., *Paeonius, pertaining to Paeon,* god of medicine; *medicinal, healing.*
palam, adv., *openly, publicly.*

Pallas, -adis, f., *Pallas Athena*, identified by the Romans with Minerva; rāmus Palladis, *the bough sacred to Pallas, the olive.*
palma, -ae, f., *hand, palm.*
palūs, -ūdis, f., *marsh, swamp; pond.*
pampineus, -a, -um, adj., *covered in vines.*
pandō, -ere, pandī, passum, *spread out, explain.*
parcō, -ere, peperci, --, *spare; refrain from.*
parens, -entis, m. or f., *parent.*
pāreō, -ēre, -uī, -itum, *obey; appear, be present.*
pariō, -ere, peperī, partum, *bring forth; give birth.*
Paris, -idis, m., *Paris, son of Priam and Hecuba.*
pariter, adv., *alike, likewise; at the same time.*
parō, -āre, -āvī, -ātum, *prepare; provide; plan.*
pars, partis, f., *part, portion.*
Parthus, -a, -um, adj., *of* or *belonging to the Parthians,* a nation occupying the country of the Medes and Persians.
partus, -ūs, m., *birth, offspring.*
parum, adv. *too little, not enough.*
parvus, -a, -um, adj., *small.*
pascō, -ere, pāvī, pastum, *feed.*
passus, -ūs, m., *pace, footstep.*
pastor, -ōris, m., *shepherd.*
pastōrālis, -e, adj., *pertaining to shepherds; rustic.*
pāstus, -ūs, m., *pasturing, feeding.*
pateō, -ēre, -uī, --, *be* or *lie open; extend; be accessible.*
pater, -tris, m., *father;* (in pl.) *patricians; senators.*

patera, -ae, f., *a saucer-shaped dish; libation cup.*
paternus, -a, -um, adj., *fatherly, paternal.*
patior, -ī, passus sum, *permit, endure, suffer.*
patria, -ae, f., *country, homeland.*
patrius, -a, -um, adj., *paternal; ancestral.*
patulus, -a, -um, adj., *opening, wide.*
paulātim, adv., *gradually, little by little.*
pavidus, -a, -um, adj., *scared, frightened.*
pavor, -ōris, m., *fear, trembling.*
pax, pācis, f., *peace; treaty of peace compact.*
pār, paris, adj., *equal, like.*
pecten, -inis, m., *comb.*
pectō, -ere, pexī, pexum, *comb.*
pectus, -oris, n., *chest, breast; heart.*
pecus, -oris, n., *farm animal; cattle.*
pedes, -itis, m., *foot soldier.*
pelagus, -ī, m., *sea, ocean.*
pellis, -is, f., *skin, hide.*
pellō, -ere, pepulī, pulsum, *strike, drive off.*
pelta, -ae, f., *light crescent-shaped shield.*
Penātēs, -ium, m., *Penates, household gods.*
pendeō, -ēre, pependī, --, *hang (down).*
pendō, pendere, pependī, pensum, *weigh; pay.*
penetrālis, -e, adj., *innermost;* (n. pl. used as subst.) *the interior of a house; sanctuary, shrine.*
penetrō, -āre, -āvī, -ātum, *penetrate, go into.*
penitus or penitē, adv., *internally; entirely.*
pēnūria, -ae, f., *want, need.*

per, prep. with acc., *through.*
percipiō, -ere, -cēpī, -ceptum, *take in, grasp.*
percurrō, -ere, -cucurrī or **-currī, -cursum,** *run through* or *over.*
percutiō, -ere, -cussī, -cussum, *strike, kill.*
perdō, -ere, -didī, -ditum, *destroy; lose.*
pererrō, -āre, -āvī, -ātum, *wander through* or *over; explore.*
perficiō, -ere, -fēcī, -fectum, *complete, accomplish.*
perfidus, -a, -um, adj., *faithless, treacherous, false.*
perfundō, -ere, -fūdī, -fūsum, *pour over* or *along; wash; spot.*
Pergama, -ōrum, n. pl., *Pergama* or *Pergamon; a city in Asia Minor; the citadel* or *walls of Troy, Troy.*
perīculum, -ī, n., *danger.*
perlābor, -ī, -lāpsus sum, *glide through* or *over.*
permisceō, -ēre, -miscuī, -mixtum, *mix completely, mingle; disturb.*
pēro, -ōnis, m., *boot* or *high shoe made of rawhide.*
perpetuus, -a, -um, adj., *continuous, uninterrupted.*
pertemptō, -āre, -āvī, -ātum, *handle completely; test.*
pervertō, -ere, -vertī, -versum, *overturn, overthrow, subvert.*
pēs, pedis, m., *foot.*
pestifer, -era, -erum, adj., *pest-bringing, pestilential.*
pestis, -is, f., *plague.*
petō, -ere, -iī and **-īvī, -ītum,** *seek, go toward; attack.*
pharetra, -ae, f., *quiver.*
Phoebigena, -ae, m., *the son of Phoebus,* Aesculapius.

Phoebus, -ī, m., *Phoebus,* Apollo.
Phrygia, -ae, f., *Phrygia, the Troad*
Phrygius, -a, -um, adj., *Phrygian; of Phrygia; Trojan.*
Phryx, -ygis, m. *a Phrygian* or *Trojan.*
pictus, -a, -um, adj., *embroidered; many-colored.*
Pīcus, -ī, m., *Picus, the son of Saturn, grandfather of Latinus, changed by Circe into a woodpecker.*
piget, -ēre, -uit, --, *it disgusts (one).*
pīlum, -ī, n., *javelin.*
pingō, -ere, pinxī, pictum, *paint, color; depict.*
pinguis, -e, adj., *fat; dull.*
pinna, -ae, f., *feather, wing.*
pīnus, -ī, f., *pine tree;* (meton.) *a ship; a torch; a pine brand* or *torch.*
pius, -a, -um, adj., *dutiful, loyal.*
plācābilis, -e, adj., *appeasable.*
placidus, -a, -um, adj., *pleasant, agreeable.*
plaga, -ae, f., *tract, region; zone.*
plāga, -ae, f., *blow, wound; lash.*
planta, -ae, f., *the sole of the foot.*
plēnus, -a, -um, adj., *full.*
plumbum, -ī, n., *lead.*
plūrimus, -a, -um, superl. adj. of **multus,** *very much, very many.*
plūs, plūris, compar. of **multus,** *more.*
Plūtō or **Plūtōn, -ōnis, m.,** *Pluto, son of Saturn, king of Hades.*
poena, -ae, f., *punishment, penalty.*
polluō, -ere, posuī, -ūtum, *soil, pollute; break; violate.*
pōmum, -ī, n., *fruit.*
pōnō, -ere, -uī, -itum, *place.*
pontus, -ī, m., *the open sea.*
populus, -ī, m., *people; populace.*
porta, -ae, f., *gate, door, entrance.*
portendō, -ere, -tendī, -tentum, *stretch; portend, foretell.*

portentum, -ī, *an omen, portent.*
portus, -ūs, m., *port, harbor, refuge, haven.*
poscō, -ere, poposcī, --, *demand; ask.*
possum, posse, potuī, --, *be able, can.*
post, prep. with acc., *behind;* adv., *afterward.*
posterus, -a, -um, adj., *next, following.*
postis, -is, m., *doorjamb; door.*
postquam, conj., *after.*
potens, -ntis, adj., *powerful, capable, mighty.*
potestās, -ātis, f., *power, rule; strength, opportunity.*
praeceps, -cipitis, adj., *headlong; rushing* (of winds, etc.)
praecipuē, adv., *especially, particularly.*
praecordia, -ōrum, n. pl., *the diaphragm* or *midriff; the vital parts; the heart.*
praeda, -ae, f., *booty, spoils; prey.*
praedō, -ōnis, m., *robber.*
praeferō, -ferre, -tulī, -lātum, *prefer.*
praefīgō, -ere, -fīxī, -fīxum, *fasten before; tip, point.*
praegnans, -antis, adj., *with young, pregnant.*
Praeneste, -is, n., *Praeneste,* a town in Latium on a lofty hill about twenty miles southeast of Rome, now Palestrina.
Praenestīnus, -a, -um, adj., *of Praeneste.*
praesēpe, -is, n., *an enclosure, stall, manger, trough.*
praesideō, -ēre, -sēdī, --, *sit before; preside over, rule over.*
praestans, -antis, adj., *outstanding, excellent.*
praeter, prep. with acc., *past; beyond; except.*
praetereā, adv., *besides.*

praeūrō, -ere, -ussī, -ustum, *burn at the point.*
praevehor, -vehī, -vectus sum, *ride before* or *past.*
praevertō, -ere, -vertī, -versum, *turn before; preoccupy; surpass.*
precor, -ārī, -ātus sum, *beg, pray.*
premō, -ere, pressī, pressum, *press* (hard); *overpower.*
prex, precis, f., *prayer, request.*
Priamēius, -a, -um, adj., *of Priam.*
Priamus, -ī, m., *Priam,* son of Laomedon, king of Troy.
prīdem, adv., *long ago.*
prīmaevus, -a, -um, adj., *first in age; eldest, youthful.*
prīmum, adv., *first, for the first time.*
prīmus, -a, -um, adj., *first, foremost, best.*
prīncipium, -ī, n., *beginning; cause.*
prior, -us, gen. **priōris,** comp. adj., *former, previous, prior.*
priscus, -a, -um, adj., *ancient.*
procella, -ae, f., *gale, storm.*
procul, adv., *at a distance.*
proelium, -ī, n., *battle.*
proficīscor, -ī, -fectus sum, *set out* or *forth.*
profugus, -a, -um, adj., *fugitive, exiled.*
profundus, -a, -um, adj., *deep; lofty;* (n. used as subst.) *the deep, the sea.*
prōgeniēs, -ēī, f., *descent, lineage, family.*
prohibeō, -ēre, -uī, -itum, *prevent; forbid.*
prōlēs, -is, f., *offspring, progeny.*
prōmissum, -ī, n., *promise.*
prōnuba, -ae, f., *bridesmaid; aiding in marriage rites; presiding over marriage.*

propero, -āre, -āvī, -ātum, *hasten.*
proprius, -a, -um, adj., *one's own.*
prōra, -ae, f., *the extreme forward part of a ship; the prow.*
prōrumpō, -ere, -rūpī, -ruptum, *cause to burst forth; cast forth.*
prōspectō, -āre, -āvī, -ātum, *look forth; look forth upon; gaze at.*
prōspiciō, -ere, -spexī, -spectum, *see in front, inspect.*
prōsum, prōdesse, -fuī, -futūrus, *be useful.*
prōtinus, adv., *at once.*
proximus, -a, um, superl. adj., *nearest, next.*
pūbēs, -is, f., *youth, young men; the groin.*
puer, -erī, m., *boy, slave.*
pugna, -ae, f., *battle, fight.*
pugnō, -āre, -āvī, -ātum, *fight.*
pulcher, -chra, -chrum, adj., *beautiful, handsome.*
pullulō, -āre, -āvī, -ātum, *spring out; sprout forth.*
pulverulentus, -a-, um, adj., *covered with dust, dusty.*
pulvis, -eris, m., *dust.*
purpura, -ae, f., *purple; crimson; purple border.*
pūrus, -a, -um, adj., *pure, unsoiled.*
putō, -āre, -āvī, -ātum, *think, suppose.*

Q

quā, adv., *where; how; anyhow; anywhere.*
quadra, -ae, f., *a quadrant section of a round cake or loaf; segment, slice.*
quadrifidus, -a, -um, adj., *split into four parts.*
quadripēs, -pedis, adj., *four-footed, on all fours; a horse.*
quaerō, -ere, -siī and **-sīvī, -sītum,** *seek, ask.*
quālis, -e, *what sort; of which sort.*
quam, adv., *than; as, how;* (with superl.) *as...as possible.*
quamvīs, adv., *even though, although.*
quandōquidem, conj., *since indeed; because.*
quantum, adv., *how much; so much as.*
quantus, -a, -um, adj., *how great; how much* or *many; of what size.*
quārē, adv., *why; therefore.*
quassō, -āre, -āvī, -ātum, *shake violently; toss; brandish.*
quatiō, -ere, --, quassum, *shake.*
quattuor, indecl. num. adj., *four.*
queō, -īre, quīvī or **quiī, quitum,** *be able.*
quercus, -ūs, f., *an oak tree;* (meton.) *oak leaf crown.*
questus, -ūs, m., *complaining; moaning; groans.*
quī, quae, quod, interrog. adj. or rel. pron., *who, what, which.*
quiēs, -ētis, f., *quiet, calm; sleep, rest.*
quiēscō, -ere, -ēvī, -ētum, *sleep, keep quiet.*
quīn, conj., *why not;* (with **etiam**), *nay even;* (introducing noun clause after negative expression of preventing) *from, but that, to prevent that.*
quīnī, -ae, -a, num. adj., *five each, five.*
quīnque, indecl. num. adj., *five.*
Quirīnālis, -e, adj., *pertaining to Quirinus* or *Romulus.*
Quirītēs, -ium, m. pl., *ancient Sabines, especially of the city of Cures; Sabines amalgamated with the Romans, thus also Roman citizens.*
quis, quid, interrog. pron., *who, what.*

quis, quae (or **qua**), **quid** (after **sī, nisī, num, nē**), indef. adj. and pron., *any; anyone/anything, someone/something.*
quisquam, quicquam, indef. pron., *anyone, anything.*
quisque, quaeque, quidque, and (as adj.) **quodque,** indef. pron., *each one, every one, everything.*
quō, adv., rel., interrog., *to where; to or for what purpose.*
quō, conj., *to the end that, in order that;* **quō magis,** *by how much more, that the more.*
quod, conj., *because;* see also **quī, quae, quod.**
quondam, adv., *formerly, at times, sometimes.*
quoque, adv., *also, too.*

R

rabidus, -a, -um, adj., *raving, savage, mad, raging.*
rabiēs, --, f., *madness, frenzy.*
radius, -ī, m., *ray; beam.*
rādō, -ere, rāsī, rāsum, *shave, scratch; inscribe.*
rāmus, -ī, m., *branch.*
rapidus, -a, -um, adj., *swift.*
rapiō, -ere, rapuī, raptum, *seize, carry off.*
raptum, -ī, n., *plunder.*
rastrum, -ī, n.; usu. in pl., **rastrī, -ōrum,** m., *rake, mattock.*
ratis, -is, f., *raft;* in poetry, *ship.*
raucus, -a, -um, adj., *harsh-sounding, noisy.*
recens, -entis, adj., *fresh, recent.*
recidīvus, -a, -um, adj., *falling back; returning; rebuilt.*
recipiō, -ere, -cēpī, -ceptum, *take back; accept.*

reclūdō, -ere, -clūsī, -clūsum, *unclose; open; reveal.*
recondō, -ere, -condidī, -conditum, *put back, put away, hide, conceal.*
recoquō, -ere, -coxī, -coctum, *boil again; recast.*
recurrō, -ere, -currī, -cursum, *run back; return.*
recurvus, -a, -um, adj., *curving back or round.*
recūsō, -āre, -āvī, -ātum, *refuse.*
reddō, -ere, -didī, -ditum, *return; restore; deliver; render.*
redeō, -īre, -iī, -itum, *go back, return.*
referō, -ferre, -tulī, -lātum, *bring back; report.*
refugiō, -ere, -fūgī, --, *flee back, run away; recoil from.*
refundō, -ere, -fūdī, -fūsum, *pour back* or *up; cast.*
rēgālis, -e, adj., *regal, kingly.*
rēgia, -ae, f., *palace.*
rēgīna, -ae, f., *queen.*
regiō, -ōnis, f., *region; neighborhood; direction.*
rēgius, -a, -um, adj., *royal, of a king, regal.*
regnātor, -ōris, m., *one who reigns; sovereign.*
regnum, -ī, n., *royal power; power; kingdom.*
regō, -ere, rēxī, rectum, *rule, control; manage; direct.*
relēgō, -āre, -āvī, -ātum, *send away, remove.*
religiō, -ōnis, f., *rite; reverence, awe; religion.*
religō, -āre, -āvī, -ātum, *tie up, bind fast.*
relinquō, -ere, -līquī, -lictum, *abandon, leave (behind).*
reliquiae, -ārum, f. pl., *remains.*

remordeō, -ēre, —, remorsum, *bite again and again;* (fig.) *harass, vex.*
reor, rērī, ratus sum, *think; suppose; believe.*
repellō, -ere, reppulī, repulsum, *drive back.*
repente, adv., *suddenly.*
reperiō, -īre, repperī, repertum, *find out, discover.*
repertor, -ōris, m., *discoverer, inventor.*
repetō, -ere, -īvī, -ītum, *return to; demand back; repeat; claim.*
repleō, -ēre, -plēvī, -plētum, *fill up again; fill.*
repōnō, -pōnere, -posuī, -positum, *put back, restore, replace.*
reportō, -āre, -āvī, -ātum, *carry back, bring again.*
reposcō, -ere, —, —, *ask again; demand back.*
requīrō, -ere, -quīsīvī or **-quīsiī, -quīsītum,** *require, seek.*
rēs, reī, f., *thing; property; matter, affair; activity; situation.*
reserō, -āre, -āvī, -ātum, *unbolt; open.*
reses, -idis, adj., *seated; inactive; dormant.*
resīdō, -ere, -sēdī, —, *sit down, sink down, shrink.*
resistō, -ere, -stitī, —, *pause; resist, withstand.*
resonō, -āre, -āvī, -ātum, *resound.*
respergō, -ere, -spersī, -spersum, *sprinkle over; besprinkle.*
respiciō, -ere, -spexī, -spectum, *look back.*
respōnsum, -ī, n., *answer.*
restō, -āre, -stitī, —, *resist.*
retrāctō, -āre, -āvī, -ātum, *handle again; gripe* or *grasp again; recall.*

revocō, -āre, -āvī, -ātum, *call back; revive.*
rex, rēgis, m., *king.*
Rhēa, -ae, f., *Rhea, a priestess, mother of Aventinus.*
rigō, -āre, -āvī, -ātum, *moisten; stain.*
rīmor, -ārī, -ātus sum, *force open in cracks;* (fig.) *ransack, explore.*
rīpa, -ae, f., *bank.*
rīte, adv., *with the proper rites; duly, correctly.*
rītus, -ūs, m., *rite; custom, manner.*
rīvus, -ī, m., *brook, stream.*
rōbur, -oris, n., *oak; strength.*
rogō, -āre, -āvī, -ātum, *ask (for).*
Rōma, -ae, f., *Rome.*
roscidus, -a, -um, adj., *dew-covered, dewy.*
Rōseus, -a, -um, adj., *of Rosea, a region or district near Reate; Rosean.*
roseus, -a, -um, adj., *rosy.*
rostrum, -ī, n., *beak, prow; speaker's platform.*
rubescō, -ere, -rubuī, —, *grow* or *turn red; begin to glow.*
rudō, -ere, -īvī, -ītum, *send forth a loud sound; bellow, roar.*
Rufrae, -ārum, f. pl., *Rufrae, a town of Campania.*
rūga, -ae, f., *wrinkle.*
rūmor, -ōris, m., *rumor.*
rumpō, -ere, rūpī, ruptum, *break; destroy.*
ruō, -ere, ruī, rūtum, *rush; fall, collapse.*
rūpēs, -is, f., *rock, crag, cliff.*
rursus or **rursum,** adv., *back, backward; on the other hand, in turn, again.*
rūs, rūris, n., *country(side).*

Rutulī, -ōrum, m. pl., *the Rutulians,* an ancient tribe of Latium dwelling south of the Tiber.
Rutulus, -ī, m., *a Rutulian,* of the tribe in Latium whose king was Turnus.

S

Sabellus, -a, -um, adj., *of the Sabelli or Sabines.*
Sabīnī, -ōrum, m. pl., *Sabines,* an ancient people occupying the hill country on the border of Latium, from whom were derived a part of the Roman people or Quirites.
Sabīnus, -a, -um, adj., *Sabine.*
sacer, -cra, -crum, adj., *holy, sacred; accursed.*
sacerdōs, -ōtis, m. or f., *priest, priestess.*
Sacrānus, -a, -um, adj., *pertaining to the Sacrani,* a Latin people; *Sacranian.*
sacrātus, -a, -um, adj., *holy.*
sacrilegus, -a, -um, adj., *guilty of impiety, sacrilegious.*
sacrō, -āre, -āvī, -ātum, *consecrate; sanctify.*
saepiō, -īre, saepsī, saeptum, *fence in; enclose.*
saeta, -ae, f., *bristle; stiff hair; fur.*
saetiger, -gera, -gerum, adj., *bristle-bearing, bristly.*
saeviō, -īre, -iī, -ītum, *rage, act savagely.*
saevus, -a, -um, adj., *savage, cruel.*
sagitta, -ae, f., *arrow.*
salignus, -a, -um, adj., *made of willow.*
saltus, -ūs, m., *pasture.*
salveō, -ēre, --, --, *be well;* imperative, *hail!*

Sāmus, -ī, f., *Samos,* an island southwest of Ephesus, near the coast of Ionia.
Samothrācia, -ae, f., *Samothrace,* a small island about thirty-eight miles south of the Thracian coast, supposed by some to have been colonized from Samos.
sanctus, -a, -um, adj., *consecrated, sacred; venerable.*
sanguineus, -a, -um, adj., *bloody, bloodshot.*
sanguis, -inis, m., *blood; family.*
Sarnus, -ī, m., *Sarnus,* a river running into the Bay of Naples near Pompeii.
Sarrastēs, -um, m. pl., *Sarrastes,* a people dwelling near the Sarnus.
Satīculus, -ī, m., *a Saticulan,* of *Saticula,* a Campanian town.
satis or **sat,** adv., *enough, sufficiently.*
Satura, -ae, f., *Satura,* an unidentified location in Latium.
Sāturnius, -a, -um, adj., *belonging to Saturn; Saturnian.*
Sāturnus, -ī, m., *Saturn,* a deified king of Latium, whose reign was the "golden age"; identified by the Romans with the Greek Cronos.
satus, -a, -um, adj., *born of, sprung from; son* or *daughter of.*
saucius, -a, -um, adj., *wounded; afflicted; drunk.*
saxum, -ī, n., *rock, boulder, stone.*
scelerō, -āre, -āvī, -ātum, *commit a crime; pollute.*
scelus, -eris, n., *crime, wicked deed, sin.*
sceptrum, -ī, n., *royal staff; scepter;* (meton.) *rule, power, realm; authority.*

scindō, -ere, scidī, scissum, *cut, rend, tear asunder.*
scopulus, -ī, m., *projecting ledge of rock; high cliff* or *rock; crag.*
scūtum, scŭtum, -ī, n., *shield.*
Scylla, -ae, f., *Scylla, dangerous rock on the Italian side of the Straits of Messana opposite Charybdis; personified as a monster, half woman and half fish.*
Sēbēthis, -idis, f., *Sebethis, the daughter of Sebethus,* a river or river-god of Campania.
secō, -āre, -uī, -ctum, *cut; cleave a path through (the sea), traverse.*
sēcrētus, -a, -um, adj., *separated, hidden, secret; unnoticed.*
secundō, -āre, -āvī, -ātum, *aid, favor.*
secundus, -a, -um, adj., *following, second; prosperous; propitious.*
secūris, -is, f., *axe.*
secūrus, -a, -um, adj., *free from care, careless.*
sed, conj., *but.*
sedeō, -ēre, sēdī, sessum, *sit, remain; settle; encamp.*
sēdēs, -is, f., *seat, chair; home, residence; settlement.*
seges, -etis, f., *field of grain; standing corn; harvest.*
segnis, -e, adj., *slow, sluggish.*
sēmen, -inis, n., *seed; breeding, propagation.*
semper, adv., *always.*
senectūs, -ūtis, f., *old age; senility.*
senex, -is, adj., *old, aged.*
senex, senis, m., *old man.*
sensus, -ūs, m., *feeling, perception; sense.*
sententia, -ae, f., *thought, feeling; opinion; verdict.*

sentiō, -īre, sensī, sensum, *perceive; feel.*
sequor, -ī, secūtus sum, *follow, come next.*
serō, -ere, sēvī, satum, *plant, sow.*
serpens, -entis, m. or **f.,** *creeping thing; snake, serpent.*
serta, -ōrum, n. pl., *things entwined; garlands, wreaths.*
sērus, -a, -um, adj., *(too) late.*
servō, -āre, -āvī, -ātum, *save, preserve.*
seu, conj., *whether; or if.*
Sevērus, -ī, m., *Severus,* a mountain in the Sabine country.
sī, conj., *if.*
sībilō, -āre, -āvī, -ātum, *hiss.*
sīc, adv., *thus, in this way, in such a way.*
Sicānī, -ōrum, m. pl., *the Sicanians* or *Sicilians.*
Siculus, -a, -um, adj., *pertaining to the Siculi,* an ancient race, part of which migrated from Latium to Sicily; *Sicilian.*
Sidicīnus, -a, -um, adj., *pertaining to the Sidicini,* or *people of Teanum and its territory* in the northern part of Campania; *Sidicinian.*
sīdus, -eris, n., *star; constellation.*
Sīgēus, -a, -um, adj., *pertaining to Sigeum,* a promontory and town in the Troad, at the mouth of the Dardanelles, about five miles northwest of Troy; *Sigean.*
signō, -āre, -āvī, -ātum, *mark, signify.*
signum, -ī, n., *mark, impression, sign; watchword, password.*
silens, -entis, adj., *still, silent.*
silva, -ae, f., *wood, forest.*
Silvia, -ae, f., *Silvia,* daughter of Tyrrhus.

similis, -e, adj., *similar.*
simul, adv., *at the same time, simultaneously; at once.*
simulācrum, -ī, n., *likeness, image, statue.*
simulō, -āre, -āvī, -ātum, *imitate; pretend.*
sine, prep. with abl., *without.*
sinister, -tra, -trum, adj., *left; adverse; inauspicious.*
sinō, -ere, sīvī, situm, *allow, permit.*
sinus, -ūs, m., *fold, pocket; chest; bay.*
situs, -ūs, m., *situation; neglect, disuse; mold.*
sīve or **seu,** conj., *whether; or if.*
socer, -erī, m., *father-in-law.*
sociō, -āre, -āvī, -ātum, *make one a* **socius***; share, associate; join in marriage.*
socius, -ī, m., *ally, comrade; friend, companion.*
sōl, sōlis, m., *sun.*
soleō, -ēre, solitus sum, *be accustomed.*
solitus, -a, -um, adj., *having been accustomed.*
solium, -ī, n., *seat; throne.*
sollicitus, -a, -um, adj., *worried, concerned.*
solum, -ī, n., *bottom, base; earth.*
sōlus, -a, -um, adj., *alone, only.*
solvō, -ere, solvī, solūtum, *loosen; release, pay; dissolve.*
somnifer, -fera, -ferum, adj., *sleep-bringing, soothing.*
somnus, -ī, m., *sleep.*
sonitus, -ūs, m., *sounding; noise.*
sonō, -āre, sonuī, sonitum, *sound, resound.*
sonor, -ōris, m., *noise, sound; din.*

Sōracte, -is, n., *Soracte,* in Etruria, northeast of Rome, on which in ancient times was a temple of Apollo.
soror, -ōris, f., *sister.*
sors, sortis, f., *fate, lot; oracular response.*
spargō, -ere, -rsī, -rsum, *scatter; hurl; sprinkle; infuse.*
spatium, -ī, n., *space; course, circuit; interval.*
speculor, -ārī, speculātus sum, *watch.*
speculum, -ī, n., *mirror.*
specus, -ūs, m. or **n.,** *cave, cavern; cavity.*
spernō, -ere, sprēvī, sprētum, *reject.*
spērō, -āre, -āvī, -ātum, *hope (for).*
spīculum, -ī, n., *sharp point, sting, arrow.*
spīrāculum, -ī, n., *breathing-hole.*
spīrō, -āre, -āvī, -ātum, *breathe; pant; exhale.*
splendeō, -ēre, --, --, *shine, gleam.*
spoliō, -āre, -āvī, -ātum, *strip, despoil.*
spons, spontis, f., *free will.*
spūma, -ae, f., *froth, foam, spray.*
spūmeus, -a, -um, adj., *foamy, frothy.*
stabulum, -ī, n., *stable, stall.*
stagnum, -ī, n., *standing water, lake, pool.*
statuō, -ere, -uī, -ūtum, *set up, establish; decide, think.*
status, -ūs, m., *position; status.*
stellō, -āre, -āvī, -ātum, *cover over with stars.*
sternō, -ere, strāvī, strātum, *spread, scatter; knock down, lay low.*
stimulus, -ī, m., *prick; spur;* (fig.) *incentive, sting.*
stīpes, -itis, m., *log* or *post; trunk of tree; club.*

stirps, stirpis, f., *stem, stalk; family tree.*
stō, stāre, stetī, statum, *stand; stand fast.*
strīdō, -ere, strīdī, --, *produce a grating* or *shrill sound; creak; roar.*
strīdor, -ōris, m., *harsh sound; creaking; rattling.*
stringō, -ere, -inxī, -ictum, *draw tight, bind fast; draw (from a scabbard, etc.).*
stupefaciō, -ere, -fēcī, -factum, *amaze, bewilder; surprise.*
stupeō, -ēre, -uī, --, *be amazed or dazed; be bewildered; wonder at.*
Stygius, -a, -um, adj., *Stygian; pertaining to the river Styx in Hades.*
sub, adv., prep. with abl. and acc., *below, under, at the foot of; near; up to;* **sub aurās,** *upward, on high.*
subdō, -ere, -didī, -ditum, *put under; place* or *fasten under; bury.*
subeō, -īre, -īvī or **-iī, -itum,** *go under* or *into; ascend.*
sūber, -eris, n., *the cork tree.*
subiciō, -ere, -iēcī, -iectum, *throw* or *place under; expose.*
subigō, -ere, -ēgī, -actum, *drive under, subject.*
subitō, adv., *suddenly; at once.*
subitus, -a, -um, adj., *having come up suddenly; sudden, unexpected.*
sublābor, -ī, -lapsus sum, adj., *slip* or *glide beneath; sink down, decline.*
sublīmis, -e, adj., *elevated, lofty, heroic, noble.*
succēdō, -ere, -cessī, -cessum, *climb; follow; succeed in.*
succendō, -ere, -cendī, -censum, *set on fire from beneath;* (fig.) *inflame, incite.*
succingō, -ere, -cinxī, -cinctum, *gird beneath; gird up; wrap.*
sudis, -is, f., *stake; palisade.*
sūdor, -ōris, m., *sweat.*
suggerō, -ere, -gessī, -gestum, *bring* or *put under* or *up to; supply.*
suī (gen.), dat. **sibi,** acc. **sē,** abl. **sē,** reflex. pron., third person, *himself, herself, itself, themselves.*
sulpureus, -a, -um, *sulphureous.*
sum, esse, fuī, futūrus, *be; exist.*
summoveō, -ēre, -mōvī, -mōtum, *move from beneath; remove; separate.*
sūmō, -ere, sumpsī, sumptum, *take up; begin; consume.*
super, adv., prep. with acc., *over.*
superbus, -a, -um, *arrogant, proud, haughty.*
superus, -a, -um, adj., *above, higher, of the upper world;* (m. pl. used as subst.) *the gods above.*
supplicium, -ī, n., *punishment; suffering; torture.*
suppōnō, -ere, -posuī, -positum, *place under; put something in the place of another, substitute.*
suprā, adv., prep. with acc., *above, beyond, over.*
surgō, -ere, surrexī, surrectum, *rise; grow.*
sūs, suis, m. or **f.,** *pig.*
suspendō, -ere, -spendī, -spensum, *hang, suspend.*
sustineō, -ēre, -tinuī, -tentum, *hold up, sustain; be able to; endure.*
suus, -a, -um, poss. adj., *his own, her own, its own, their own.*
Syrtis, -is, f., *shoals on the N. African coast between Carthage and Cyrene.*

T

tacitus, -a, -um, *silent.*
tactus, -ūs, m., *touching; touch.*
taeda, -ae, f., *torch.*
taenia, -ae, f., *headband, fillet; ribbon.*
tālis, -e, *such, of such a sort.*
tam, adv., *so.*
tandem, adv., *finally.*
tangō, -ere, tetigī, tactum, *touch; strike.*
tantum, adv., *so much; only; to such a degree* or *height;* **tantum... quantum,** *so great (such, so much)...as....*
tantus, -a, -um, adj., *so much, so great, of such size.*
tapēte, -is, n., *a coverlet; hanging; a carpet; horse housings* or *cloths;* abl. pl., **tapētīs** (perhaps from **tapētum, -ī**), *with housings.*
Tartareus, -a, -um, adj., *pertaining to Tartarus; Tartarean; infernal.*
tēctum, -ī, n., *building, house.*
tegmen, -inis, n., *means of covering; skin; hide.*
tegō, -ere, tēxī, tēctum, *cover, protect; defend.*
tēla, -ae, f., *web.*
Tēleboae, -ārum or **-um, m. pl.,** *Teleboae, a people of Acarnania, a part of whom migrated to the island of Capreae in the Bay of Naples.*
tellūs, -ūris, f., *earth.*
Telōn, -ōnis, m., *Telon, king of the Teleboans on the island of Capreae.*
tēlum, -ī, n., *spear, weapon.*
temnō, -ere, --, --, *despise, scorn.*
tempestās, -ātis, f., *season, time; weather; storm.*

templum, -ī, n., *temple.*
tempus, -oris, n., *temple (of the forehead).*
tempus, -oris, n., *time.*
tendō, -ere, tetendī, tentum, *stretch, extend, direct.*
tenebrae, -ārum, f. pl., *darkness.*
teneō, -ēre, tenuī, tentum, *hold; possess; occupy.*
tener, -era, -erum, *tender.*
tenuis, -e, adj., *thin; delicate.*
ter, num. adv., *three times.*
teres, -etis, adj. *tapering, polished; tapering.*
tergeō, -ēre, -tersī, -tersum, *wipe; clean; burnish.*
tergum, -ī, n., *the back of men* or *animals; hide, skin.*
terra, -ae, f., *land.*
terribilis, -e, adj., *terrifying.*
terror, -ōris, m., *fear.*
tessera, -ae, f., *square tablet; watchword, password.*
testor, -ārī, -ātus sum, *testify; call to witness, appeal to.*
Tetrica, -ae, m., *Tetrica, a mountain in the Sabine country.*
Teucrī, -ōrum, m. pl., *descendants of Teucer, Teucrians, Trojans.*
Teutonicus, -a, -um, *of the Teutons; Teutonic; Germanic.*
thalamus, -ī, m., *marriage bed; bedchamber.*
thiasus, -ī, m., *dance in honor of Bacchus; wild dance.*
thōrāx, -ācis, m., (acc. pl., **thōrācas**), *corselet.*
Thrēicius, -a, -um, adj., *Thracian; northern.*

Thȳbris, -idis, m., *Thybris/Tiber,* an ancient king of Latium; *the Tiber river* (based on Greek spelling); see also **Tiberis.**
thyrsus, -ī, m., *the stalk of a plant; a staff wreathed with ivy and vine-leaves.*
tiāras, -ae, m., *an Eastern headband or crown; tiara.*
Tiberīnus, -a, -um, *pertaining to the Tiber.* **Tiberīnus, -ī, m.,** *the river-god Tiber; the Tiber.*
Tiberis, -is, m., *the Tiber river;* see also **Thȳbris.**
Tībur, -uris, n., *Tibur,* a city on the eastern border of Latium.
Tīburtius, -a, -um, adj., *of Tibur.*
Tīburtus, -ī, m., *Tiburtus,* a founder of Tibur.
tingō, -ere, tinxī, tinctum, *wet, moisten; dye, color.*
Tīrynthius, -a, -um, adj., *of Tiryns,* a town in Argolis, where Hercules was brought up; *Tirynthian.*
tollō, -ere, sustulī, sublātum, *lift, raise; destroy; remove.*
tonsa, -ae, f., an *oar.*
torqueō, -ēre, torsī, tortum, *twist.*
torrens, -entis, m., *a rushing stream, torrent.*
torreō, -ēre, -uī, tostum, *burn; rush, roll.*
torris, -is, m., *firebrand; brand.*
tortilis, -e, adj., *twisted, winding.*
torum, -ī, n., (also, **torus, -ī, m.),** *bed, couch, cushion.*
torvus, -a, -um, *stern; wild; savage, fierce.*
tot, indecl. adj., *so many.*
totiens, adv, *so often, so many times.*
tōtus, -a, -um, adv., *whole.*

trabea, -ae, f., adj., *a short purple (or partly so) mantle,* Etruscan in origin; *robe of state (of kings, augurs, knights, etc.).*
trahō, -ere, trāxī, tractum, *drag, haul; derive.*
trans, prep. with acc., *across, over; beyond.*
transcrībō, -ere, -scripsī, -scriptum, *transfer by writing; enroll; transfer.*
transformō, -āre, -āvī, -ātum, *change the form, transform.*
tremō, -ere, -uī, --, *tremble.*
tremor, -ōris, m., *trembling; quaking; tremor.*
tremulus, -a, -um, adj., *trembling, shaking, quivering.*
trepidus, -a, -um, adj., *agitated, fearful.*
tribus, -ūs, f., *tribe.*
trilix, -līcis, adj., *of three threads, triple.*
triplex, -plicis, adj., *threefold.*
tristis, -e, adj., *sad; gloomy.*
Trivia, -ae, f., *Trivia;* an epithet of Hecate or Diana, whose images were placed at the forks of roads (> **trivium**).
Trōes, -um, m., *Trojans.*
Trōia, -ae, f., *Troy.*
Trōiānus, -a, -um, *Trojan.*
Trōius, -a, -um, adj., *of Troy; Trojan.*
tū, gen. **tuī,** dat. **tibi,** acc. **tē,** abl. **tē,** pers. pron. sing., *you.*
tuba, -ae, f., *trumpet; trumpet-signal.*
tueor, -ērī, tūtus sum, *look at, watch; protect.*
tum or **tunc,** adv., *then, at that time.*
tumeō, -ēre, --, --, *swell, puff up.*
tumulus, -ī, m., *mound.*
turba, -ae, f., *uproar.*

Vocabulary

turbō, -inis, f., *whirlwind; spinning top.*
Turnus, -ī, m., *Turnus, the chief of the Rutulians.*
turriger, -gera, -gerum, *tower-crowned.*
turris, -is, f., *tower.*
tūtor, -ārī, -ātus sum, *protect.*
tūtus, -a, -um, adj., *safe; secure, protected.*
tuus, -a, -um, poss. adj., *your.*
tyrannus, -ī, m., *tyrant.*
Tyrrhēnus, -a, -um, adj., *Tyrrhenian; Etruscan; Tuscan.*
Tyrrheus, -eī, m. or **Tyrrhus, -ī, m.,** *Tyrrheus, a shepherd in Latium, working for Latinus.*
Tyrrhīdae, -ārum, m. pl., *the sons of Tyrrheus.*

U

ūber, -eris, adj., *fertile, rich.*
ūber, -eris, n., *udder; fruitfulness.*
ubī, interrog., rel., indef. adv., *where, when.*
ūdus, -a, -um, adj., *wet, damp.*
Ūfens, -entis, m., *Ufen, a river of Latium flowing into the sea west of Terracina; Ufens, a chief of the Aequi.*
ultimus, -a, -um, superl. adj., *farther; farthest.*
ultrō, adv., *furthermore, beyond; voluntarily.*
ululātus, -ūs, m., *howling; wailing, shrieking.*
ululō, -āre, -āvī, -ātum, *howl; wail, shriek.*
umbō, -ōnis, m., *the boss of a shield; a shield*
umbra, -ae, f., *shadow, shade.*
Umbrō, -ōnis, m., *Umbro, a priest of the Marsi.*
ūmeō, -ēre, --, --, *be wet, moist.*
umerus, -ī, m., *shoulder.*
ūnā, adv., *together; at the same time.*
ūnanimus, -a, -um, adj., *of one mind.*
unda, -ae, f., *wave.*
unde, adv., *from where, whence.*
undique, adv., *from* or *on all sides; everywhere.*
undō, -āre, -āvī, -ātum, *rise in waves, surge.*
ūnus, -a, -um, adj., *one.*
urbs, urbis, f., *city.*
urgeō, urgēre, ursī, --, *press; spur on, urge.*
urna, -ae, f., *urn.*
ūrō, -ere, ussī, ustum, *burn.*
ursus, -ī, m., *bear.*
usquam, adv., *anywhere.*
usque, adv., *all the way, right on; continuously.*
ut or **utī,** adv., conj., *so that; as, when; that; how? In what manner?*
uterque, utraque, utrumque, adj. or pron., *each of two.*
uterus, -ī, m., *the womb, belly.*
utrimque, adv., *on* or *from either side; on both sides.*

V

vacuus, -a, -um, adj., *empty, vacant; free of.*
vadōsus, -a, -um, adj., *shallow, that can be forded.*
vadum, -ī, n., *ford; shallow; wave.*
valeō, -ēre, -uī, -itum, *be strong, be able; be well, fare well.*
vallēs, -is, f., *valley.*
vapor, -ōris, m., *vapor, steam; heat.*
varius, -a, -um, adj., *various; different.*
vastus, -a, -um, adj., *empty; desolate.*

vātēs, -is, m., *seer, prophet; poet.*
-ve, enclit. conj. *or;* **-ve…-ve…,** *whether…or, either…or.*
vectis, -is, m., *lever, bar, bolt.*
vehō, -ere, vexī, vectum, *carry; convey;* pass., *ride, sail, fly.*
vel, conj., *or;* **vel…vel,** *either…or.*
Velīnus, -ī, m., conj., *Velinus, a lake in the country of the Sabines.*
vellus, -eris, n., *fleece; woolen band or fillet; skin.*
vēlō, -āre, -āvī, -ātum, *cover, conceal.*
vēlum, -ī, n., *sail, awning.*
velut or **velutī,** adv., *just as, even as, like.*
vēnātus, -ūs, m., adv., *hunting.*
venēnum, -ī, n., *poison; drug.*
veneror, -ārī, venerātus sum, *venerate.*
veniō, -īre, vēnī, ventum, *come.*
venōr, -ārī, venātus sum, *hunt, go hunting.*
ventus, -ī, m., *wind.*
Venus, -eris, f., *Venus, goddess of love and beauty, identified by the Romans with Aphrodite, daughter of Jupiter and Dione;* (meton.) *love, lust.*
verber, -eris, n., *whip; a beating or blow with a whip.*
verbum, ī, n., *word.*
vērō, adv., *certainly, in truth, surely.*
versō, -āre, -āvī, -ātum, *keep turning; agitate.*
vertex, -icis, m., *whirlpool; peak, summit; (top of the) head.*
vertō, -ere, vertī, versum, *turn; change; destroy;* middle sense, *move about.*
verū, -ūs, n., *spit; tapering lance.*
vērum, conj., *but (indeed), yet.*

vērum, -ī, n., *that which is true; truth, justice.*
vērus, -a, -um, adj., *real, true.*
vester, -tra, -trum, poss. adj. pl., *your.*
vestibulum, -ī, n., *entrance, vestibule.*
vestīgium, -ī, n., *step, track; footstep.*
vestīgō, -āre, -āvī, -ātum, *track; trace, explore; hunt.*
vestis, -is, f., *clothing, garment; robe.*
vetus, -eris, adj., *old.*
via, -ae, f., *street, road, way.*
vicissim, adv., *in turn.*
victor, -ōris, m., *conqueror, victor;* (appos.) *victorious.*
victrix, -īcis, f., *female conqueror;* adj., *victorious.*
videō, -ēre, vīdī, vīsum, *see;* pass., *be seen, seem.*
vincō, -ere, vīcī, victum, *conquer.*
vinculum, -ī, n., *bond, fetter.*
vīnum, vīnī, n., *wine.*
violō, -āre, -āvī, -ātum, *violate, dishonor; outrage.*
vīpereus, -a, -um, adj., *viperous.*
vir, -ī, m., *man, husband.*
Virbius, -ī, m., *Virbius, a Latin warrior, son of Hippolytus and Aricia.*
virga, -ae, f., *twig; wand.*
virgeus, -a, -um, *of twigs.*
virgō, -inis, f., *maiden, girl of marriageable age; virgin.*
virgultum, -ī, n., *brambles, a thicket.*
viridis, -e, adj., *green.*
viridō, -āre, -āvī, -ātum, *be green.*
virīlis, -e, adj., *manly, virile.*
virtūs, -ūtis, f., *manliness, courage.*
vīs, acc. sing. **vim,** abl. sing. **vī;** pl. **vīrēs, vīrium, f.,** (sing.) *force, power; violence;* (pl.) *(physical) strength.*

vīscus, -eris, n., *innards, viscera, guts.*
vīta, -ae, f., *life.*
vītisator, -ōris, m., *vine-planter.*
vitreus, -a, -um, *made of glass; glassy, clear.*
vitta, -ae, f., *ribbon.*
vīvō, -ere, vīxī, victum, *live, be alive.*
vix, adv., *hardly, scarcely.*
vōciferor, -ārī, -ferātus sum, *raise the voice; cry out.*
vocō, -āre, -āvī, -ātum, *call; summon.*
Volcānus (Vulcānus), -ī, m., *Vulcan, the god of fire and of the forge.*
volitō, -āre, -āvī, -ātum, *fly around.*
volō, velle, voluī, --, *be willing, want.*
volō, -āre, -āvī, -ātum, *fly.*
Volscus, -a, -um, adj., *Volscian.*
Volturnus, -ī, m., *Vulturnus,* a river of Campania.

volūbilis, -e, adj., *turning, spinning.*
volucris, -is, m. or f., *bird.*
voluntās, -ātis, f., *will, desire; wish, favor; delight.*
volvō, -ere, voluī, volūtum, *roll; ponder.*
vōmer, -eris, m., *plowshare, plow.*
vorāgō, -inis, f., *chasm, abyss; whirlpool; torrent.*
vōs, gen. vestrum, vestrī, dat. vōbīs, acc. vōs, abl. vōbīs, pers. pron. pl., *you.*
vōtum, -ī, n., *vow, solemn promise.*
vox, vōcis, f., *voice; word.*
vulnus, -eris, n., *wound.*
vultus, -ūs, m., *expression; face.*

Index

Please note: This index contains major references to the listed terms but is not intended to be comprehensive. References to pages in the "General Introduction" are preceded by "p." or "pp." (e.g. p. 14, pp. 2-3); references to notes in the commentary are made by line number/numbers (e.g. 4, 10-24). An asterisk (*) indicates terms included in Appendix 2.

ablative:
    absolute: 5, 6, 112-13, 125, 249, 261, 385, 510, 520, 649-50, 661-2
    attendant circumstance: 45-6, 50-1, 249, 284
    cause: 31, 202-4, 464-5, 473-4, 517
    comparison: 383, 649-50
    degree of difference: 784
    description: 30, 162, 483, 783
    manner: 216, 487
    means: 12, 14, 19-20, 23, 34, 41-2, 58, 71, 202-4, 211, 236-8, 289, 318-19, 354, 373-4, 411-12, 480, 488, 525-6, 531-2, 538-9, 566-7, 589-90, 644, 692, 726, 733, 748-9
    origin or source: 152, 679-80, 331, 734-5
    personal agent: 310
    place where: 12, 34, 76-7, 140, 192-3, 300, 302-3, 353, 387, 401-2, 659, 679-80, 793
    price: 317
    quality: 525-6, 746-7
    separation: 217-18, 292, 299, 313, 369-70
    specification: 64-5, 78, 483, 660, 666-8
    supine: 64-5
    time: 45-6, 50-1, 102-3, 414, 492
accusative:
    adverbial: 358, 510
    direction: 216
    double construction: 189-91, 606
    Greek: 34, 64-5, 90-1, 288, 305-6, 324, 641
    internal: 460
    motion toward/place to which: 492
    predicate: 507-8
    respect: 60, 74, 75, 796
Achilles: 649-50, 807
Actium: p. 4; 43-4, 318-19
adjectives:
    adjective/noun arrangements: 10-14, 10, 13, 14, 217-18, 422, 642-4, 792
    adverbial meaning: 10, 117-18, 141, 194, 354, 503, 510, 554, 593, 598
    diminutive: 681
    epic compound: 17-18, 81-2, 93, 324, 758; App. 2

Index

prolepsis: 350-1, 498, 509, 626-7, 797, App. 2
substantive: 30, 54-5, 182, 280-1, 538-9, 726
Aeneas: pp. 4-6, 9-14; 1-285, 5, 286-640, *passim*
Aequiculi: 744-9
aetiology*: 1-4, 1-2, 761-82
AG = *Allen and Greenough's New Latin Grammar*: see 1-285 n. 1
Alba: 601-3, 655-69
Alexandrian poetry/style: p. 7. See also Hellenistic poetry/style
Allecto: pp. 12-13; 286-640, 323-40, 324, 328, 341-72, 405, 462-6, 528-30, 622, *passim*
alliteration*: 8-9, 21-2, 25-6, 79-80, 148, 164-5, 394, 397, 531-2, 632-3
Amata: 57, 68, 321, 341-72, 367-72, 405, *passim*
ambiguity: p. 13; 1-285, 157, 286-640, 405
anachronism: 173-5, 601-40, 664, 712-14
anaphora*: 41-2, 53, 251-3, 302-3, 315-16, 329, 351-2, 460, 473-4, 499, 516, 695-6, 759, 814-17
anastrophe*: 30, 234, 296, 379, 441, 803
Anchises: 12, 96-101, 107-34, 123, 126-7, 128, 140, 152, 282-3, 651, 682-3, 712-14
antithesis*: 140, 72
Antony, Marc: pp. 2-4; 43-4, 678-90
apodosis: 311, 371-2
Apollo: 12, 59, 61-2, 105, 241, 475-510, 761-82, 769, 772-3
Apollonius of Rhodes (*Argonautica*): pp. 7-8; 37-45, 37-8, 518, 699-702, 703-5, 718-21, 808-11
apostrophe*: 1-2, 48-9, 120-1, 318-19, 389-91, 684, 685-6, 733-43, 733, 744, 759, 797

archaism*: 27-8, 41-2, 50-1, 69-70, 96-7, 109, 126-7, 153, 192-3, 272-3, 378, 395, 446, 458, 464-5, 500, 583, 592, 703, 787-8
Ardea: 38, 409-10, 411-12
Argonautica: see Apollonius of Rhodes
Aricia: 761-82
arsis*, lengthening in: 173-5, 186, 398
Ascanius: see Iulus
assonance*: 8-9, 17-18, 25-6, 345, 651
asyndeton*: 8-9, 41-2, 53, 75, 150-1, 156, 170, 202-4, 219-20, 241, 294-5, 302-3, 305-6, 309, 327, 329, 337-8, 338-9, 351-2, 394, 404, 460, 468-9, 473-4, 516, 578-9, 625, 710-11, 742-3, 759
attraction (grammatical/syntactic): 799
augury: 69-70, 173-5, 187-8, 259-60, 272-3
Augustus/Octavian: pp. 2-6, 9-11; 12, 43-4, 59, 107, 153, 170, 604-6, 607, 609, 678-90, 706-22
Aurunci: 39, 206, 795
Ausonia: 39, 54-5, 105, 231-3, 547, 623. See also Italy
Aventinus: 655-69
Bacchus (Liber): 389-91, 403, 580-2
Caeculus: 678-90
Caesar, Julius: pp. 2, 4, 9; 107
caesura*: 178
Caieta: p. 13; 1-4
Callimachus: pp. 4, 7; 261, 378-83, 761-82, 803
Calybe: 406-34
Camilla: p. 13; 641-817, 803-817
Campania: 39, 691-705, 723-32, 733-43
Catillus and Corus: 670-7
Cato the Elder: 1-285, 180-1, 647-54, 678-90
Catullus: pp. 7-8; 228, 261, 335-7, 356, 362, 718-21, 807

Celaeno: 105, 107-34, 112-15, 447-8
chiasmus*: 7, 337-8, 344, 384, 651, 742-3
Circe: 8-9, 10-24, 15-18, 189-91, 282-3, 328, 511-12
civil wars: pp. 1-5, 14; 317, 318-19, 335-7, 545, 678-90
Clausus: 706-22
Cleopatra: pp. 3-4; 377, 450
coinage*: *see* neologism*
compound or epic adjective: 17-18, 81-2, 93, 179, 277, 324, 335-7, 500, 674-5, 758
conditional sentences: 21-2 (participle), 311, 371-2
connective relative: 21-2, 330, 785-6
consonance*: 8-9, 164-5, 173-5, 345, 651
Creusa: 30, 501-2
Cumae: 1-4
cum clauses:
   circumstantial: 61-2, 246-8, 427-8, 494-5, 734-5
   temporal with indicative: 124, 148, 166-7, 700, 720
   whenever: 87-8
Cupid: p. 13; 350-1, 355, 415-16, 693
Cybele: 139
dactyl*: 173-5, 395
Dardanus: 206, 207, 208, 209, 211, 219-20, 239-40, 255, 289
dative:
   advantage: 724
   agent: 411-12, 444, 507-8
   compound verbs: 35-6, 39, 87-8, 110, 160-1, 213-14, passim
   indirect object: 1-2, 24, 63, 359, 709
   possessor: 50-1, 268-70, 329, 337-8, 371-2, 538-9, 676-7
   purpose: 325-6, 481-2, 551, 611, 637, 642, 761-2
   reference: 48-9, 79-80, 173-5, 231-3, 293-4, 325-6, passim
   separation: 282-3, 388

Diana: 305-6, 308, 516, 761-82 764, 774
dicolon abundans* (also theme and variation*): 7, 21-2, 27-8, 51, 53, 265-6, 321, 504, 529-30, 555, 676-7
Dido: p. 13; 104, 105, 122, 147, 148, 212-48, 239-40, 309, 318-19, 348, 350-1, 376, 377, 392-6, 399, 409-10, 415-16, 427-8, 448-9, 456-7, 461-2, 500, 548, 693, 803-17, 814-17
Dionysius of Halicarnassus: p. 18; 81-2, 107-34, 343, 647-54
Donatus, Tiberius Claudius: p. 1; 129
elision*: 41-2, 69-70, 170, 294-5, 311, 345, 472, 623
ellipsis*: 117-18, 156, 552
enallage*: 73, 164-5, 329, 343, 533-4, 574-6, 796. *See also* transferred epithet*
enjambment*: 30, 37-8, 54-5, 79-80, 141, 157, 297-8, 302-3, 347, 424, 451, 533-4, 736-7
Ennius: p. 8; 4, 294-5, 545, 592, 622, 691, 699-702, *passim*
epithet*: 5, 29, 139, 141, 179, 286, 329, 337-8, 343, 427-8, 516, 533-4
Etruscan: 43-4, 173-5, 207, 423, 641, 647-54, 691-705, *passim*
etymology/etymological wordplay*: 41-2, 48-9, 79-80, 192-3, 256-8, 413, 517, 592, 645-6, 682-3, 684, 706-7, 734-5, 767-8, 776-7
fate: 1-4, 123, 293-4, 313, 314, 584, 750-60, *passim*
FRH = *The Fragments of the Roman Historians*: *see* 1-285 n. 1
FRL = *Fragmentary Republican Latin*: *see* 1-285 n. 1
Fury/fury/*furor*: p. 10; 312, 386, 607, 609, *passim*. *See also* passions

genitive:
   archaic: 50-1, 464-5
   cause of pity: 360-1
   description: 687-8
   lack or need: 197-8, 440
   objective: 304-5, 365-6, 401-2, 438-9
   partitive: 272-3, 552, 601-3
   synonymous: 351-2
gerund: 112-13
golden age: 44-5, 48-9, 202-4, 492
golden line*: 10-14, 10, 14, 422, 615
Halaesus: 723-32
half line: p. 6; 129
Harpies: 107-34, 114-15
Hecate: see Trivia
Hector: 157, 378-83, 414, 427-8, 444, 586-90
Hecuba: 319-20, 321, 363-4
Helen: 319-20, 363-4, 481-2
Helenus: 10-24, 107-34
Hellenistic poetry/style: pp. 3, 7; 14, 261, *passim*
hendiadys*: 15, 94-5, 142-3, 277, 419, 577, 658, 751, 772-3, 775
Hercules: 655-69, 658, 661-2, 663, 666-8, 674-7
heroism: pp. 5, 8, 10, 14; 5, 10-24, *passim*
Hesperia: 4, 30, 43-4, 120-1, 262, 563. See also Italy
hiatus*: 178, 225-7, 631
Hippolytus: 761-82
Homer: see *Iliad* and *Odyssey*
hypallage*: see enallage
hyperbaton*: 10-14, 13, 64-5, 142-3, 166-7, 236-8, 331, 404, 464-5, 477-8, 488, 498, 519, 531-2, 566-7, 612, 616-17, 783
hyperbole*: 271-2, 377, 529-30
hypermetric line*: 160-1, 470
hysteron proteron*: 208
ictus* and word accent*, clash of: 398, 555, 592

Iliad (Homer): pp. 6-7; 37-45, 44-45, 57, 462-6, 481-2, 528-30, 586-90, 641-817, 641-6, 649-50, 699-702, 756-7, 808-11, *passim*
Ilioneus: 98-9, 212-48, 222-27, 243, 262, 304-5
imperative:
   ago/agite: 307-8
   archaic with *ne*: 96-7, 202-4
   future: 126-7, 313
impersonal construction: 692, 730-1, 748-9
impersonal verb: 360-1, 523-4, 553, 734-5
incomplete line: see half line
indirect command: 35-6, 546
indirect questions: 130-1, 222-4, 642-4, 679-80
indirect statement:
   accusative and infinitive: 255, 389-91, 470, 578-9, 765
   implied: 150-1
infinitive:
   archaic: 69-70
   epexegetic: 35-6
   historical: 15-18, 76-7, 78
   for indirect command: 35-6
   with infinitive: see indirect statement
   poetic usages: 35-6
interlocking word order* (also synchysis*): 5, 10-14, 10, 11, 342, 346, 525-6, 649-50, 770-1
intertextuality: 6-9 with n. 36, *passim*
irony*: 21-2, 44-5, 129, 246-8, 285, 288, 297-8, 409-10, 496, 751
Italy: 4, 23, 31, 39 (*Ausonia*), 85 (*Oenotria*), 641-817, *passim*. See also Hesperia
Iulus (=Ascanius): p. 13; 107, 475-510, 477-8, 552

Juno: pp. 12-14; 117-18, 166-7, 286-640, 293-4, 308, 323-40, 386, 427-8, 557-8, 592, 620-1, *passim*
Jupiter: pp. 10, 14; 44, 107, 117-18, 141, 166-7, 219-20, 607, *passim*
Latinus: p. 12; 1-285, 45-80, 45-6, 47, 50-1, 81-106, 347-72, 586-90, *passim*
Laurentum: 47
Lausus: 5, 473-4, 641-817, 647-54
Lavinia: 37-45, 45-80, 50-1, 73-6, 79-80, 96-7, 251-3, 318-19, 321, 389-91, *passim*
Lavinium: 158
litotes*: 8-9, 195-6, 202-4, 231-3, 261, 466, 498, 557-8, 610, 678, 733
Livy: p. 18; 607, 647-54, 655-69, 706-22, *passim*
Lucretius: p. 9; 89, 550, *passim*
Maecenas: pp. 3-4
Marcellus (Augustus' nephew and son-in-law): 473-4, 706-22
Mars: 187-8, 304-5, 318-19, 550, 601-3
Medea: 37-45, 73-6, 699-702, 759
Messapus: 691-705
metaphor*: 14, 16, 27-8, 64-5, 312, 319-20, 329, 343, 345, 393, 405, 422, 481-2, 496, 551, 572-3, 577, 588, 592, 594, 598, 600, 644, 785-6
meter: *see* Appendix 1: Vergil's Meter
metonymy*: 53, 76-7, 90-1, 112-13, 246-8, 381-2, 386, 381-2, 497, 601-3, 606, 655, 670, 725
Mezentius: 265-6, 586-90, 641-817, 647-54
Minerva (=Pallas Athena): 154-5, 363-4, 503, 805-6
Misenus/Misenum: 1-2
monosyllable, lines ending in a: 310, 592, 790
Muse, invocation of: 37-45, 37-8, 41-2, 641-6, 641, 645-6
Naevius: p. 8; 557-8

neologism* (also coinage*): 1-2, 308, 363-4, 505-6, 560, 623, 651, 674-5, 740, 748-9, 758, 787-8, 796, 814-17
neoteric poetry/style: 7. *See also* Hellenistic poetry/style
Neptune: 10-24, 23, 105, 586-90, 691-705, 692
Odyssey (Homer)/Odysseus: pp. 6, 8, 12-13; 10-24, *passim*
Oebalus: 733-43
OLD = *Oxford Latin Dictionary*: *see* 1-285 n. 1
omens: 21-2, 68, 119, 173-5
onomatopoeia*: 17-18, 632-3
optimism vs. pessimism (in interpretation): pp. 10-11
oracles: 79-80, 81-106, 81-2, 86, 96-101, 107-34, 251-3, 254, 268-70, 367-72, 368, 392, 584
oxymoron*: 1-2, 550, 615
Palinurus: 1-2, 23
Pallas: *see* Minerva
parataxis*: 287
Paris: p. 13; 319-20, 321, 363-4, 481-2
paronomasia* (also wordplay*): 41-2, 208, 386, 411-12, 413, 517, 645-6, 684, 706-7, 712-14, 740, 767-8, 784, 791
passions: p. 8; 37-45, 57, 347, 356, 373-4, 386, 644, *passim*. *See also furor*
pathetic fallacy*: 722
patronymic*: 152, 484, 560, 622
penates: 120-1, 459
periphrasis*: 56, 152, 287, 305-6, 308, 331, 342, 409-10, 464-5, 466, 479, 556, 620-1, 632-3, 656-7, 761-2, 772-3
personification*: 386, 676-7, 722
pietas: 5, 386 (vs. *furor*), *passim*
polyptoton*: 44-5, 48-9, 69-70, 117-18, 120-1, 122, 136-8, 150-1, 173-5, 197-8, 241, 251-3, 327, 386, 548, 555, 642-2, 653-4, 715-17, 742-3

polysyndeton*: 325-6, 725-32, 794
Praeneste: 678-90
Priam: 45-50, 59, 105, 183-4, 246-8, 251-3
prolepsis*: 350-1, 498, 509, 626-7, 797
prophecy: 31, 41-2, 81-2, 96-101, 102-3, 107-34, 112-15, 123, 255, 271-2, 272-3, 409-10, 447-8
Punic Wars: p. 8; 545, 607, 723-32
purpose clause: 21-2, 332-3, 481-2. *See also* relative clause of purpose
Quirinus: 187-8, 612
Quirites: 710-11
relative clause of characteristic: 653-4
relative clause of purpose: 98-9, 144-5, 256-8, 271-2, 348, 388
Remus: p. 11; 655-9
Rhea Silvia: 487, 659, 661-2
rhetorical question*: 294-5, 302-3
Rome: pp. 1-6, 9-10; 96-101, 641-817, *passim*
Romulus: p. 10; 197-8, 487, 612, 655-69, 706-22, 709
Rutulians: 318-19, 342, 475, 647-54, 748-9, 783-802
Sabines: 178, 179, 631, 706-22
sacrifice: 87-8, 93, 304-5, 305-6, 744-9, 764
Saturnus: 47, 48-9, 180-1
Scylla and Charybdis: 302-3, 588
Sibyl: 31, 41-2, 107-34
Silvia: 475-510
simile*: 378-83, 378, 405, 462-6, 500, 528-30, 586-90, 594, 674-7, 698, 699-702, 609
Social (or Marsic) Wars: pp. 1, 14; 641-817, 670-7, 678-90, 723-32, 750-60
spondaic line*: 631, 634
spondee*: 153, 164-5, 170

subjunctive:
condition: 371-2
cum-circumstantial: 61-2, 494-5
deliberative: 359
hortatory: 132
indirect question: 222-4, 642-4
jussive: 265-6, 317, 340, 434
optative: 259-60
potential: 703-5, 808-9
purpose: 21-2, 334, 481-2, 776-7
relative causal clause: 348
relative clause of purpose: 256-8
substantive clause: 207
substantive clause: 207
supine: 64-5
syllepsis*: 187-8, 431, 477-8. *See also* zeugma*
synchysis*: *see* interlocking word order*
syncope*: 6, 61-2, 201, 207, 409-10, 766
synecdoche*: 245, 431, 632-3
synizesis*: 33, 189-91, 249, 262, 302-3, 609
theme and variation*: *see* dicolon abundans*
Tibur: 630, 670-7
tmesis*: 104, 559, 589-90
tragedy: pp. 8-9, 12-13; *passim*
transferred epithet*: 164-5, 329, 343, 533-4. *See also* enallage*
tricolon*: 15-18, 126-7, 149, 150-1, 154-5, 170, 197-8, 219-20, 229-30, 231-3, 290-1, 294-5, 302-3, 315-16, 335-7, 338-9, 340, 468-9, 473-4, 574-6, 578-9, 604-6, 710-17, 725-32, 738-41, 739
Trivia: 516, 774, 781-2
Troy: 1-2, 23, 105, 157 207, 225-7, *passim*

Turnus: p. 13; 54-5, 96-7, 318-19, 321,
    341-72, 367-72, 406-34, 420, 462-6,
    467, 641-817, 783-802, *passim*
Ufens: 744-9
Umbro: 750-60
Venus: pp. 9-10; 46, 321, *passim*
Vergil (*see* General Introduction):
    Aeneid: pp. 5-6; *passim*
    Eclogues: pp. 2-5, 7; *passim*
    Georgics: pp. 4-5, 7-8; *passim*
    life and death: pp. 1-6

VE = *The Virgil Encyclopedia*: *see* 1-285
    n. 1
Virbius: 761-82
Volsci: 803-17
word accent*: *see* ictus* and word
    accent*
wordplay: *see* paronomasia*
zeugma*: 187-8, 430-1, 477-8, 712-14.
    See also syllepsis*